Anne Happy♪

unhappy go lucky!

5

COTOJI

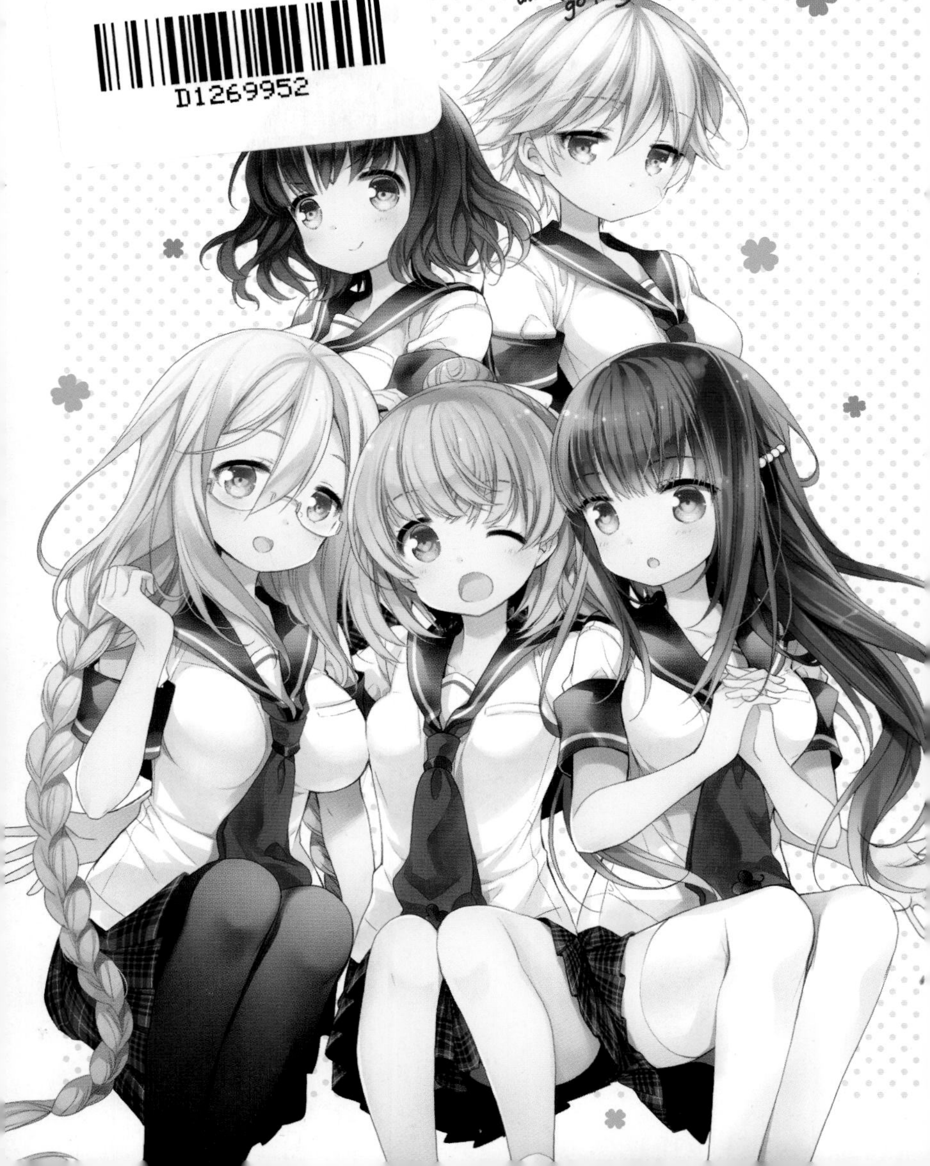

CONTENTS
ANNE HAPPY
VOLUME FIVE
COTOJI

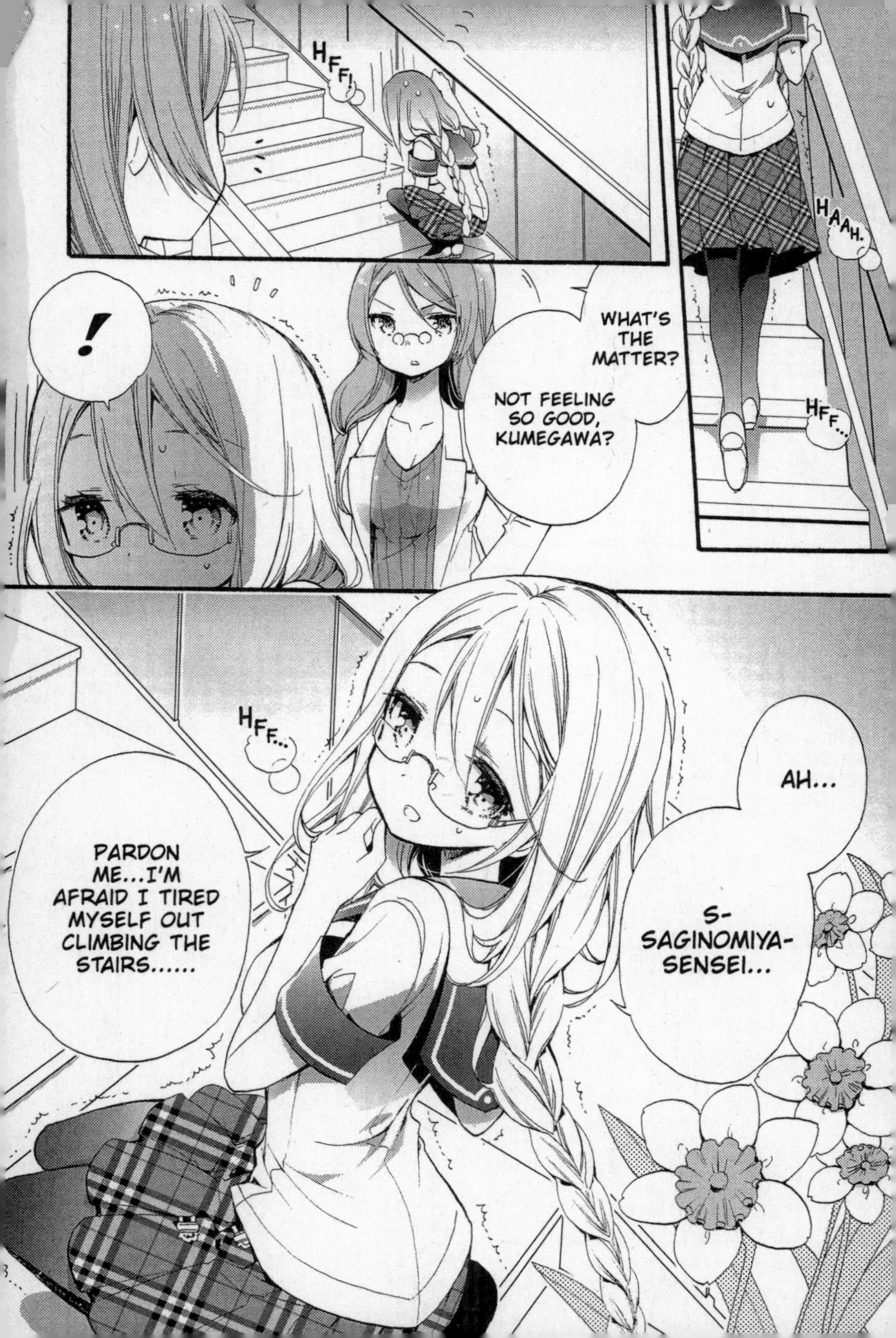
HAAH.
HFF...
HFF!
WHAT'S THE MATTER?
NOT FEELING SO GOOD, KUMEGAWA?
!
AH...
S-SAGINOMIYA-SENSEI...
HFF...
PARDON ME...I'M AFRAID I TIRED MYSELF OUT CLIMBING THE STAIRS......

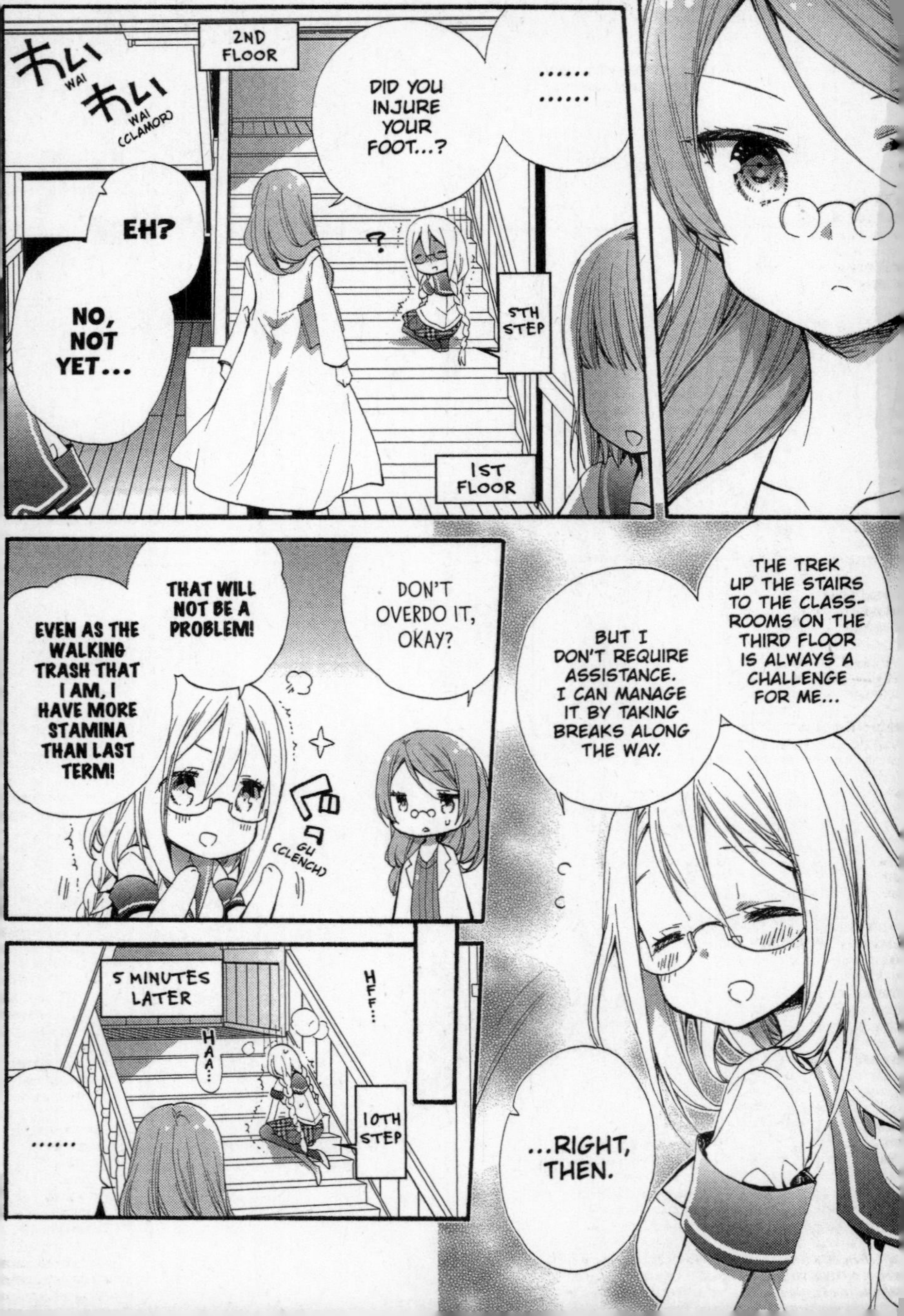
......
......
DID YOU INJURE YOUR FOOT...?
2ND FLOOR
わい WAI わい WAI (CLAMOR)
?
5TH STEP
EH?
NO, NOT YET...
1ST FLOOR
THE TREK UP THE STAIRS TO THE CLASS-ROOMS ON THE THIRD FLOOR IS ALWAYS A CHALLENGE FOR ME...
BUT I DON'T REQUIRE ASSISTANCE. I CAN MANAGE IT BY TAKING BREAKS ALONG THE WAY.
...RIGHT, THEN.
DON'T OVERDO IT, OKAY?
THAT WILL NOT BE A PROBLEM!
EVEN AS THE WALKING TRASH THAT I AM, I HAVE MORE STAMINA THAN LAST TERM!
GU (CLENCH)
HFF...
5 MINUTES LATER
HAA...
10TH STEP
......

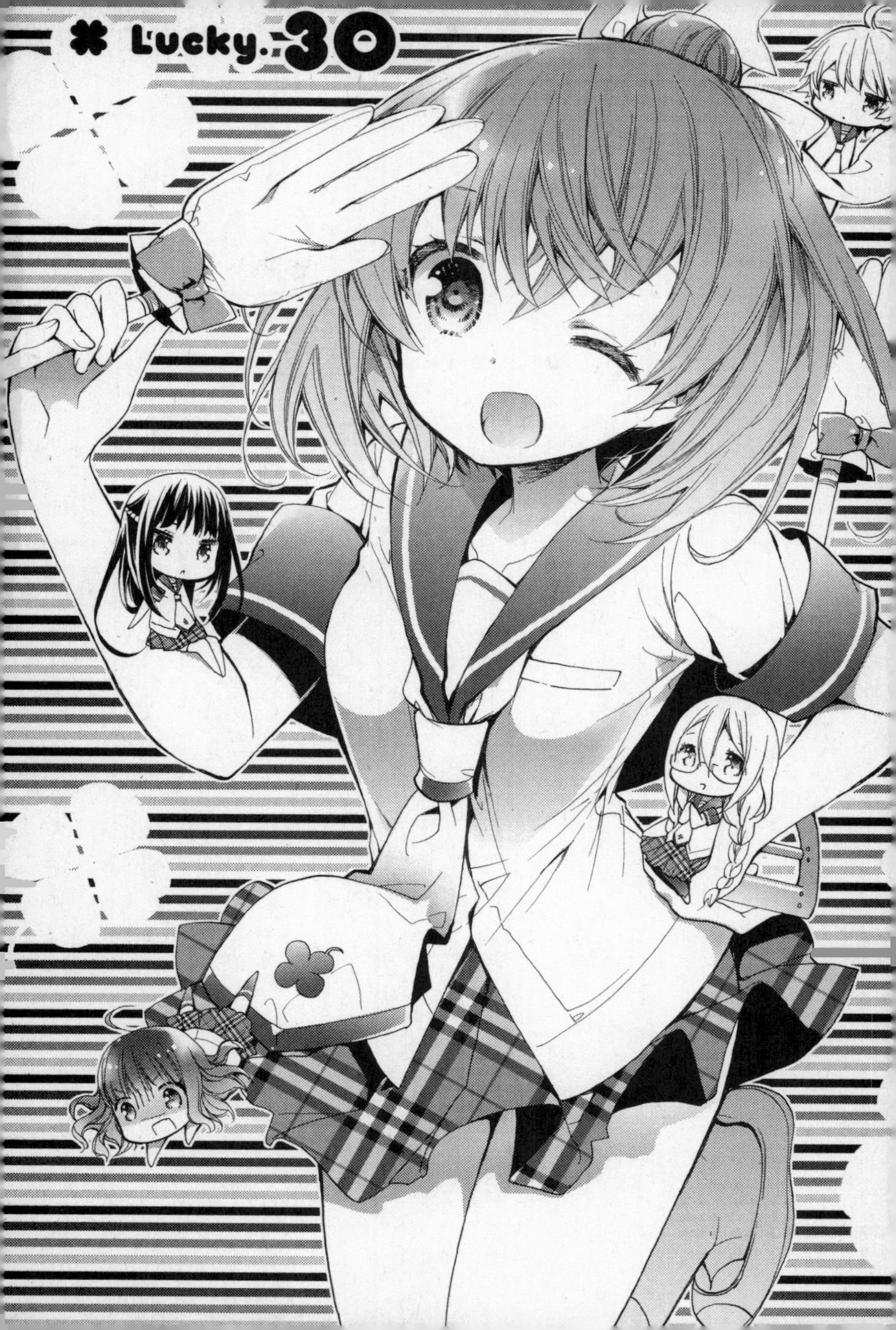
Lucky. 30

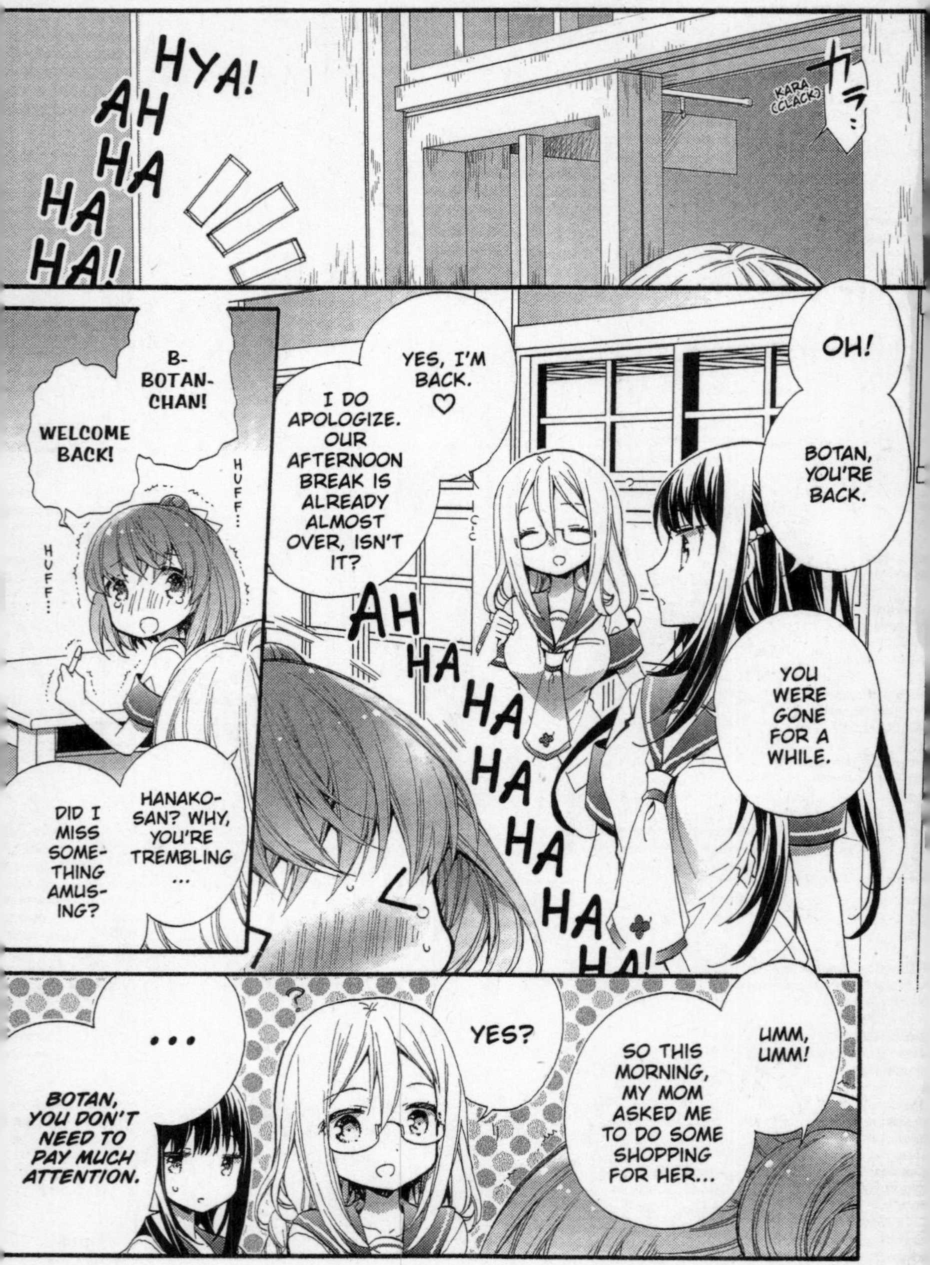
KARA (CLACK)
HYA! AH HA HA HA HA!
OH!
BOTAN, YOU'RE BACK.
YOU WERE GONE FOR A WHILE.
YES, I'M BACK. ♡
I DO APOLOGIZE. OUR AFTERNOON BREAK IS ALREADY ALMOST OVER, ISN'T IT?
AH HA HA HA HA HA HA!
B-BOTAN-CHAN!
WELCOME BACK!
HUFF...
HUFF...
HANAKO-SAN? WHY, YOU'RE TREMBLING...
DID I MISS SOMETHING AMUSING?
UMM, UMM!
SO THIS MORNING, MY MOM ASKED ME TO DO SOME SHOPPING FOR HER...
YES?
...
BOTAN, YOU DON'T NEED TO PAY MUCH ATTENTION.

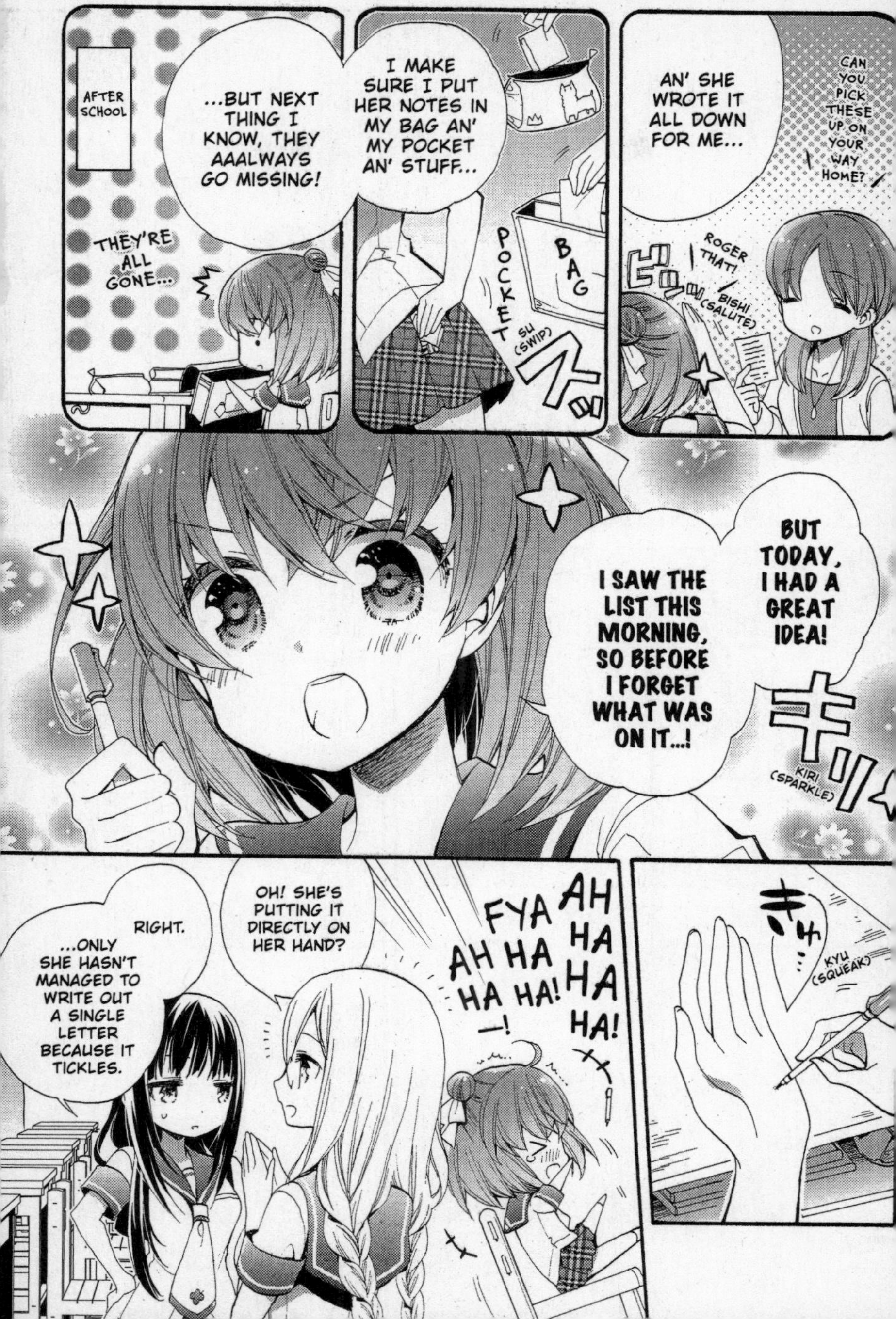

CAN YOU PICK THESE UP ON YOUR WAY HOME?
AN' SHE WROTE IT ALL DOWN FOR ME...
ROGER THAT!
BISHI (SALUTE)
I MAKE SURE I PUT HER NOTES IN MY BAG AN' MY POCKET AN' STUFF...
BAG
POCKET
SU (SWIP)
AFTER SCHOOL
...BUT NEXT THING I KNOW, THEY AAALWAYS GO MISSING!
THEY'RE ALL GONE...
BUT TODAY, I HAD A GREAT IDEA!
I SAW THE LIST THIS MORNING, SO BEFORE I FORGET WHAT WAS ON IT...!
KIRI (SPARKLE)
KYU (SQUEAK)
AH HA HA HA HA!
FYA AH HA HA HA! —!
OH! SHE'S PUTTING IT DIRECTLY ON HER HAND?
RIGHT.
...ONLY SHE HASN'T MANAGED TO WRITE OUT A SINGLE LETTER BECAUSE IT TICKLES.

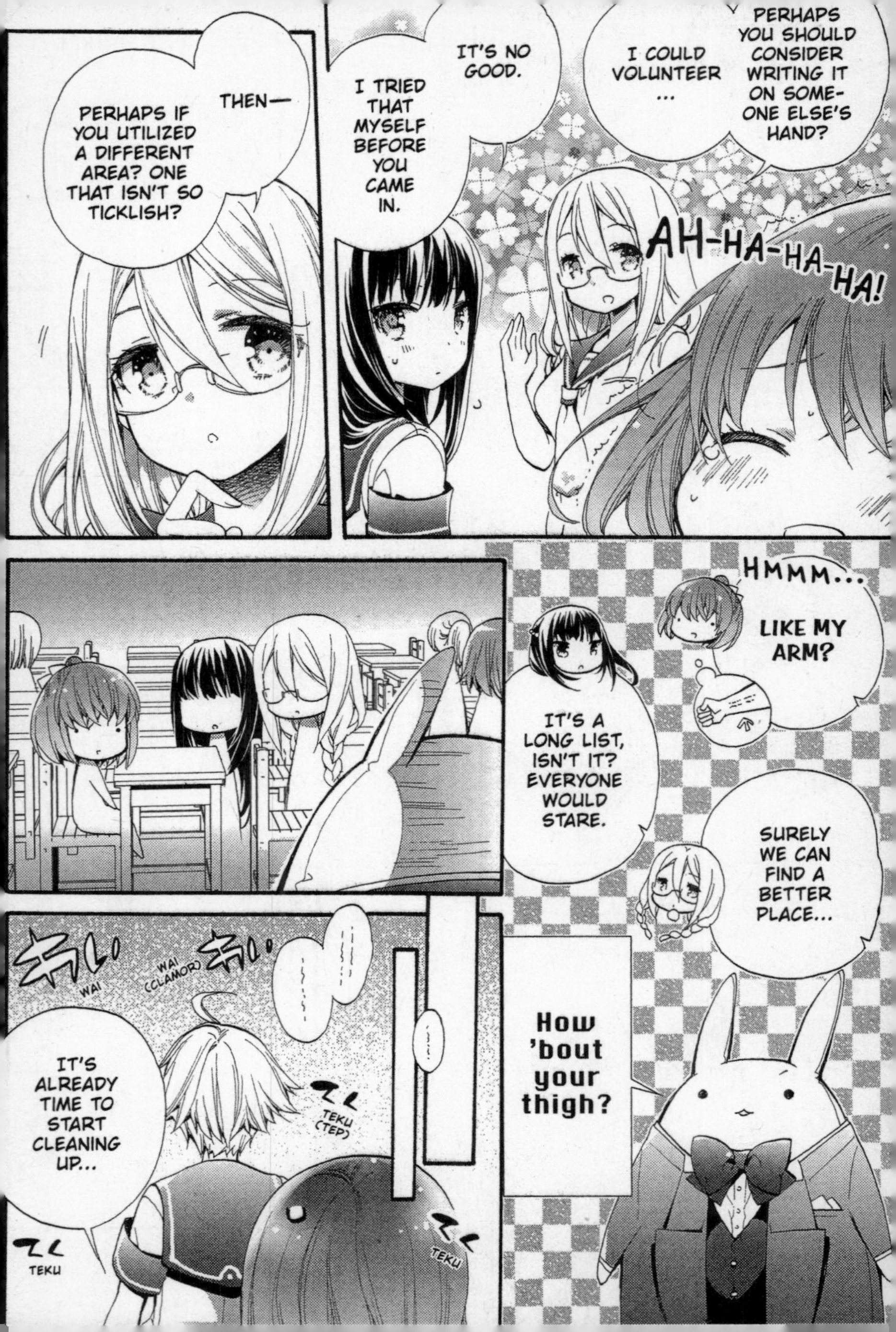

PERHAPS YOU SHOULD CONSIDER WRITING IT ON SOME-ONE ELSE'S HAND?
I COULD VOLUNTEER ...
AH-HA-HA-HA!
IT'S NO GOOD.
I TRIED THAT MYSELF BEFORE YOU CAME IN.
THEN—
PERHAPS IF YOU UTILIZED A DIFFERENT AREA? ONE THAT ISN'T SO TICKLISH?
HMMM...
LIKE MY ARM?
IT'S A LONG LIST, ISN'T IT? EVERYONE WOULD STARE.
SURELY WE CAN FIND A BETTER PLACE...
How 'bout your thigh?
WAI
WAI (CLAMOR)
IT'S ALREADY TIME TO START CLEANING UP...
TEKU (TEP)
TEKU
TEKU

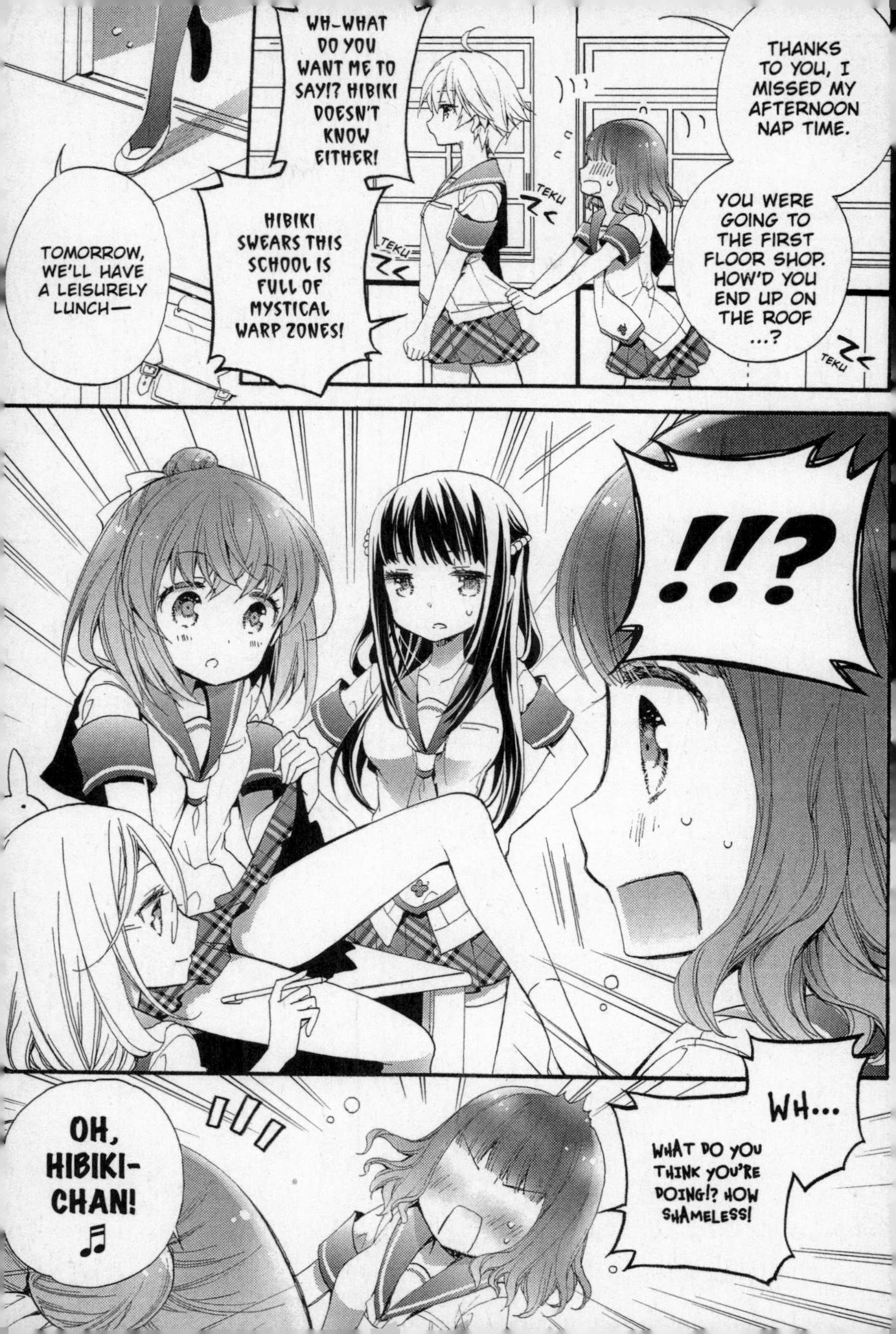
THANKS TO YOU, I MISSED MY AFTERNOON NAP TIME.
YOU WERE GOING TO THE FIRST FLOOR SHOP. HOW'D YOU END UP ON THE ROOF ...?
TEKU
TEKU
WH-WHAT DO YOU WANT ME TO SAY!? HIBIKI DOESN'T KNOW EITHER!
HIBIKI SWEARS THIS SCHOOL IS FULL OF MYSTICAL WARP ZONES!
TEKU
TOMORROW, WE'LL HAVE A LEISURELY LUNCH—
!!?
WH...
WHAT DO YOU THINK YOU'RE DOING!? HOW SHAMELESS!
OH, HIBIKI-CHAN! ♫

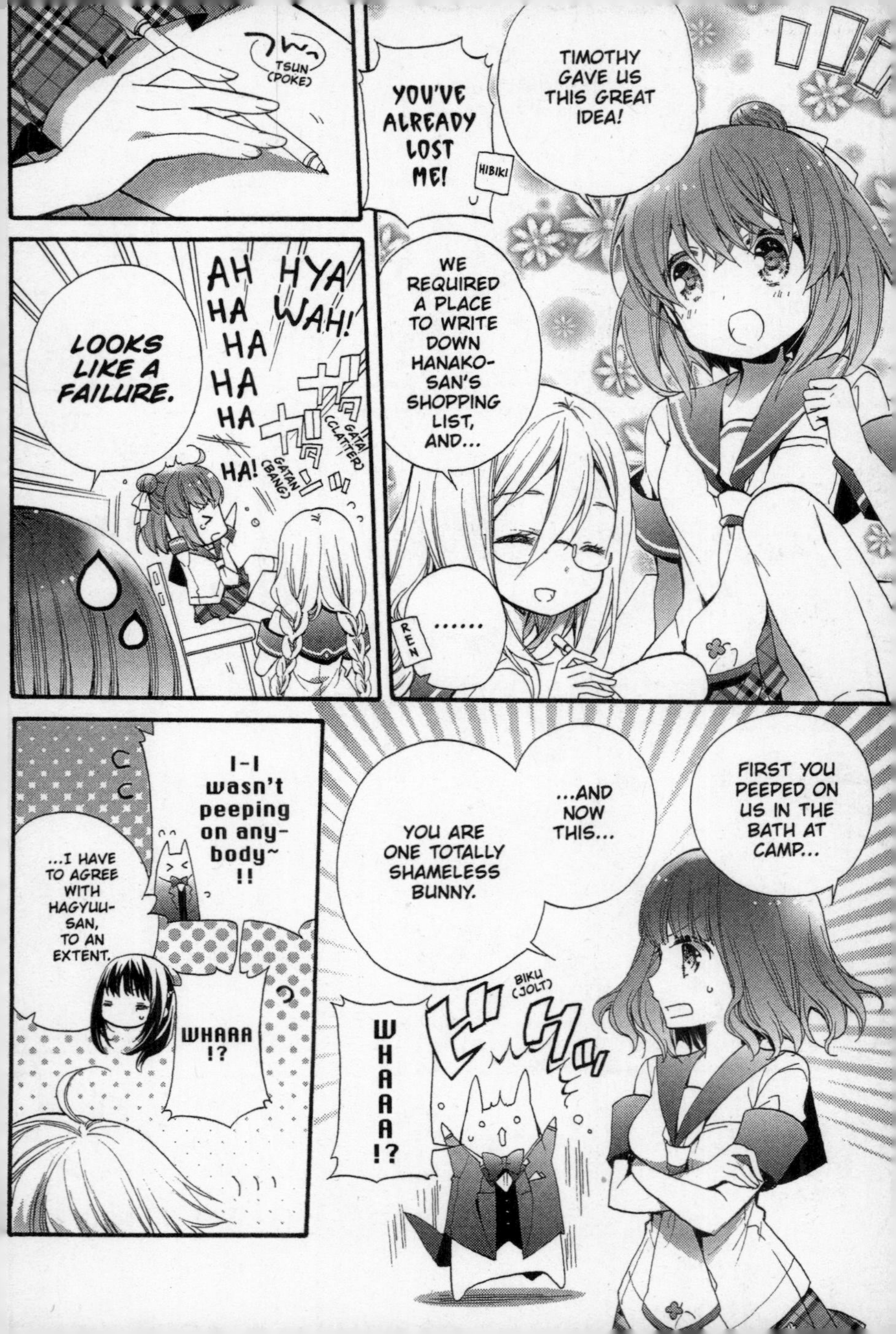

TIMOTHY GAVE US THIS GREAT IDEA!
YOU'VE ALREADY LOST ME!
HIBIKI
WE REQUIRED A PLACE TO WRITE DOWN HANAKO-SAN'S SHOPPING LIST, AND...
REN
......
TSUN (POKE)
HYA WAH!
AH HA HA HA HA HA!
GATA! (CLATTER)
GATAN (BANG)
LOOKS LIKE A FAILURE.
FIRST YOU PEEPED ON US IN THE BATH AT CAMP...
...AND NOW THIS...
YOU ARE ONE TOTALLY SHAMELESS BUNNY.
BIKU (JOLT)
WHAAAA!?
I-I wasn't peeping on any-body~!!
WHAAA!?
...I HAVE TO AGREE WITH HAGYUU-SAN, TO AN EXTENT.

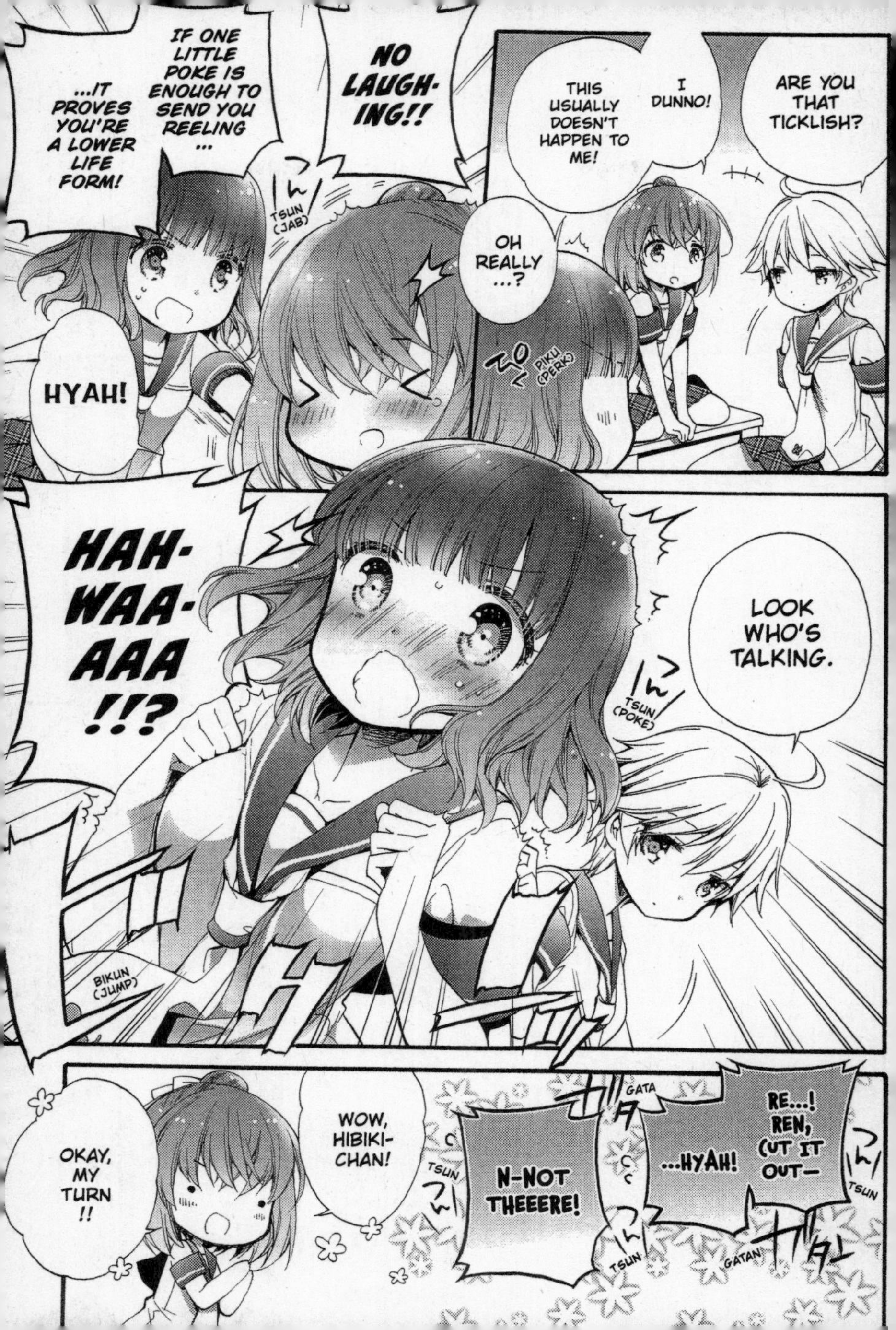
ARE YOU THAT TICKLISH?
I DUNNO!
THIS USUALLY DOESN'T HAPPEN TO ME!
OH REALLY ...?
PIKU (PERK)
TSUN (JAB)
HYAH!
NO LAUGH-ING!!
IF ONE LITTLE POKE IS ENOUGH TO SEND YOU REELING ...
...IT PROVES YOU'RE A LOWER LIFE FORM!
LOOK WHO'S TALKING.
TSUN (POKE)
HAH-WAA-AAA!!?
BIKUN (JUMP)
RE...! REN, CUT IT OUT—
TSUN
GATAN
...HYAH!
GATA
N-NOT THEEERE!
TSUN
TSUN
WOW, HIBIKI-CHAN!
OKAY, MY TURN!!

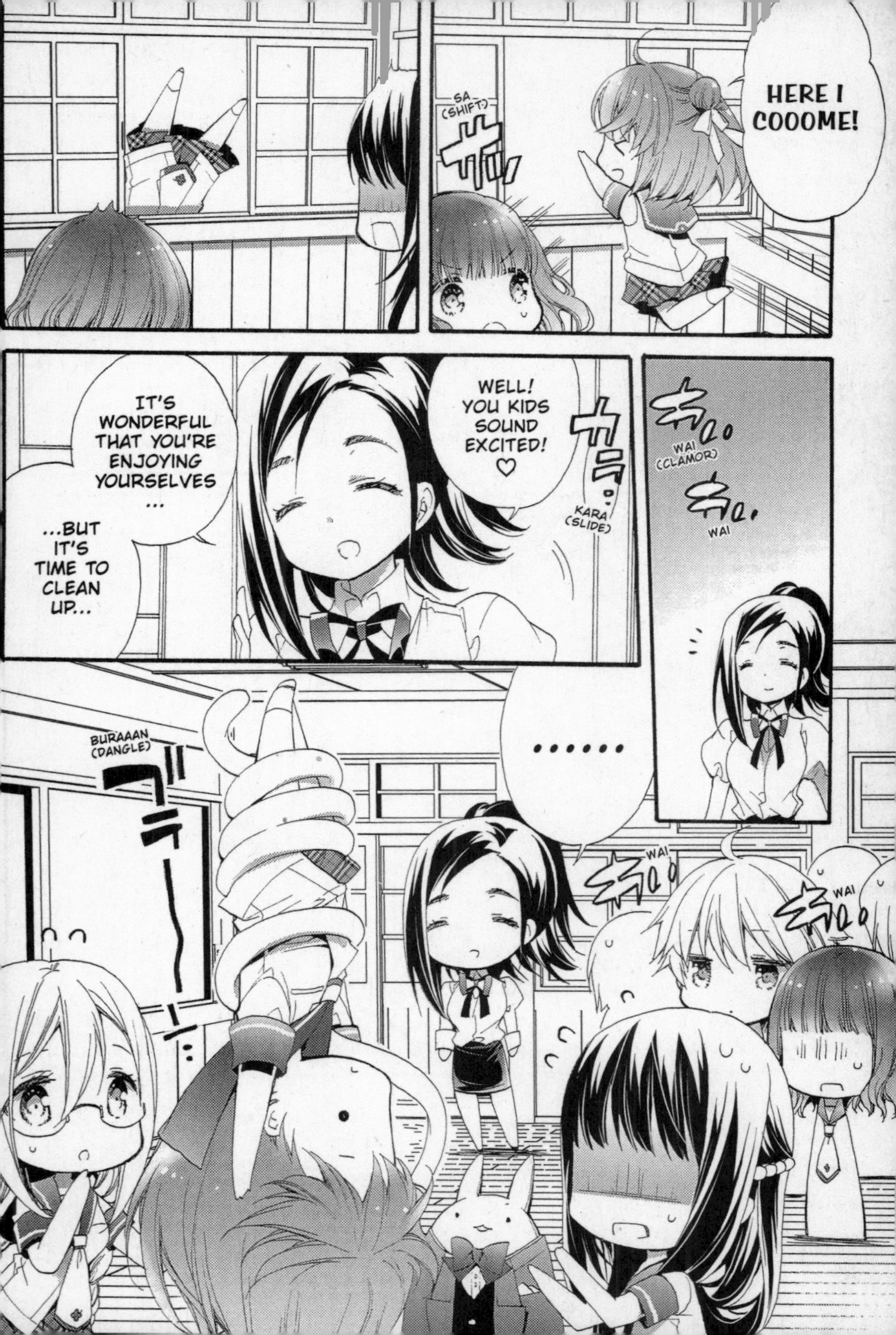
HERE I COOOME!
SA (SHIFT)
WAI (CLAMOR)
WAI
WELL! YOU KIDS SOUND EXCITED! ♡
KARA (SLIDE)
IT'S WONDERFUL THAT YOU'RE ENJOYING YOURSELVES ...
...BUT IT'S TIME TO CLEAN UP...
......
WAI
WAI
BURAAAN (DANGLE)

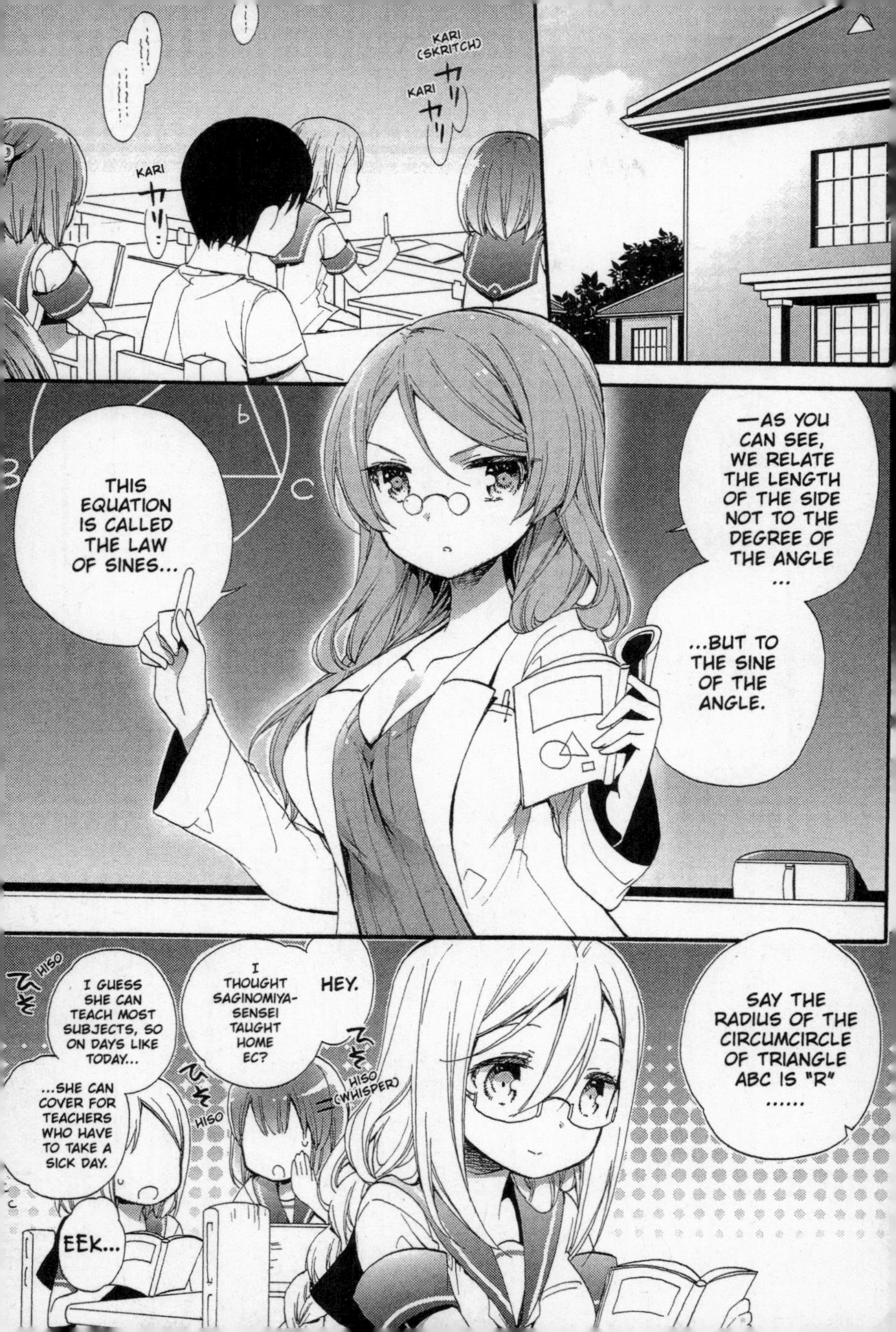
KARI (SKRITCH)
KARI
KARI
—AS YOU CAN SEE, WE RELATE THE LENGTH OF THE SIDE NOT TO THE DEGREE OF THE ANGLE ...
...BUT TO THE SINE OF THE ANGLE.
THIS EQUATION IS CALLED THE LAW OF SINES...
SAY THE RADIUS OF THE CIRCUMCIRCLE OF TRIANGLE ABC IS "R" ......
HEY.
I THOUGHT SAGINOMIYA-SENSEI TAUGHT HOME EC?
HISO (WHISPER)
HISO
HISO
I GUESS SHE CAN TEACH MOST SUBJECTS, SO ON DAYS LIKE TODAY...
...SHE CAN COVER FOR TEACHERS WHO HAVE TO TAKE A SICK DAY.
EEK...

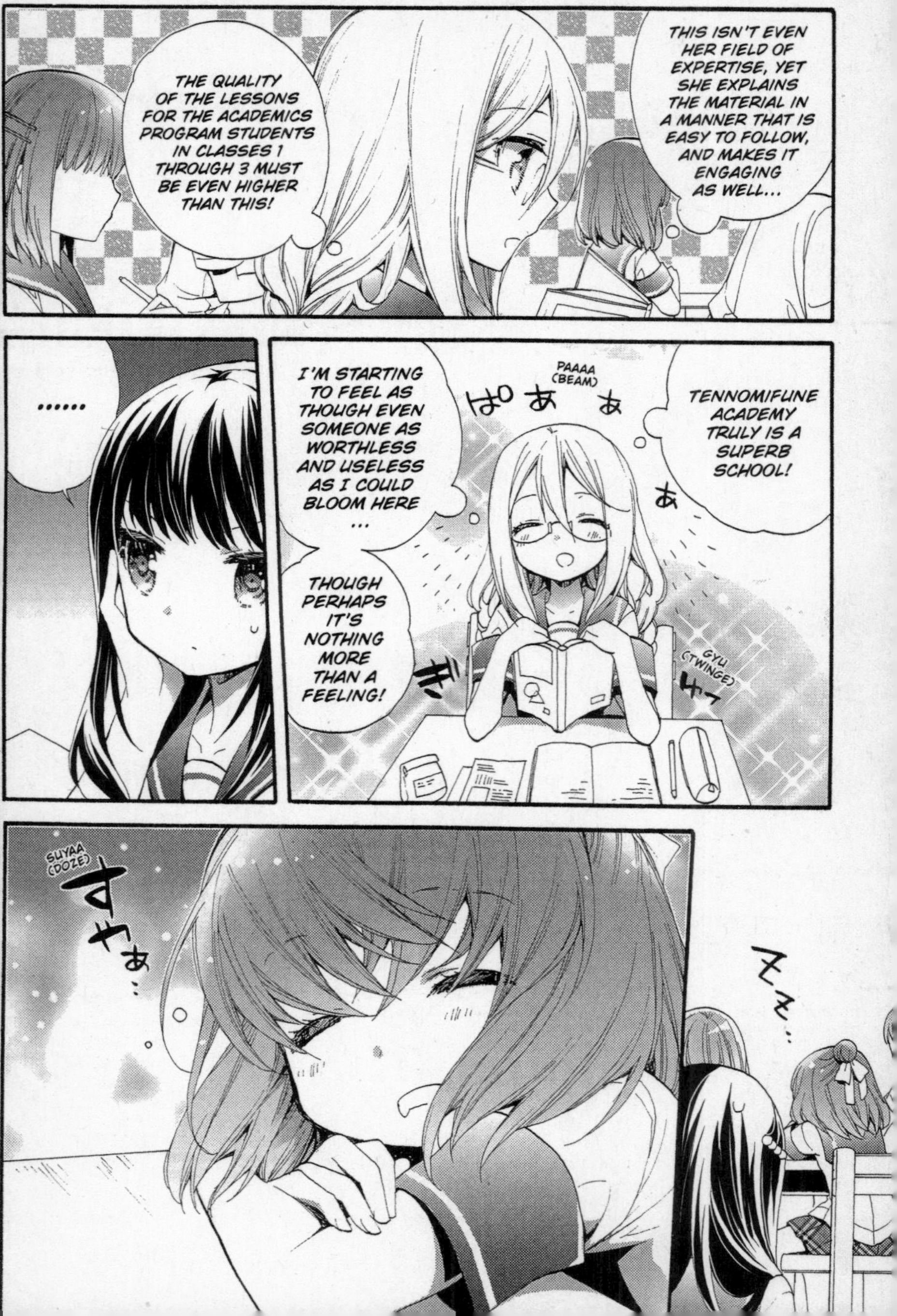
THIS ISN'T EVEN HER FIELD OF EXPERTISE, YET SHE EXPLAINS THE MATERIAL IN A MANNER THAT IS EASY TO FOLLOW, AND MAKES IT ENGAGING AS WELL...
THE QUALITY OF THE LESSONS FOR THE ACADEMICS PROGRAM STUDENTS IN CLASSES 1 THROUGH 3 MUST BE EVEN HIGHER THAN THIS!
TENNOMIFUNE ACADEMY TRULY IS A SUPERB SCHOOL!
PAAAA (BEAM)
ぱあぁぁ
I'M STARTING TO FEEL AS THOUGH EVEN SOMEONE AS WORTHLESS AND USELESS AS I COULD BLOOM HERE ...
THOUGH PERHAPS IT'S NOTHING MORE THAN A FEELING!
GYU (TWINGE)
ぎゅっ
......
ぞぞ...
SUYAA (DOZE)
すやぁ..

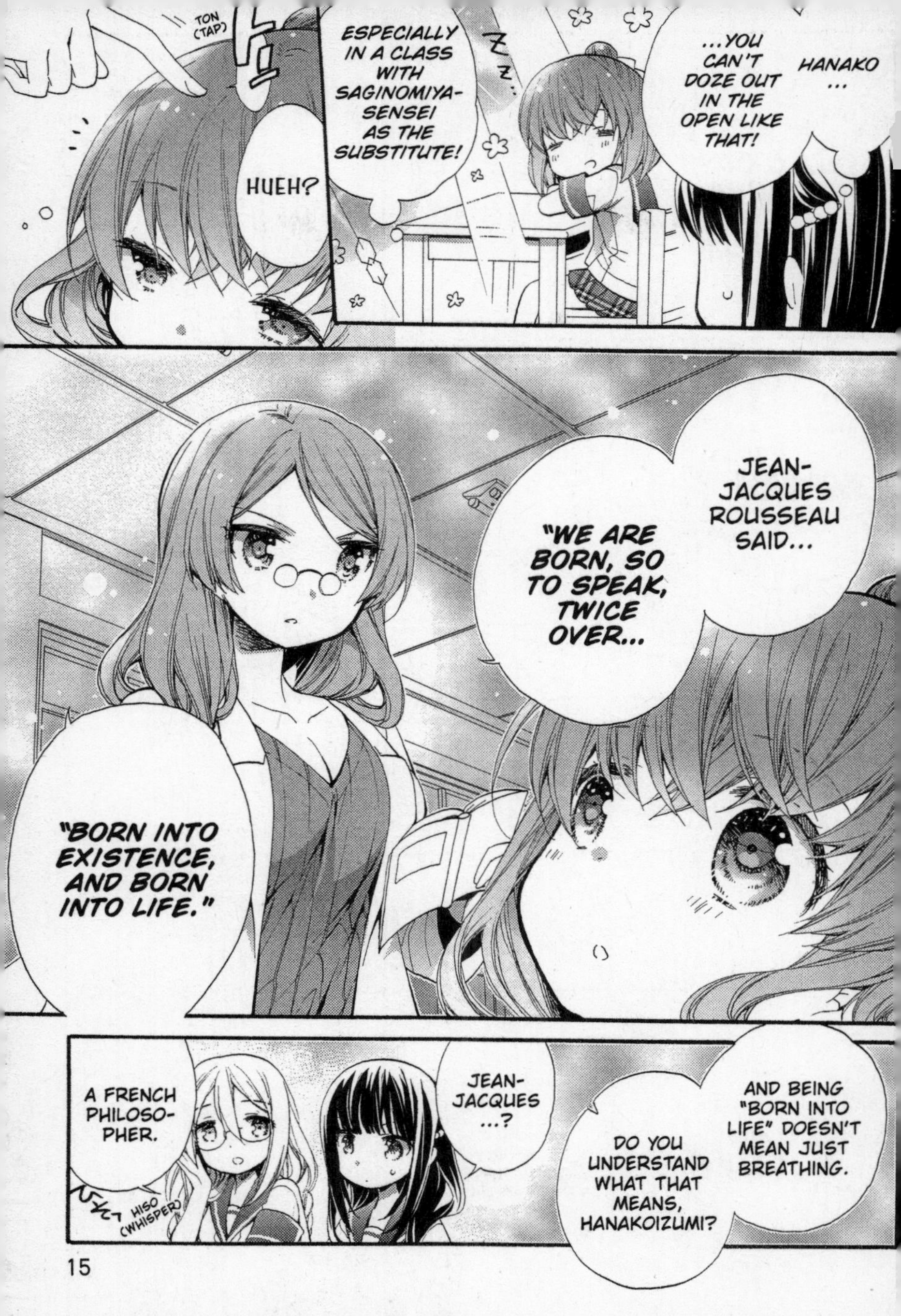
HANAKO ...
...YOU CAN'T DOZE OUT IN THE OPEN LIKE THAT!
ESPECIALLY IN A CLASS WITH SAGINOMIYA-SENSEI AS THE SUBSTITUTE!
TON (TAP)
HUEH?
JEAN-JACQUES ROUSSEAU SAID...
"WE ARE BORN, SO TO SPEAK, TWICE OVER...
"BORN INTO EXISTENCE, AND BORN INTO LIFE."
AND BEING "BORN INTO LIFE" DOESN'T MEAN JUST BREATHING.
DO YOU UNDERSTAND WHAT THAT MEANS, HANAKOIZUMI?
JEAN-JACQUES ...?
A FRENCH PHILOSOPHER.
HISO (WHISPER)

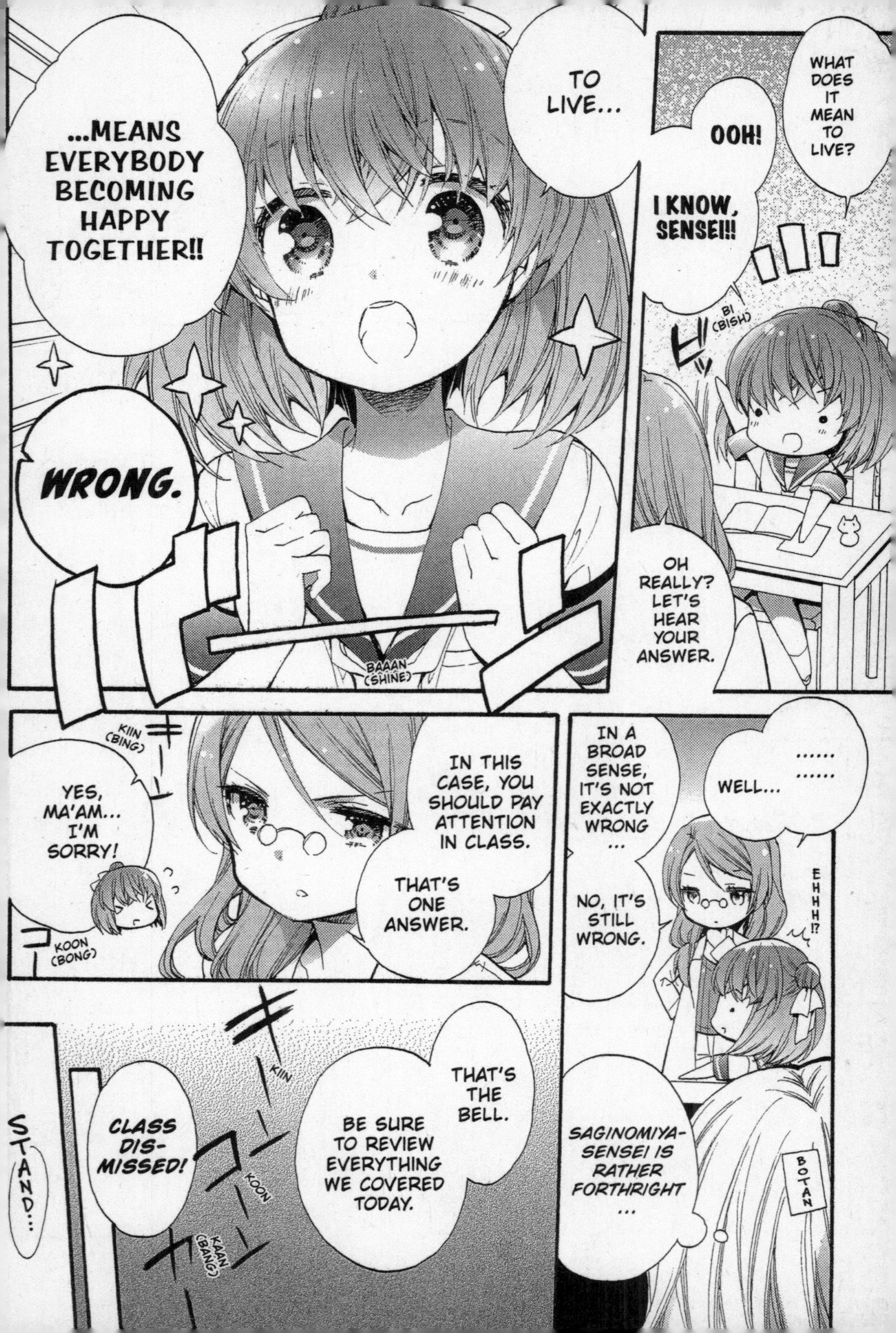
WHAT DOES IT MEAN TO LIVE?
OOH!
I KNOW, SENSEI!!!
BI (BISH)
OH REALLY? LET'S HEAR YOUR ANSWER.
TO LIVE...
...MEANS EVERYBODY BECOMING HAPPY TOGETHER!!
WRONG.
BAAAN (SHINE)
......
......
WELL...
IN A BROAD SENSE, IT'S NOT EXACTLY WRONG ...
EHHH!?
NO, IT'S STILL WRONG.
IN THIS CASE, YOU SHOULD PAY ATTENTION IN CLASS.
THAT'S ONE ANSWER.
KIIN (BING)
YES, MA'AM... I'M SORRY!
KOON (BONG)
BOTAN
SAGINOMIYA-SENSEI IS RATHER FORTHRIGHT ...
THAT'S THE BELL.
BE SURE TO REVIEW EVERYTHING WE COVERED TODAY.
KIIN
KOON
KAAN (BANG)
CLASS DIS-MISSED!
STAND...

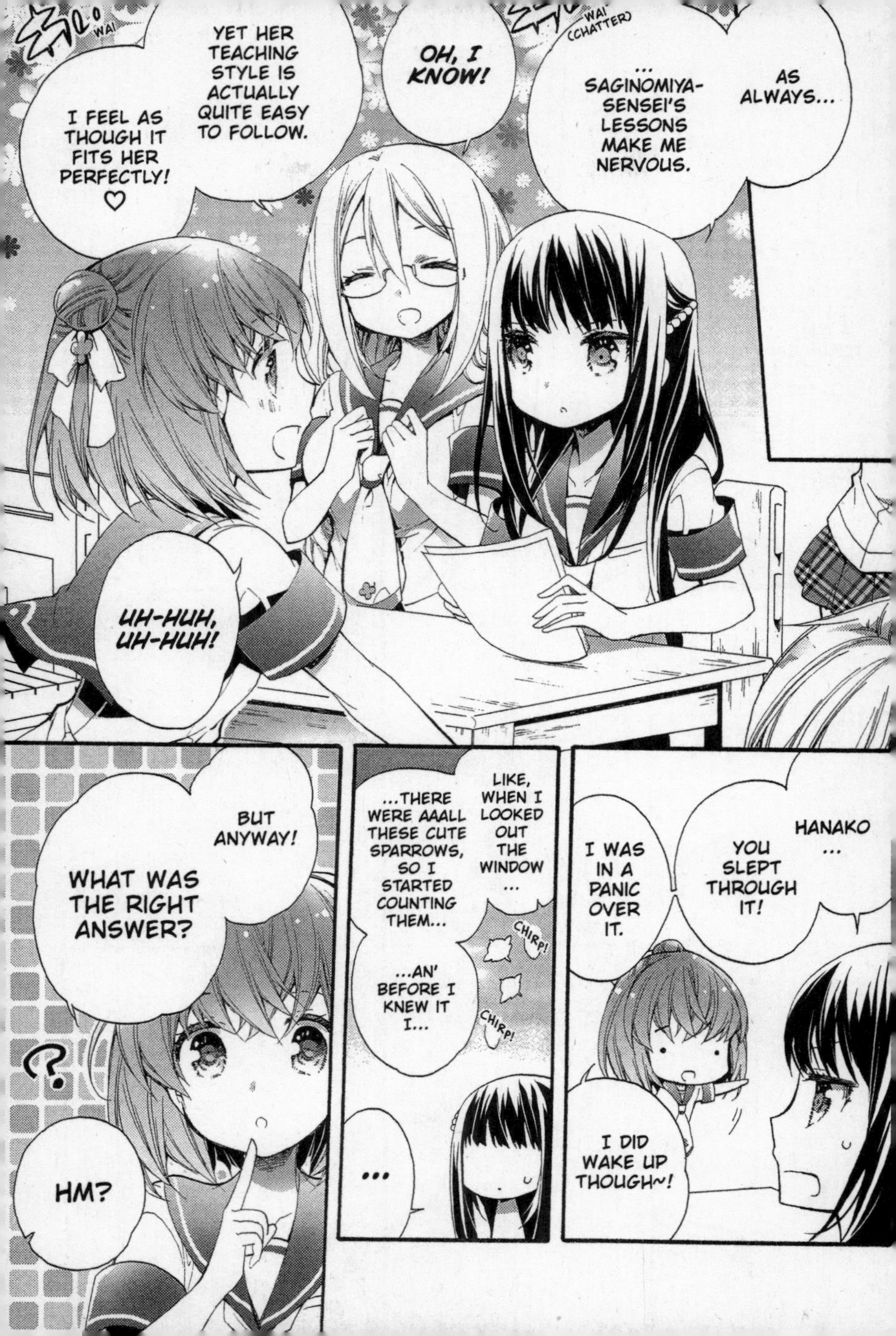
WAI (CHATTER)
AS ALWAYS...
...SAGINOMIYA-SENSEI'S LESSONS MAKE ME NERVOUS.
OH, I KNOW!
YET HER TEACHING STYLE IS ACTUALLY QUITE EASY TO FOLLOW.
WAI
I FEEL AS THOUGH IT FITS HER PERFECTLY! ♡
UH-HUH, UH-HUH!
HANAKO...
YOU SLEPT THROUGH IT!
I WAS IN A PANIC OVER IT.
I DID WAKE UP THOUGH~!
LIKE, WHEN I LOOKED OUT THE WINDOW...
...THERE WERE AAALL THESE CUTE SPARROWS, SO I STARTED COUNTING THEM...
CHIRP!
...AN' BEFORE I KNEW IT I...
CHIRP!
...
BUT ANYWAY!
WHAT WAS THE RIGHT ANSWER?
HM?

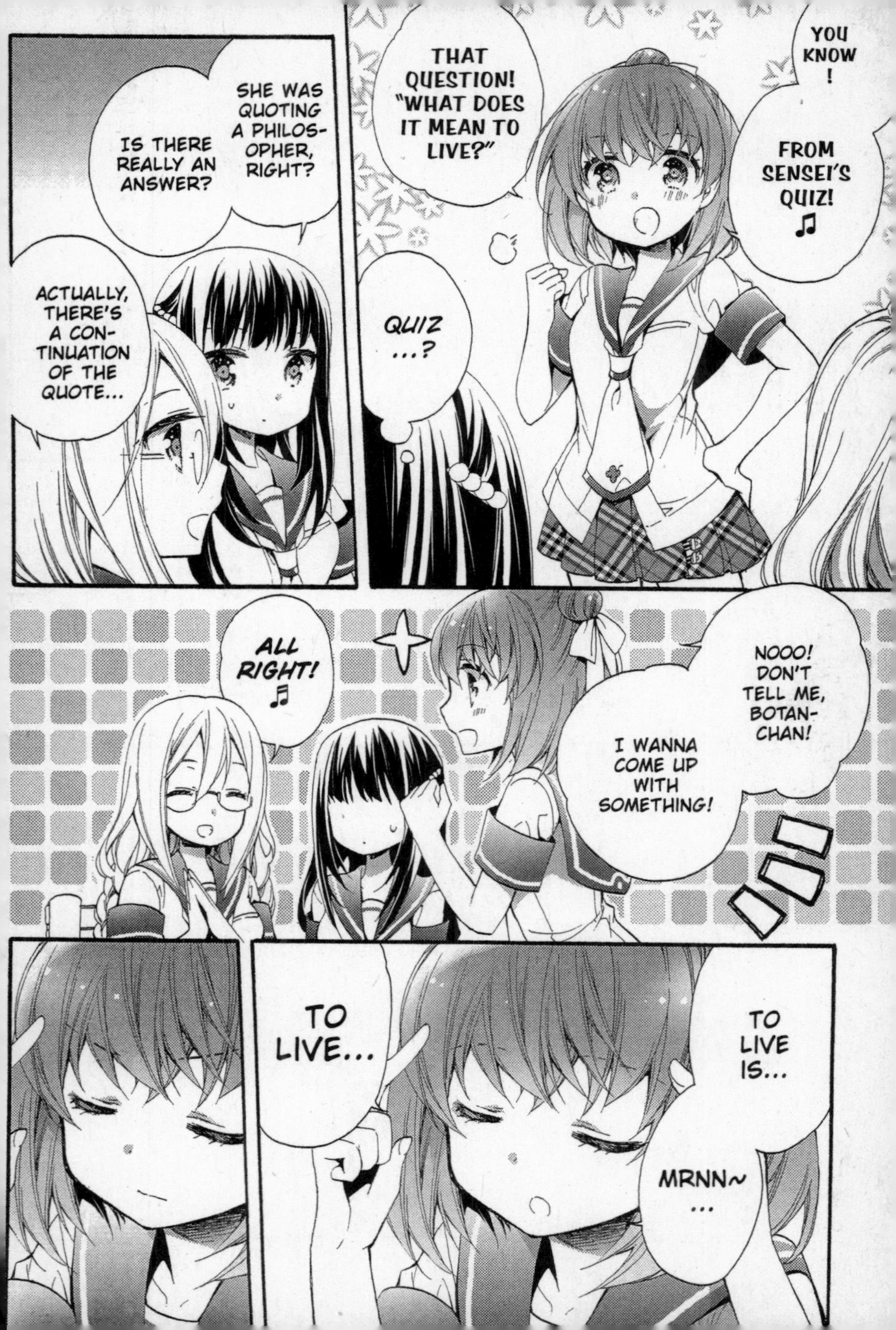
YOU KNOW!
FROM SENSEI'S QUIZ! ♫
THAT QUESTION! "WHAT DOES IT MEAN TO LIVE?"
QUIZ ...?
SHE WAS QUOTING A PHILOS-OPHER, RIGHT?
IS THERE REALLY AN ANSWER?
ACTUALLY, THERE'S A CON-TINUATION OF THE QUOTE...
NOOO! DON'T TELL ME, BOTAN-CHAN!
I WANNA COME UP WITH SOMETHING!
ALL RIGHT! ♫
TO LIVE IS...
TO LIVE...
MRNN~ ...

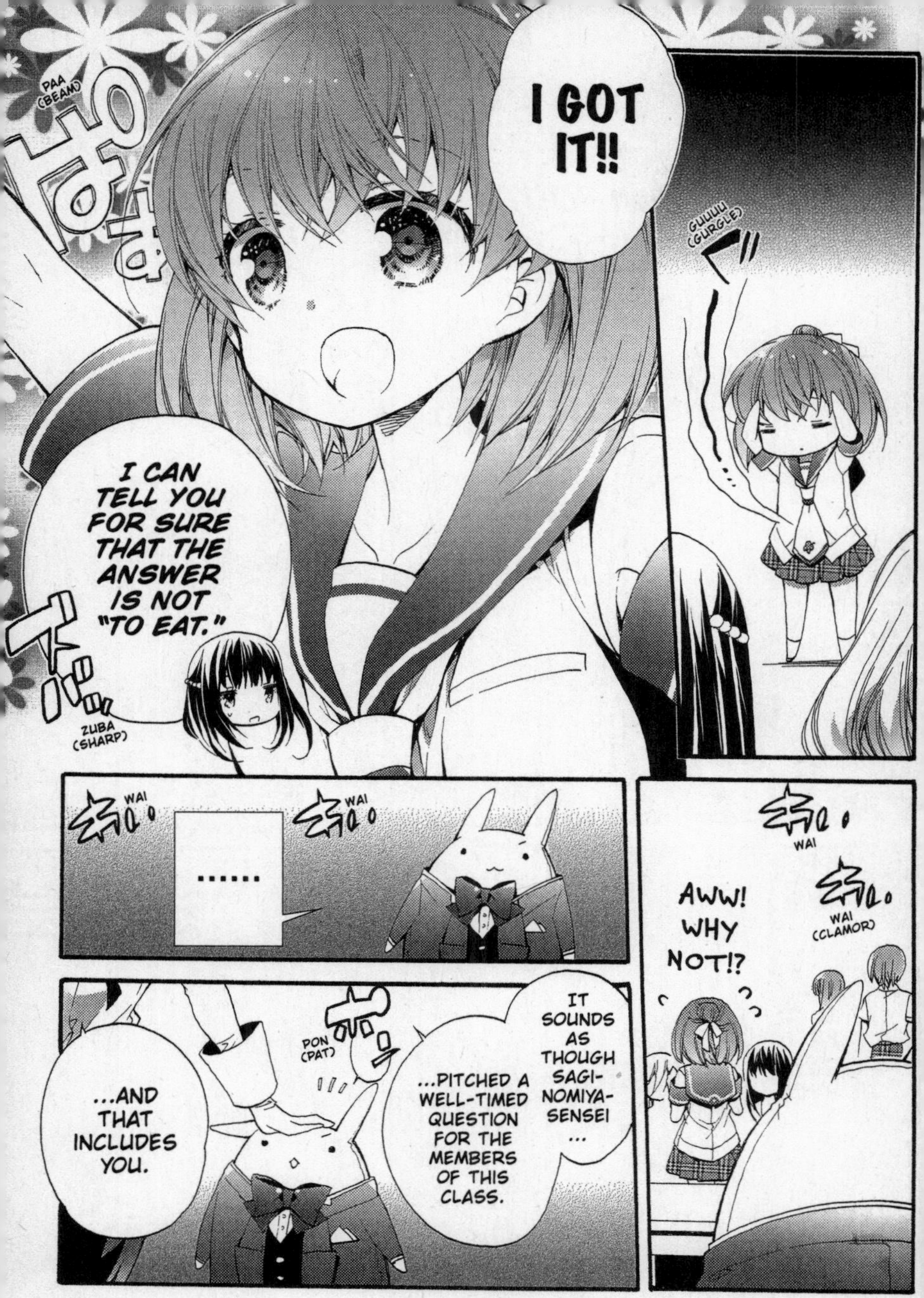
GUUUU (GURGLE)
I GOT IT!!
PAA (BEAM)
I CAN TELL YOU FOR SURE THAT THE ANSWER IS NOT "TO EAT."
ZUBA (SHARP)
WAI
AWW! WHY NOT!?
WAI (CLAMOR)
WAI
WAI
......
IT SOUNDS AS THOUGH SAGI-NOMIYA-SENSEI ...
...PITCHED A WELL-TIMED QUESTION FOR THE MEMBERS OF THIS CLASS.
PON (PAT)
...AND THAT INCLUDES YOU.

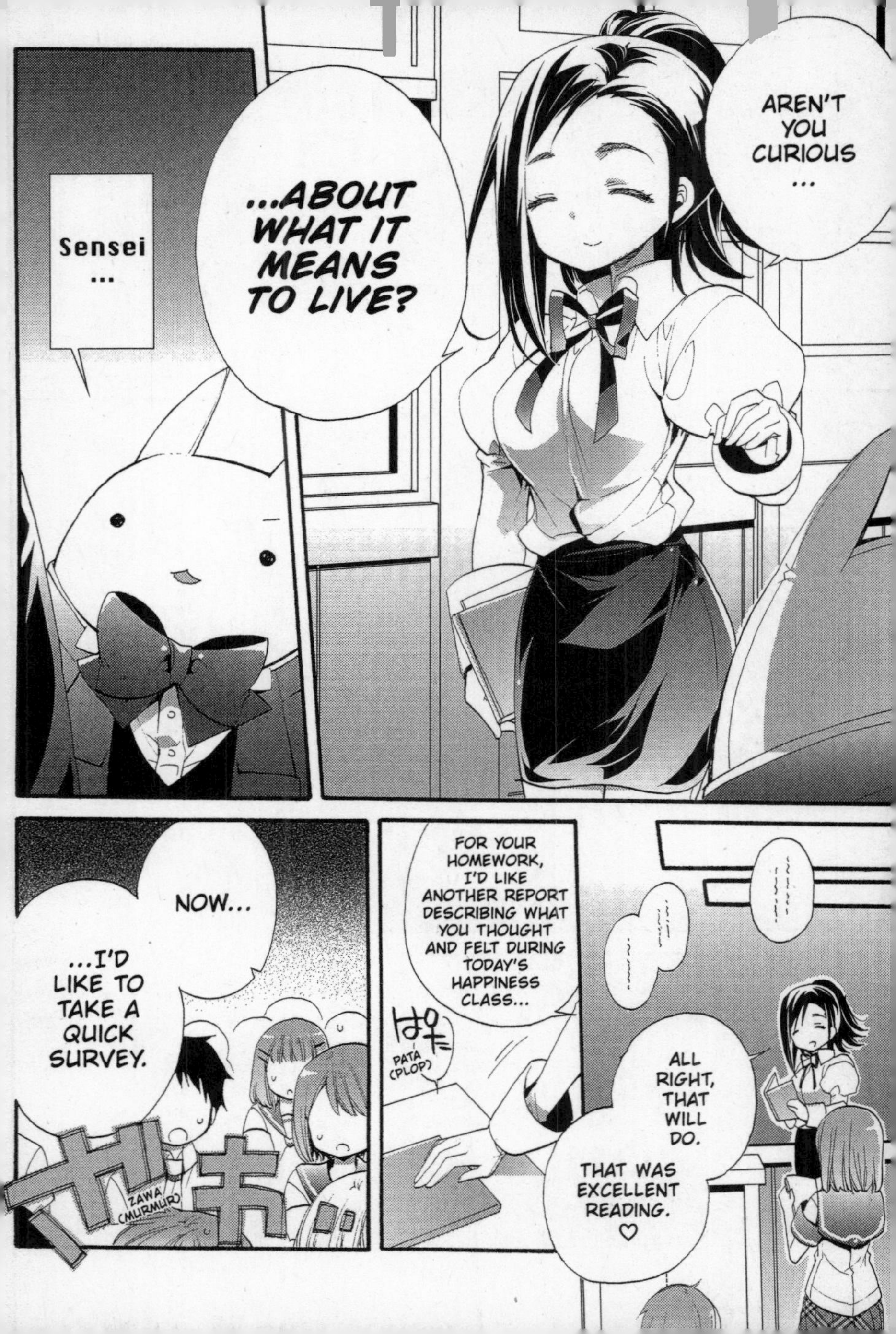
AREN'T YOU CURIOUS ...
...ABOUT WHAT IT MEANS TO LIVE?
Sensei ...
ALL RIGHT, THAT WILL DO.
THAT WAS EXCELLENT READING. ♡
FOR YOUR HOMEWORK, I'D LIKE ANOTHER REPORT DESCRIBING WHAT YOU THOUGHT AND FELT DURING TODAY'S HAPPINESS CLASS...
PATA (PLOP)
NOW...
...I'D LIKE TO TAKE A QUICK SURVEY.
ZAWA (MURMUR)

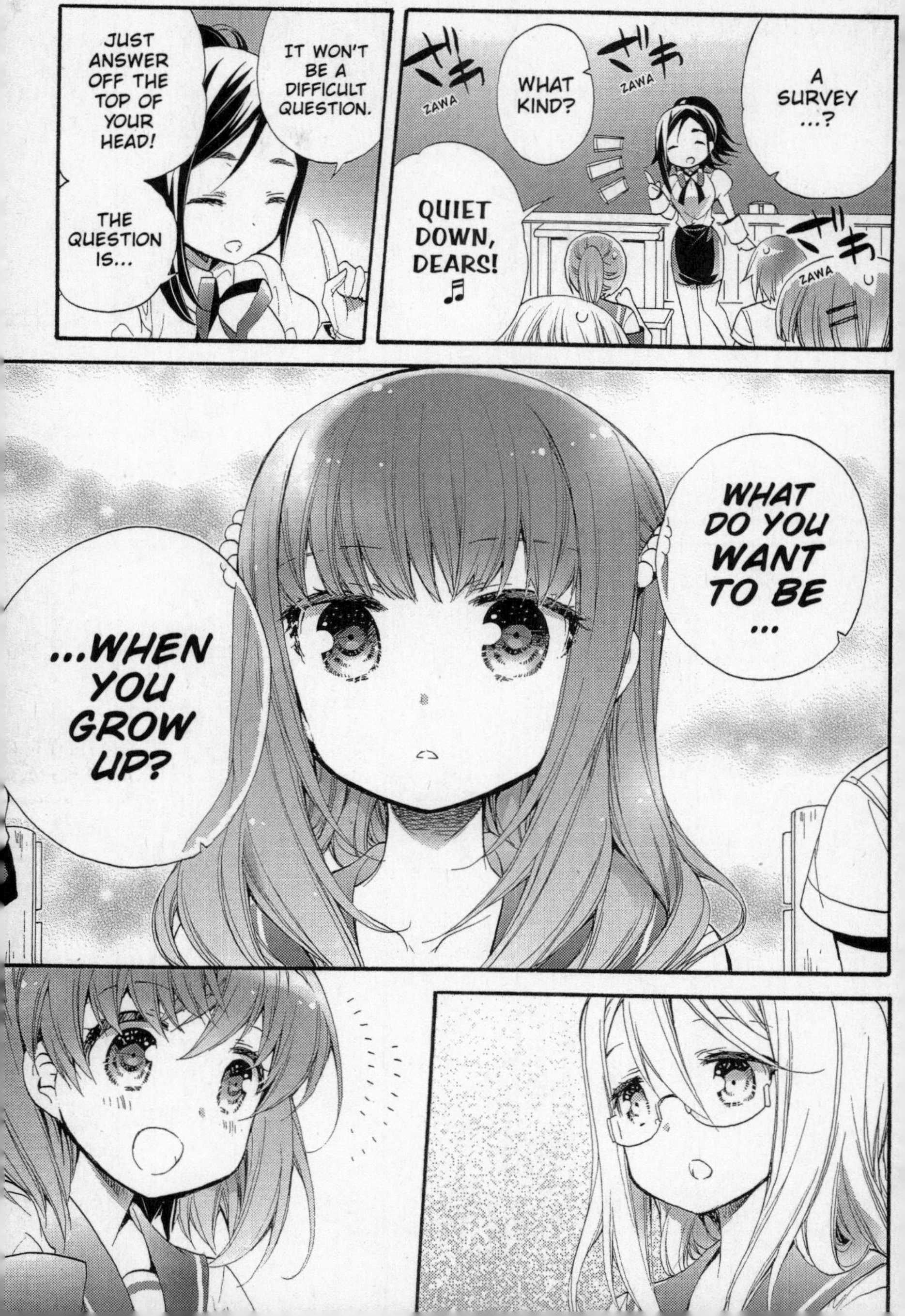
A SURVEY ...?
ZAWA
WHAT KIND?
ZAWA
ZAWA
QUIET DOWN, DEARS! ♫
IT WON'T BE A DIFFICULT QUESTION.
JUST ANSWER OFF THE TOP OF YOUR HEAD!
THE QUESTION IS...
WHAT DO YOU WANT TO BE ...
...WHEN YOU GROW UP?

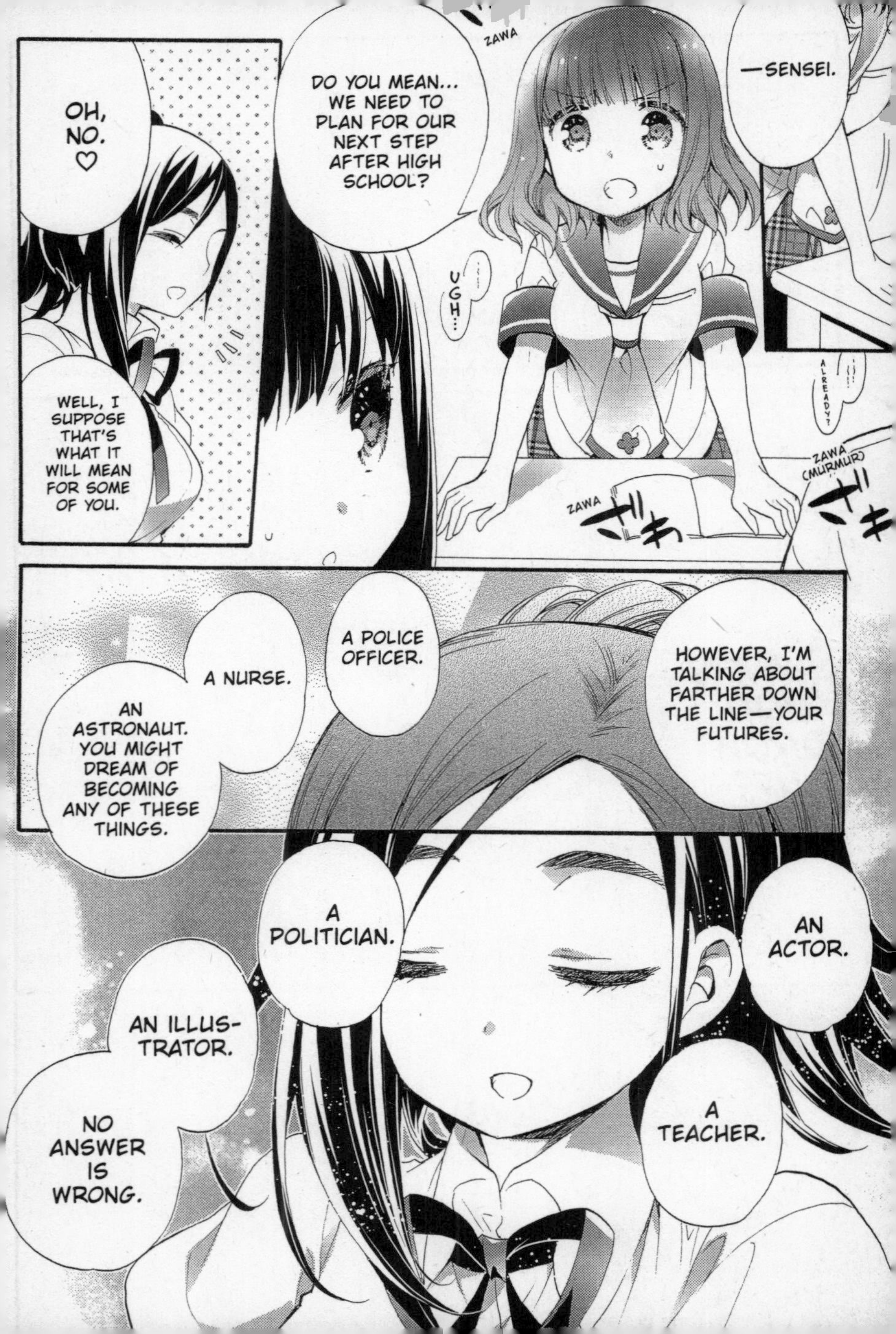
—SENSEI.
ZAWA
DO YOU MEAN... WE NEED TO PLAN FOR OUR NEXT STEP AFTER HIGH SCHOOL?
UGH...
ALREADY?
ZAWA (MURMUR)
ZAWA
OH, NO. ♡
WELL, I SUPPOSE THAT'S WHAT IT WILL MEAN FOR SOME OF YOU.
HOWEVER, I'M TALKING ABOUT FARTHER DOWN THE LINE—YOUR FUTURES.
A POLICE OFFICER.
A NURSE.
AN ASTRONAUT. YOU MIGHT DREAM OF BECOMING ANY OF THESE THINGS.
AN ACTOR.
A POLITICIAN.
A TEACHER.
AN ILLUS-TRATOR.
NO ANSWER IS WRONG.

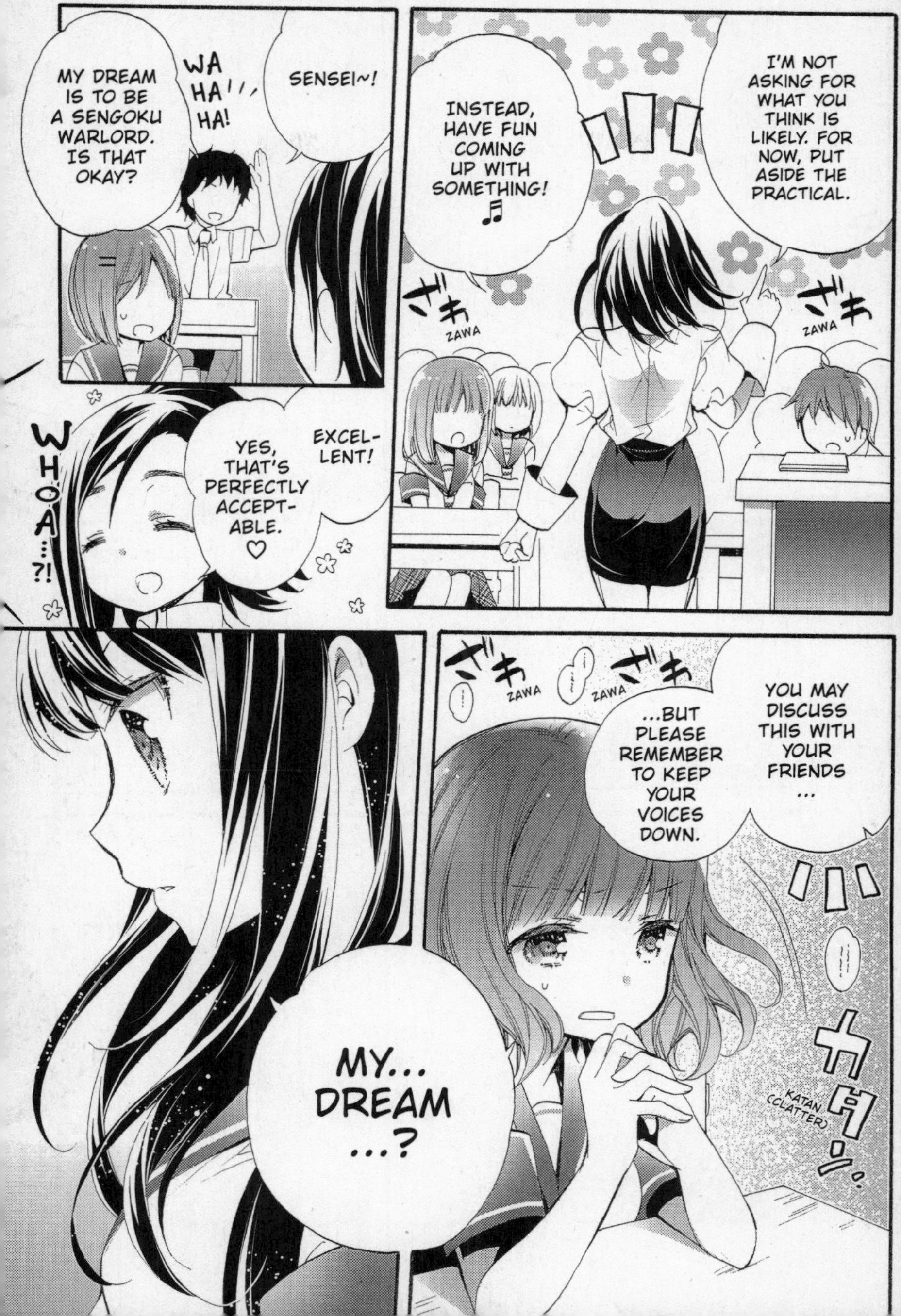
I'M NOT ASKING FOR WHAT YOU THINK IS LIKELY. FOR NOW, PUT ASIDE THE PRACTICAL.
INSTEAD, HAVE FUN COMING UP WITH SOMETHING! ♬
ZAWA
ZAWA
SENSEI~!
WA HA HA!
MY DREAM IS TO BE A SENGOKU WARLORD. IS THAT OKAY?
EXCEL-LENT!
YES, THAT'S PERFECTLY ACCEPT-ABLE. ♡
WHOA...?!
YOU MAY DISCUSS THIS WITH YOUR FRIENDS ...
...BUT PLEASE REMEMBER TO KEEP YOUR VOICES DOWN.
ZAWA
ZAWA
KATAN (CLATTER)
MY... DREAM ...?

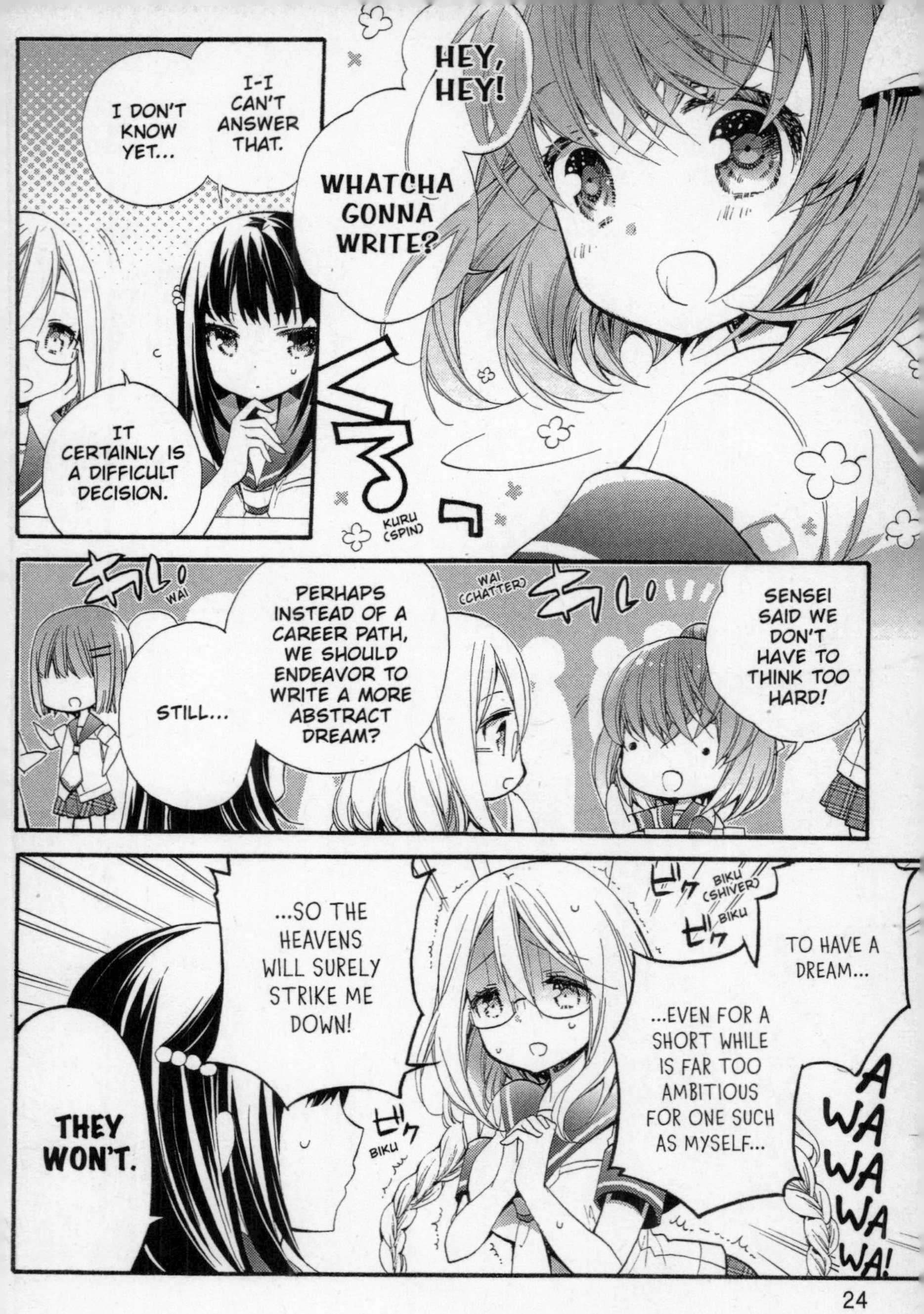
HEY, HEY!
WHATCHA GONNA WRITE?
KURU (SPIN)
I-I CAN'T ANSWER THAT.
I DON'T KNOW YET...
IT CERTAINLY IS A DIFFICULT DECISION.
SENSEI SAID WE DON'T HAVE TO THINK TOO HARD!
WAI (CHATTER)
PERHAPS INSTEAD OF A CAREER PATH, WE SHOULD ENDEAVOR TO WRITE A MORE ABSTRACT DREAM?
STILL...
WAI
BIKU (SHIVER)
BIKU
TO HAVE A DREAM...
...EVEN FOR A SHORT WHILE IS FAR TOO AMBITIOUS FOR ONE SUCH AS MYSELF...
AWAWAWAWA!
...SO THE HEAVENS WILL SURELY STRIKE ME DOWN!
BIKU
THEY WON'T.

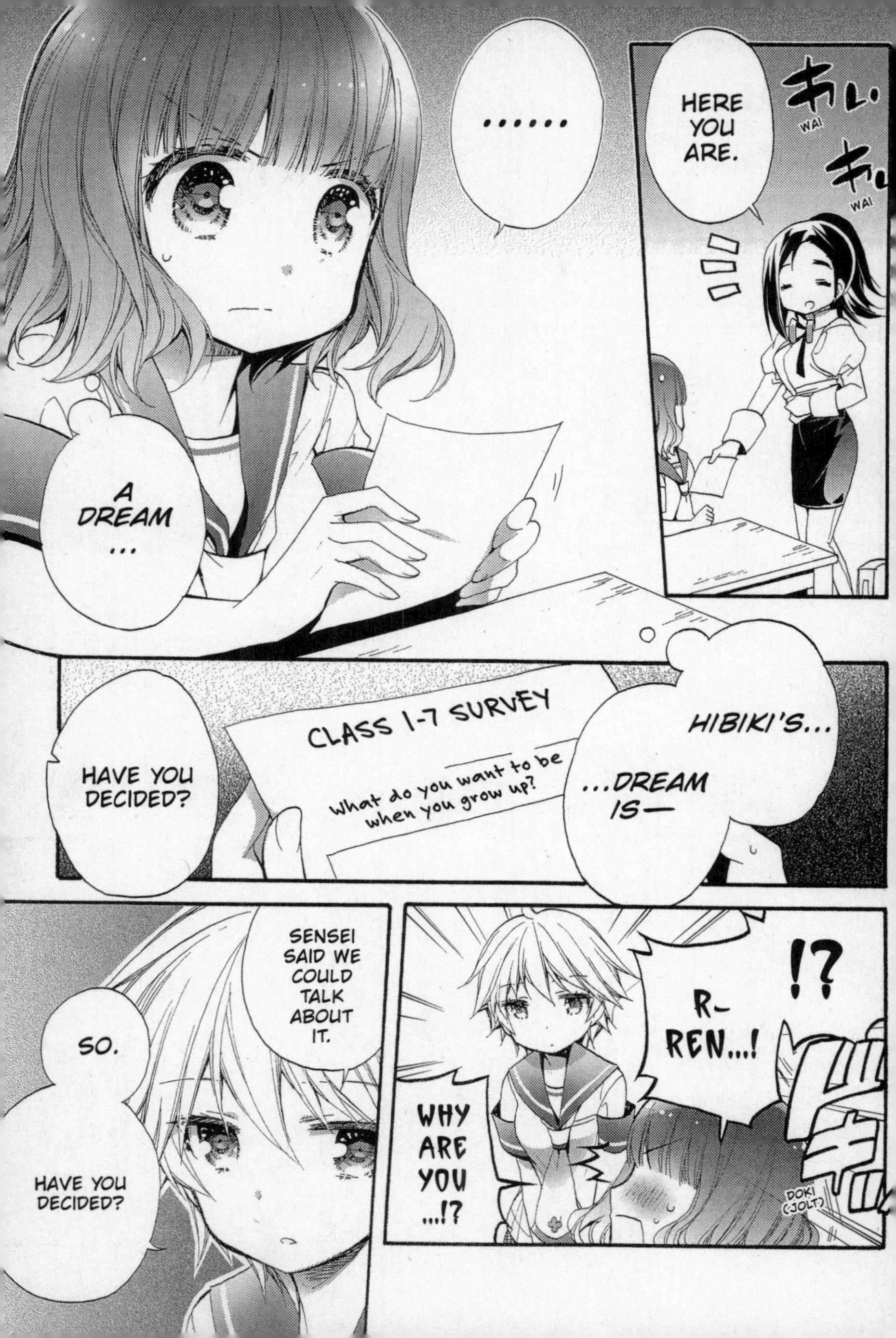
WAI
WAI
HERE YOU ARE.
......
A DREAM ...
HIBIKI'S...
...DREAM IS—
CLASS 1-7 SURVEY
What do you want to be when you grow up?
HAVE YOU DECIDED?
!?
R-REN...!
DOKI (-JOLT-)
WHY ARE YOU ...!?
SENSEI SAID WE COULD TALK ABOUT IT.
SO.
HAVE YOU DECIDED?

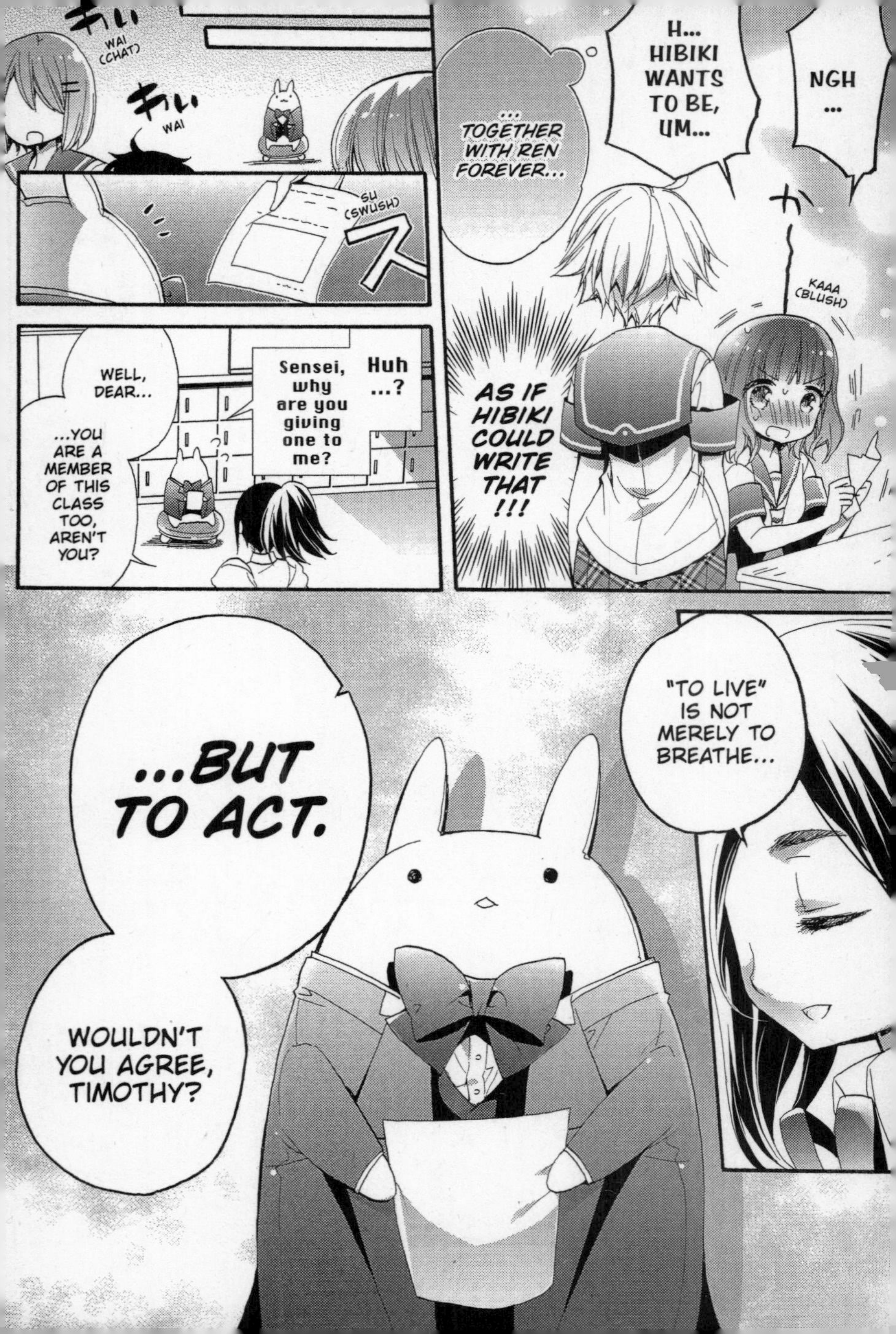
NGH ...
H... HIBIKI WANTS TO BE, UM...
...TOGETHER WITH REN FOREVER...
KAAA (BLUSH)
AS IF HIBIKI COULD WRITE THAT!!!
WAI (CHAT)
WAI
SU (SWUSH)
Huh ...?
Sensei, why are you giving one to me?
WELL, DEAR...
...YOU ARE A MEMBER OF THIS CLASS TOO, AREN'T YOU?
"TO LIVE" IS NOT MERELY TO BREATHE...
...BUT TO ACT.
WOULDN'T YOU AGREE, TIMOTHY?

Anne Happy

unhappy go lucky!

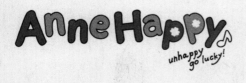

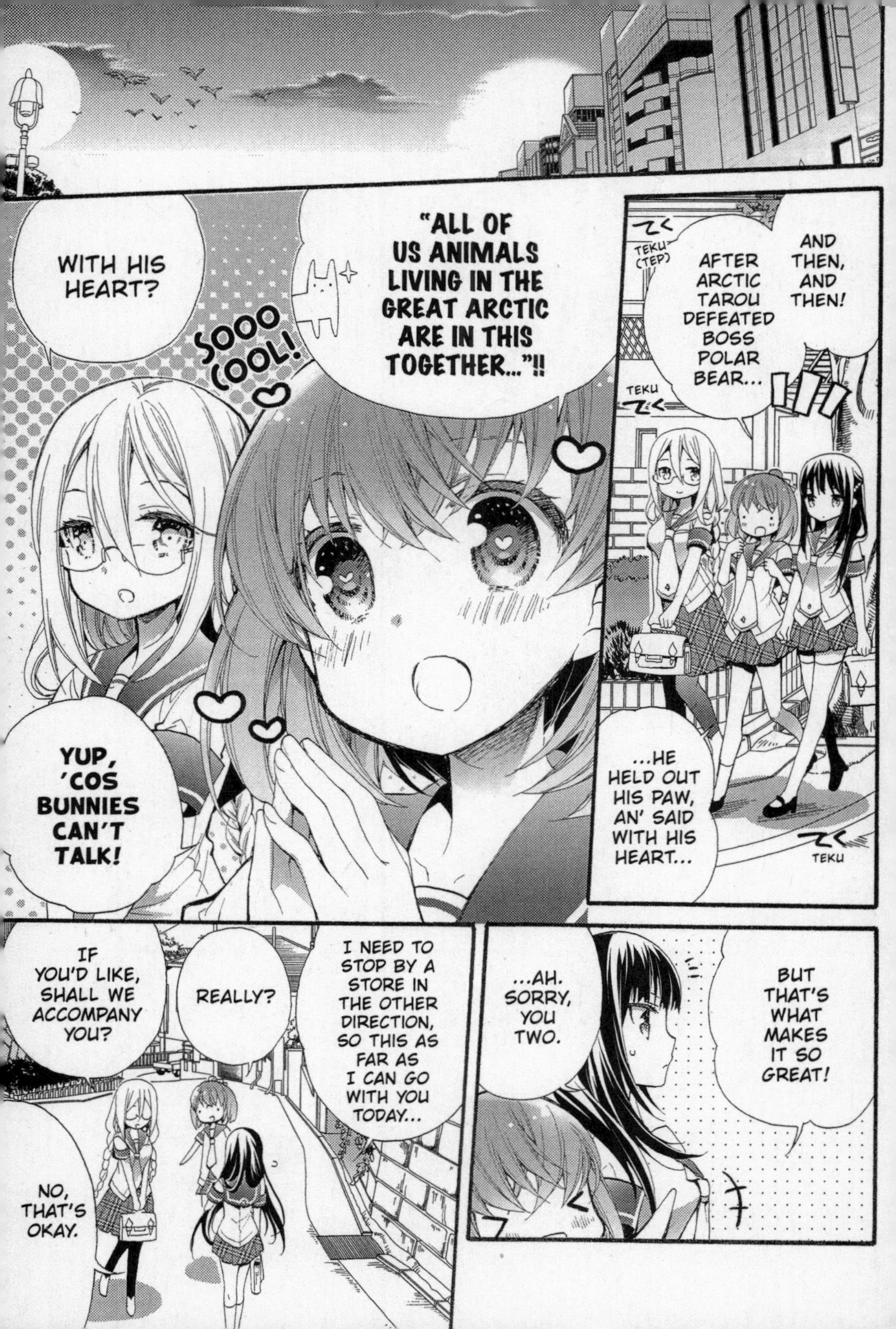
AND THEN, AND THEN!
TEKU (TEP)
AFTER ARCTIC TAROU DEFEATED BOSS POLAR BEAR...
TEKU
...HE HELD OUT HIS PAW, AN' SAID WITH HIS HEART...
TEKU
"ALL OF US ANIMALS LIVING IN THE GREAT ARCTIC ARE IN THIS TOGETHER..."!!
SOOO COOL!
WITH HIS HEART?
YUP, 'COS BUNNIES CAN'T TALK!
BUT THAT'S WHAT MAKES IT SO GREAT!
...AH. SORRY, YOU TWO.
I NEED TO STOP BY A STORE IN THE OTHER DIRECTION, SO THIS AS FAR AS I CAN GO WITH YOU TODAY...
REALLY?
IF YOU'D LIKE, SHALL WE ACCOMPANY YOU?
NO, THAT'S OKAY.

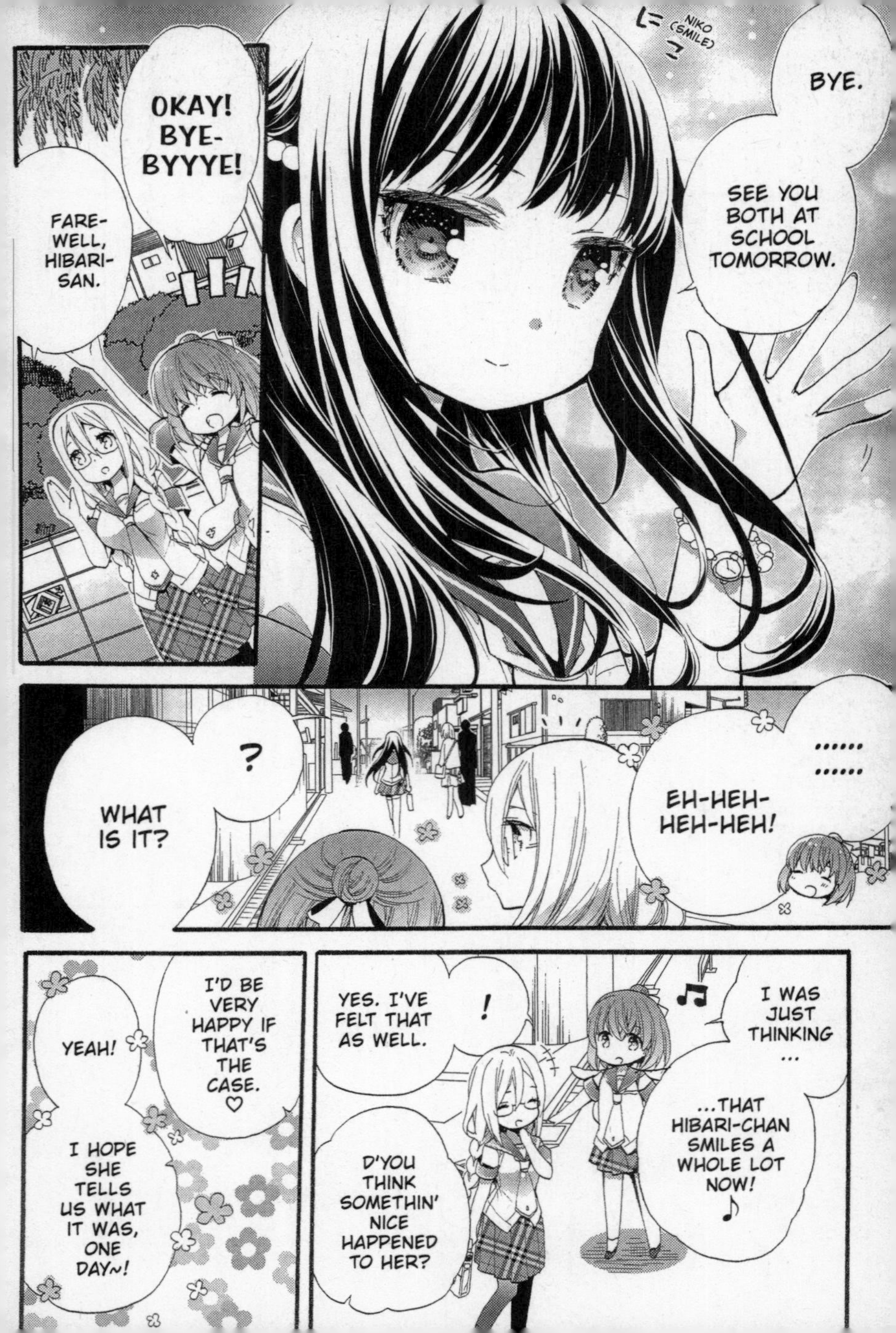
NIKO (SMILE)
BYE.
SEE YOU BOTH AT SCHOOL TOMORROW.
OKAY! BYE-BYYYE!
FARE-WELL, HIBARI-SAN.
......
......
EH-HEH-HEH-HEH!
?
WHAT IS IT?
I WAS JUST THINKING ...
...THAT HIBARI-CHAN SMILES A WHOLE LOT NOW! ♪
!
YES. I'VE FELT THAT AS WELL.
D'YOU THINK SOMETHIN' NICE HAPPENED TO HER?
I'D BE VERY HAPPY IF THAT'S THE CASE. ♡
YEAH!
I HOPE SHE TELLS US WHAT IT WAS, ONE DAY~!

✽ Lucky. 31

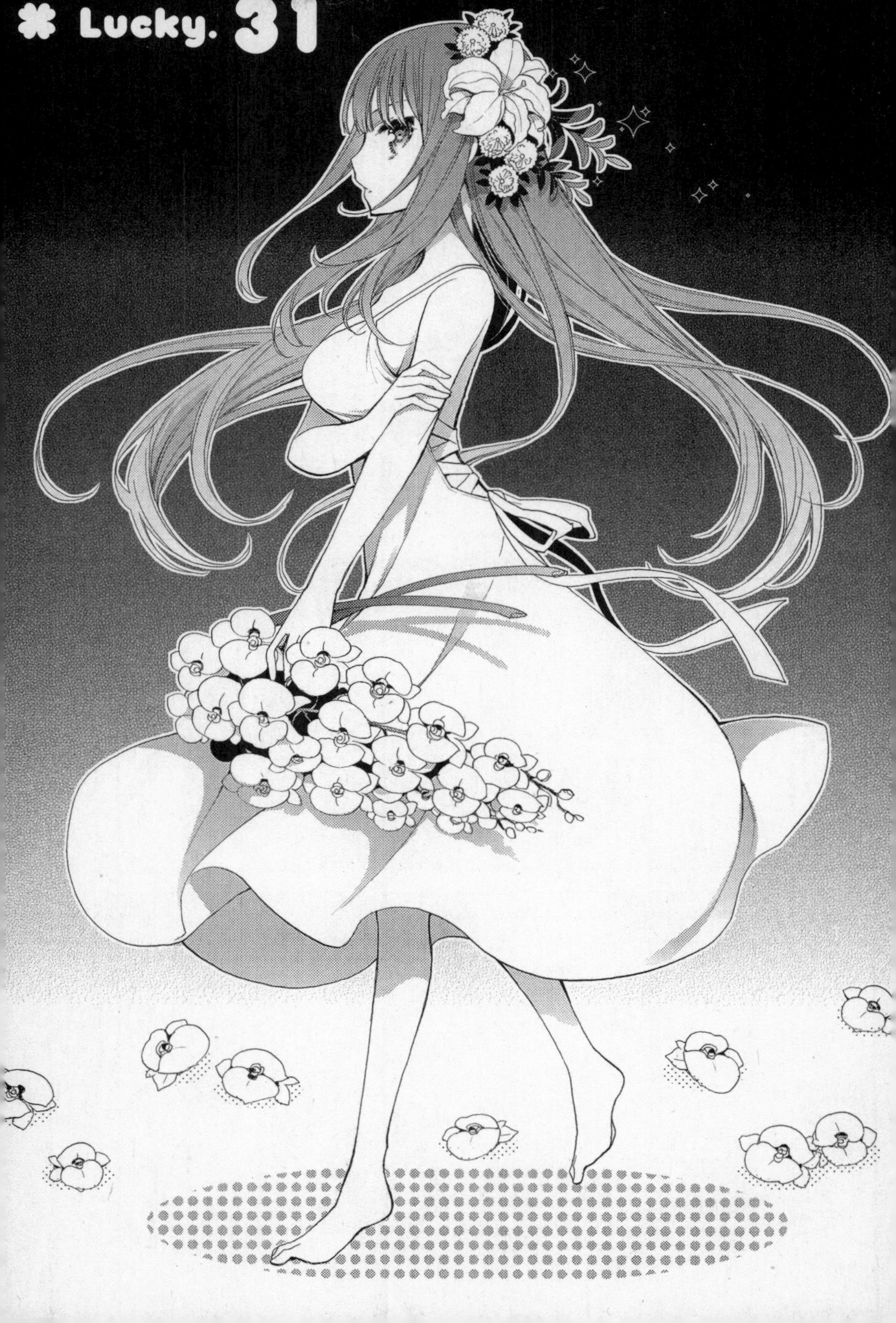

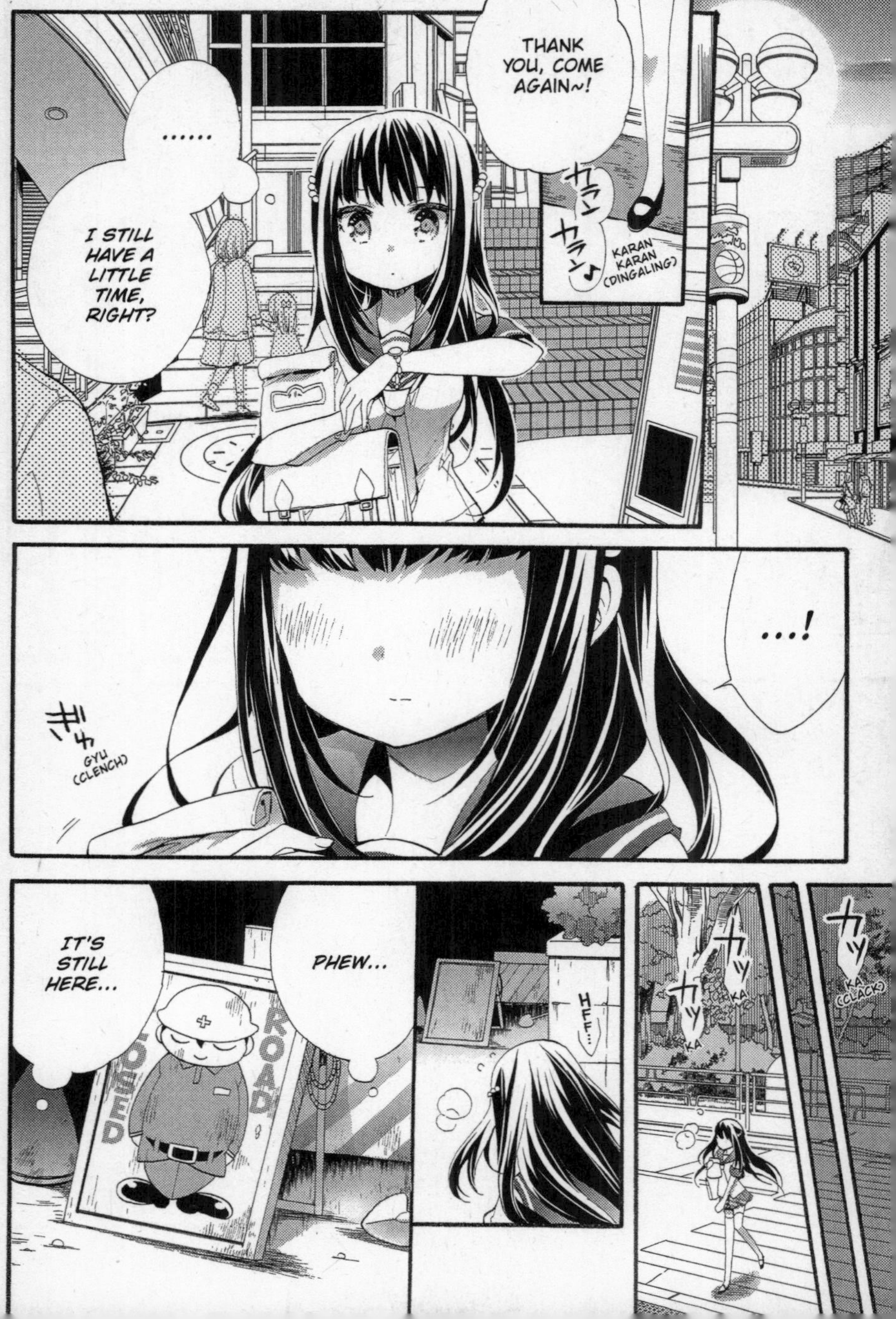
THANK YOU, COME AGAIN~!
カランカラン♪
KARAN KARAN (DINGALING)
......
I STILL HAVE A LITTLE TIME, RIGHT?
...!
ぎゅ
GYU (CLENCH)
カッ
KA (CLACK)
カッ
KA
カッ
KA
HFF...
PHEW...
IT'S STILL HERE...
ROAD

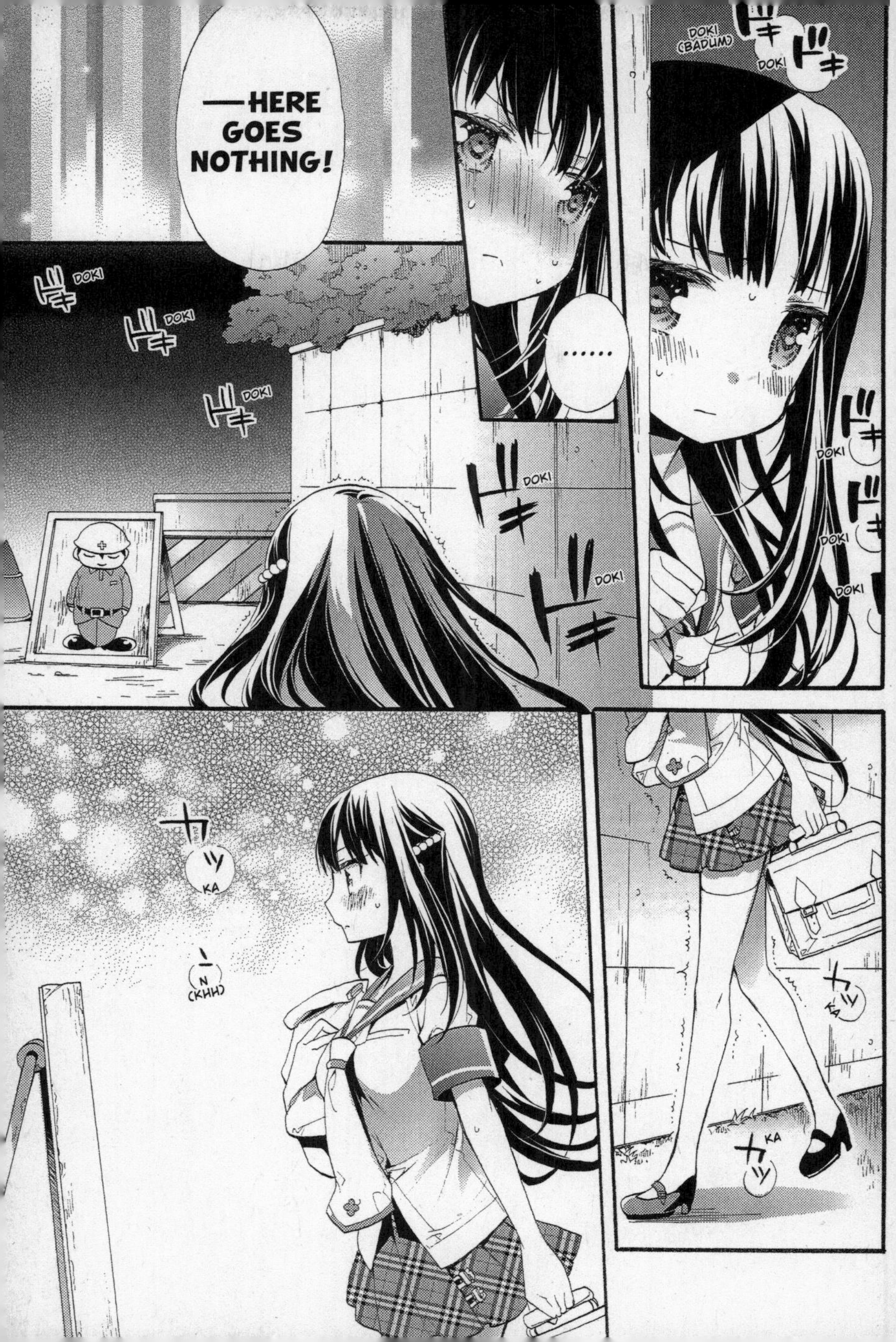
DOKI (BADUM)
DOKI
DOKI
DOKI
DOKI
......
—HERE GOES NOTHING!
DOKI
DOKI
DOKI
DOKI
DOKI
KA
KA
KA
N (KHH)

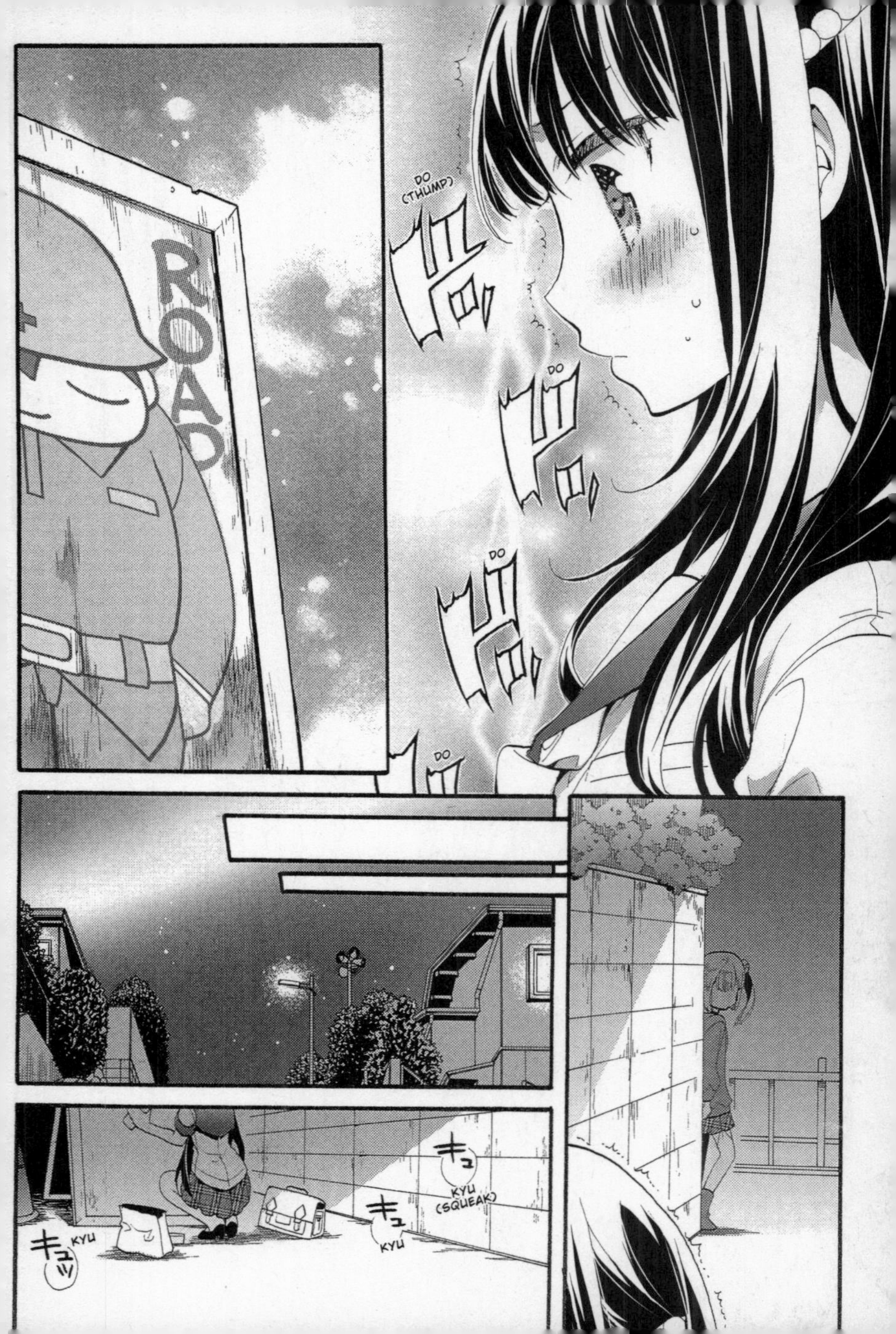
DO (THUMP)
DO
DO
DO
ROAD
キュ
KYU (SQUEAK)
キュ
KYU
キュッ
KYU

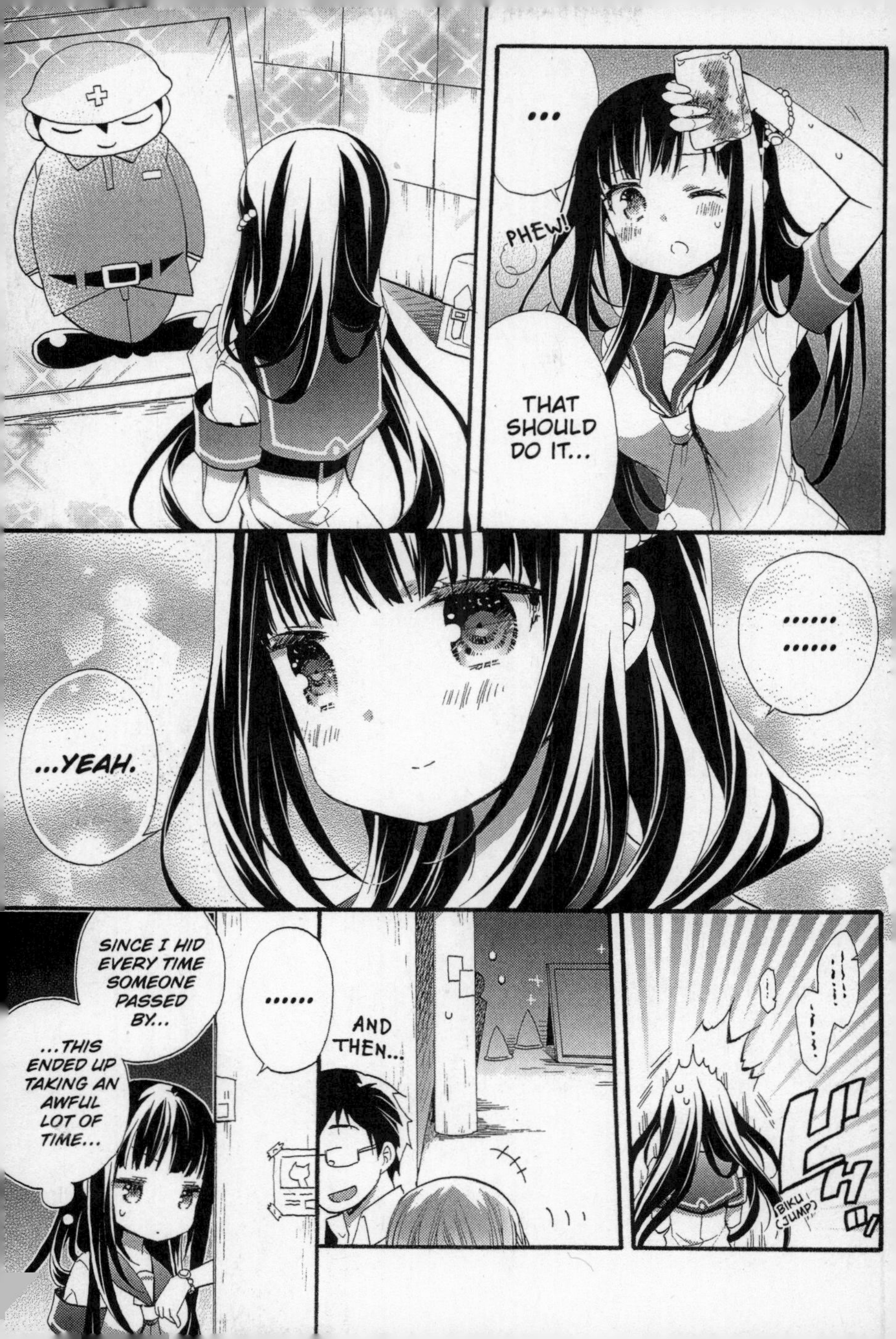
...
PHEW!
THAT SHOULD DO IT...
......
......
...YEAH.
BIKU (JUMP)
AND THEN...
......
SINCE I HID EVERY TIME SOMEONE PASSED BY...
...THIS ENDED UP TAKING AN AWFUL LOT OF TIME...

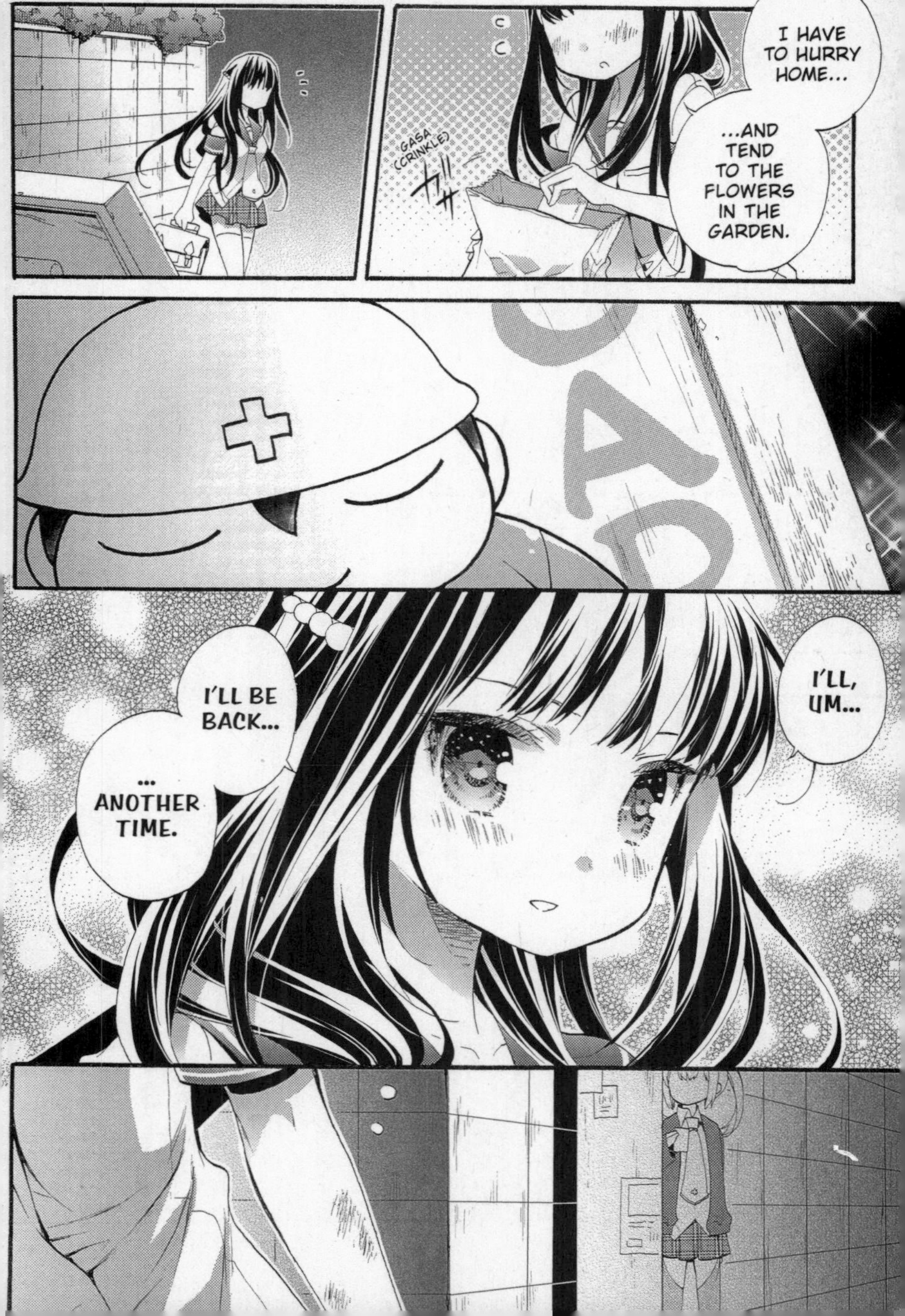
I HAVE TO HURRY HOME...
...AND TEND TO THE FLOWERS IN THE GARDEN.
GASA (CRINKLE)
I'LL, UM...
I'LL BE BACK...
... ANOTHER TIME.

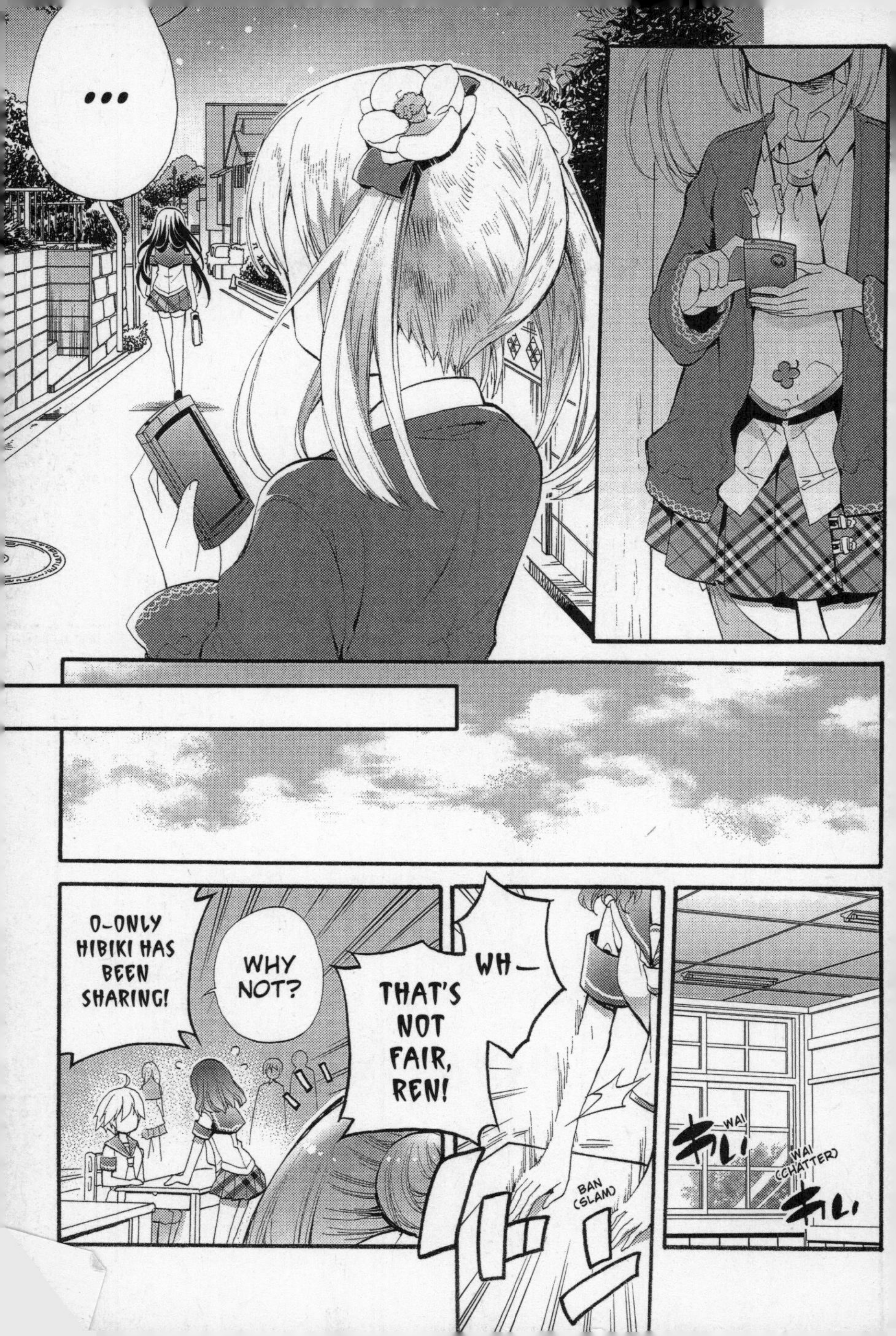
...
WAI
WAI (CHATTER)
WH—
THAT'S NOT FAIR, REN!
BAN (SLAM)
WHY NOT?
O-ONLY HIBIKI HAS BEEN SHARING!

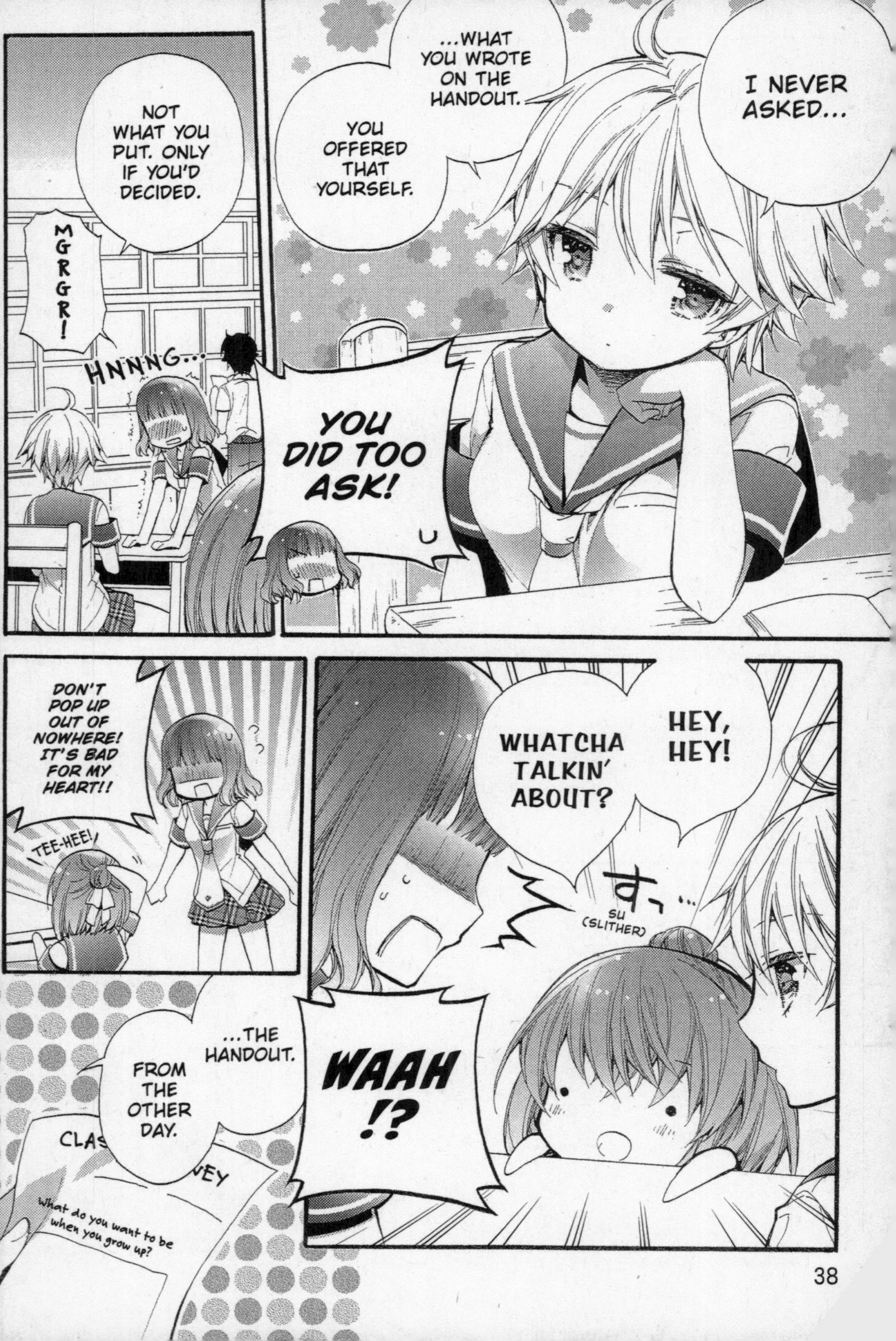
I NEVER ASKED...
...WHAT YOU WROTE ON THE HANDOUT.
YOU OFFERED THAT YOURSELF.
YOU DID TOO ASK!
NOT WHAT YOU PUT. ONLY IF YOU'D DECIDED.
MGRGR!
HNNNG...
HEY, HEY!
WHATCHA TALKIN' ABOUT?
すっ…
SU (SLITHER)
WAAH !?
DON'T POP UP OUT OF NOWHERE! IT'S BAD FOR MY HEART!!
TEE-HEE!
...THE HANDOUT.
FROM THE OTHER DAY.
What do you want to be when you grow up?

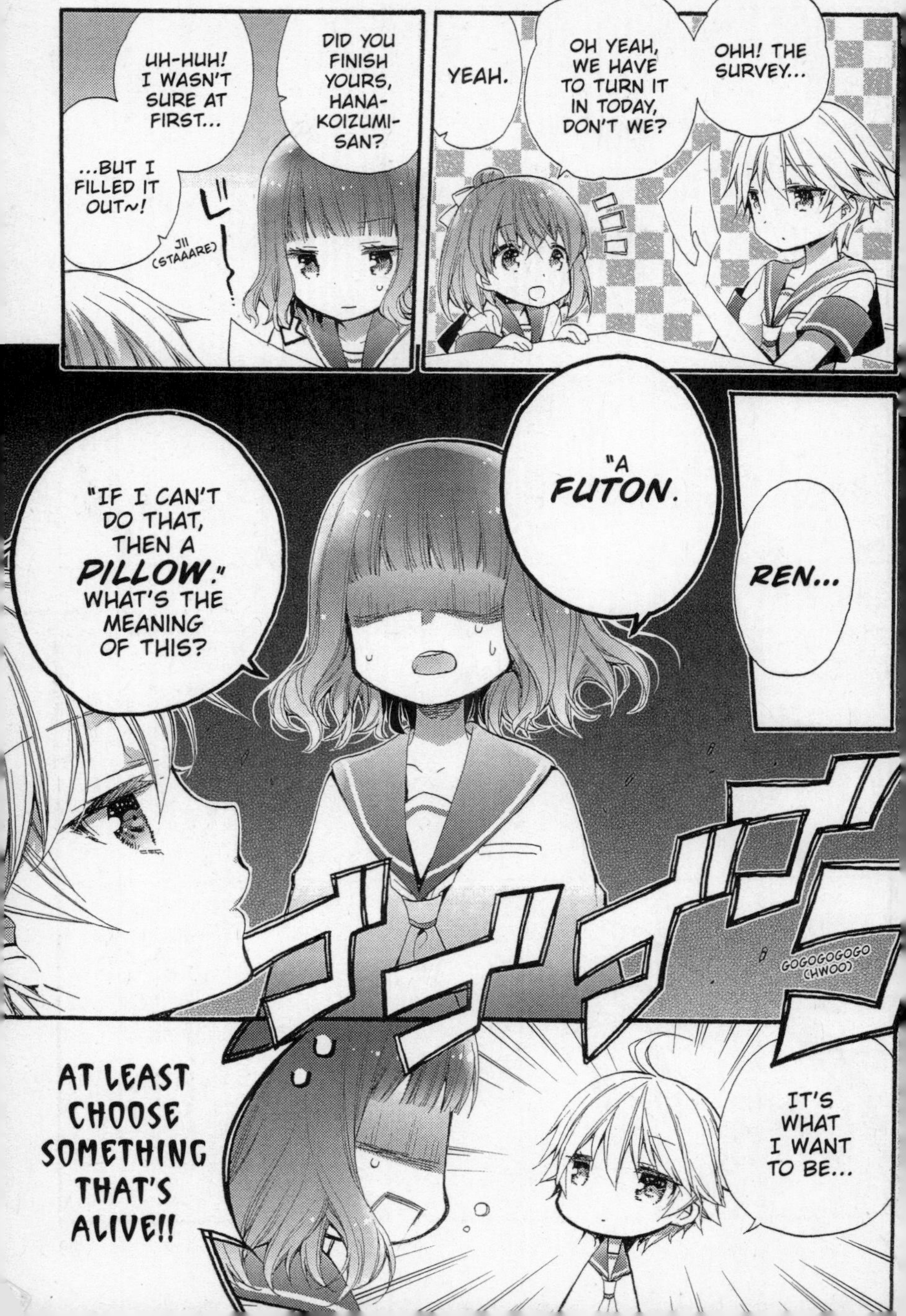
OHH! THE SURVEY...
OH YEAH, WE HAVE TO TURN IT IN TODAY, DON'T WE?
YEAH.
DID YOU FINISH YOURS, HANA-KOIZUMI-SAN?
UH-HUH! I WASN'T SURE AT FIRST...
...BUT I FILLED IT OUT~!
JII (STAAARE)
REN...
"A FUTON.
"IF I CAN'T DO THAT, THEN A PILLOW." WHAT'S THE MEANING OF THIS?
GOGOGOGOGO (CHWOO)
IT'S WHAT I WANT TO BE...
AT LEAST CHOOSE SOMETHING THAT'S ALIVE!!

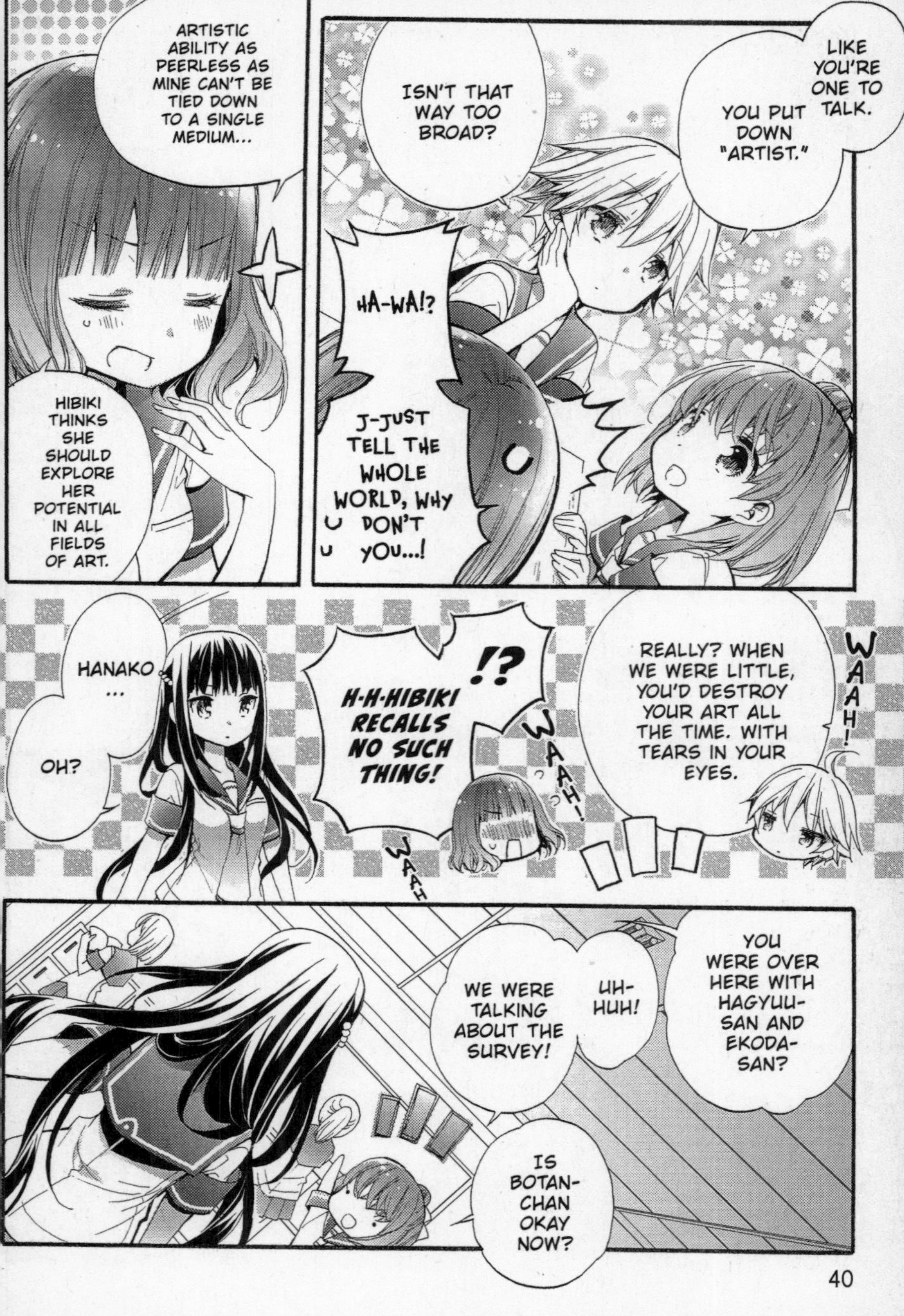
LIKE YOU'RE ONE TO TALK.
YOU PUT DOWN "ARTIST."
ISN'T THAT WAY TOO BROAD?
HA-WA!?
J-JUST TELL THE WHOLE WORLD, WHY DON'T YOU...!
ARTISTIC ABILITY AS PEERLESS AS MINE CAN'T BE TIED DOWN TO A SINGLE MEDIUM...
HIBIKI THINKS SHE SHOULD EXPLORE HER POTENTIAL IN ALL FIELDS OF ART.
WAAH!
REALLY? WHEN WE WERE LITTLE, YOU'D DESTROY YOUR ART ALL THE TIME. WITH TEARS IN YOUR EYES.
WAAH!
!?
H-H-HIBIKI RECALLS NO SUCH THING!
WAAH
HANAKO...
OH?
YOU WERE OVER HERE WITH HAGYUU-SAN AND EKODA-SAN?
UH-HUH!
WE WERE TALKING ABOUT THE SURVEY!
IS BOTAN-CHAN OKAY NOW?

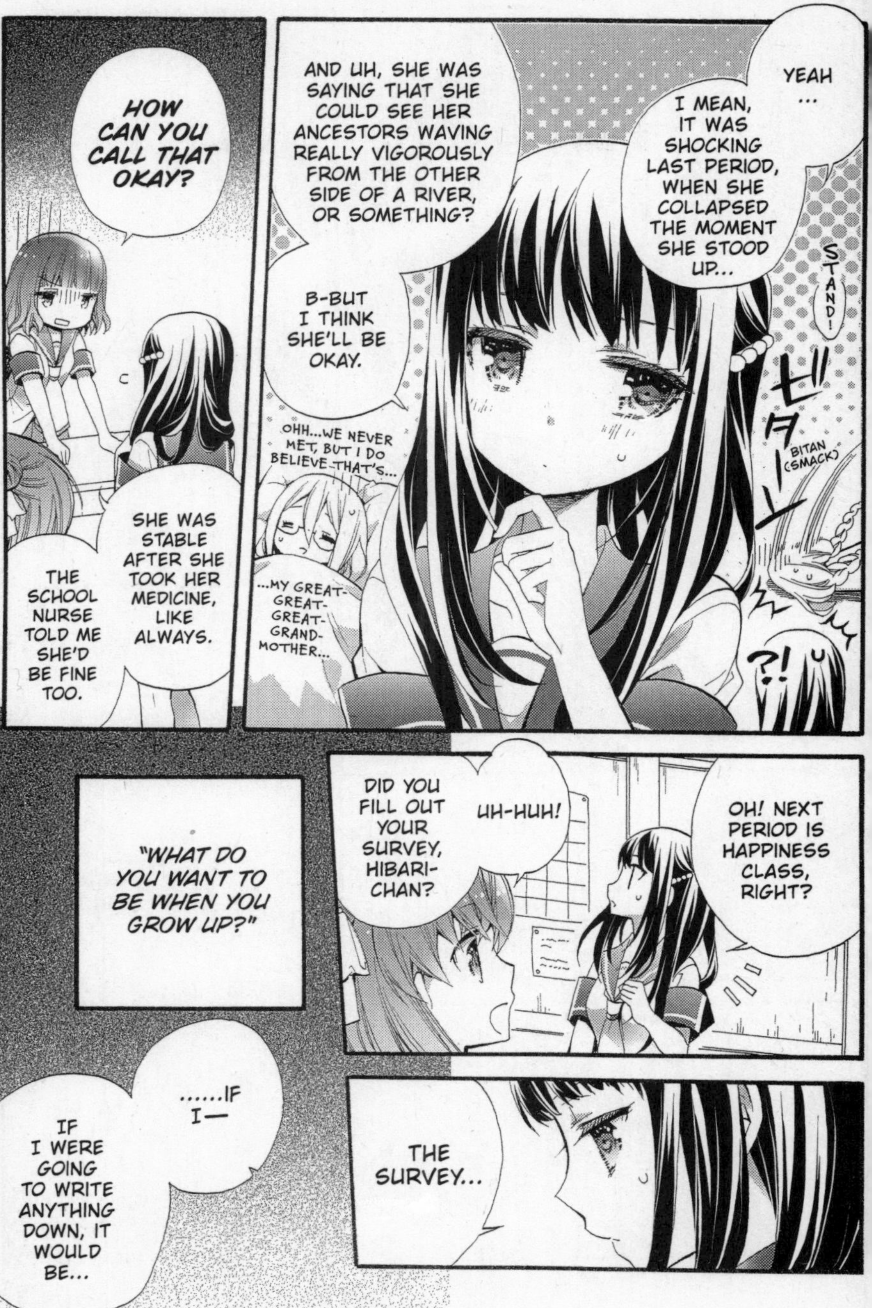
YEAH...
I MEAN, IT WAS SHOCKING LAST PERIOD, WHEN SHE COLLAPSED THE MOMENT SHE STOOD UP...
STAND!
BITAN (SMACK)
?!
AND UH, SHE WAS SAYING THAT SHE COULD SEE HER ANCESTORS WAVING REALLY VIGOROUSLY FROM THE OTHER SIDE OF A RIVER, OR SOMETHING?
B-BUT I THINK SHE'LL BE OKAY.
OHH...WE NEVER MET, BUT I DO BELIEVE THAT'S...
...MY GREAT-GREAT-GREAT-GRANDMOTHER...
HOW CAN YOU CALL THAT OKAY?
SHE WAS STABLE AFTER SHE TOOK HER MEDICINE, LIKE ALWAYS.
THE SCHOOL NURSE TOLD ME SHE'D BE FINE TOO.
OH! NEXT PERIOD IS HAPPINESS CLASS, RIGHT?
UH-HUH!
DID YOU FILL OUT YOUR SURVEY, HIBARI-CHAN?
"WHAT DO YOU WANT TO BE WHEN YOU GROW UP?"
THE SURVEY...
......IF I—
IF I WERE GOING TO WRITE ANYTHING DOWN, IT WOULD BE...

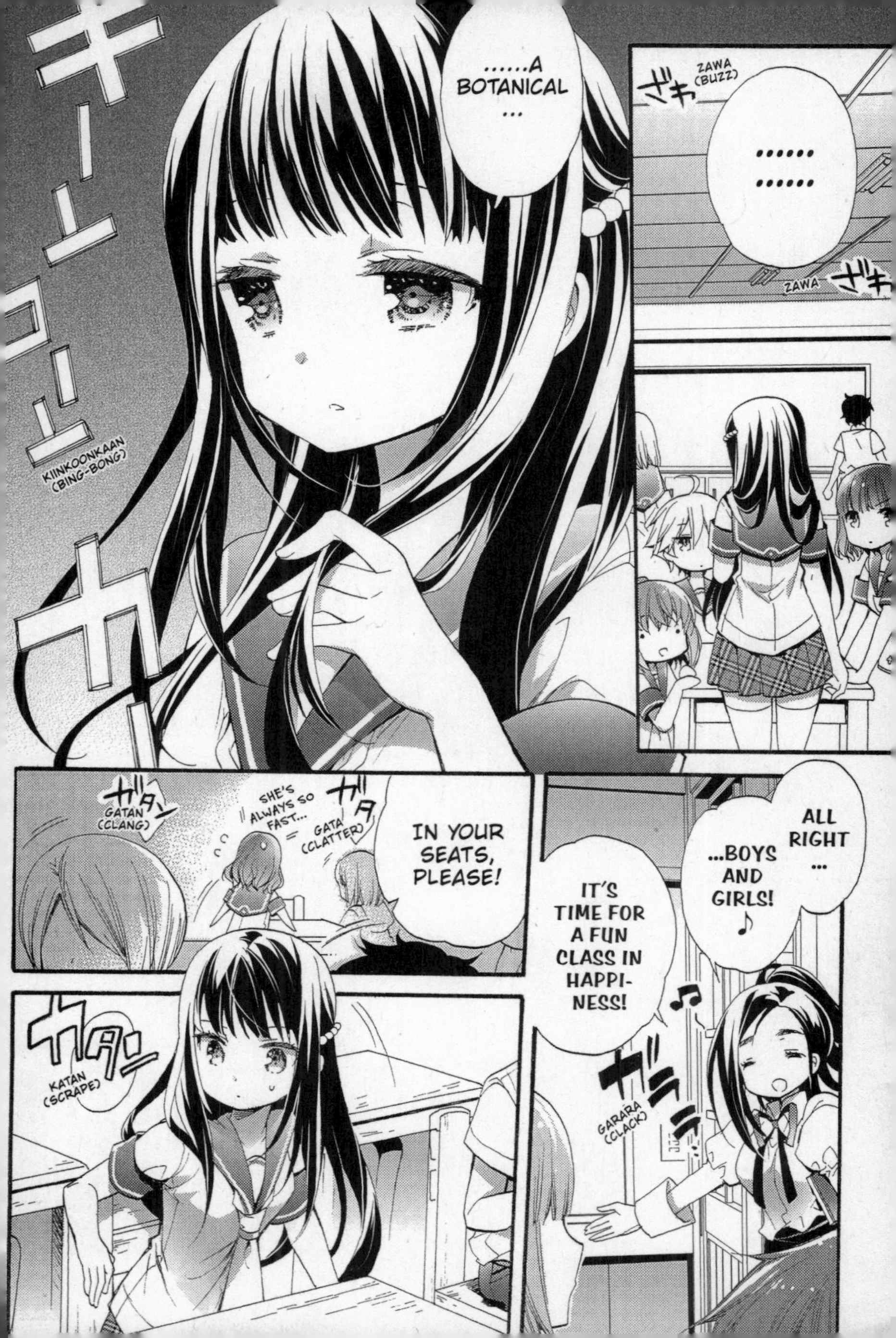

ざわ
ZAWA (BUZZ)
....
ZAWA
ざわ
......A BOTANICAL ...
キーンコーンカーン
KIINKOONKAAN (BING-BONG)
ALL RIGHT ...
...BOYS AND GIRLS! ♪
IT'S TIME FOR A FUN CLASS IN HAPPINESS!
ガララ
GARARA (CLACK)
IN YOUR SEATS, PLEASE!
ガタ
GATA (CLATTER)
SHE'S ALWAYS SO FAST...
ガタン
GATAN (CLANG)
カタン
KATAN (SCRAPE)

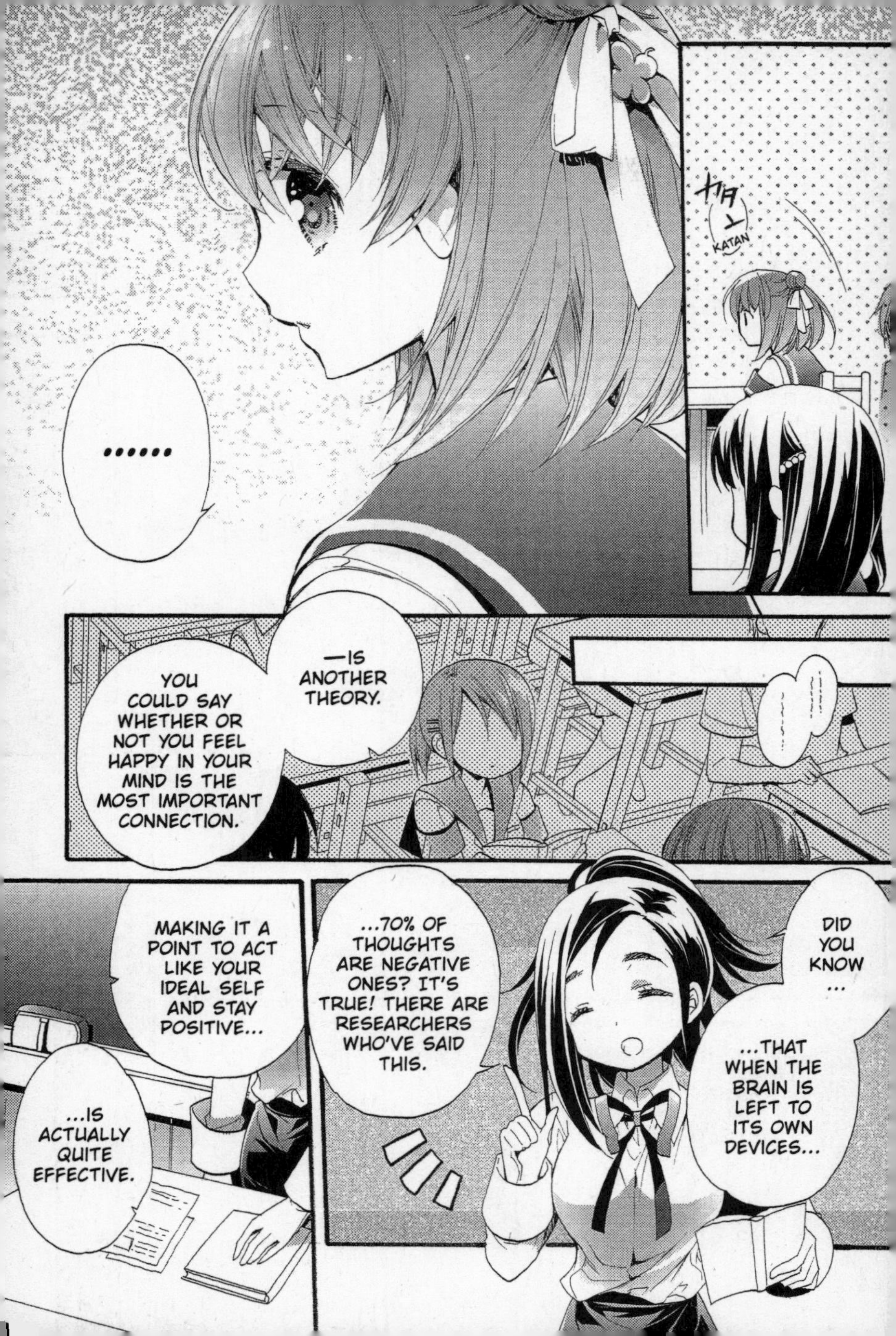
KATAN
......
—IS ANOTHER THEORY.
YOU COULD SAY WHETHER OR NOT YOU FEEL HAPPY IN YOUR MIND IS THE MOST IMPORTANT CONNECTION.
DID YOU KNOW...
...THAT WHEN THE BRAIN IS LEFT TO ITS OWN DEVICES...
...70% OF THOUGHTS ARE NEGATIVE ONES? IT'S TRUE! THERE ARE RESEARCHERS WHO'VE SAID THIS.
MAKING IT A POINT TO ACT LIKE YOUR IDEAL SELF AND STAY POSITIVE...
...IS ACTUALLY QUITE EFFECTIVE.

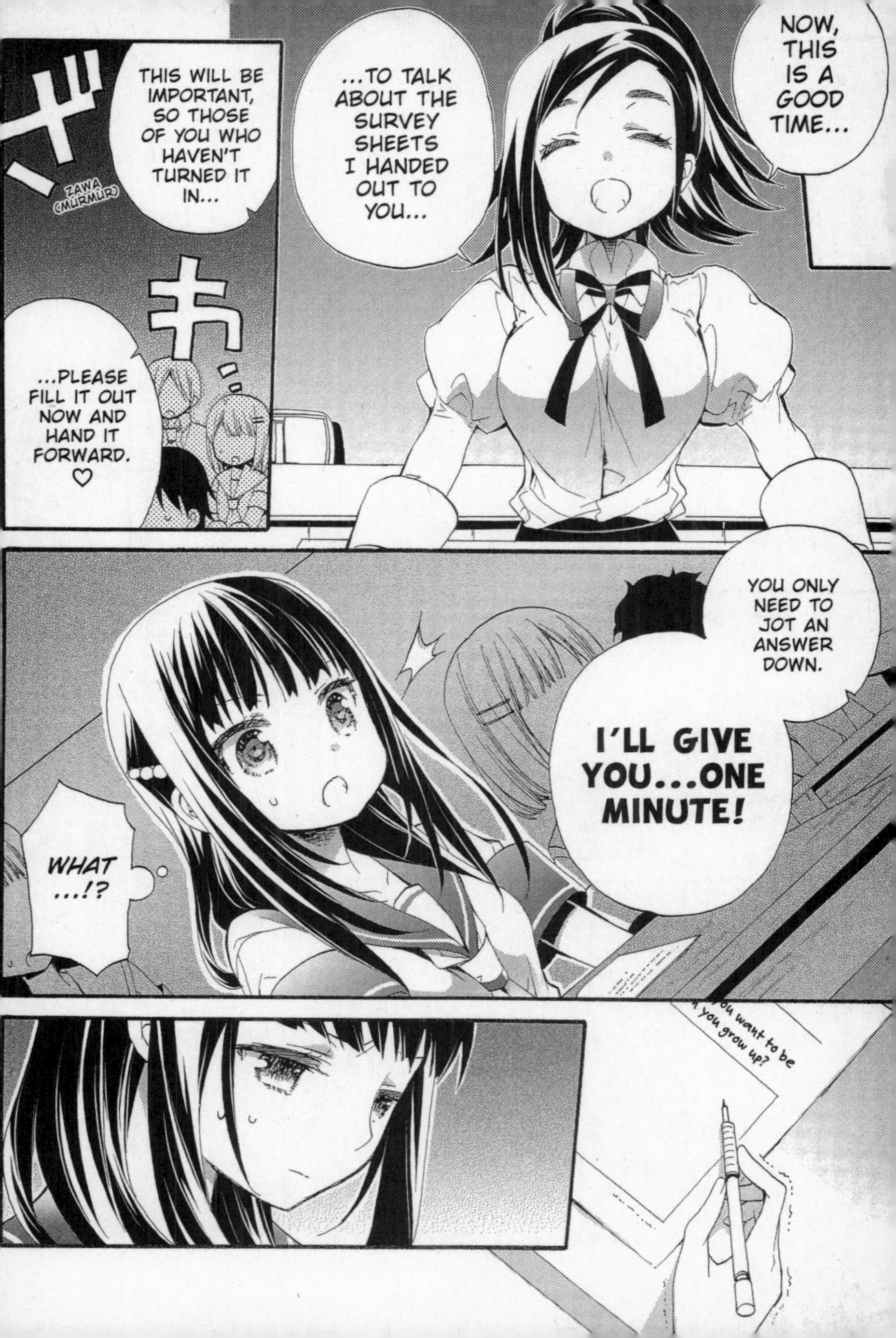
NOW, THIS IS A GOOD TIME...
...TO TALK ABOUT THE SURVEY SHEETS I HANDED OUT TO YOU...
THIS WILL BE IMPORTANT, SO THOSE OF YOU WHO HAVEN'T TURNED IT IN...
ZAWA (MURMUR)
...PLEASE FILL IT OUT NOW AND HAND IT FORWARD. ♡
YOU ONLY NEED TO JOT AN ANSWER DOWN.
I'LL GIVE YOU...ONE MINUTE!
WHAT ...!?
you want to be
you grow up?

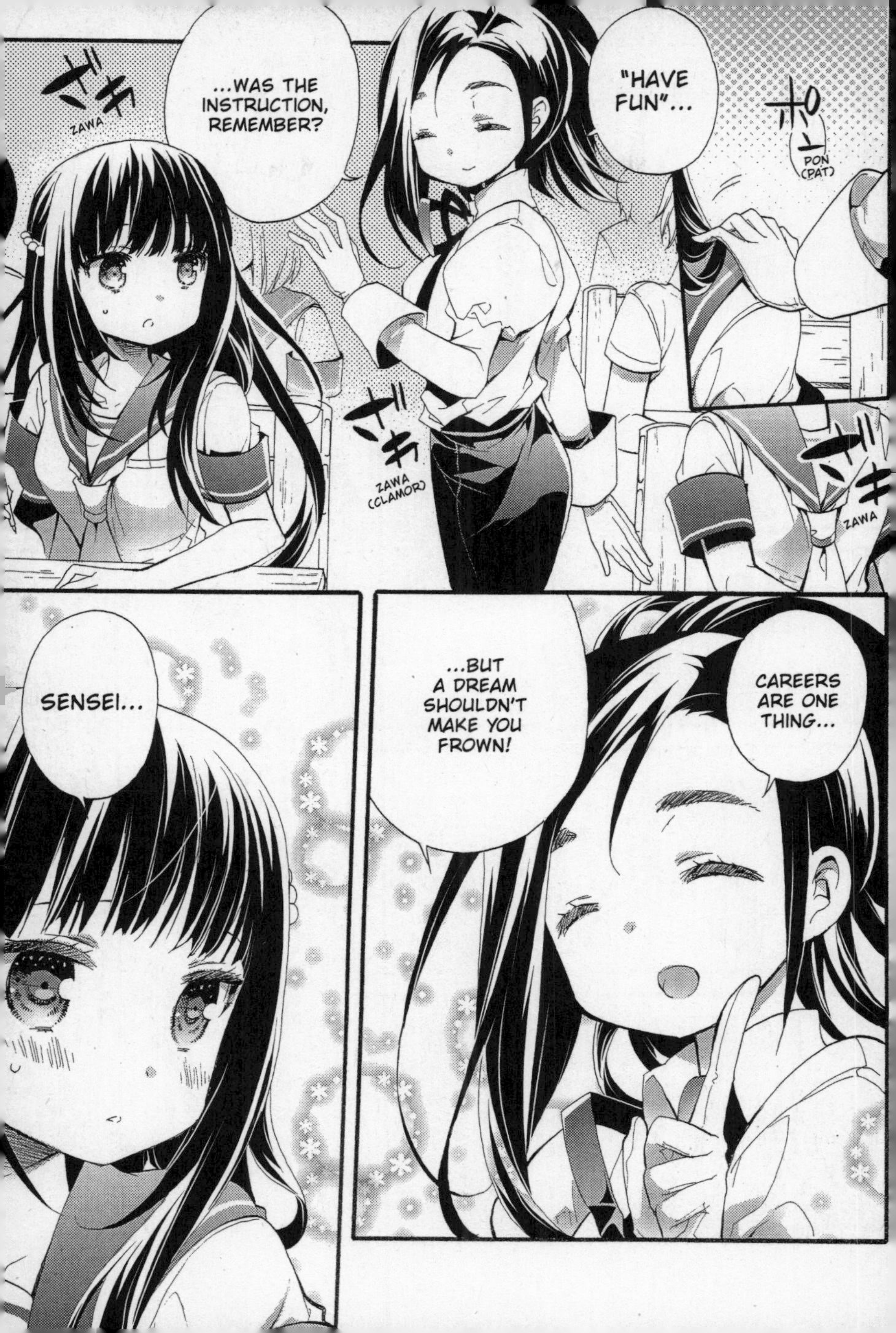
"HAVE FUN"...
PON (PAT)
...WAS THE INSTRUCTION, REMEMBER?
ZAWA
ZAWA
ZAWA (CLAMOR)
ZAWA
CAREERS ARE ONE THING...
...BUT A DREAM SHOULDN'T MAKE YOU FROWN!
SENSEI...

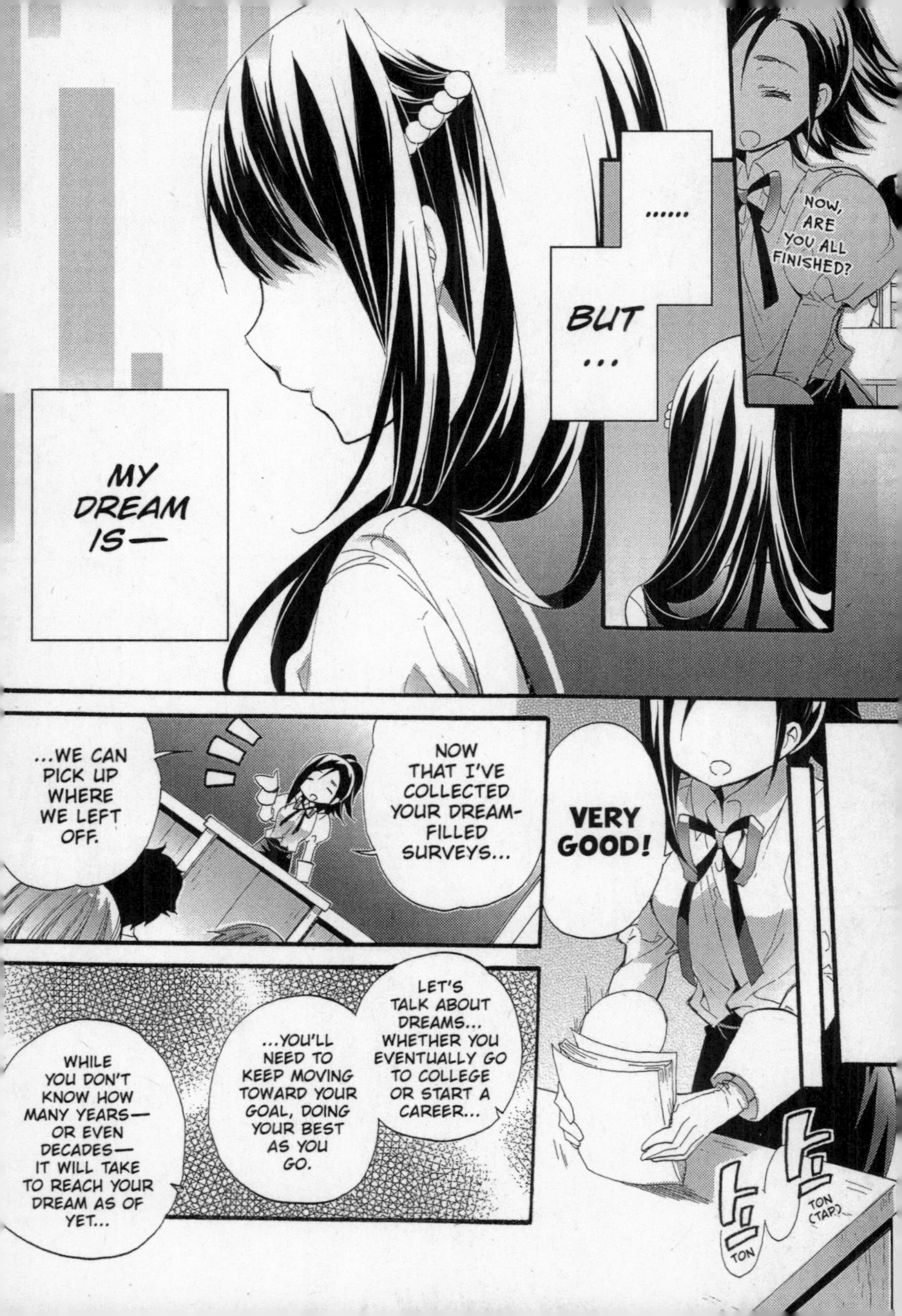
NOW, ARE YOU ALL FINISHED?
......
BUT ...
MY DREAM IS—
VERY GOOD!
NOW THAT I'VE COLLECTED YOUR DREAM-FILLED SURVEYS...
...WE CAN PICK UP WHERE WE LEFT OFF.
LET'S TALK ABOUT DREAMS... WHETHER YOU EVENTUALLY GO TO COLLEGE OR START A CAREER...
...YOU'LL NEED TO KEEP MOVING TOWARD YOUR GOAL, DOING YOUR BEST AS YOU GO.
WHILE YOU DON'T KNOW HOW MANY YEARS— OR EVEN DECADES— IT WILL TAKE TO REACH YOUR DREAM AS OF YET...
TON (TAP)
TON

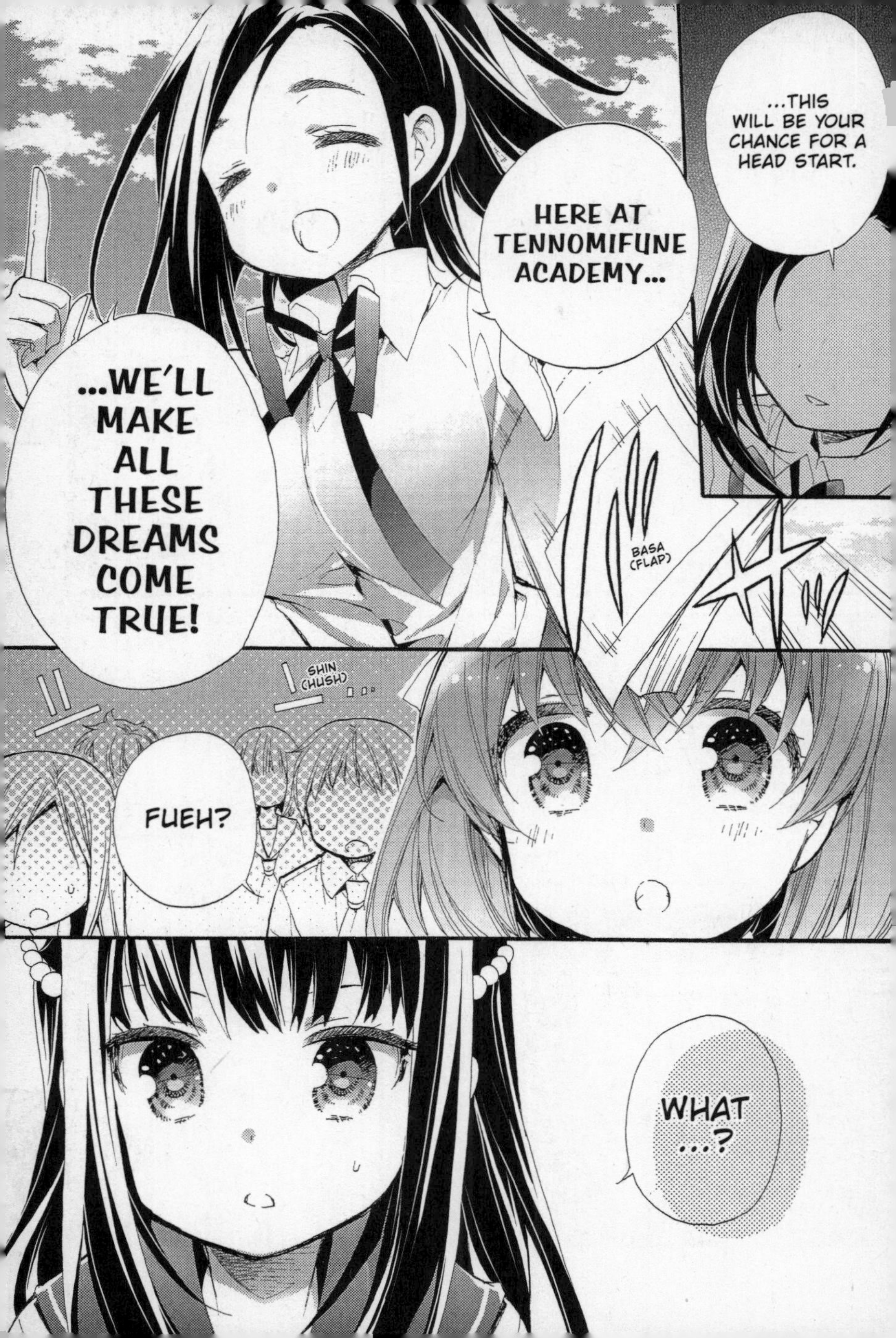
...THIS WILL BE YOUR CHANCE FOR A HEAD START.
HERE AT TENNOMIFUNE ACADEMY...
...WE'LL MAKE ALL THESE DREAMS COME TRUE!
BASA (FLAP)
SHIN (HUSH)
FUEH?
WHAT ...?

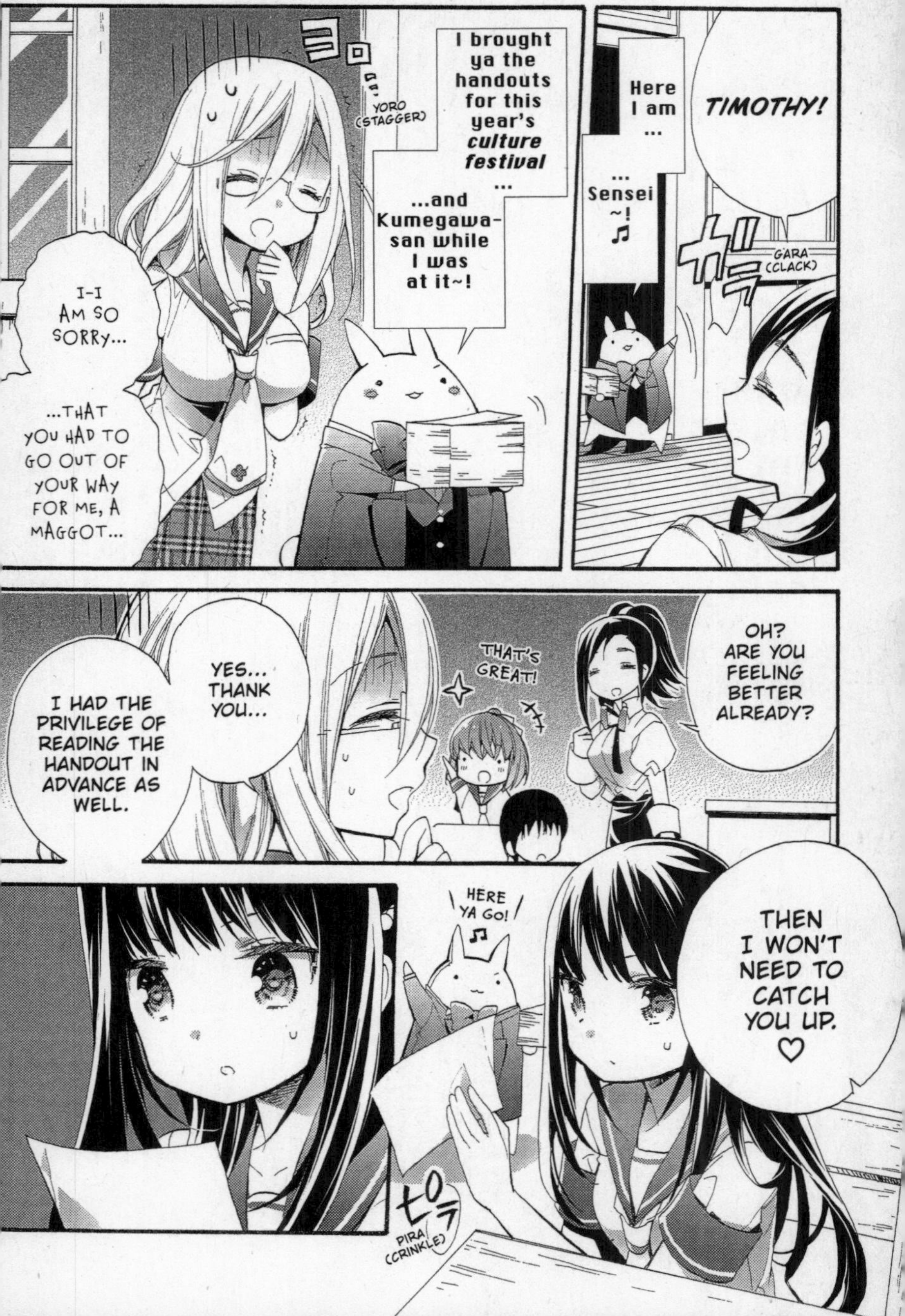
TIMOTHY!
GARA (CLACK)
Here I am ...
... Sensei ~! ♫
I brought ya the handouts for this year's *culture festival* ...
YORO (STAGGER)
...and Kumegawa-san while I was at it~!
I-I AM SO SORRY...
...THAT YOU HAD TO GO OUT OF YOUR WAY FOR ME, A MAGGOT...
OH? ARE YOU FEELING BETTER ALREADY?
THAT'S GREAT!
YES... THANK YOU...
I HAD THE PRIVILEGE OF READING THE HANDOUT IN ADVANCE AS WELL.
THEN I WON'T NEED TO CATCH YOU UP. ♡
HERE YA GO! ♫
PIRA (CRINKLE)

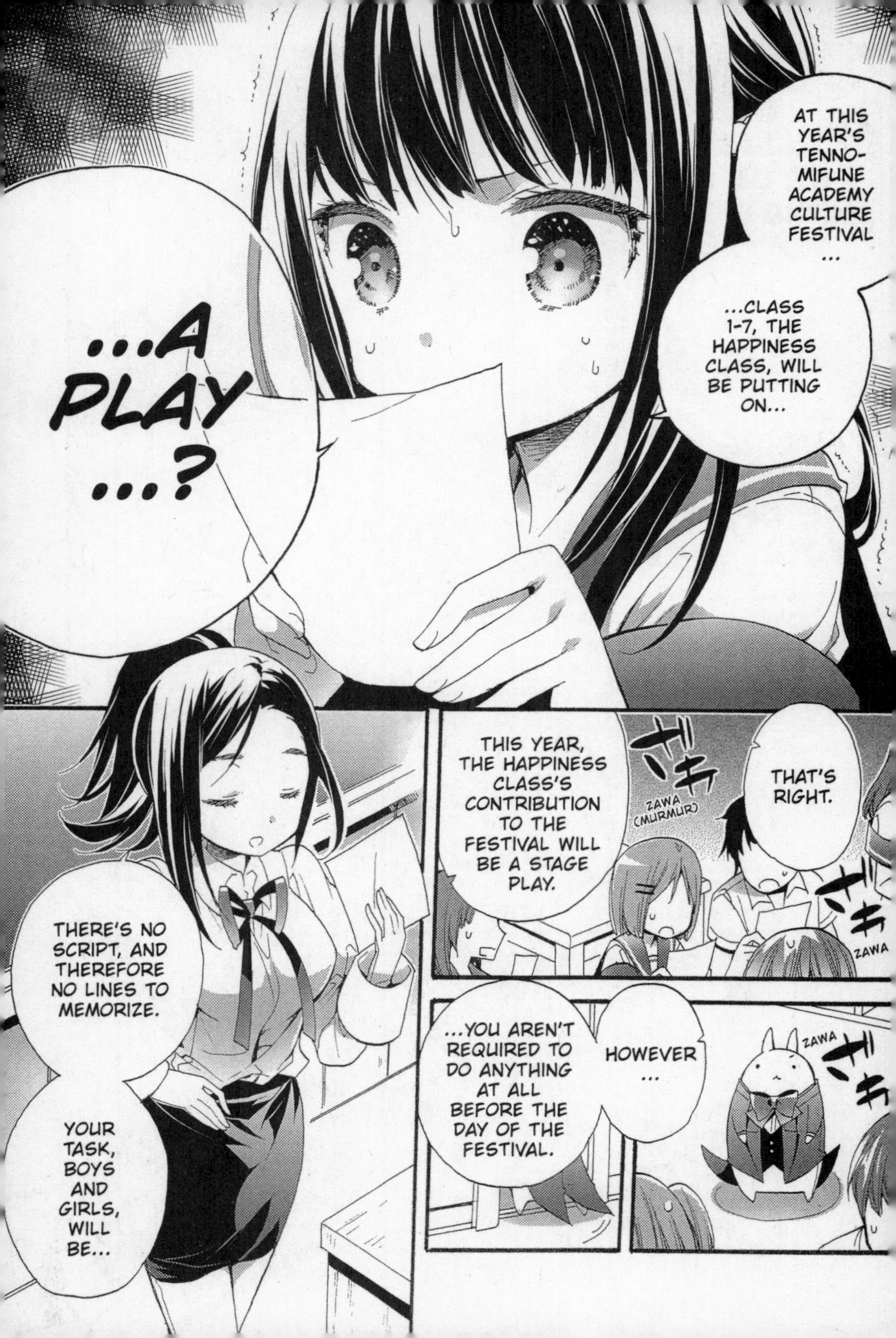
AT THIS YEAR'S TENNO-MIFUNE ACADEMY CULTURE FESTIVAL...
...CLASS 1-7, THE HAPPINESS CLASS, WILL BE PUTTING ON...
...A PLAY...?
THAT'S RIGHT.
ZAWA
THIS YEAR, THE HAPPINESS CLASS'S CONTRIBUTION TO THE FESTIVAL WILL BE A STAGE PLAY.
ZAWA (MURMUR)
ZAWA
HOWEVER...
...YOU AREN'T REQUIRED TO DO ANYTHING AT ALL BEFORE THE DAY OF THE FESTIVAL.
THERE'S NO SCRIPT, AND THEREFORE NO LINES TO MEMORIZE.
YOUR TASK, BOYS AND GIRLS, WILL BE...

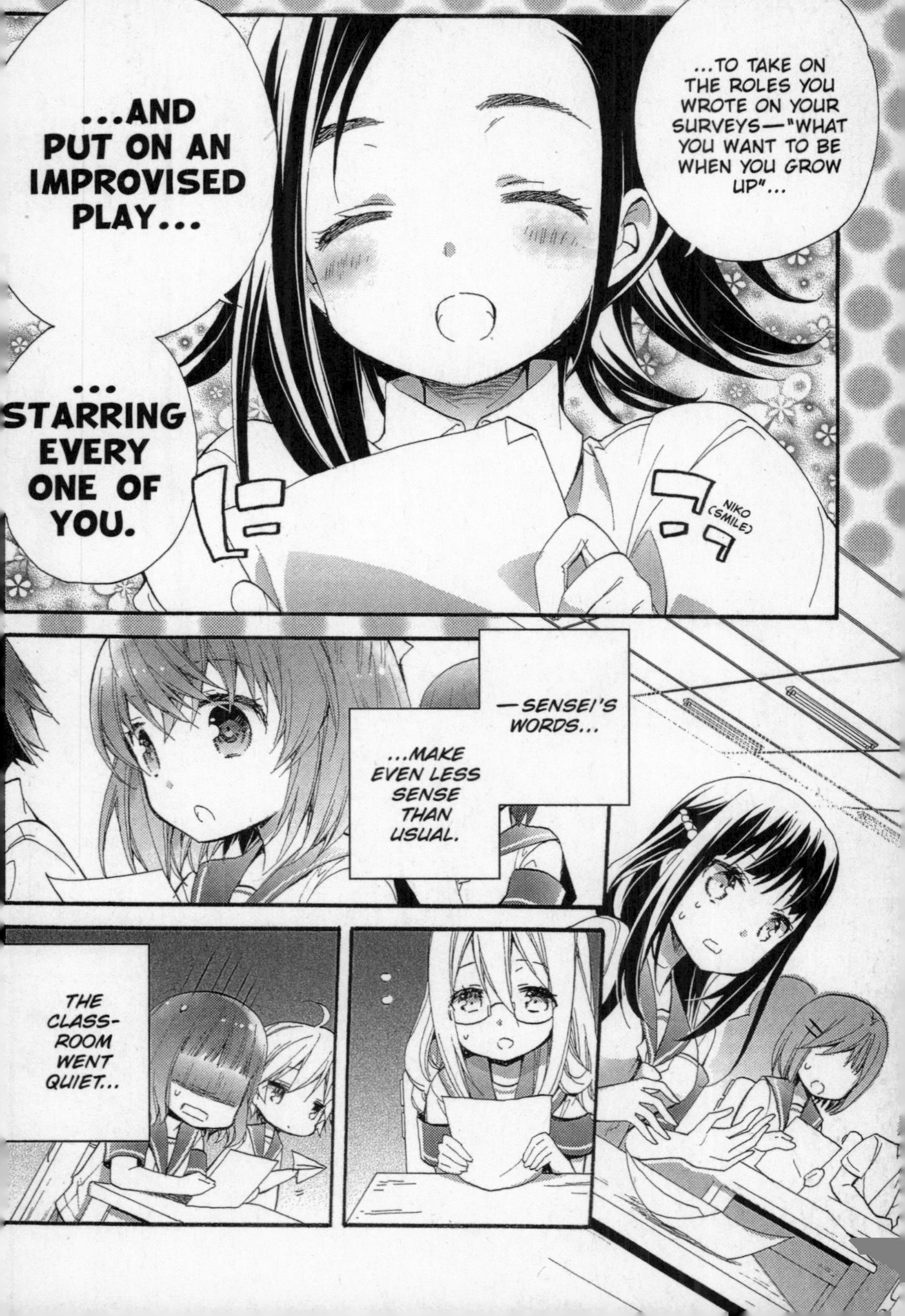
...TO TAKE ON THE ROLES YOU WROTE ON YOUR SURVEYS—"WHAT YOU WANT TO BE WHEN YOU GROW UP"...
...AND PUT ON AN IMPROVISED PLAY...
...STARRING EVERY ONE OF YOU.
NIKO (SMILE)
—SENSEI'S WORDS...
...MAKE EVEN LESS SENSE THAN USUAL.
THE CLASS-ROOM WENT QUIET...

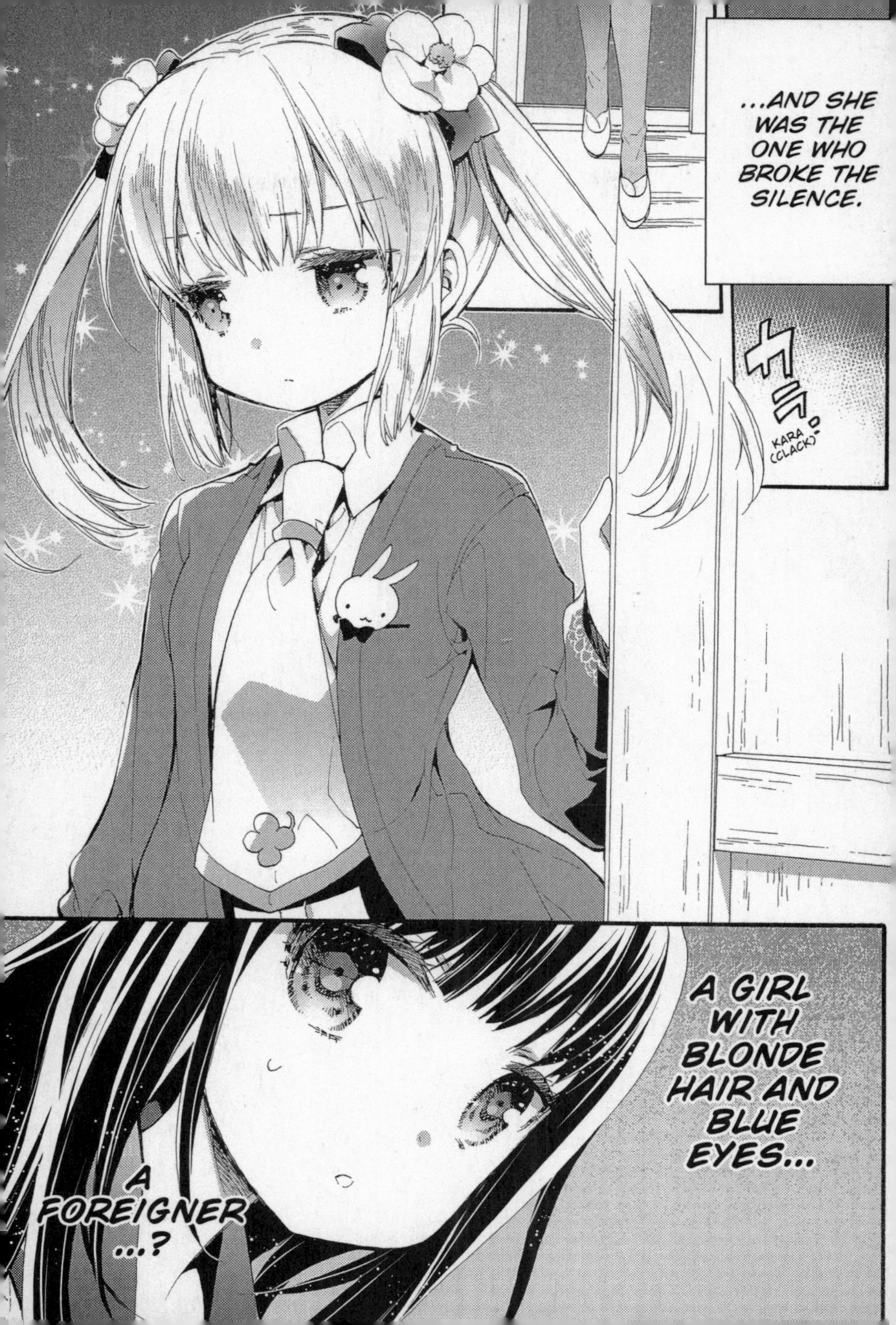
...AND SHE WAS THE ONE WHO BROKE THE SILENCE.
KARA (CLACK)
A GIRL WITH BLONDE HAIR AND BLUE EYES...
A FOREIGNER ...?

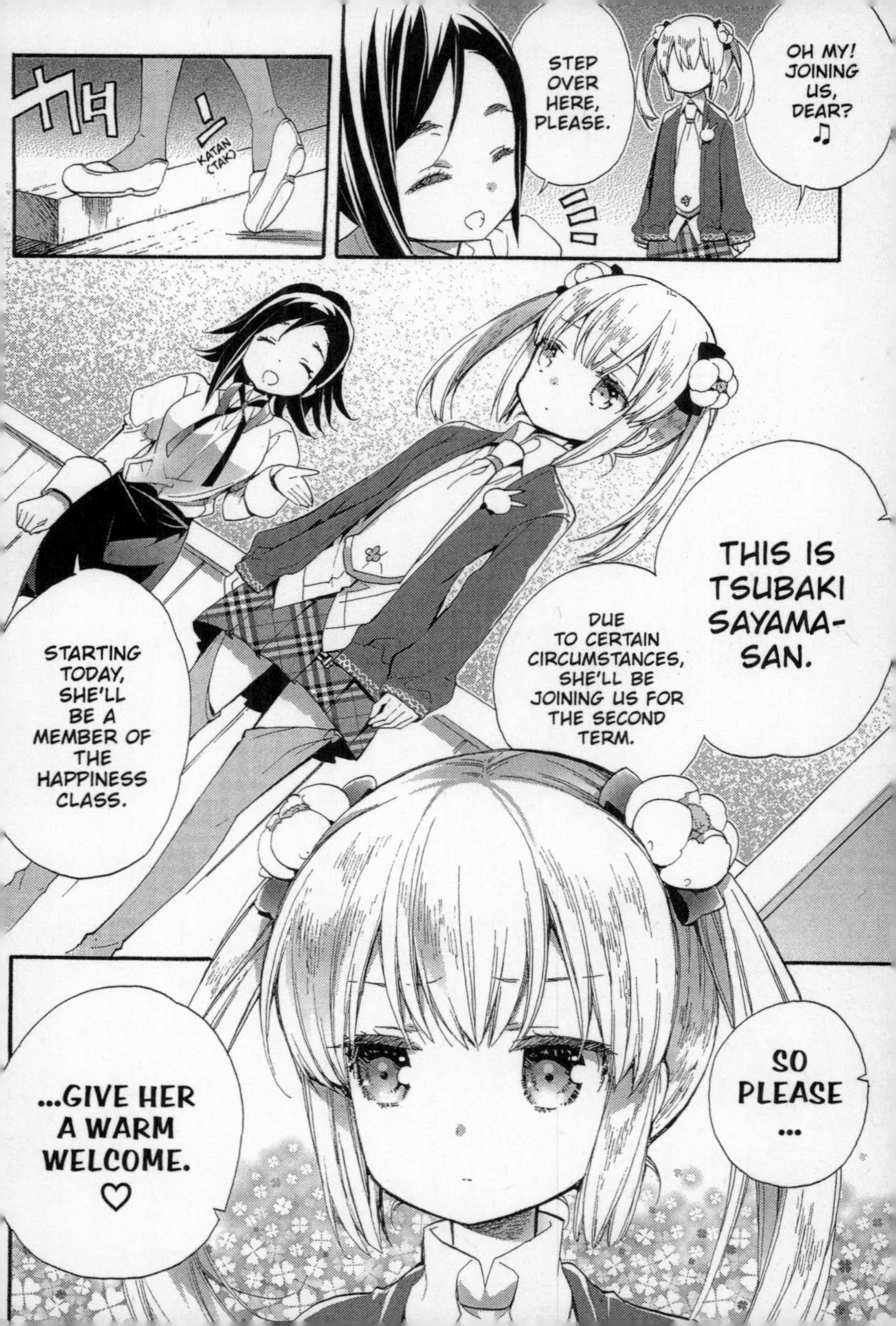
OH MY! JOINING US, DEAR? ♫
STEP OVER HERE, PLEASE.
KATAN (TAK)
THIS IS TSUBAKI SAYAMA-SAN.
DUE TO CERTAIN CIRCUMSTANCES, SHE'LL BE JOINING US FOR THE SECOND TERM.
STARTING TODAY, SHE'LL BE A MEMBER OF THE HAPPINESS CLASS.
SO PLEASE...
...GIVE HER A WARM WELCOME. ♡

AnneHappy♪

unhappy go lucky!

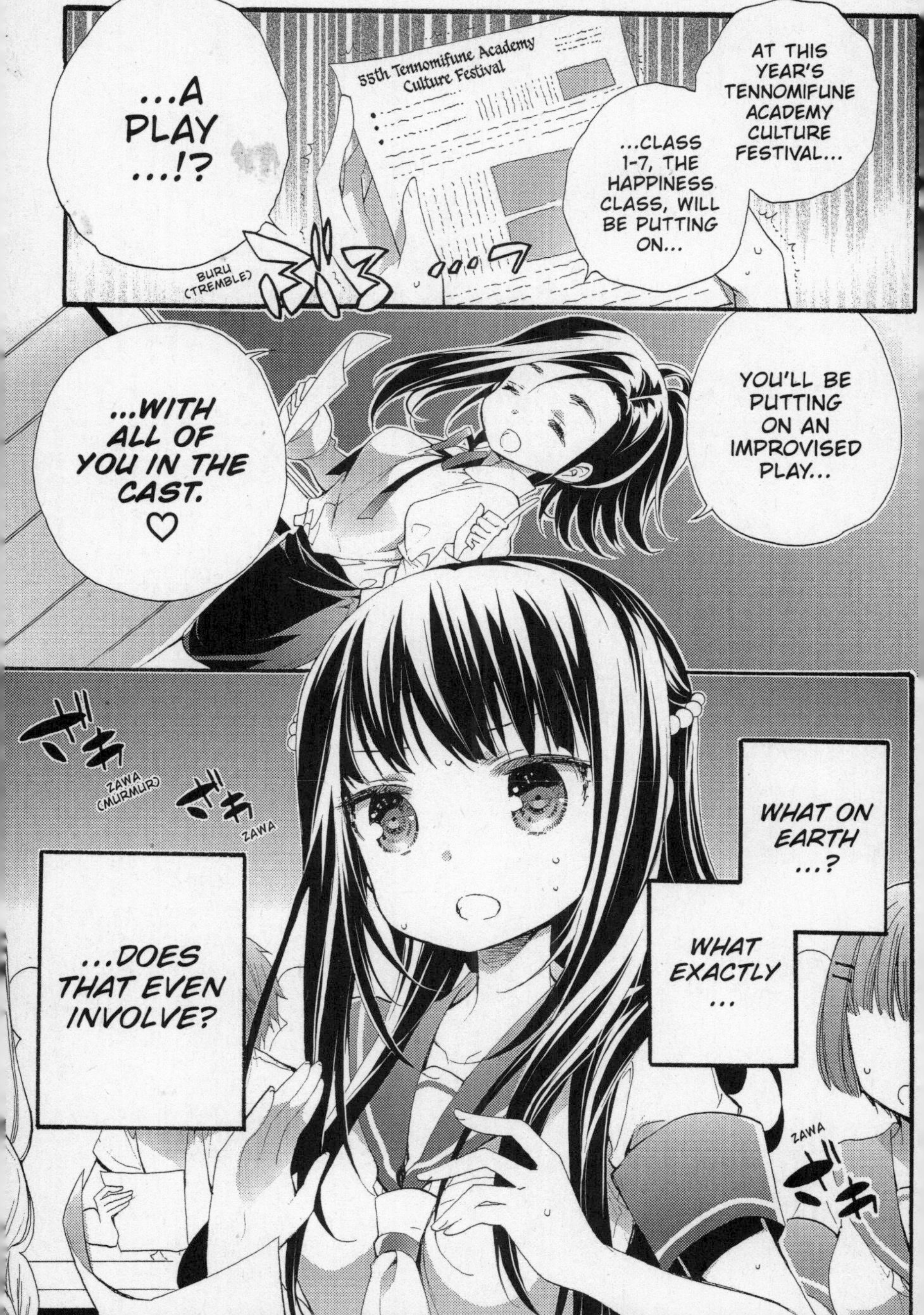
AT THIS YEAR'S TENNOMIFUNE ACADEMY CULTURE FESTIVAL...
...CLASS 1-7, THE HAPPINESS CLASS, WILL BE PUTTING ON...
55th Tennomifune Academy Culture Festival
...A PLAY ...!?
BURU (TREMBLE)
YOU'LL BE PUTTING ON AN IMPROVISED PLAY...
...WITH ALL OF YOU IN THE CAST. ♡
ZAWA
WHAT ON EARTH ...?
WHAT EXACTLY ...
ZAWA
ZAWA (MURMUR)
...DOES THAT EVEN INVOLVE?

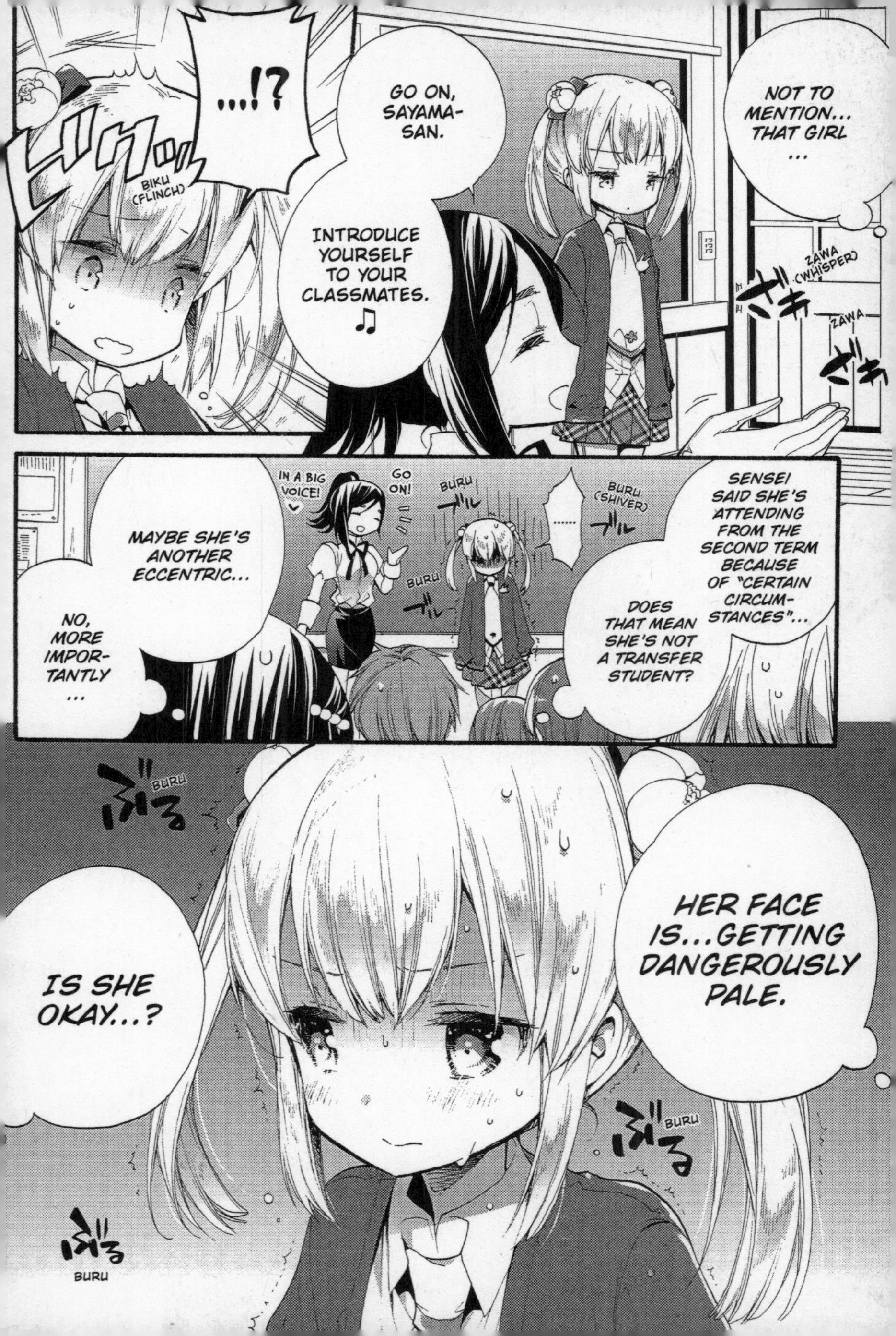

NOT TO MENTION... THAT GIRL ...
ZAWA (WHISPER)
ZAWA
GO ON, SAYAMA-SAN.
INTRODUCE YOURSELF TO YOUR CLASSMATES. ♫
...!?
BIKU (FLINCH)
SENSEI SAID SHE'S ATTENDING FROM THE SECOND TERM BECAUSE OF "CERTAIN CIRCUMSTANCES"...
DOES THAT MEAN SHE'S NOT A TRANSFER STUDENT?
BURU (SHIVER)
......
BURU
GO ON!
IN A BIG VOICE! ♥
BURU
MAYBE SHE'S ANOTHER ECCENTRIC...
NO, MORE IMPORTANTLY ...
HER FACE IS...GETTING DANGEROUSLY PALE.
BURU
BURU
IS SHE OKAY...?
BURU

Lucky. 32

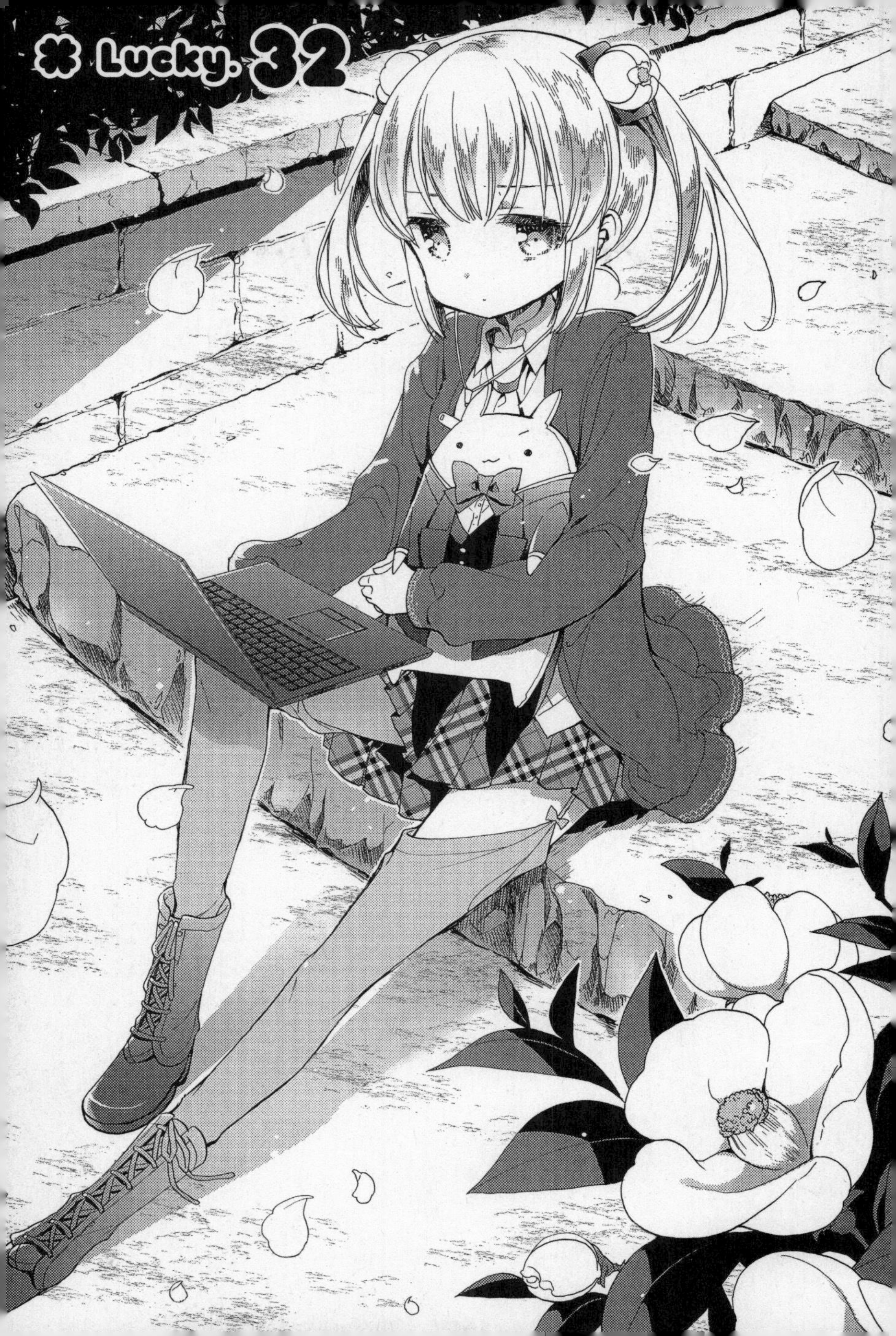

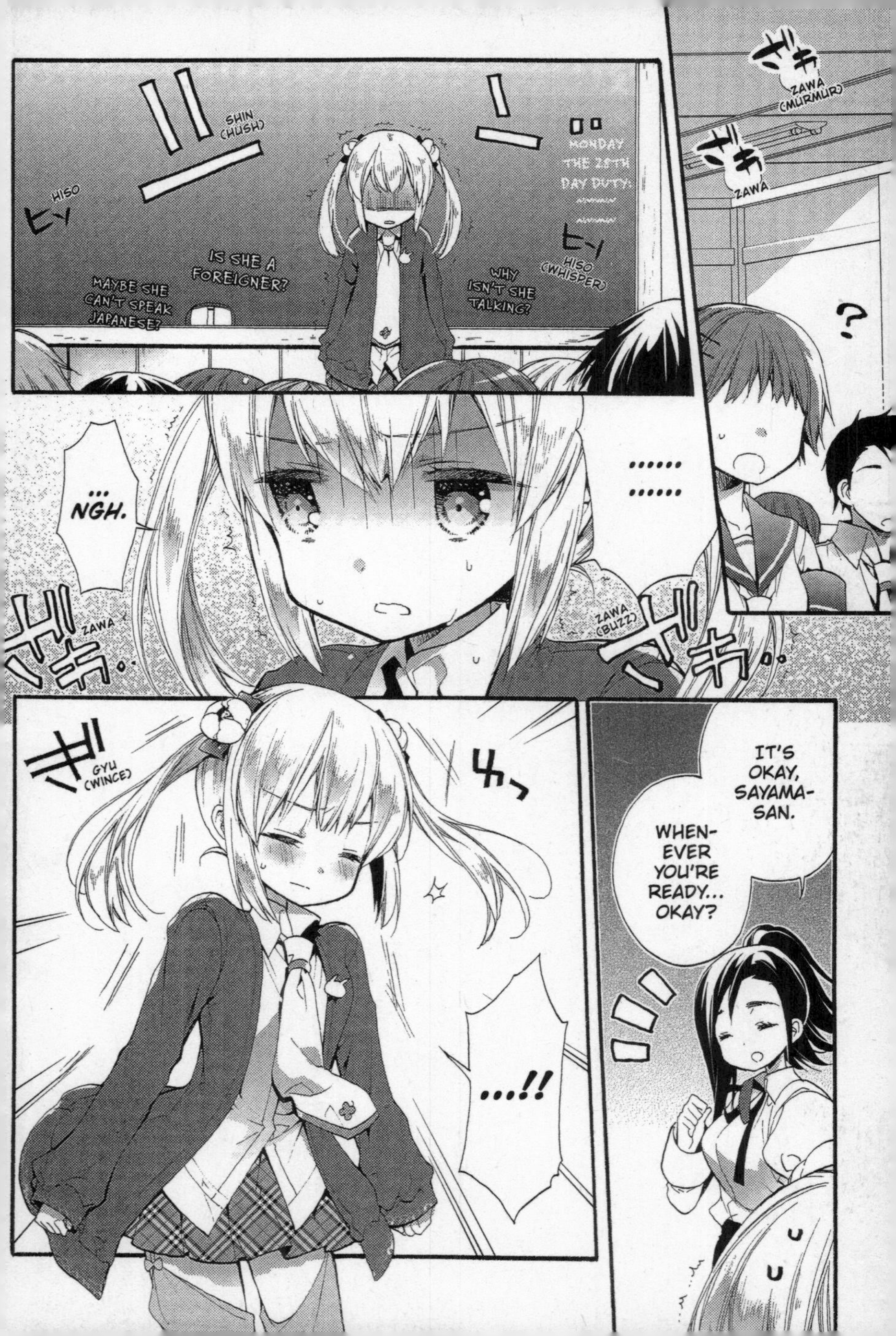
ZAWA (MURMUR)
ZAWA
?
SHIN (HUSH)
MONDAY THE 25TH DAY DUTY:
HISO (WHISPER)
WHY ISN'T SHE TALKING?
IS SHE A FOREIGNER?
MAYBE SHE CAN'T SPEAK JAPANESE?
HISO
......
......
... NGH.
ZAWA (BUZZ)
ZAWA
IT'S OKAY, SAYAMA-SAN.
WHEN-EVER YOU'RE READY... OKAY?
...!!
GYU (WINCE)

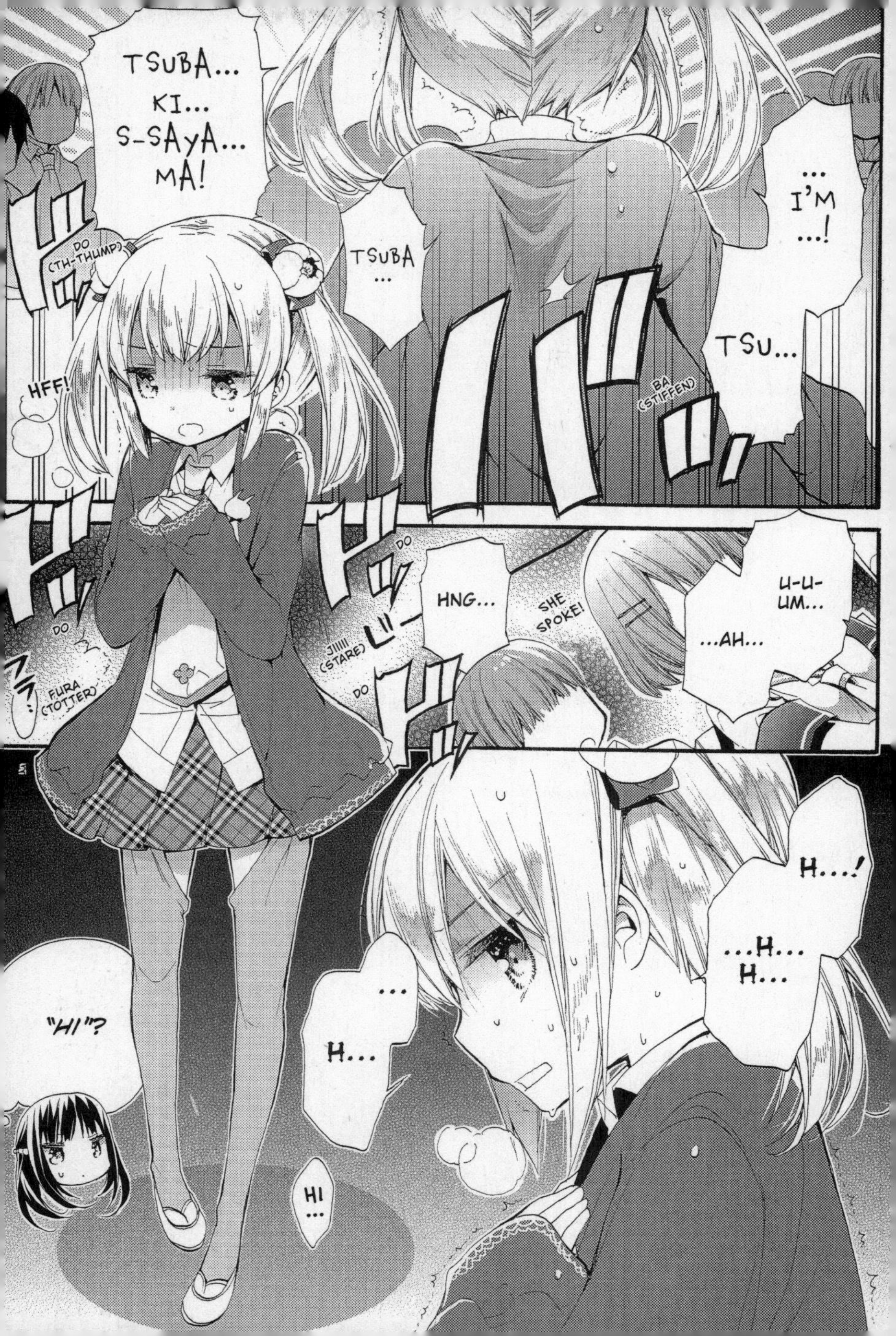
...I'M ...!
TSUBA...
TSU...
BA (STIFFEN)
U-U-UM... ...AH...
SHE SPOKE!
HNG...
JIIIII (STARE)
DO
H...!
...H... H...
... H...
TSUBA... KI... S-SAYA... MA!
DO (TH-THUMP)
HFF!
DO
FURA (TOTTER)
"HI"?
HI ...

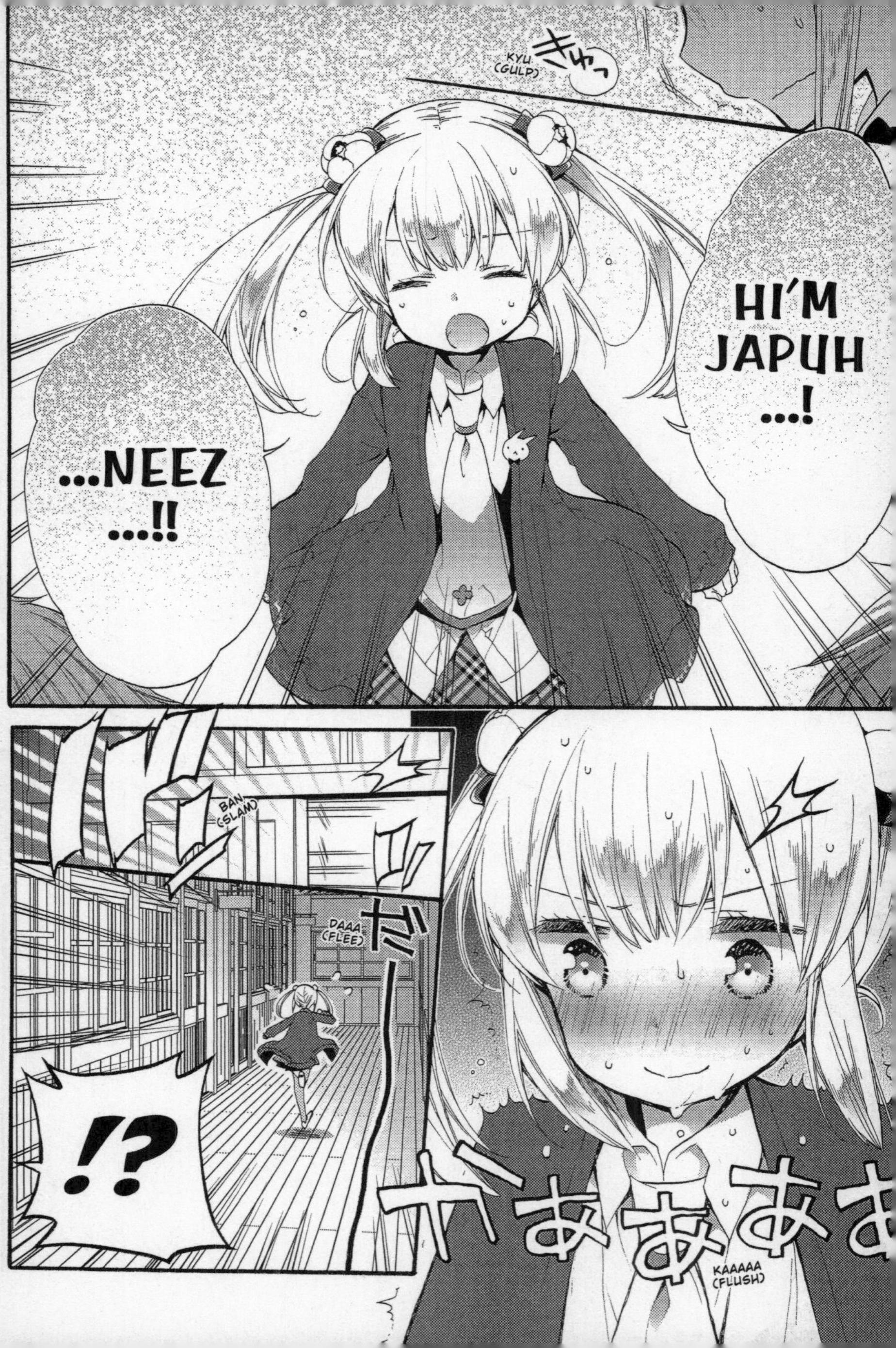
きゅっ
KYU (GULP)
HI'M JAPUH ...!
...NEEZ ...!!
KAAAAA (FLUSH)
BAN (SLAM)
だー
DAAA (FLEE)
!?

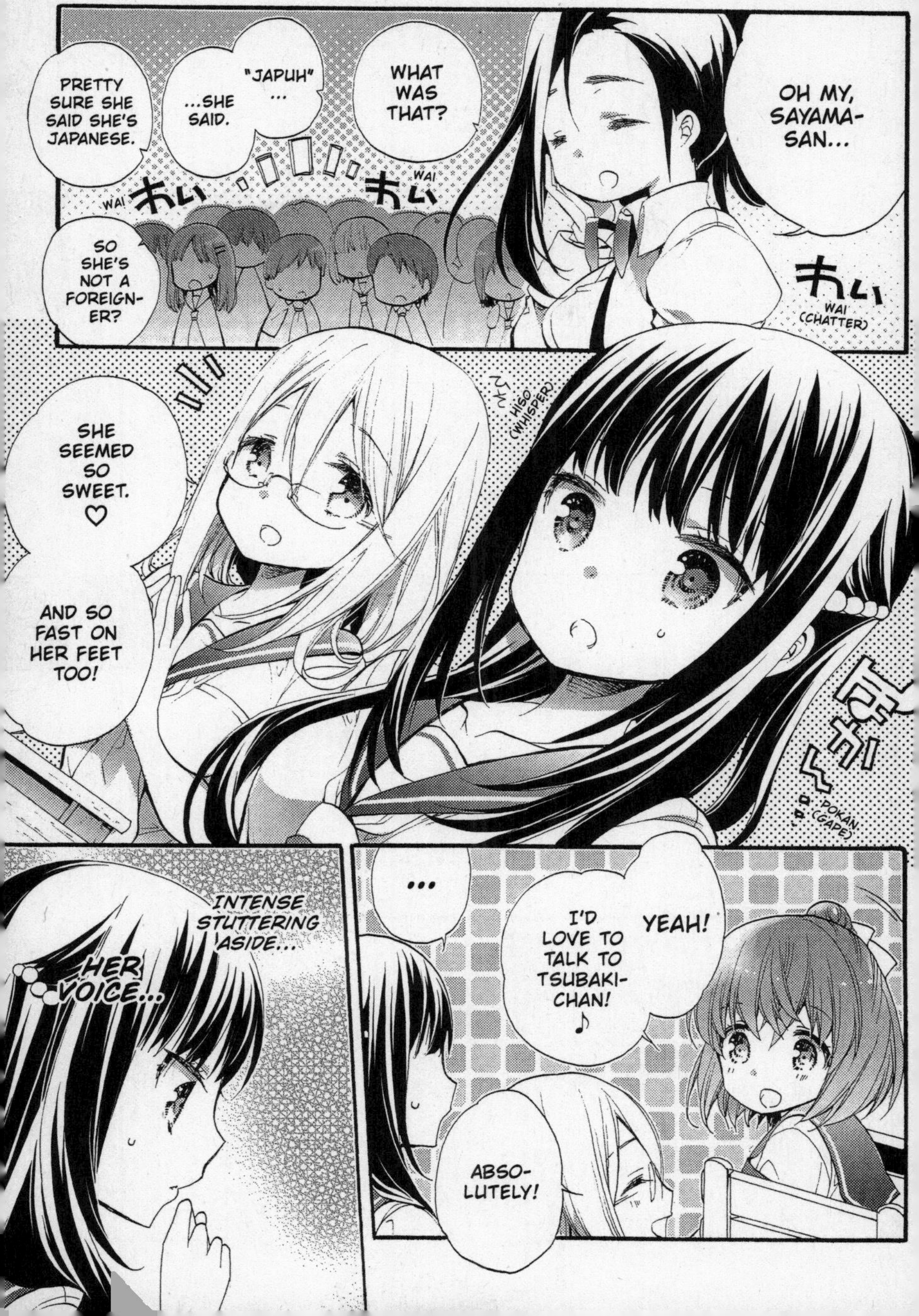
OH MY, SAYAMA-SAN...
WAI (CHATTER)
WHAT WAS THAT?
"JAPUH" ...
...SHE SAID.
PRETTY SURE SHE SAID SHE'S JAPANESE.
WAI
WAI
SO SHE'S NOT A FOREIGNER?
POKAN (GAPE)
HISO (WHISPER)
SHE SEEMED SO SWEET. ♡
AND SO FAST ON HER FEET TOO!
YEAH!
I'D LOVE TO TALK TO TSUBAKI-CHAN! ♪
...
ABSO-LUTELY!
INTENSE STUTTERING ASIDE...
HER VOICE...

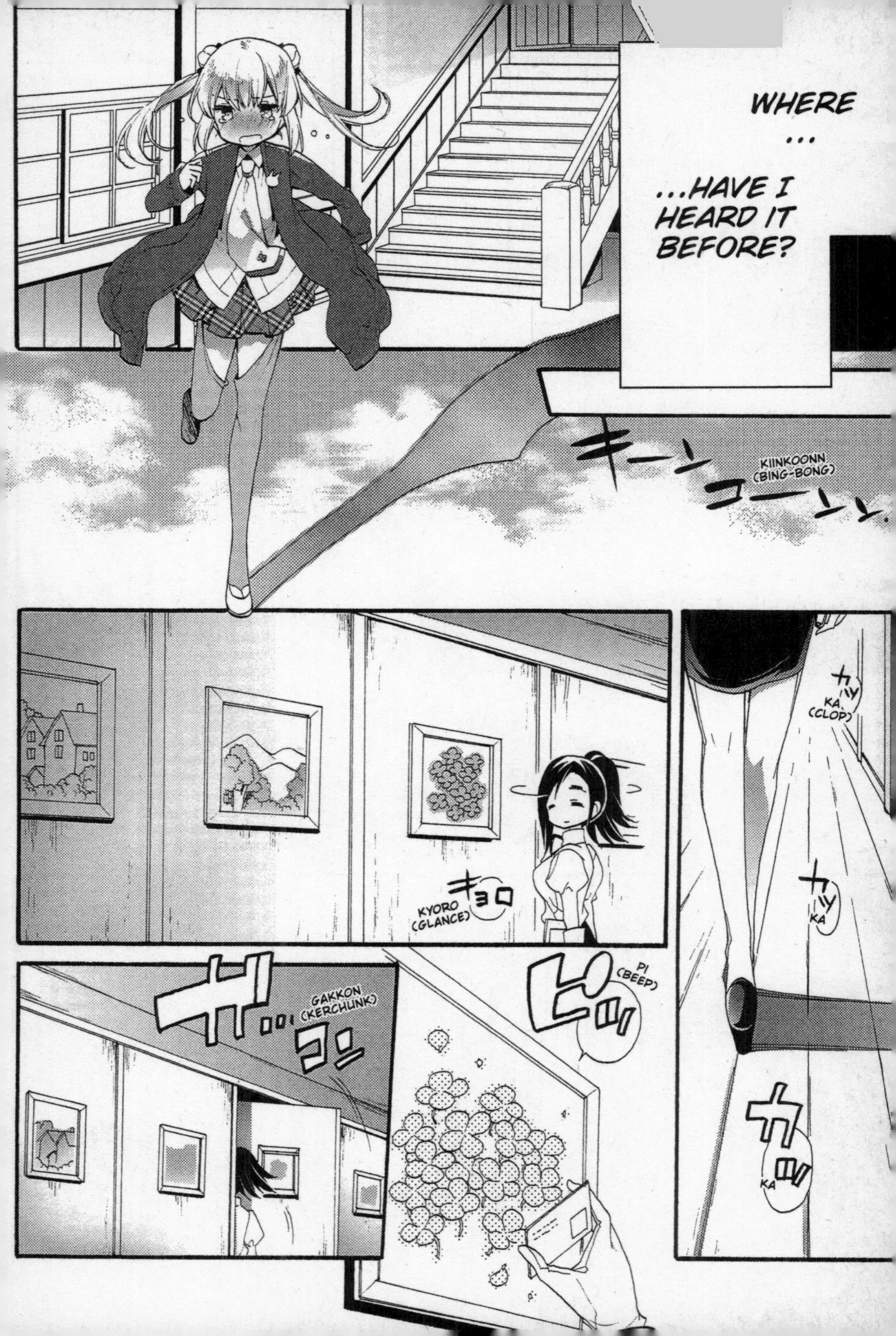
WHERE ...
...HAVE I HEARD IT BEFORE?
キーンコーンン
KIINKOONN (BING-BONG)
カッ
KA (CLOP)
カッ
KA
カッ
KA
キョロ
KYORO (GLANCE)
ピッ
PI (BEEP)
ガッコン
GAKKON (KERCHUNK)

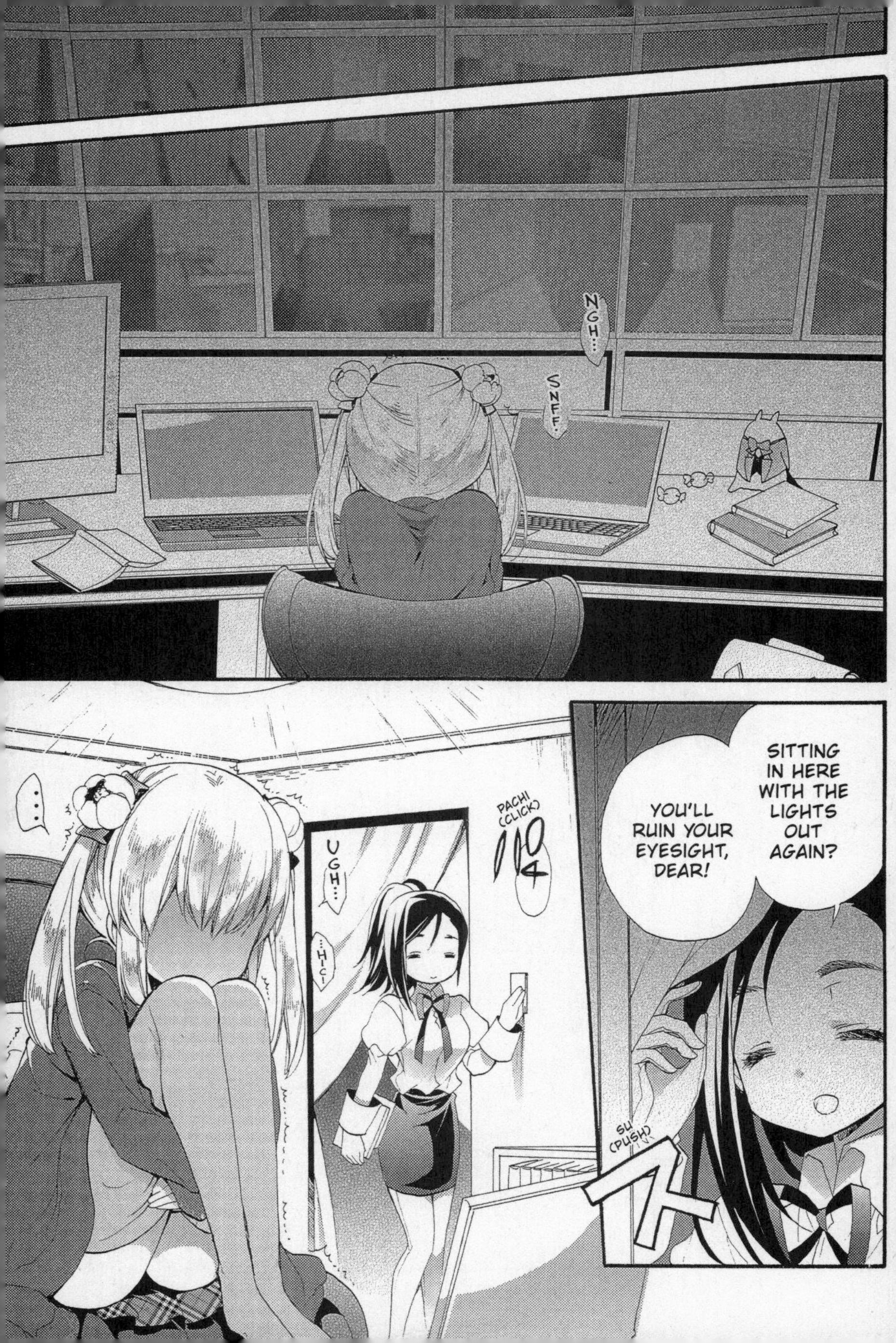
NGH...
SNFF.
SITTING IN HERE WITH THE LIGHTS OUT AGAIN?
YOU'LL RUIN YOUR EYESIGHT, DEAR!
SU (PUSH)
PACHI (CLICK)
UGH...
...HIC!
...

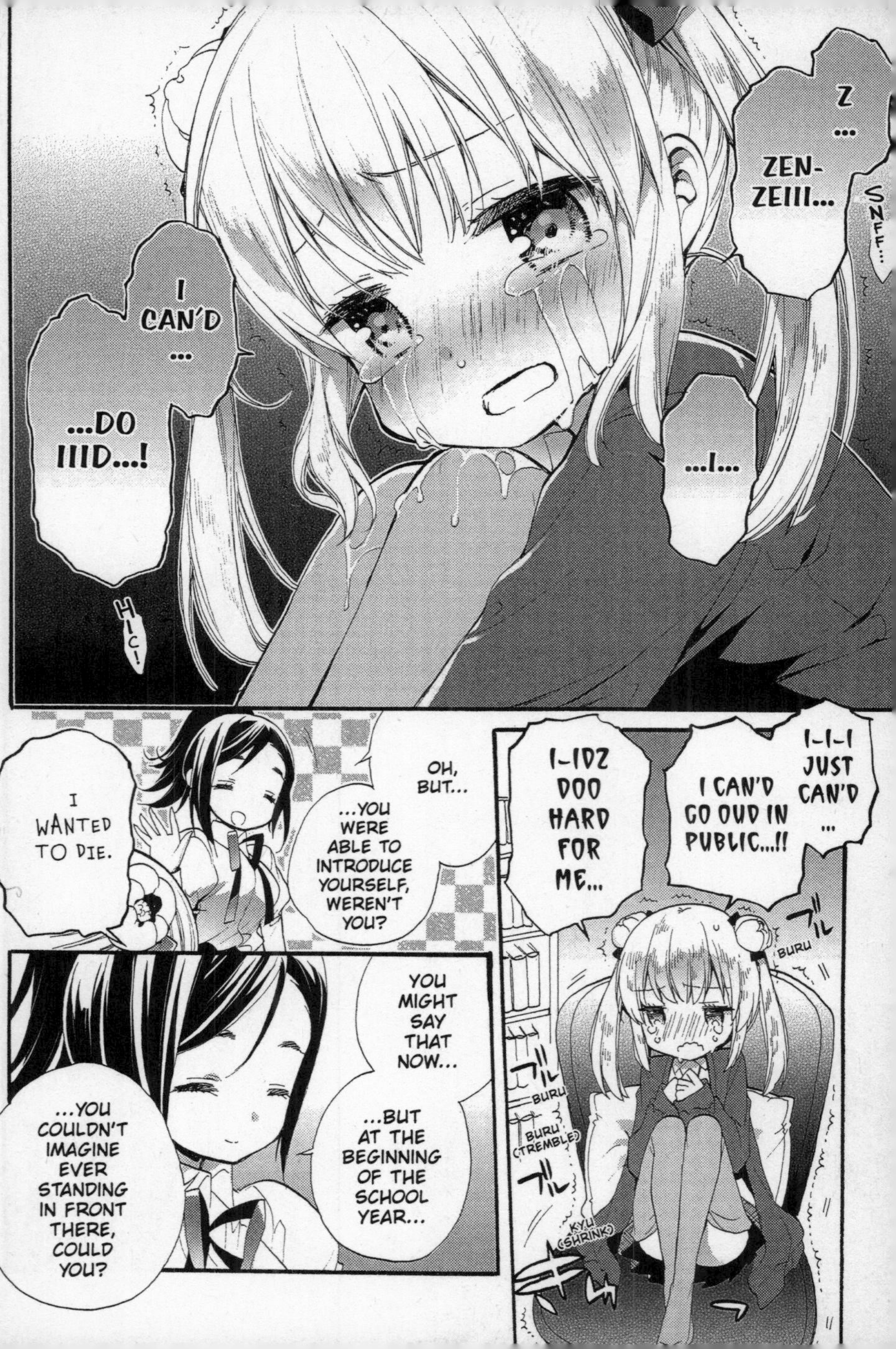
Z ... ZEN-ZEIII...
SNFF...
...I...
I CAN'D ...
...DO IIID...!
HIC!
I-I-I JUST CAN'D ...
I CAN'D GO OUD IN PUBLIC...!!
I-IDZ DOO HARD FOR ME...
BURU
BURU
BURU (TREMBLE)
KYU (SHRINK)
OH, BUT...
...YOU WERE ABLE TO INTRODUCE YOURSELF, WEREN'T YOU?
I WANTED TO DIE.
YOU MIGHT SAY THAT NOW...
...BUT AT THE BEGINNING OF THE SCHOOL YEAR...
...YOU COULDN'T IMAGINE EVER STANDING IN FRONT THERE, COULD YOU?

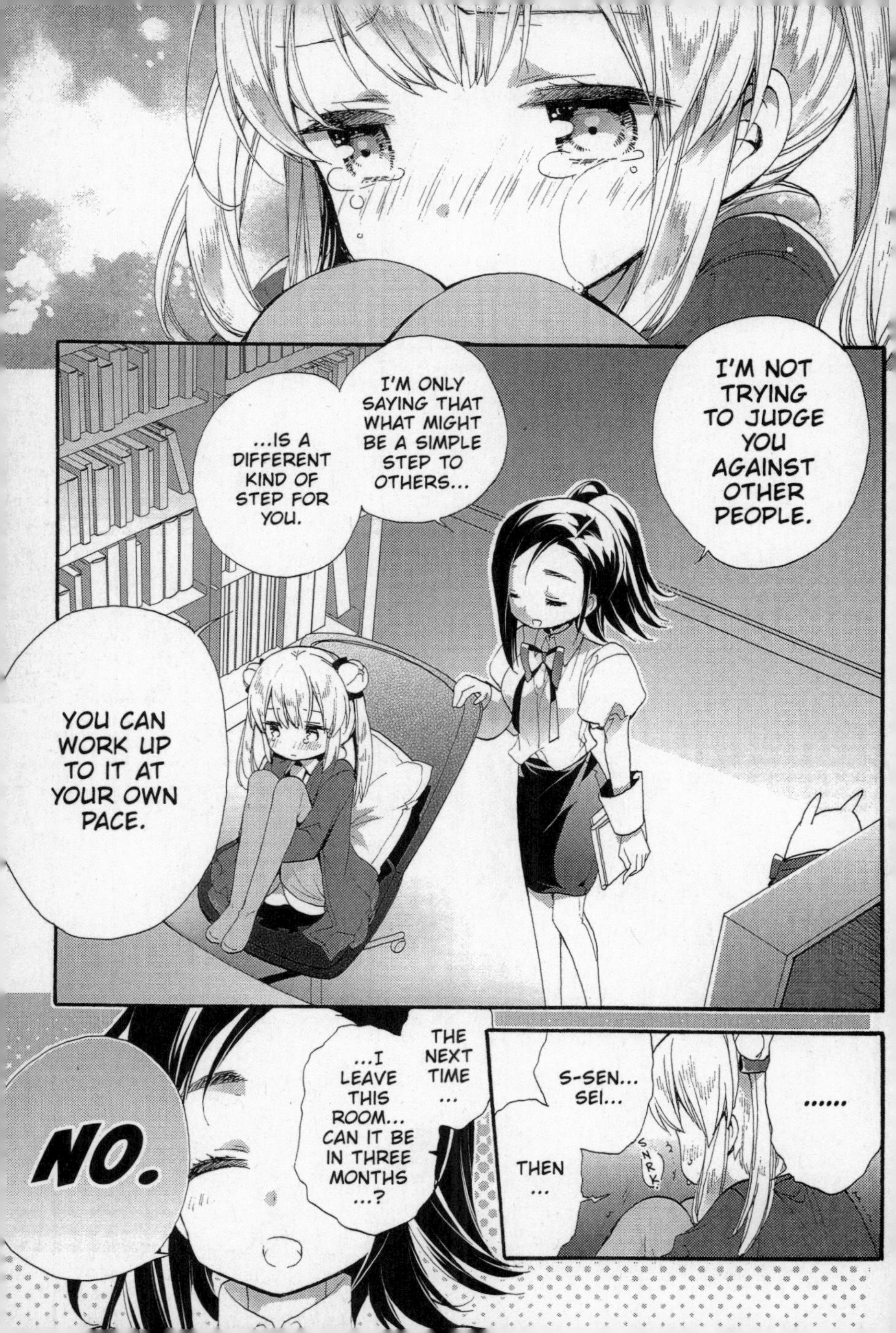
I'M NOT TRYING TO JUDGE YOU AGAINST OTHER PEOPLE.
I'M ONLY SAYING THAT WHAT MIGHT BE A SIMPLE STEP TO OTHERS...
...IS A DIFFERENT KIND OF STEP FOR YOU.
YOU CAN WORK UP TO IT AT YOUR OWN PACE.
......
S-SEN... SEI...
SNRK
THEN ...
THE NEXT TIME ...
...I LEAVE THIS ROOM... CAN IT BE IN THREE MONTHS ...?
NO.

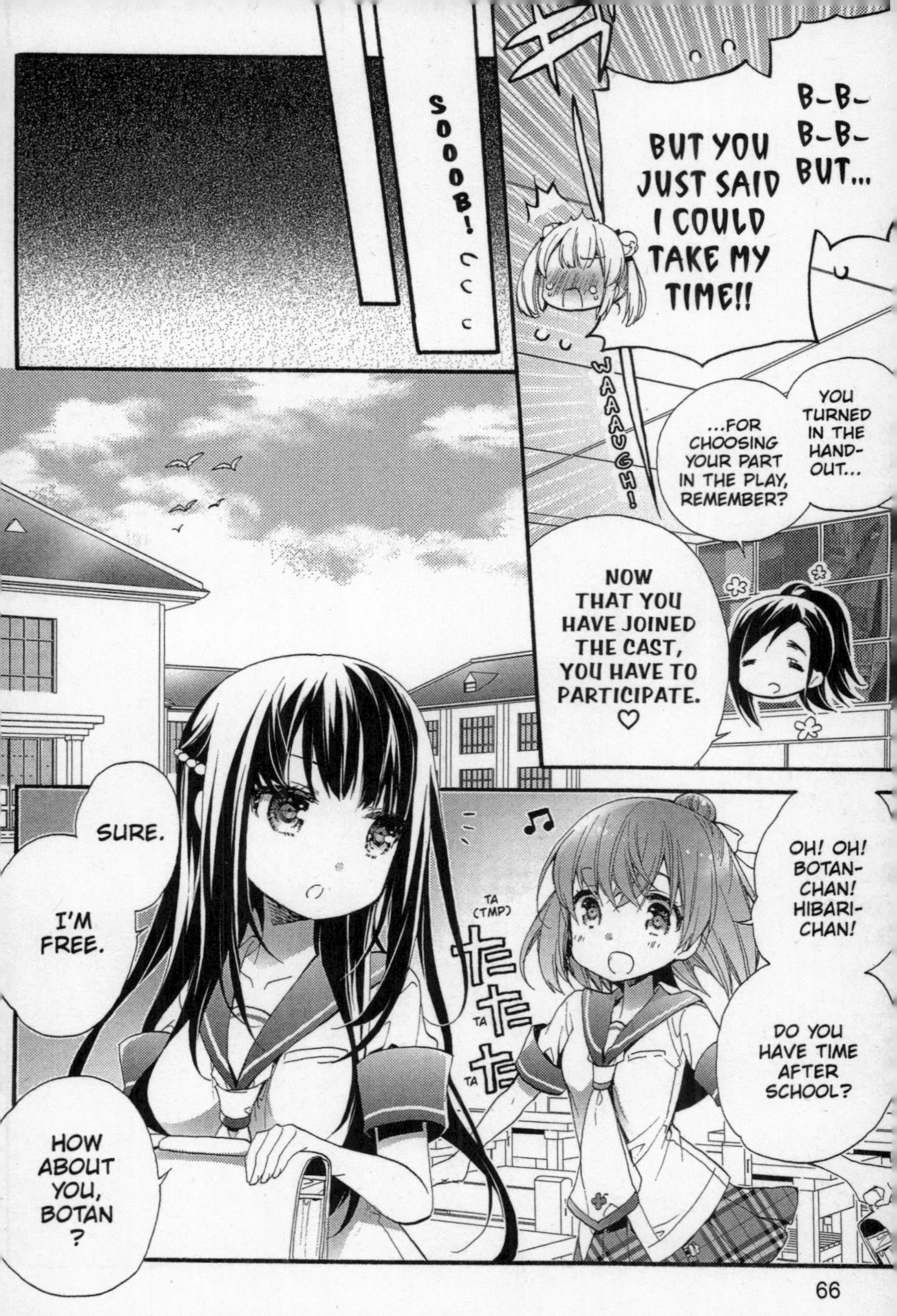

B-B-B-B-BUT...
BUT YOU JUST SAID I COULD TAKE MY TIME!!
WAAAAUGH!
YOU TURNED IN THE HAND-OUT...
...FOR CHOOSING YOUR PART IN THE PLAY, REMEMBER?
NOW THAT YOU HAVE JOINED THE CAST, YOU HAVE TO PARTICIPATE. ♡
SOOOB!
OH! OH! BOTAN-CHAN! HIBARI-CHAN!
DO YOU HAVE TIME AFTER SCHOOL?
TA (TMP)
TA
TA
SURE.
I'M FREE.
HOW ABOUT YOU, BOTAN?

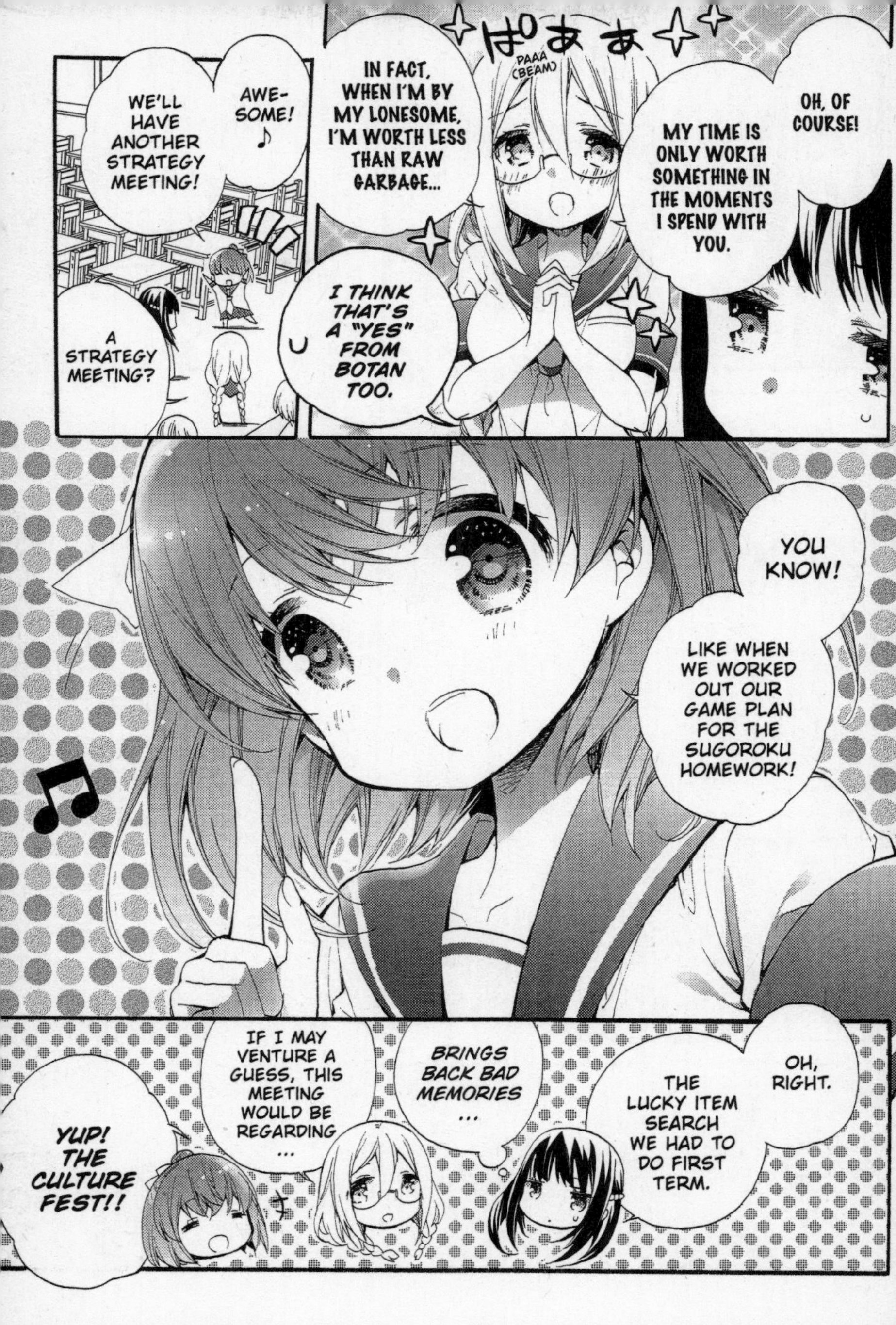
OH, OF COURSE!
MY TIME IS ONLY WORTH SOMETHING IN THE MOMENTS I SPEND WITH YOU.
ぱあぁ
PAAA (BEAM)
IN FACT, WHEN I'M BY MY LONESOME, I'M WORTH LESS THAN RAW GARBAGE...
I THINK THAT'S A "YES" FROM BOTAN TOO.
AWE-SOME! ♪
WE'LL HAVE ANOTHER STRATEGY MEETING!
A STRATEGY MEETING?
YOU KNOW!
LIKE WHEN WE WORKED OUT OUR GAME PLAN FOR THE SUGOROKU HOMEWORK!
OH, RIGHT.
THE LUCKY ITEM SEARCH WE HAD TO DO FIRST TERM.
BRINGS BACK BAD MEMORIES...
IF I MAY VENTURE A GUESS, THIS MEETING WOULD BE REGARDING...
YUP! THE CULTURE FEST!!

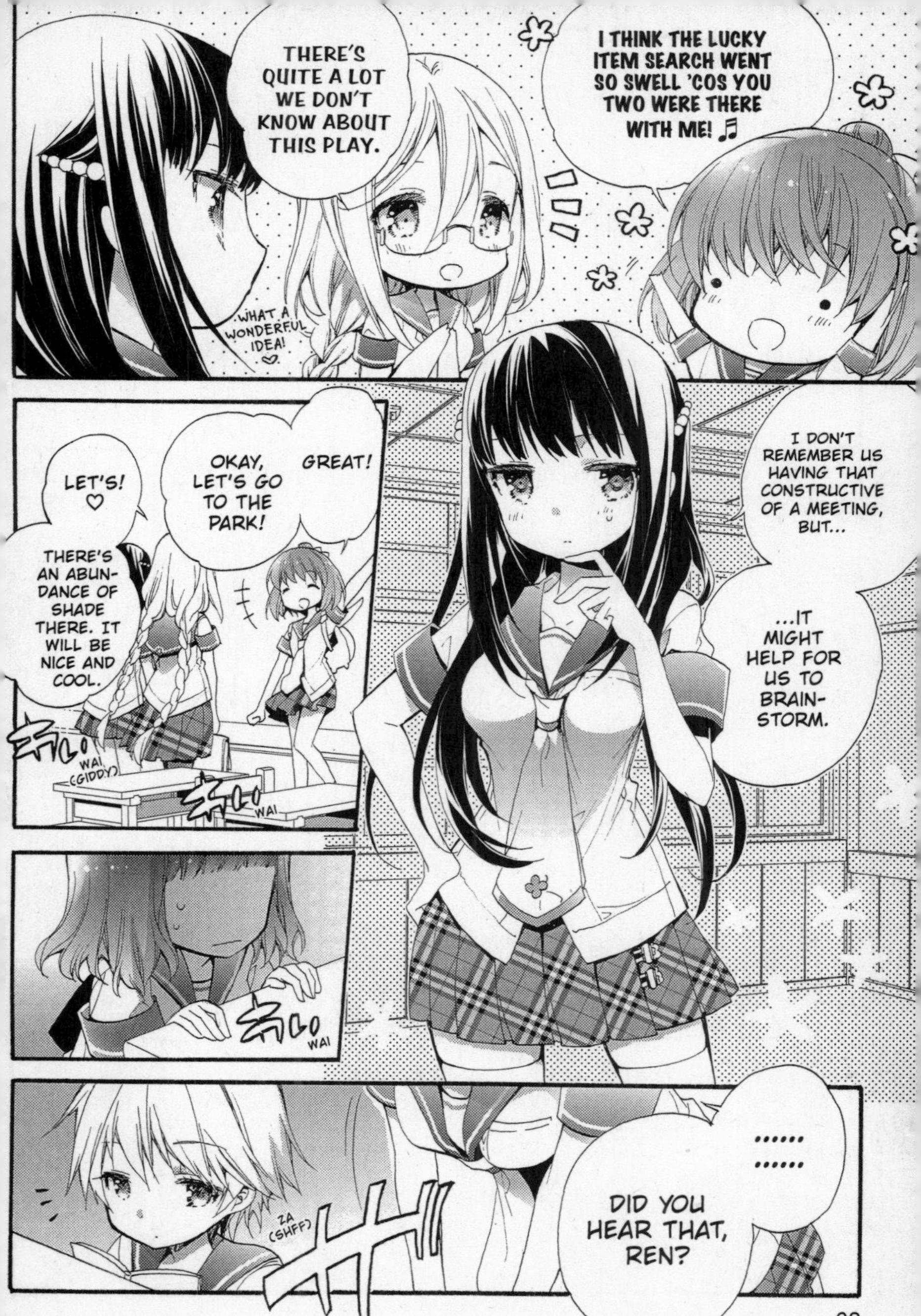
I THINK THE LUCKY ITEM SEARCH WENT SO SWELL 'COS YOU TWO WERE THERE WITH ME! ♫
THERE'S QUITE A LOT WE DON'T KNOW ABOUT THIS PLAY.
WHAT A WONDERFUL IDEA! ♡
I DON'T REMEMBER US HAVING THAT CONSTRUCTIVE OF A MEETING, BUT...
...IT MIGHT HELP FOR US TO BRAIN-STORM.
GREAT!
OKAY, LET'S GO TO THE PARK!
LET'S! ♡
THERE'S AN ABUN-DANCE OF SHADE THERE. IT WILL BE NICE AND COOL.
WAI (GIDDY)
WAI
WAI
......
......
DID YOU HEAR THAT, REN?
ZA (SHFF)

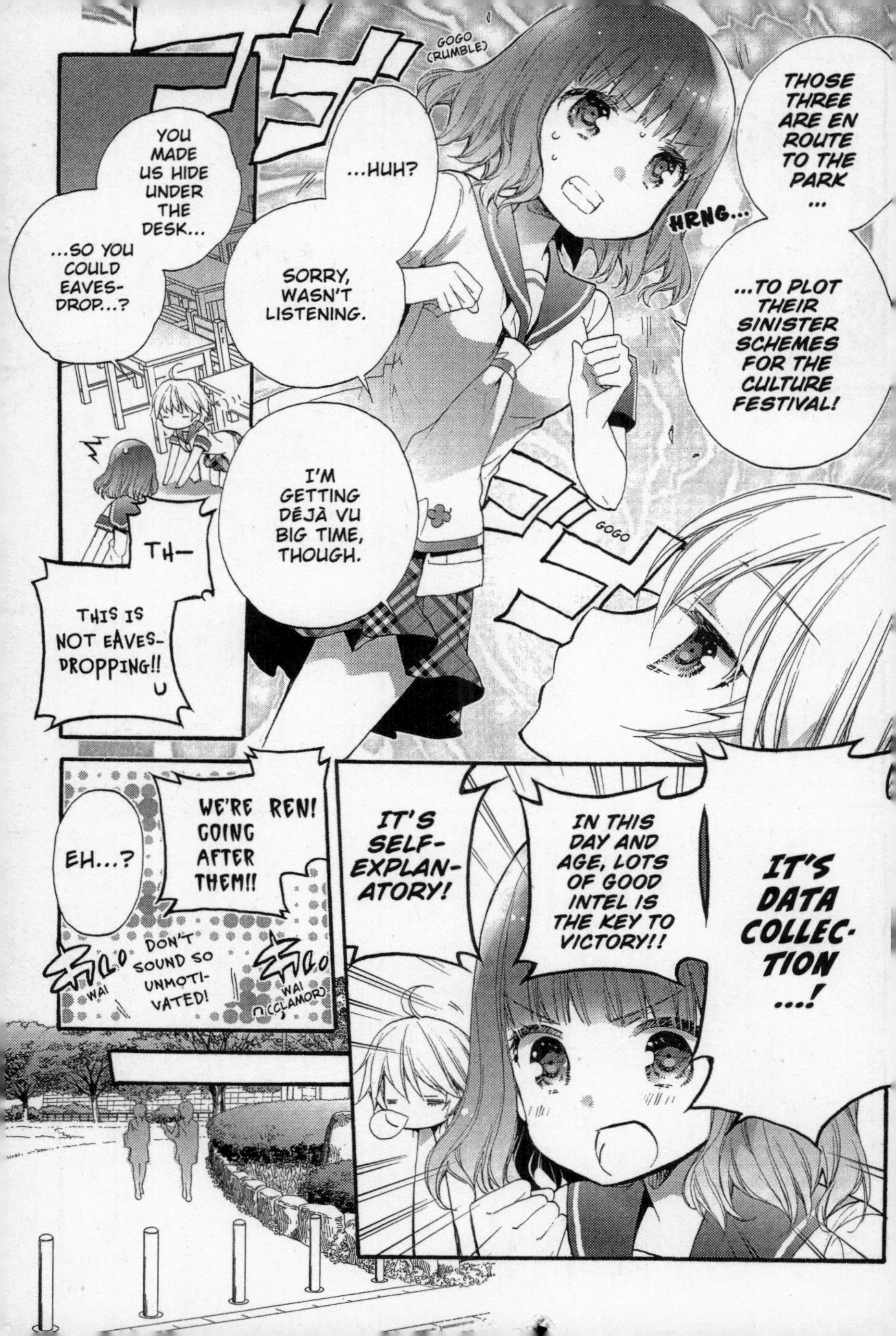
GOGO (RUMBLE)
THOSE THREE ARE EN ROUTE TO THE PARK...
HRNG...
...TO PLOT THEIR SINISTER SCHEMES FOR THE CULTURE FESTIVAL!
GOGO
...HUH?
SORRY, WASN'T LISTENING.
I'M GETTING DÉJÀ VU BIG TIME, THOUGH.
YOU MADE US HIDE UNDER THE DESK...
...SO YOU COULD EAVES-DROP...?
TH—
THIS IS NOT EAVES-DROPPING!!
IT'S DATA COLLEC-TION...!
IN THIS DAY AND AGE, LOTS OF GOOD INTEL IS THE KEY TO VICTORY!!
IT'S SELF-EXPLAN-ATORY!
REN!
WE'RE GOING AFTER THEM!!
EH...?
DON'T SOUND SO UNMOTI-VATED!
WAI WAI (CLAMOR)

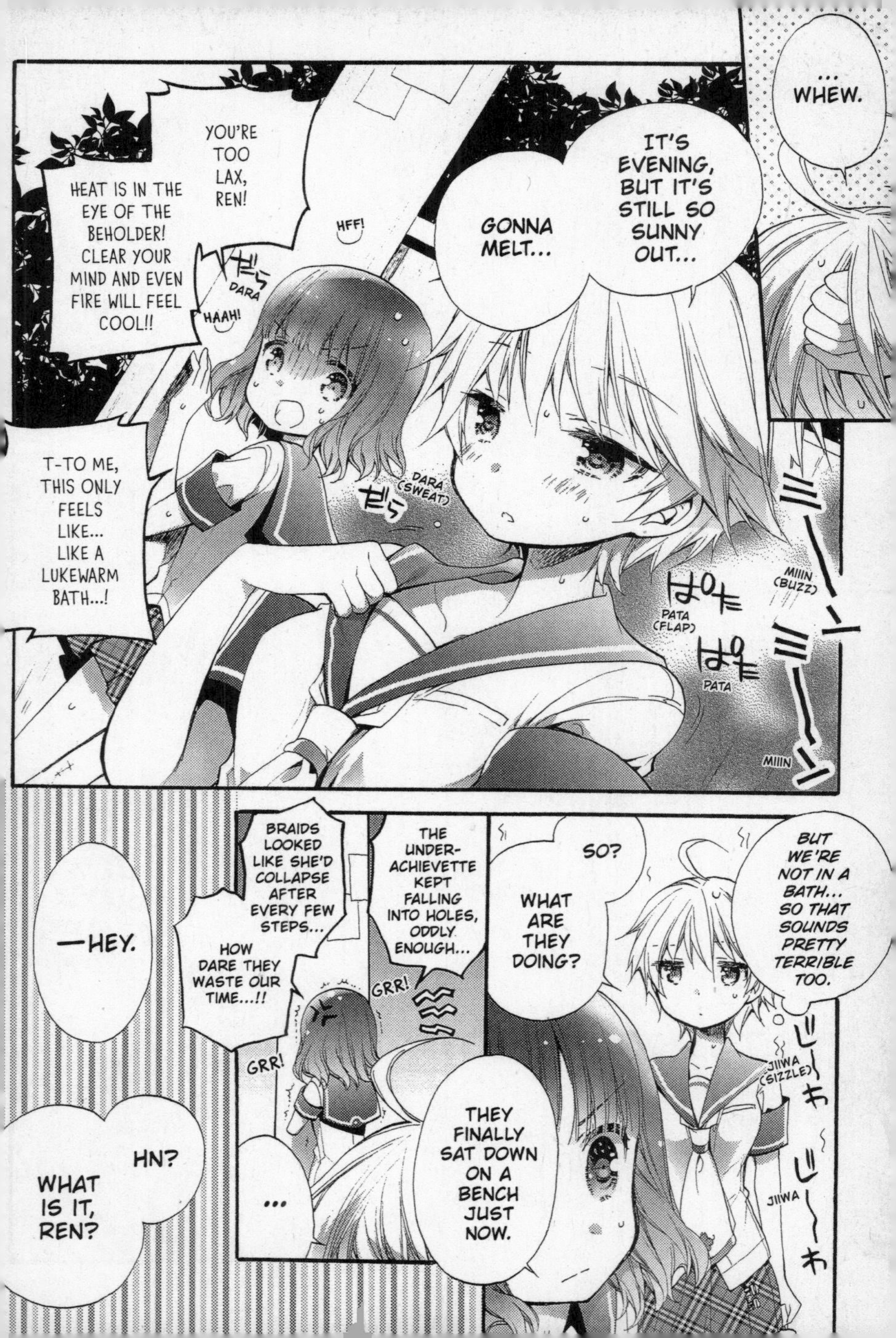

...WHEW.
IT'S EVENING, BUT IT'S STILL SO SUNNY OUT...
GONNA MELT...
MIIIN (BUZZ)
PATA (FLAP)
PATA
MIIIN
DARA (SWEAT)
YOU'RE TOO LAX, REN!
HEAT IS IN THE EYE OF THE BEHOLDER! CLEAR YOUR MIND AND EVEN FIRE WILL FEEL COOL!!
HFF!
DARA
HAAH!
T-TO ME, THIS ONLY FEELS LIKE... LIKE A LUKEWARM BATH...!
BUT WE'RE NOT IN A BATH... SO THAT SOUNDS PRETTY TERRIBLE TOO.
SO?
WHAT ARE THEY DOING?
JIIWA (SIZZLE)
JIIWA
THEY FINALLY SAT DOWN ON A BENCH JUST NOW.
...
THE UNDER-ACHIEVETTE KEPT FALLING INTO HOLES, ODDLY ENOUGH...
BRAIDS LOOKED LIKE SHE'D COLLAPSE AFTER EVERY FEW STEPS...
HOW DARE THEY WASTE OUR TIME...!!
GRR!
GRR!
—HEY.
HN? WHAT IS IT, REN?

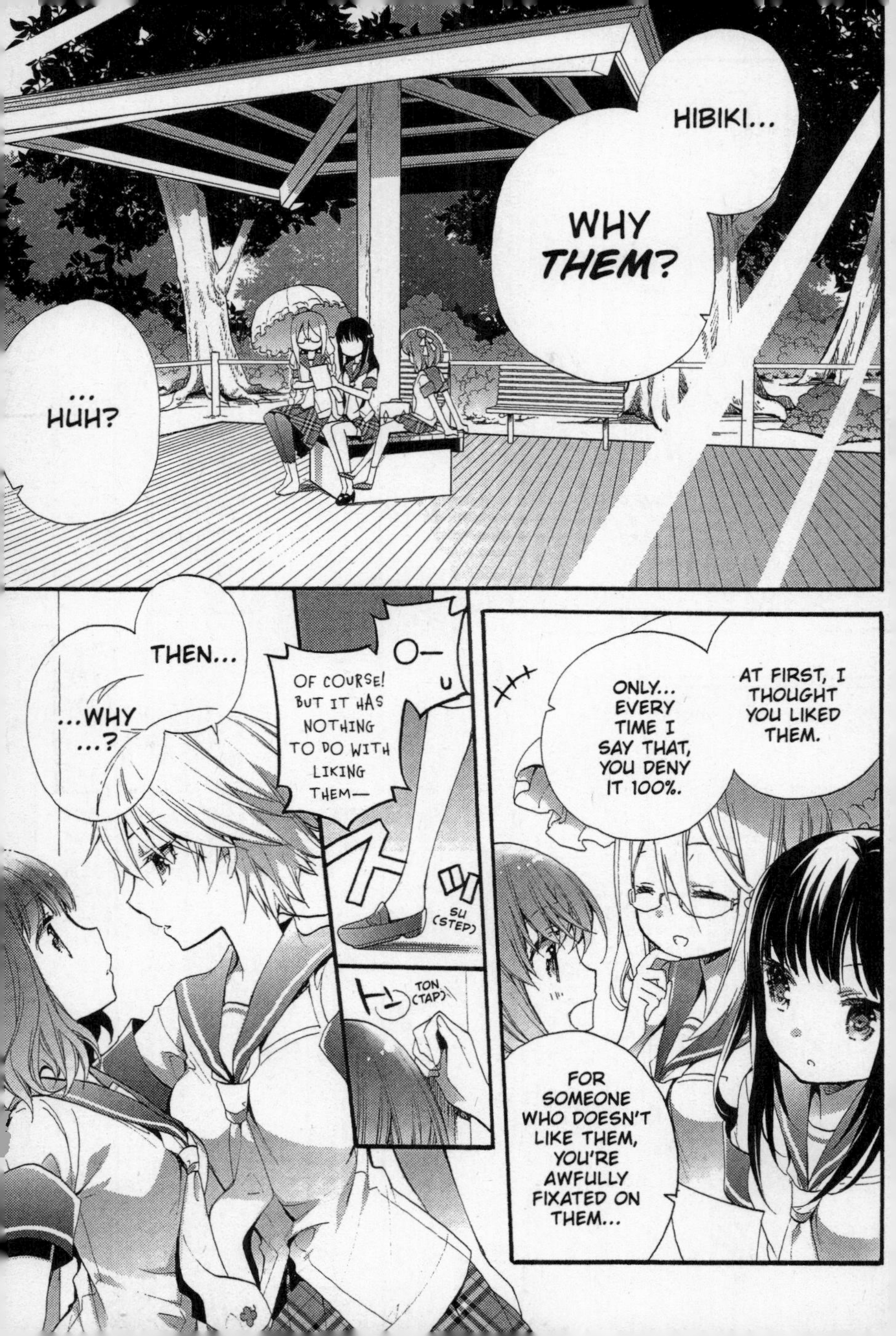
HIBIKI...
WHY *THEM*?
... HUH?
AT FIRST, I THOUGHT YOU LIKED THEM.
ONLY... EVERY TIME I SAY THAT, YOU DENY IT 100%.
FOR SOMEONE WHO DOESN'T LIKE THEM, YOU'RE AWFULLY FIXATED ON THEM...
O— U
OF COURSE! BUT IT HAS NOTHING TO DO WITH LIKING THEM—
SU (STEP)
TON (TAP)
THEN...
...WHY ...?

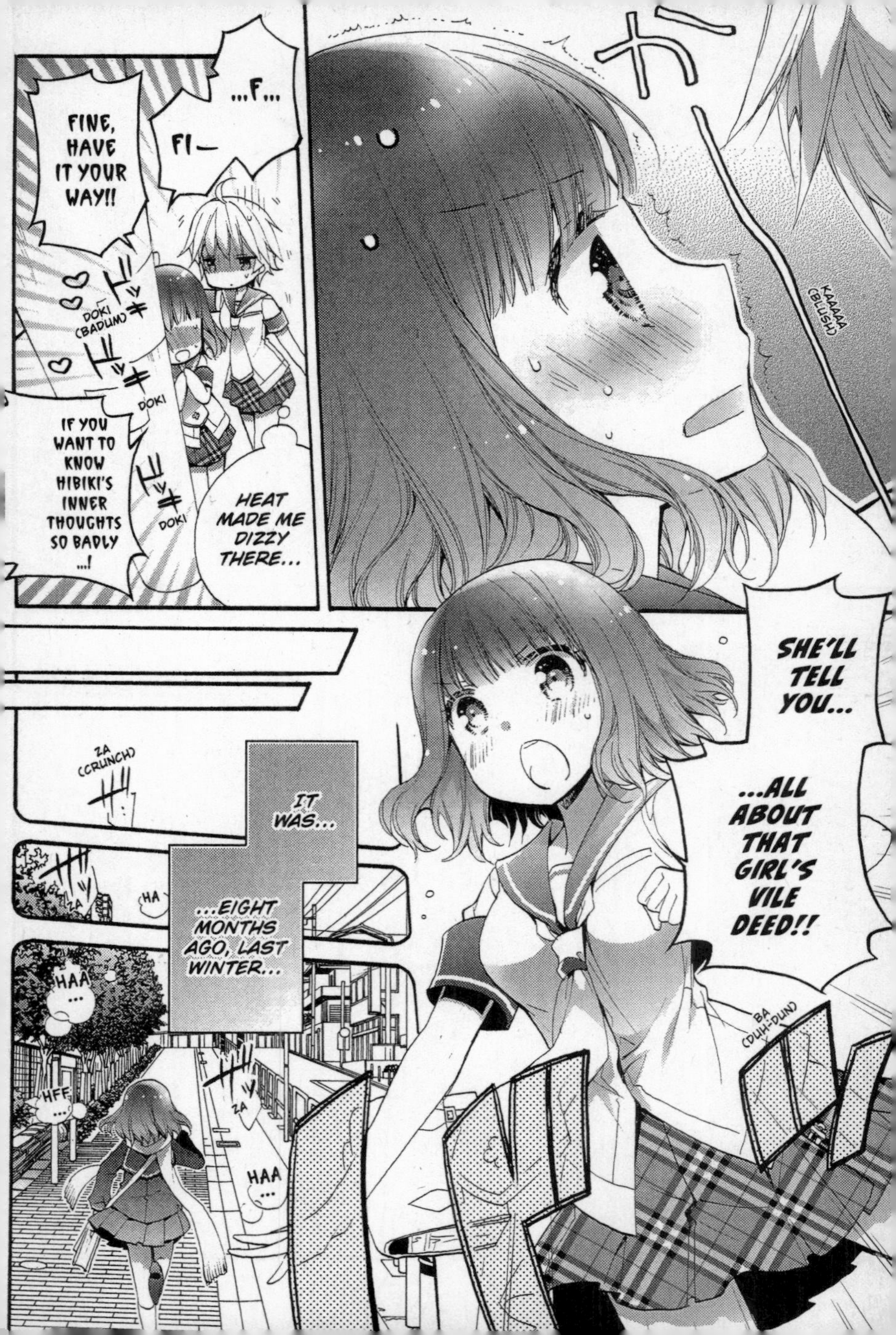

KAAAAA (BLUSH)
...F...
FI—
FINE, HAVE IT YOUR WAY!!
DOKI (BADUM)
DOKI
DOKI
HEAT MADE ME DIZZY THERE...
IF YOU WANT TO KNOW HIBIKI'S INNER THOUGHTS SO BADLY ...!
SHE'LL TELL YOU...
...ALL ABOUT THAT GIRL'S VILE DEED!!
BA (DUH-DUND)
ZA (CRUNCH)
IT WAS...
...EIGHT MONTHS AGO, LAST WINTER...
ZA
HA
HAA ...
HFF ....
ZA
HAA ...

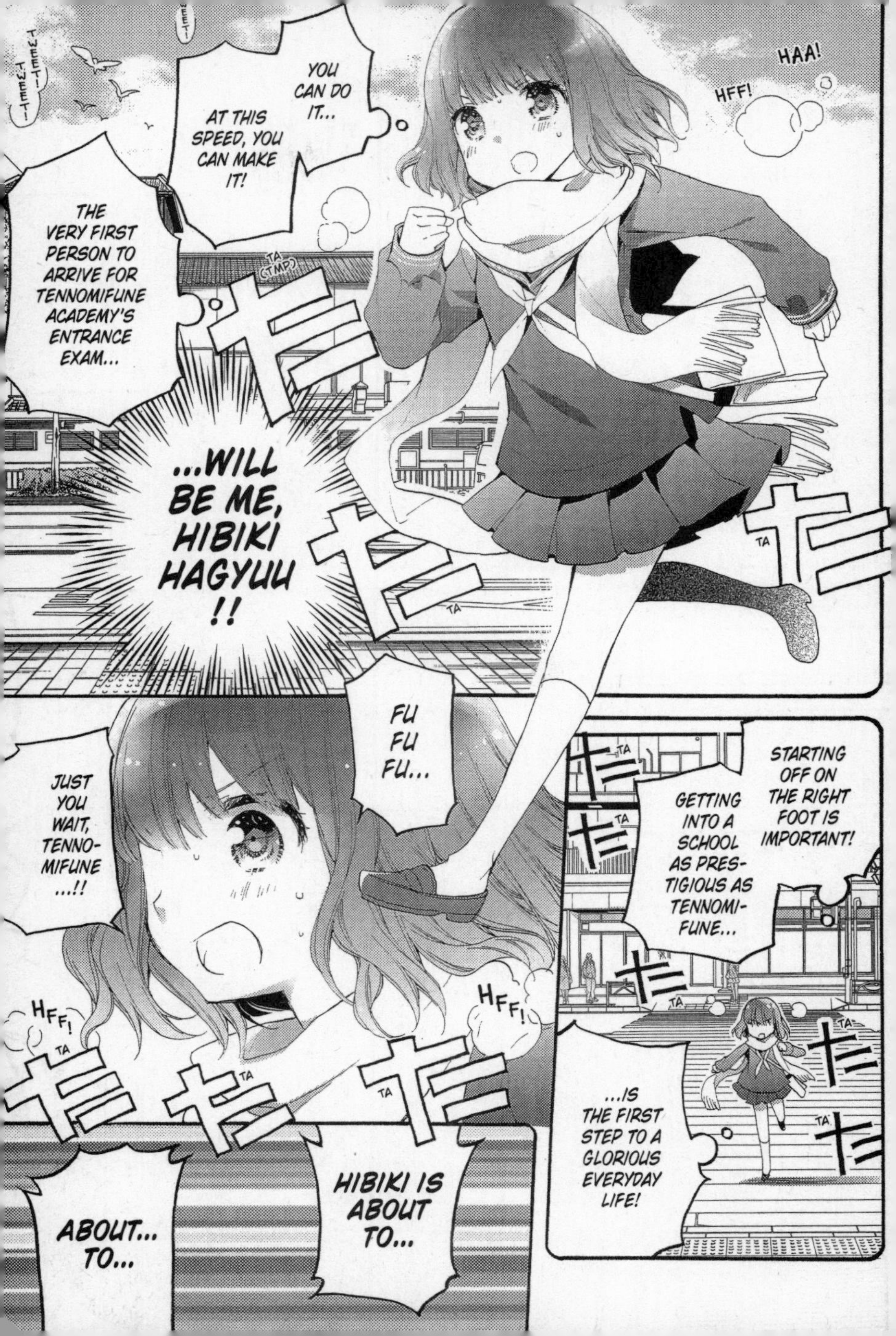
HAA!
HFF!
YOU CAN DO IT...
AT THIS SPEED, YOU CAN MAKE IT!
TWEET! TWEET!
THE VERY FIRST PERSON TO ARRIVE FOR TENNOMIFUNE ACADEMY'S ENTRANCE EXAM...
TA (TMP)
...WILL BE ME, HIBIKI HAGYUU!!
TA
TA
STARTING OFF ON THE RIGHT FOOT IS IMPORTANT!
GETTING INTO A SCHOOL AS PRESTIGIOUS AS TENNOMIFUNE...
TA
TA
TA
...IS THE FIRST STEP TO A GLORIOUS EVERYDAY LIFE!
TA
TA
FU FU FU...
JUST YOU WAIT, TENNOMIFUNE...!!
HFF!
HFF!
TA
TA
TA
HIBIKI IS ABOUT TO...
ABOUT... TO...

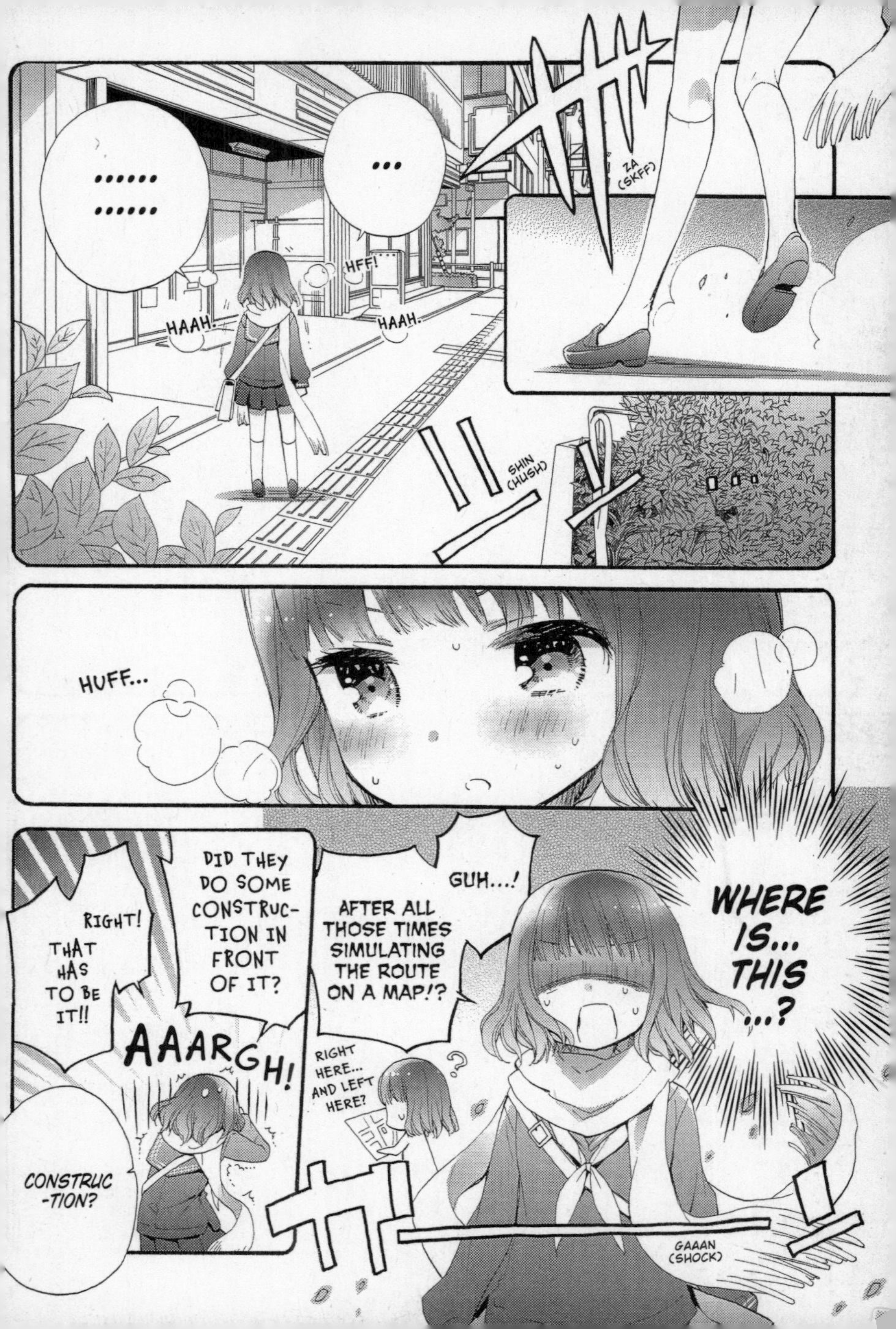
ZA (SKFF)
SHIN (HUSH)
...
......
......
HFF!
HAAH.
HAAH.
HUFF...
WHERE IS... THIS ...?
GAAAN (SHOCK)
GUH...!
AFTER ALL THOSE TIMES SIMULATING THE ROUTE ON A MAP!?
DID THEY DO SOME CONSTRUC-TION IN FRONT OF IT?
RIGHT! THAT HAS TO BE IT!!
AAARGH!
RIGHT HERE... AND LEFT HERE?
CONSTRUC-TION?

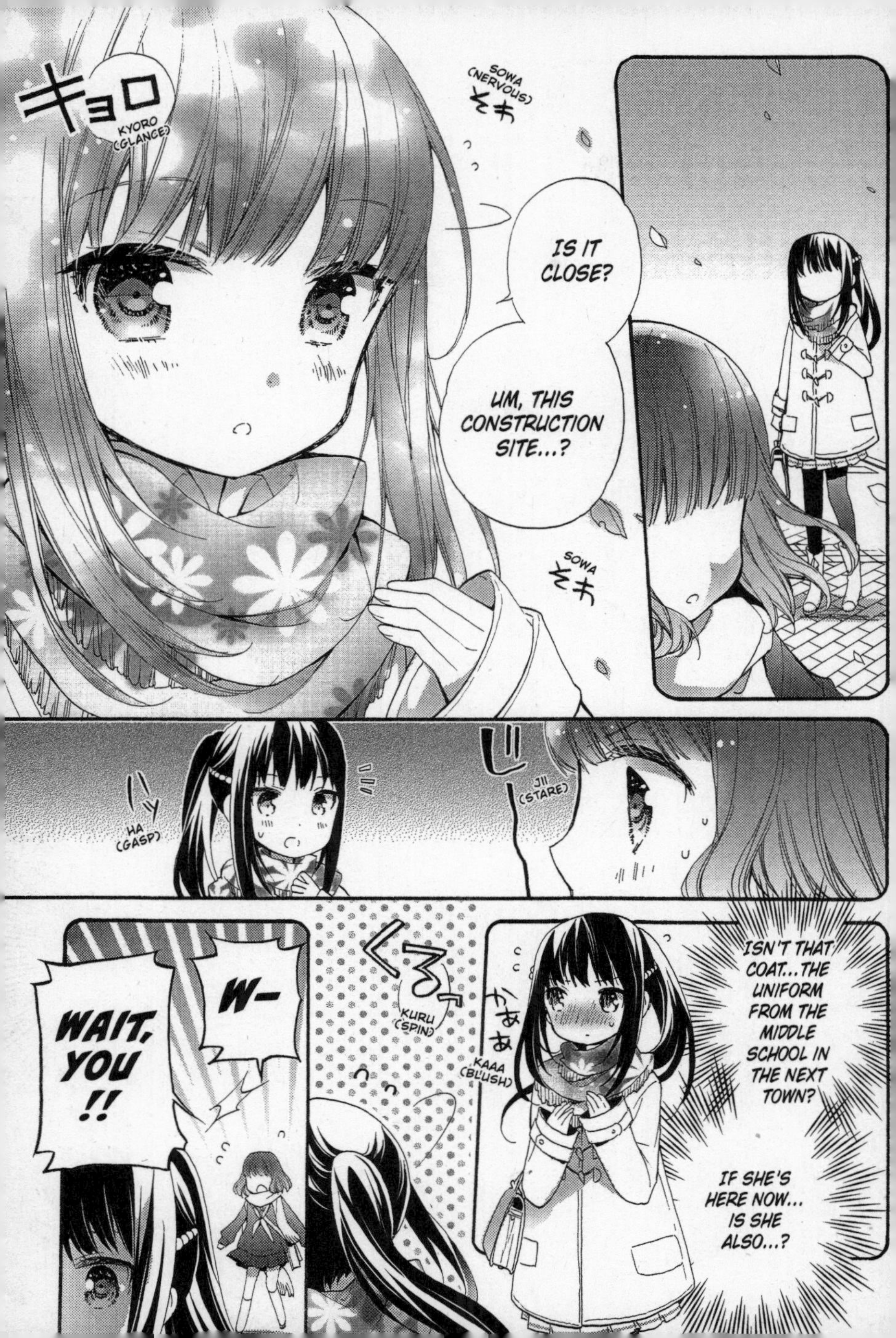
そわ
SOWA (NERVOUS)
IS IT CLOSE?
UM, THIS CONSTRUCTION SITE...?
キョロ
KYORO (GLANCE)
そわ
SOWA
じー
JII (STARE)
ハッ
HA (GASP)
ISN'T THAT COAT...THE UNIFORM FROM THE MIDDLE SCHOOL IN THE NEXT TOWN?
かあぁ
KAAA (BLUSH)
IF SHE'S HERE NOW... IS SHE ALSO...?
くるっ
KURU (SPIN)
W-
WAIT, YOU!!

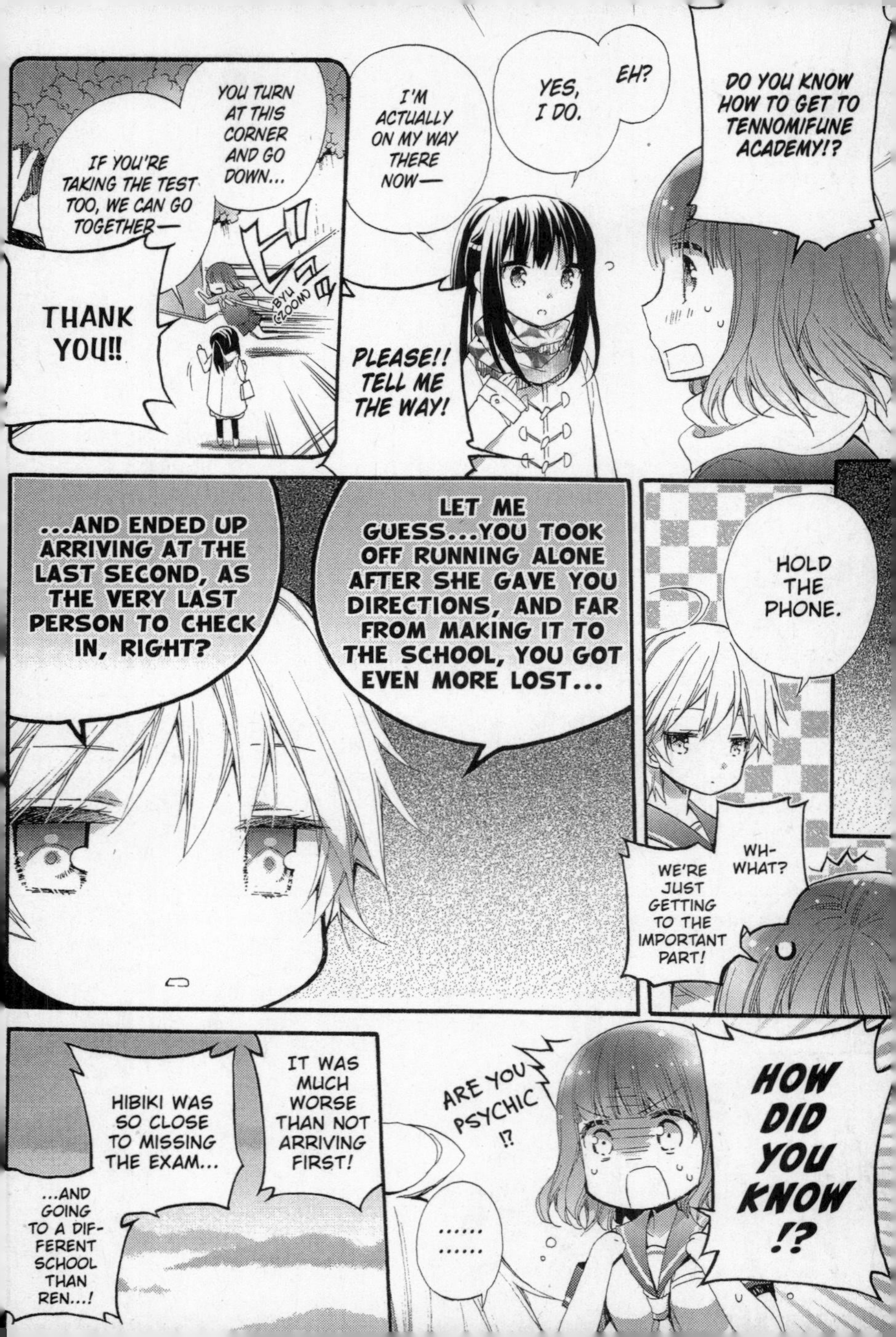

DO YOU KNOW HOW TO GET TO TENNOMIFUNE ACADEMY!?
EH?
YES, I DO.
I'M ACTUALLY ON MY WAY THERE NOW—
PLEASE!! TELL ME THE WAY!
YOU TURN AT THIS CORNER AND GO DOWN...
IF YOU'RE TAKING THE TEST TOO, WE CAN GO TOGETHER—
BYU (ZOOM)
THANK YOU!!
HOLD THE PHONE.
WH-WHAT?
WE'RE JUST GETTING TO THE IMPORTANT PART!
LET ME GUESS...YOU TOOK OFF RUNNING ALONE AFTER SHE GAVE YOU DIRECTIONS, AND FAR FROM MAKING IT TO THE SCHOOL, YOU GOT EVEN MORE LOST...
...AND ENDED UP ARRIVING AT THE LAST SECOND, AS THE VERY LAST PERSON TO CHECK IN, RIGHT?
HOW DID YOU KNOW!?
ARE YOU PSYCHIC!?
......
......
IT WAS MUCH WORSE THAN NOT ARRIVING FIRST!
HIBIKI WAS SO CLOSE TO MISSING THE EXAM...
...AND GOING TO A DIF-FERENT SCHOOL THAN REN...!

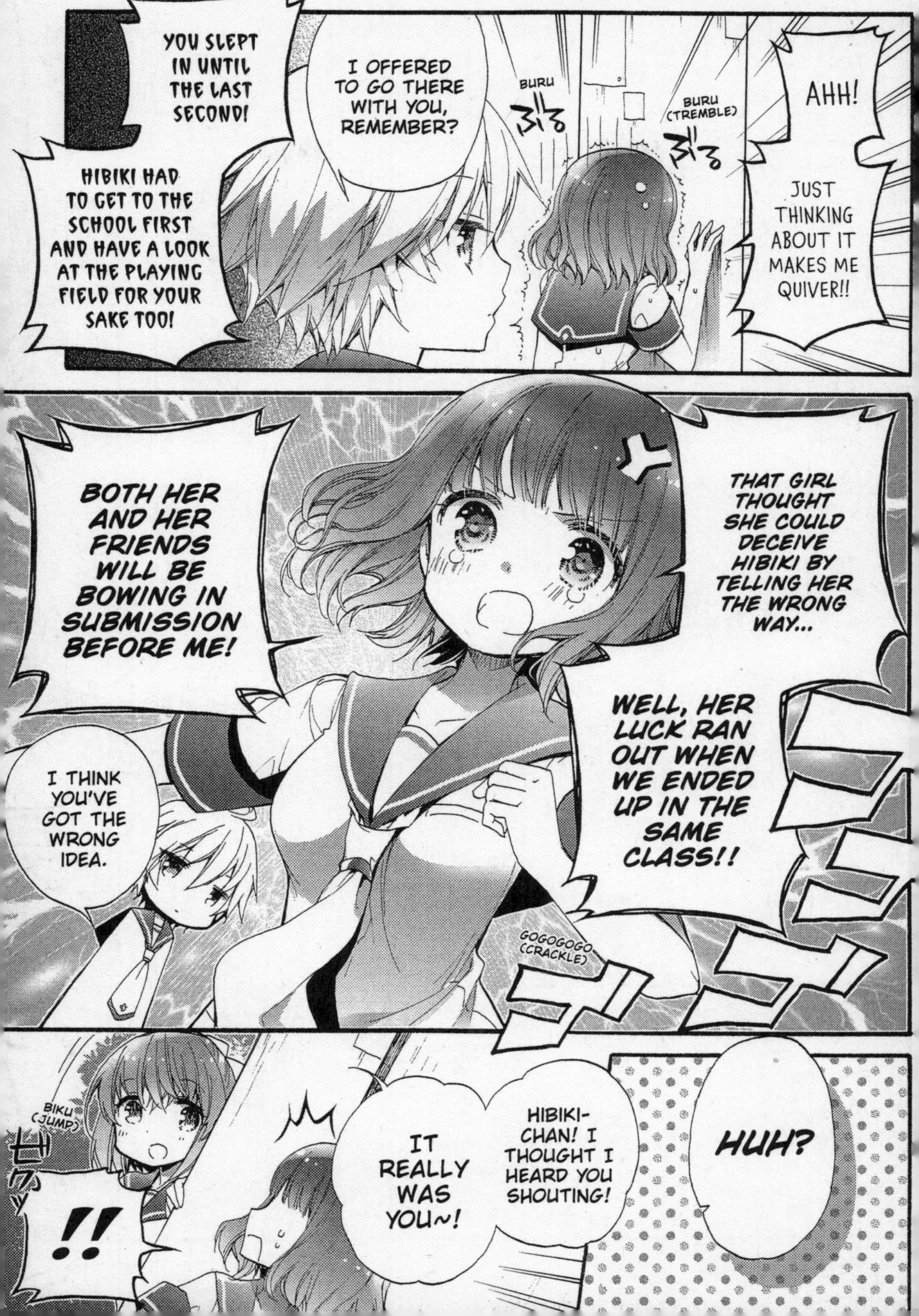
AHH!
JUST THINKING ABOUT IT MAKES ME QUIVER!!
BURU (TREMBLE)
ぶる
BURU
ぶる
I OFFERED TO GO THERE WITH YOU, REMEMBER?
YOU SLEPT IN UNTIL THE LAST SECOND!
HIBIKI HAD TO GET TO THE SCHOOL FIRST AND HAVE A LOOK AT THE PLAYING FIELD FOR YOUR SAKE TOO!
THAT GIRL THOUGHT SHE COULD DECEIVE HIBIKI BY TELLING HER THE WRONG WAY...
WELL, HER LUCK RAN OUT WHEN WE ENDED UP IN THE SAME CLASS!!
BOTH HER AND HER FRIENDS WILL BE BOWING IN SUBMISSION BEFORE ME!
GOGOGOGO (CRACKLE)
I THINK YOU'VE GOT THE WRONG IDEA.
HUH?
HIBIKI-CHAN! I THOUGHT I HEARD YOU SHOUTING!
IT REALLY WAS YOU~!
BIKU (JUMP)
!!

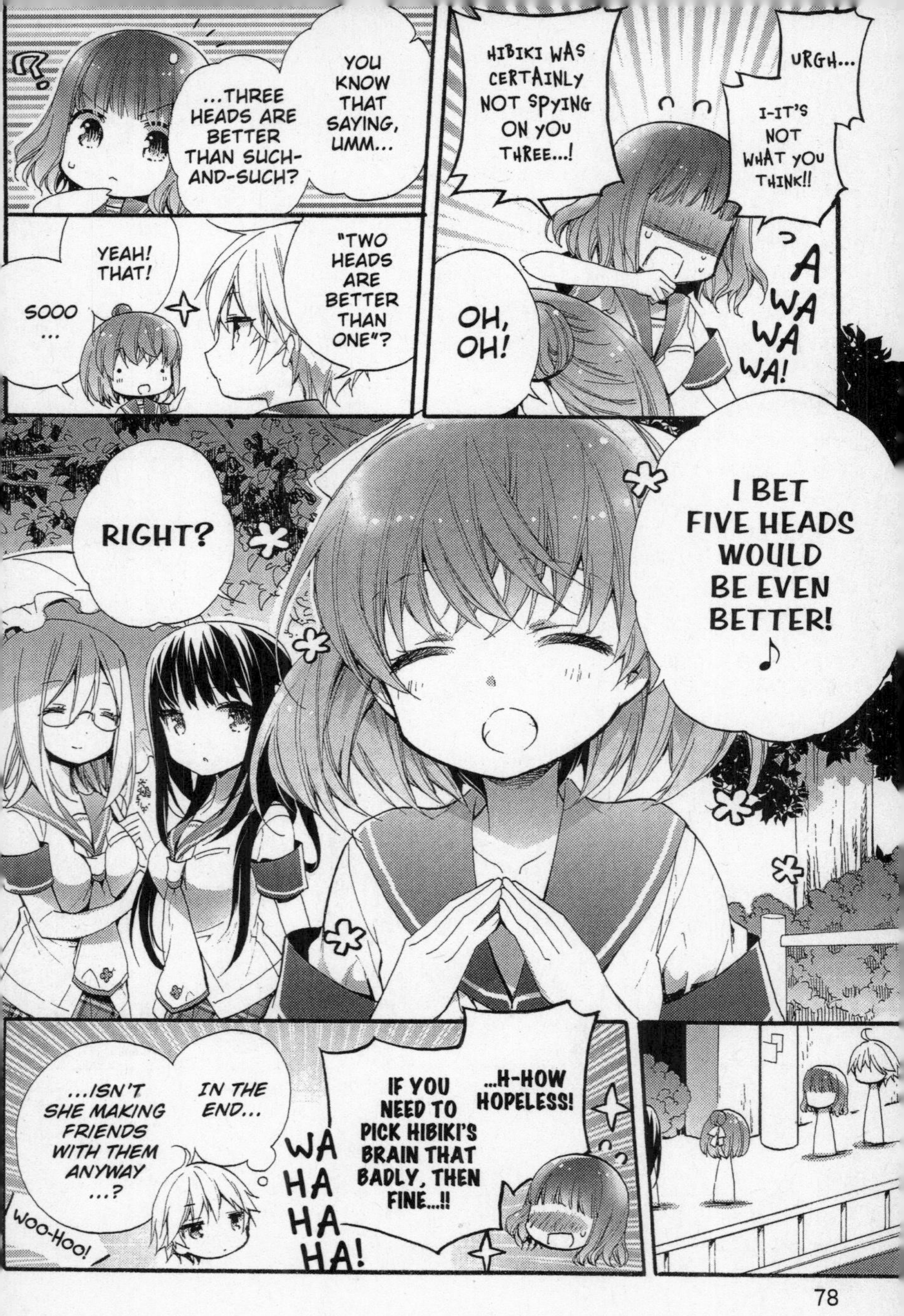
HIBIKI WAS CERTAINLY NOT SPYING ON YOU THREE...!
URGH...
I-IT'S NOT WHAT YOU THINK!!
AWAWAWAWA!
OH, OH!
YOU KNOW THAT SAYING, UMM...
...THREE HEADS ARE BETTER THAN SUCH-AND-SUCH?
"TWO HEADS ARE BETTER THAN ONE"?
YEAH! THAT!
SOOO ...
I BET FIVE HEADS WOULD BE EVEN BETTER! ♪
RIGHT?
...H-HOW HOPELESS!
IF YOU NEED TO PICK HIBIKI'S BRAIN THAT BADLY, THEN FINE...!!
WA HA HA HA HA!
IN THE END...
...ISN'T SHE MAKING FRIENDS WITH THEM ANYWAY ...?
WOO-HOO!

Anne Happy

unhappy go lucky!

✽ Lucky. 33

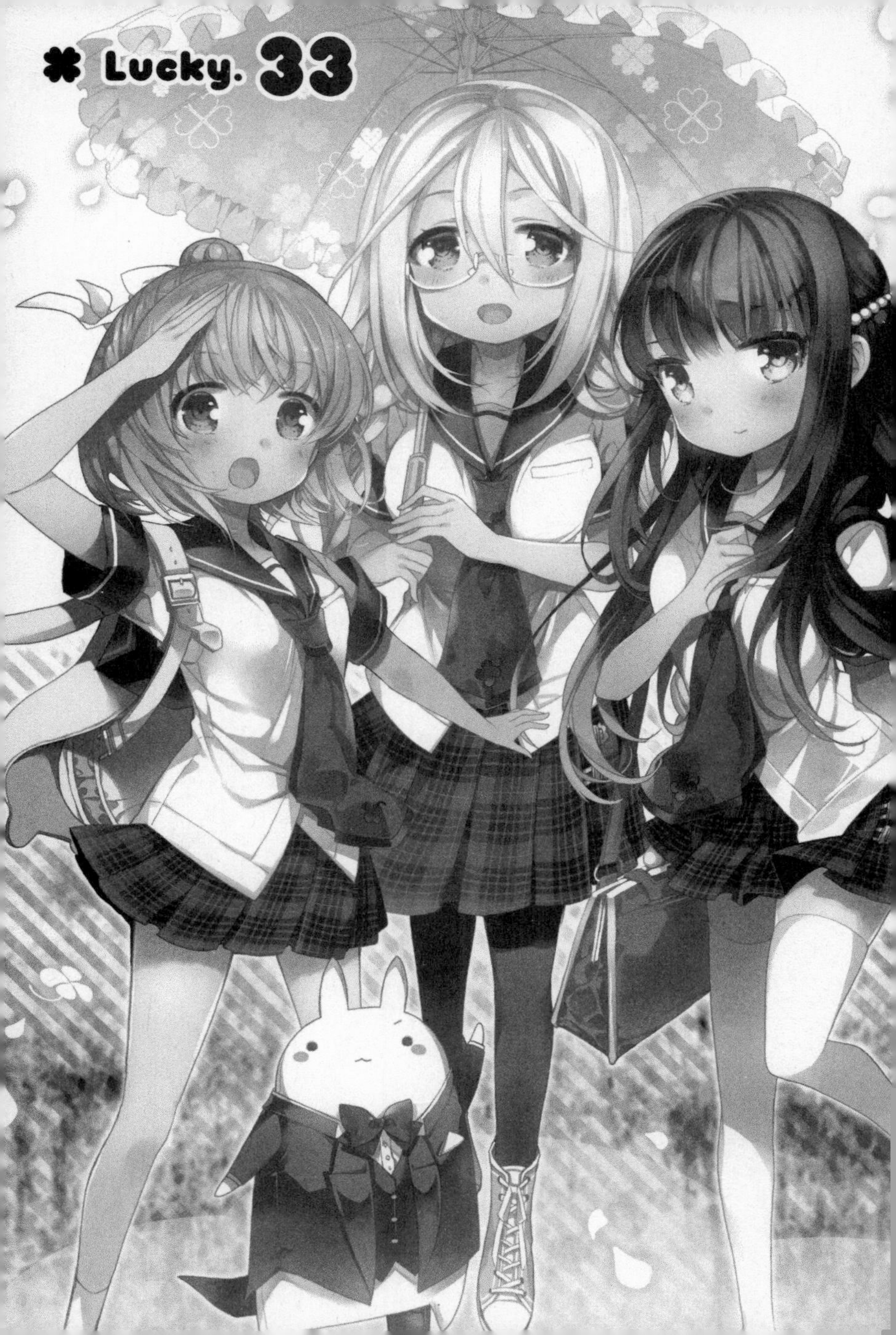

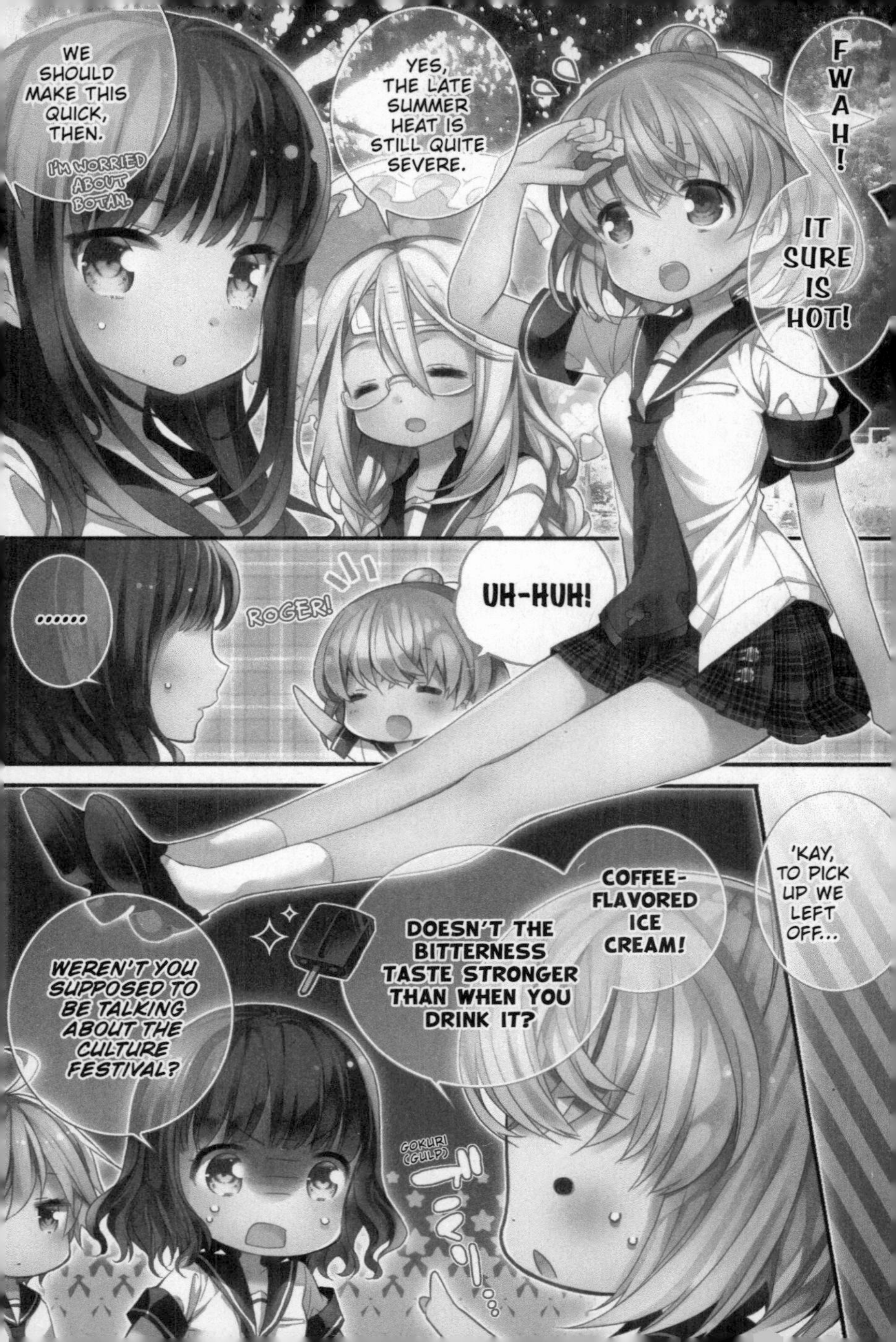
FWAH!
IT SURE IS HOT!
YES, THE LATE SUMMER HEAT IS STILL QUITE SEVERE.
WE SHOULD MAKE THIS QUICK, THEN.
I'M WORRIED ABOUT BOTAN.
UH-HUH!
ROGER!
......
'KAY, TO PICK UP WE LEFT OFF...
COFFEE-FLAVORED ICE CREAM!
DOESN'T THE BITTERNESS TASTE STRONGER THAN WHEN YOU DRINK IT?
WEREN'T YOU SUPPOSED TO BE TALKING ABOUT THE CULTURE FESTIVAL?
GOKURI (GULP)

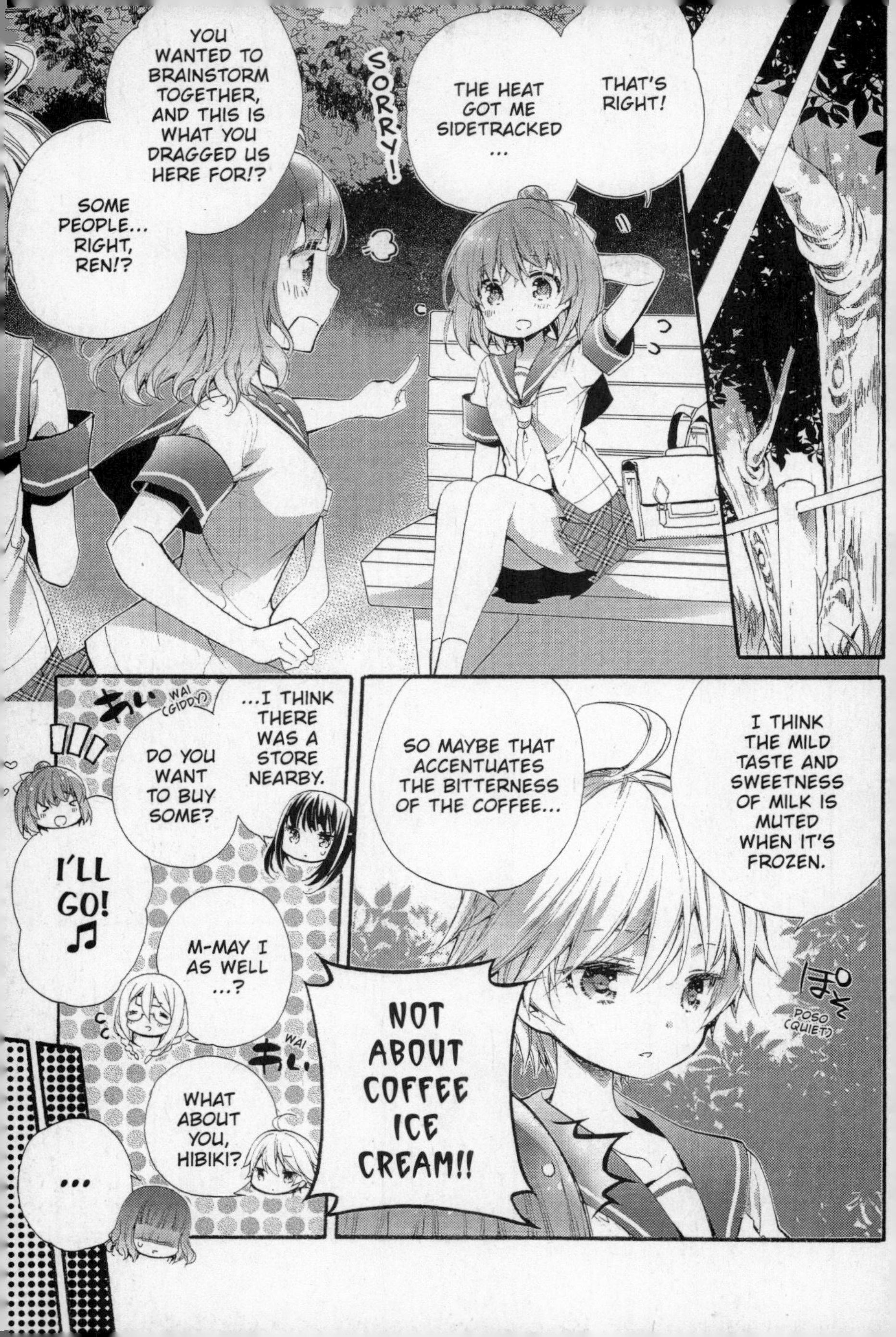
THAT'S RIGHT!
THE HEAT GOT ME SIDETRACKED ...
SORRY!
YOU WANTED TO BRAINSTORM TOGETHER, AND THIS IS WHAT YOU DRAGGED US HERE FOR!?
SOME PEOPLE... RIGHT, REN!?
I THINK THE MILD TASTE AND SWEETNESS OF MILK IS MUTED WHEN IT'S FROZEN.
SO MAYBE THAT ACCENTUATES THE BITTERNESS OF THE COFFEE...
POSO (QUIET)
NOT ABOUT COFFEE ICE CREAM!!
...I THINK THERE WAS A STORE NEARBY.
DO YOU WANT TO BUY SOME?
WAI (GIDDY)
I'LL GO! ♫
M-MAY I AS WELL ...?
WAI
WHAT ABOUT YOU, HIBIKI?
...

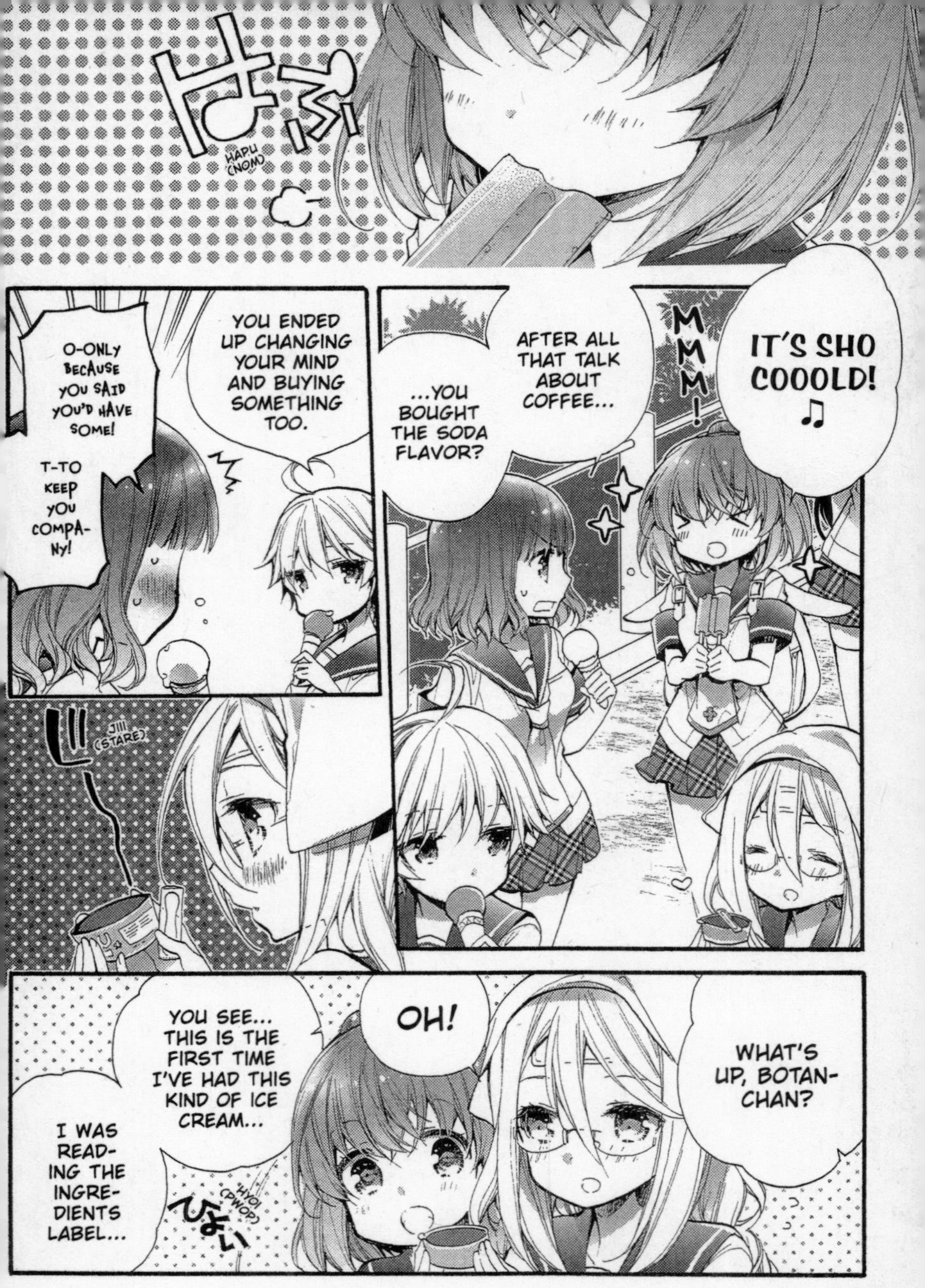
はぷ
HAPU (NOM)
MMM!
IT'S SHO COOOLD! ♫
AFTER ALL THAT TALK ABOUT COFFEE...
...YOU BOUGHT THE SODA FLAVOR?
YOU ENDED UP CHANGING YOUR MIND AND BUYING SOMETHING TOO.
O-ONLY BECAUSE YOU SAID YOU'D HAVE SOME!
T-TO KEEP YOU COMPA-NY!
じー
JIII (STARE)
WHAT'S UP, BOTAN-CHAN?
OH!
YOU SEE... THIS IS THE FIRST TIME I'VE HAD THIS KIND OF ICE CREAM...
I WAS READ-ING THE INGRE-DIENTS LABEL...
ひょい
HYOI (PWOP)

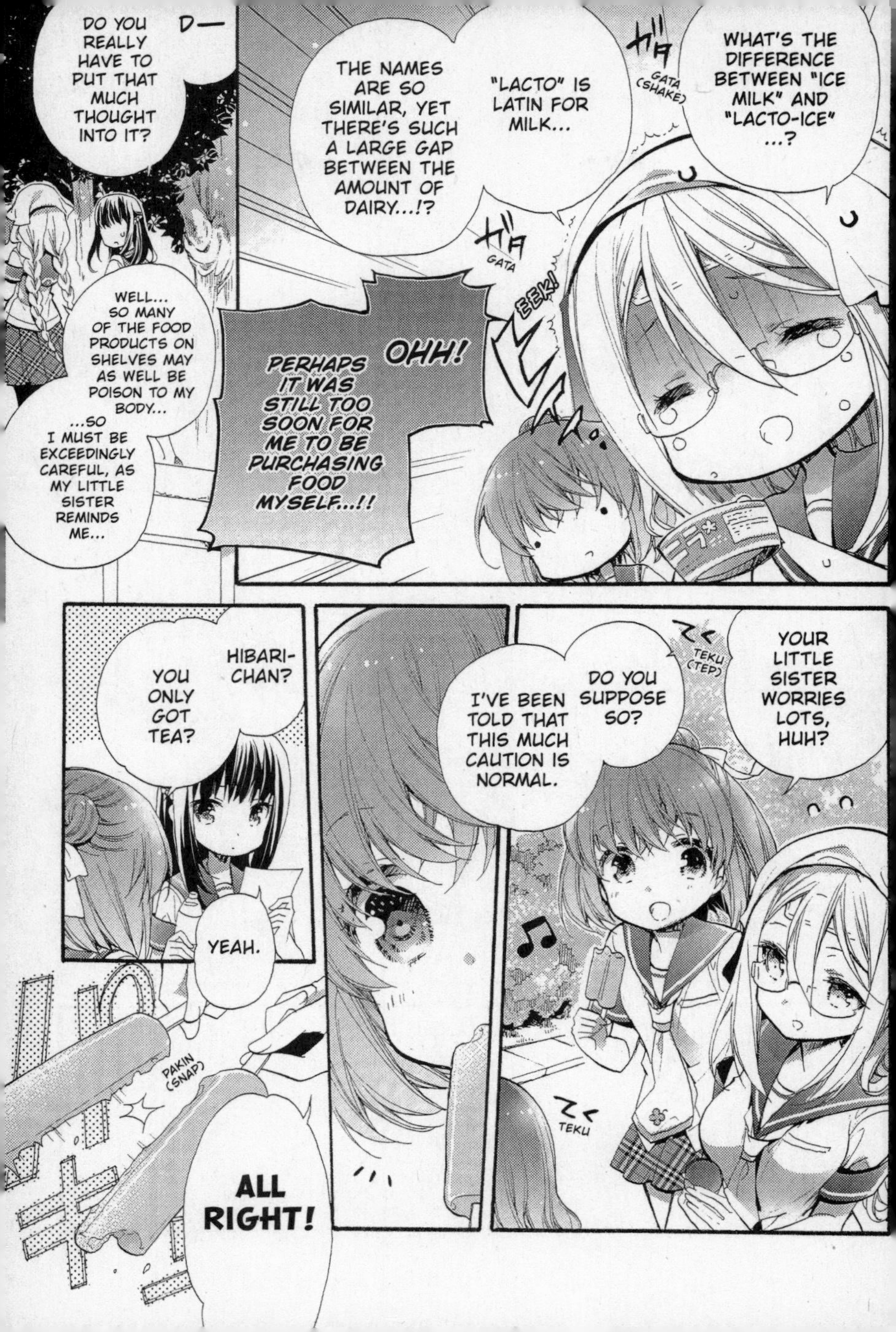
WHAT'S THE DIFFERENCE BETWEEN "ICE MILK" AND "LACTO-ICE" ...?
GATA (SHAKE)
"LACTO" IS LATIN FOR MILK...
THE NAMES ARE SO SIMILAR, YET THERE'S SUCH A LARGE GAP BETWEEN THE AMOUNT OF DAIRY...!?
GATA
EEK!
OHH!
PERHAPS IT WAS STILL TOO SOON FOR ME TO BE PURCHASING FOOD MYSELF...!!
D—
DO YOU REALLY HAVE TO PUT THAT MUCH THOUGHT INTO IT?
WELL... SO MANY OF THE FOOD PRODUCTS ON SHELVES MAY AS WELL BE POISON TO MY BODY...
...SO I MUST BE EXCEEDINGLY CAREFUL, AS MY LITTLE SISTER REMINDS ME...
TEKU (TEP)
YOUR LITTLE SISTER WORRIES LOTS, HUH?
DO YOU SUPPOSE SO?
I'VE BEEN TOLD THAT THIS MUCH CAUTION IS NORMAL.
TEKU
HIBARI-CHAN?
YOU ONLY GOT TEA?
YEAH.
PAKIN (SNAP)
ALL RIGHT!

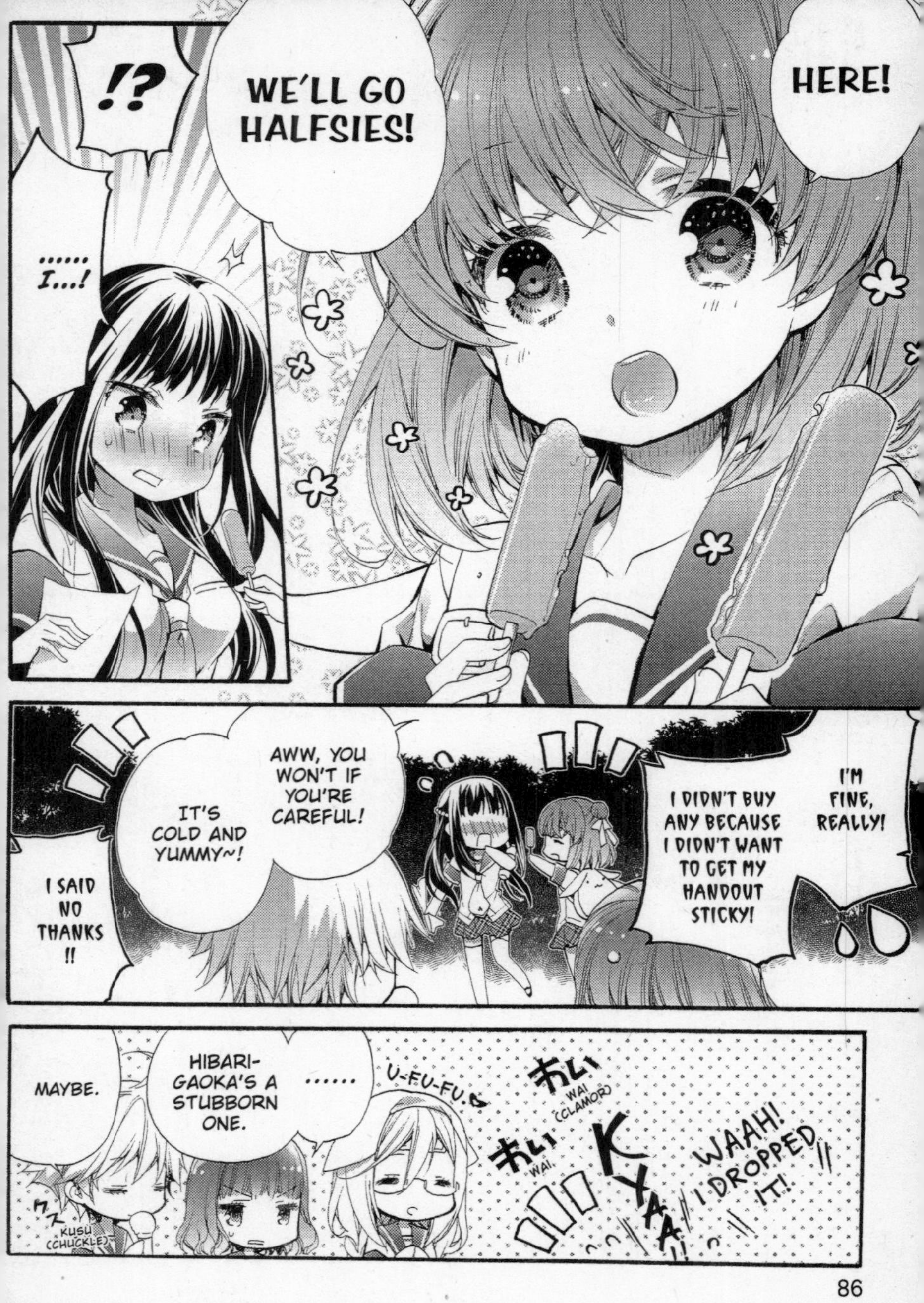
HERE!
WE'LL GO HALFSIES!
!?
...... I...!
I'M FINE, REALLY!
I DIDN'T BUY ANY BECAUSE I DIDN'T WANT TO GET MY HANDOUT STICKY!
AWW, YOU WON'T IF YOU'RE CAREFUL!
IT'S COLD AND YUMMY~!
I SAID NO THANKS !!
WAAH! I DROPPED IT! !!
KYAA!
わい WAI (CLAMOR)
わい WAI
U-FU-FU.
......
HIBARI-GAOKA'S A STUBBORN ONE.
MAYBE.
クス KUSU (CHUCKLE)

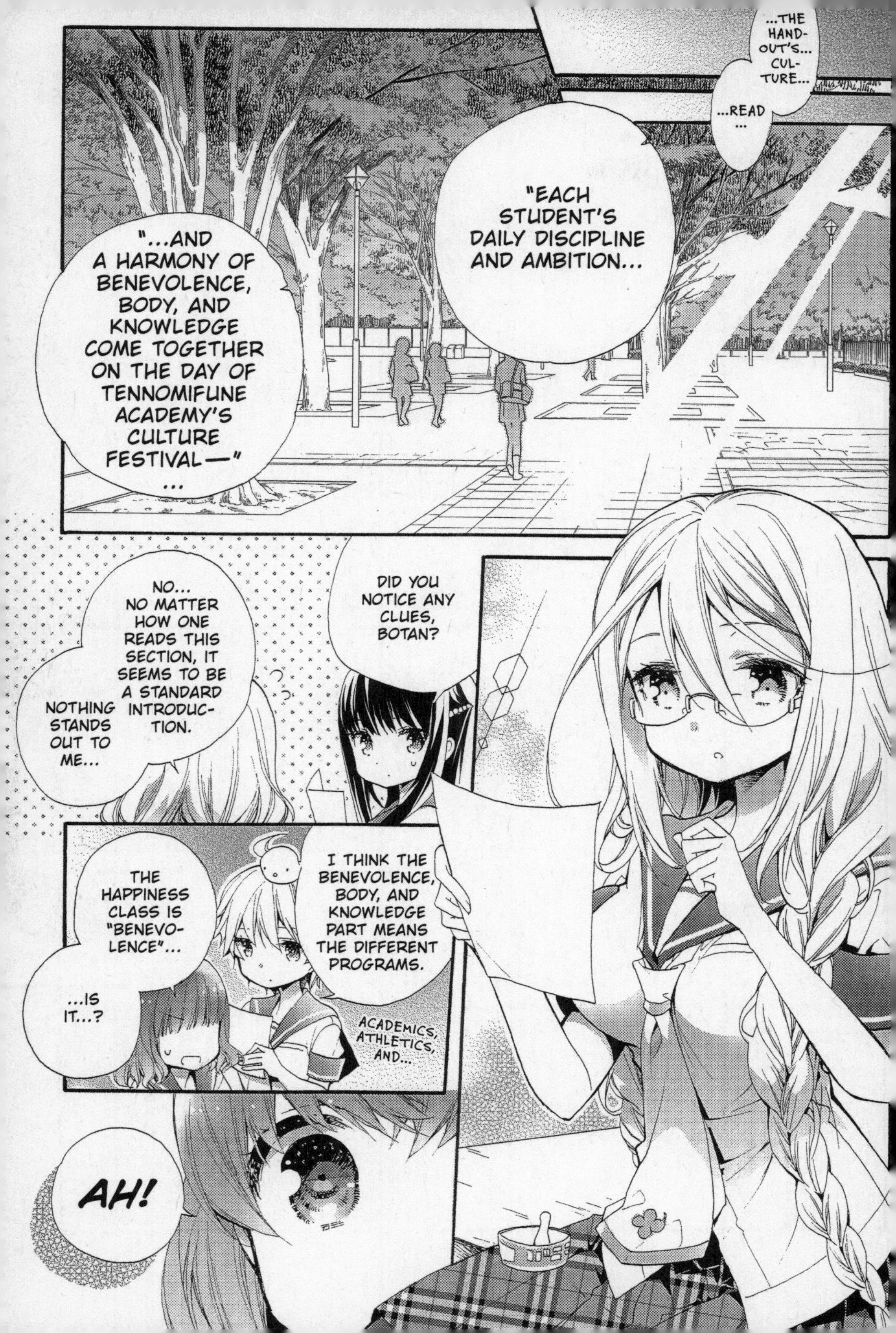
...THE HAND-OUT'S... CUL-TURE...
...READ ...
"EACH STUDENT'S DAILY DISCIPLINE AND AMBITION...
"...AND A HARMONY OF BENEVOLENCE, BODY, AND KNOWLEDGE COME TOGETHER ON THE DAY OF TENNOMIFUNE ACADEMY'S CULTURE FESTIVAL—" ...
DID YOU NOTICE ANY CLUES, BOTAN?
NO... NO MATTER HOW ONE READS THIS SECTION, IT SEEMS TO BE A STANDARD INTRODUC-TION.
NOTHING STANDS OUT TO ME...
I THINK THE BENEVOLENCE, BODY, AND KNOWLEDGE PART MEANS THE DIFFERENT PROGRAMS.
ACADEMICS, ATHLETICS, AND...
THE HAPPINESS CLASS IS "BENEVO-LENCE"...
...IS IT...?
AH!

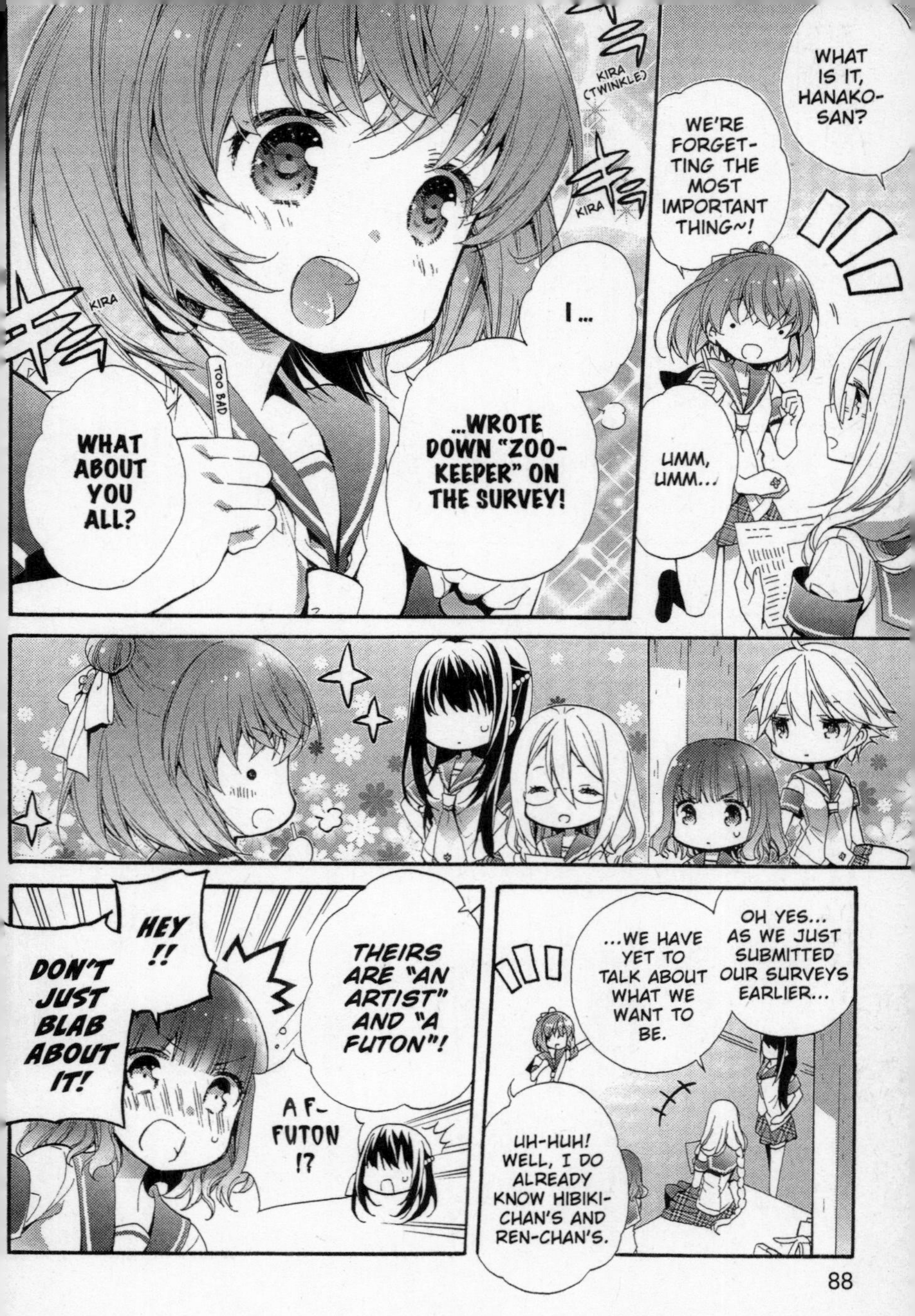
WHAT IS IT, HANAKO-SAN?
WE'RE FORGETTING THE MOST IMPORTANT THING~!
UMM, UMM...
KIRA (TWINKLE)
KIRA
KIRA
I...
...WROTE DOWN "ZOO-KEEPER" ON THE SURVEY!
TOO BAD
WHAT ABOUT YOU ALL?
OH YES... AS WE JUST SUBMITTED OUR SURVEYS EARLIER...
...WE HAVE YET TO TALK ABOUT WHAT WE WANT TO BE.
UH-HUH! WELL, I DO ALREADY KNOW HIBIKI-CHAN'S AND REN-CHAN'S.
THEIRS ARE "AN ARTIST" AND "A FUTON"!
A F-FUTON!?
HEY!!
DON'T JUST BLAB ABOUT IT!

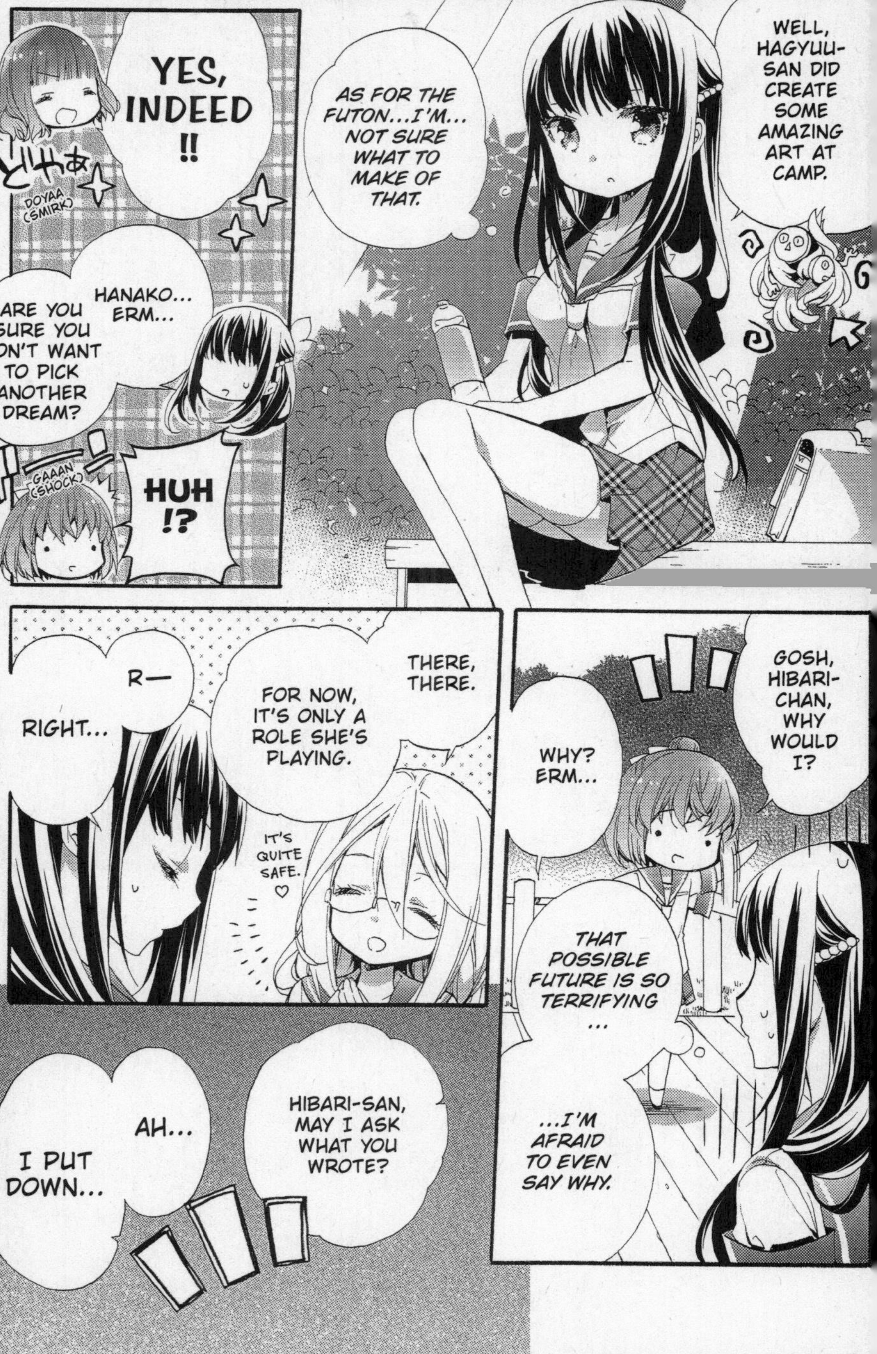
WELL, HAGYUU-SAN DID CREATE SOME AMAZING ART AT CAMP.
AS FOR THE FUTON...I'M... NOT SURE WHAT TO MAKE OF THAT.
YES, INDEED!!
どやあ
DOYAA (SMIRK)
HANAKO... ERM...
ARE YOU SURE YOU DON'T WANT TO PICK ANOTHER DREAM?
HUH!?
GAAAN (SHOCK)
GOSH, HIBARI-CHAN, WHY WOULD I?
WHY? ERM...
THAT POSSIBLE FUTURE IS SO TERRIFYING...
...I'M AFRAID TO EVEN SAY WHY.
THERE, THERE.
FOR NOW, IT'S ONLY A ROLE SHE'S PLAYING.
IT'S QUITE SAFE. ♡
R—
RIGHT...
HIBARI-SAN, MAY I ASK WHAT YOU WROTE?
AH...
I PUT DOWN...

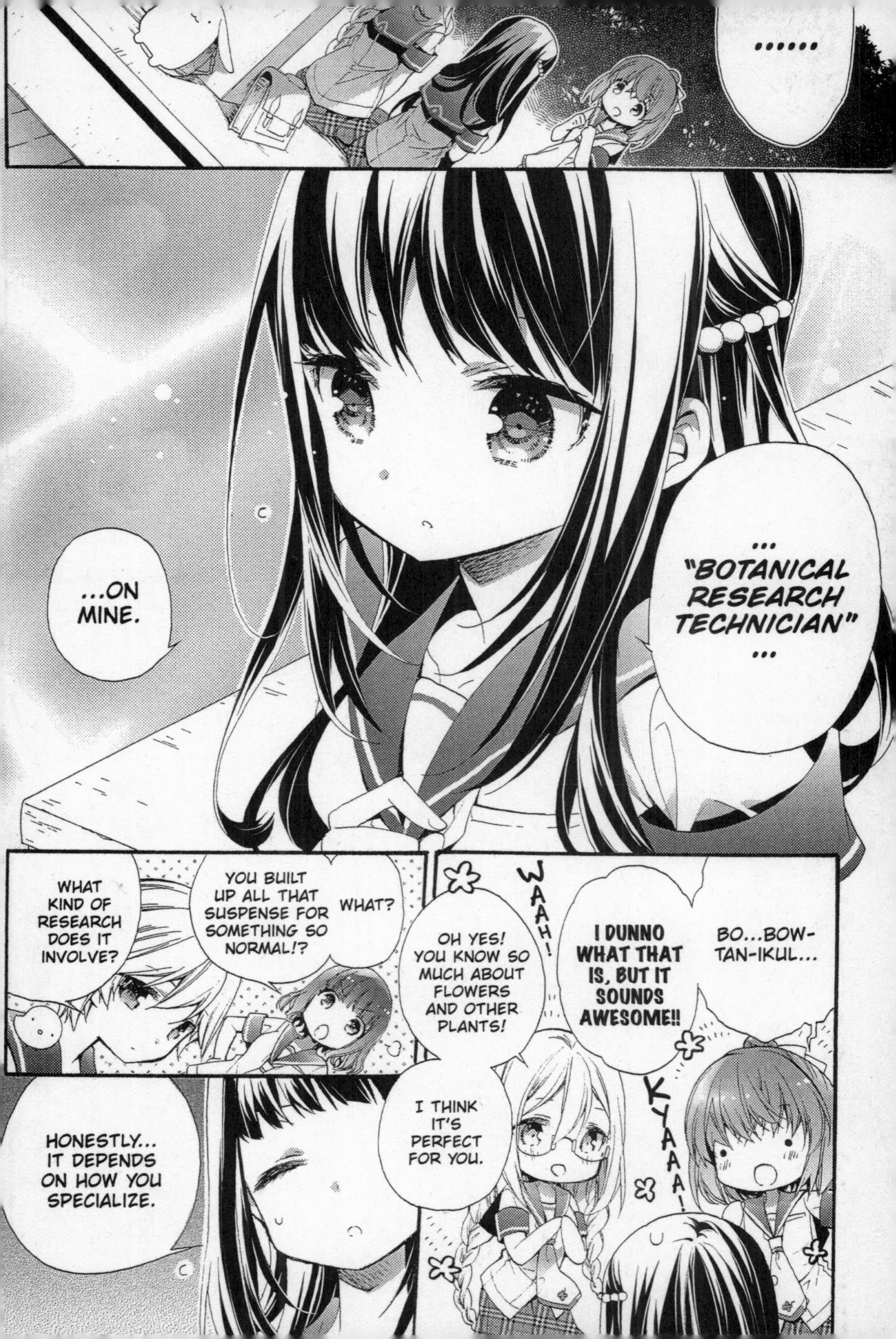
......
... "BOTANICAL RESEARCH TECHNICIAN" ...
...ON MINE.
BO...BOW-TAN-IKUL...
I DUNNO WHAT THAT IS, BUT IT SOUNDS AWESOME!!
WAAAH!
OH YES! YOU KNOW SO MUCH ABOUT FLOWERS AND OTHER PLANTS!
KYAAAA!
I THINK IT'S PERFECT FOR YOU.
WHAT?
YOU BUILT UP ALL THAT SUSPENSE FOR SOMETHING SO NORMAL!?
WHAT KIND OF RESEARCH DOES IT INVOLVE?
HONESTLY... IT DEPENDS ON HOW YOU SPECIALIZE.

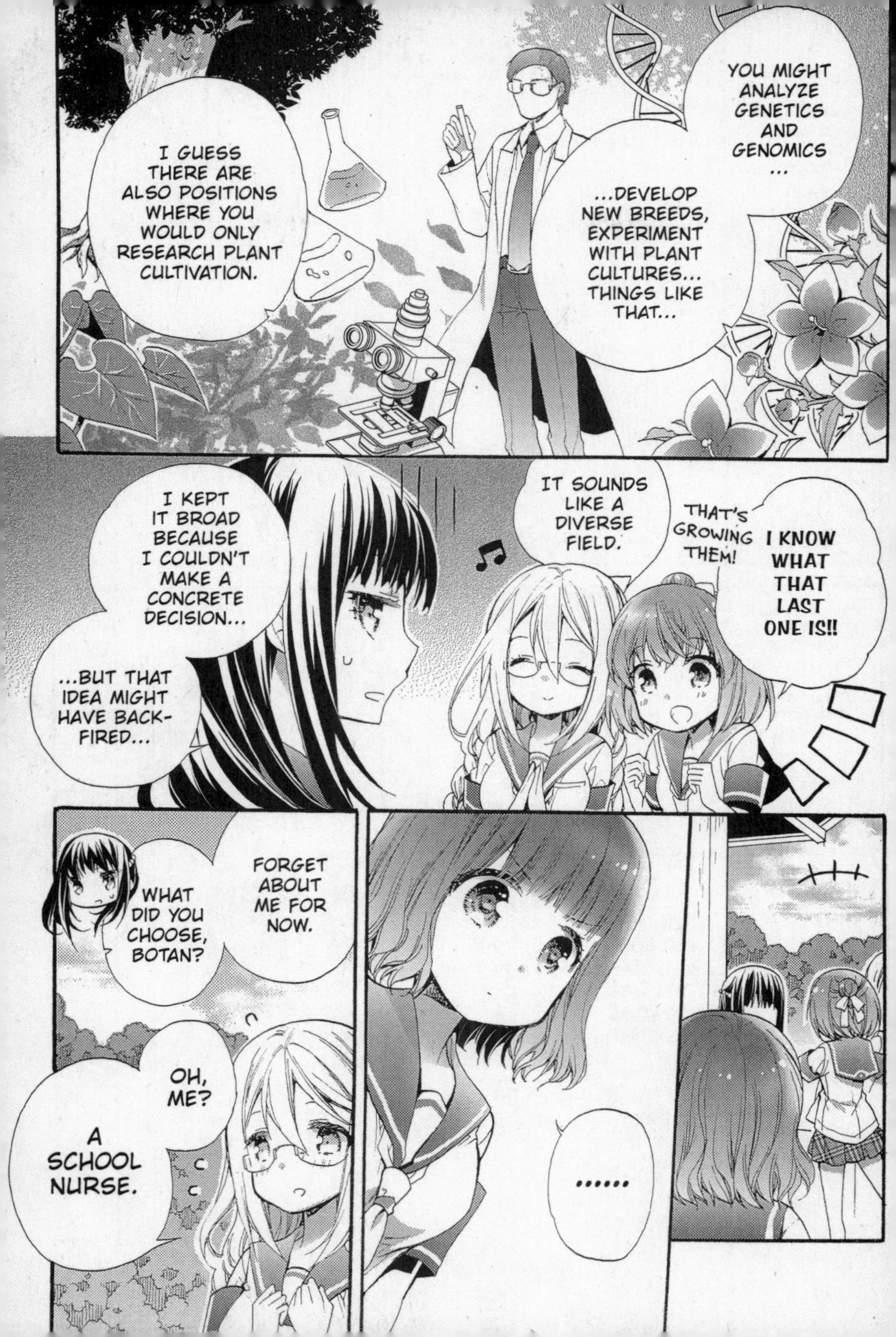
YOU MIGHT ANALYZE GENETICS AND GENOMICS ...
...DEVELOP NEW BREEDS, EXPERIMENT WITH PLANT CULTURES... THINGS LIKE THAT...
I GUESS THERE ARE ALSO POSITIONS WHERE YOU WOULD ONLY RESEARCH PLANT CULTIVATION.
I KNOW WHAT THAT LAST ONE IS!!
THAT'S GROWING THEM!
IT SOUNDS LIKE A DIVERSE FIELD.
I KEPT IT BROAD BECAUSE I COULDN'T MAKE A CONCRETE DECISION...
...BUT THAT IDEA MIGHT HAVE BACK-FIRED...
......
FORGET ABOUT ME FOR NOW.
WHAT DID YOU CHOOSE, BOTAN?
OH, ME?
A SCHOOL NURSE.

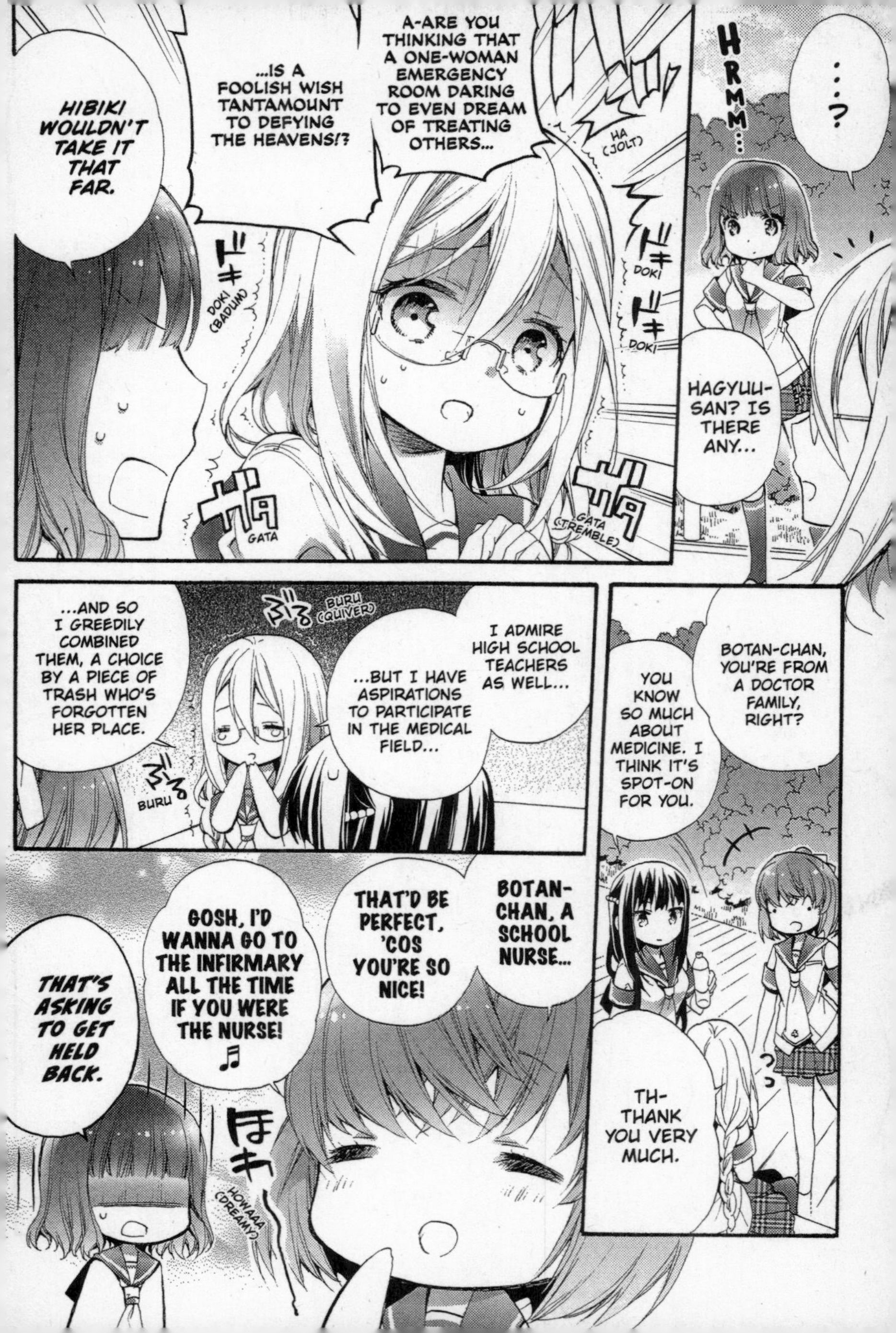
...?
HRMM...
HAGYUU-SAN? IS THERE ANY...
HA (JOLT)
DOKI
DOKI
GATA (TREMBLE)
A-ARE YOU THINKING THAT A ONE-WOMAN EMERGENCY ROOM DARING TO EVEN DREAM OF TREATING OTHERS...
...IS A FOOLISH WISH TANTAMOUNT TO DEFYING THE HEAVENS!?
DOKI (BADUM)
GATA
HIBIKI WOULDN'T TAKE IT THAT FAR.
BOTAN-CHAN, YOU'RE FROM A DOCTOR FAMILY, RIGHT?
YOU KNOW SO MUCH ABOUT MEDICINE. I THINK IT'S SPOT-ON FOR YOU.
TH-THANK YOU VERY MUCH.
I ADMIRE HIGH SCHOOL TEACHERS AS WELL...
...BUT I HAVE ASPIRATIONS TO PARTICIPATE IN THE MEDICAL FIELD...
BURU (QUIVER)
...AND SO I GREEDILY COMBINED THEM, A CHOICE BY A PIECE OF TRASH WHO'S FORGOTTEN HER PLACE.
BURU
BOTAN-CHAN, A SCHOOL NURSE...
THAT'D BE PERFECT, 'COS YOU'RE SO NICE!
GOSH, I'D WANNA GO TO THE INFIRMARY ALL THE TIME IF YOU WERE THE NURSE! ♫
HOWAAA (DREAMY)
THAT'S ASKING TO GET HELD BACK.

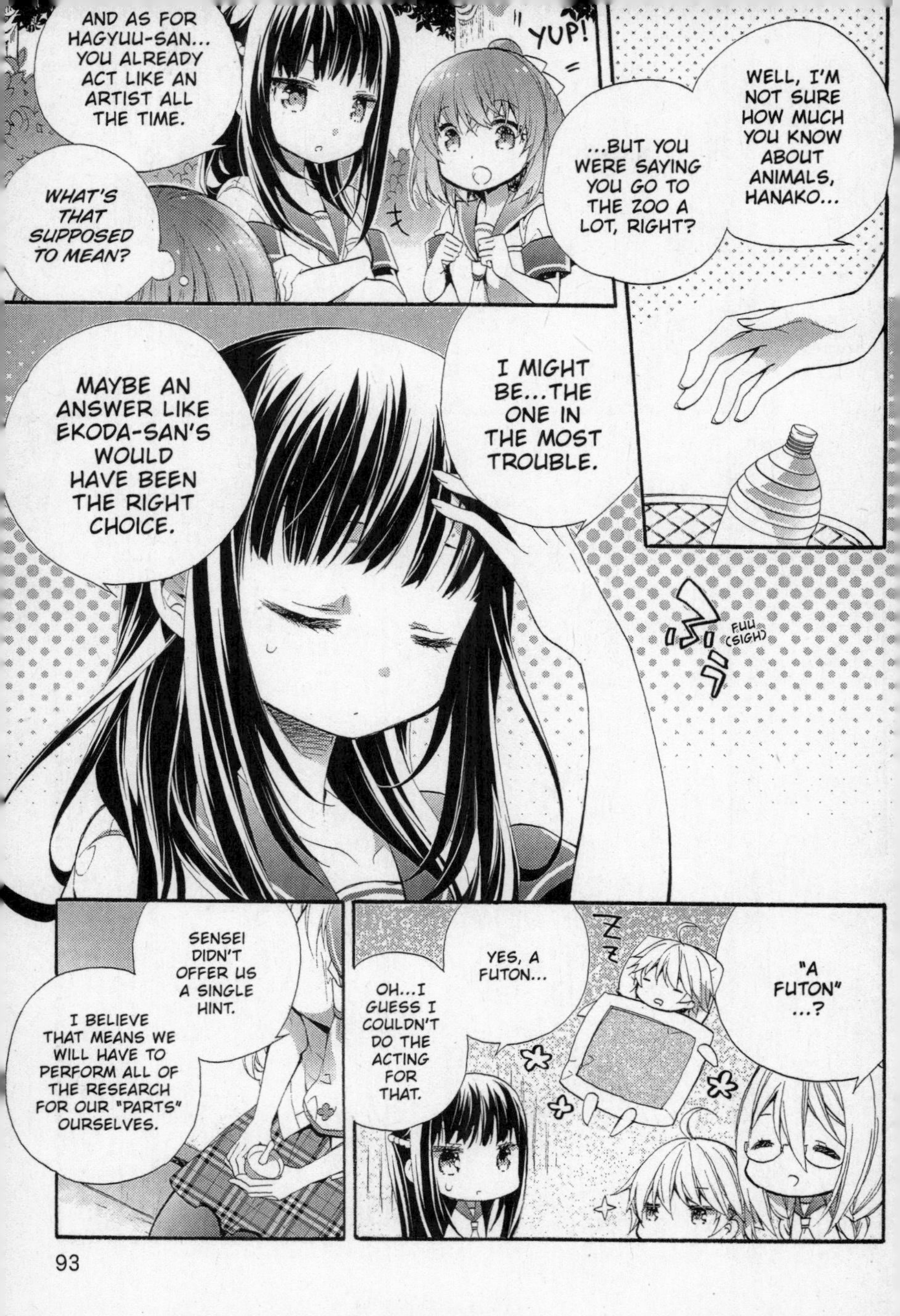
WELL, I'M NOT SURE HOW MUCH YOU KNOW ABOUT ANIMALS, HANAKO...
...BUT YOU WERE SAYING YOU GO TO THE ZOO A LOT, RIGHT?
YUP!
AND AS FOR HAGYUU-SAN... YOU ALREADY ACT LIKE AN ARTIST ALL THE TIME.
WHAT'S THAT SUPPOSED TO MEAN?
I MIGHT BE...THE ONE IN THE MOST TROUBLE.
MAYBE AN ANSWER LIKE EKODA-SAN'S WOULD HAVE BEEN THE RIGHT CHOICE.
FUU (SIGH)
"A FUTON" ...?
YES, A FUTON...
OH...I GUESS I COULDN'T DO THE ACTING FOR THAT.
SENSEI DIDN'T OFFER US A SINGLE HINT.
I BELIEVE THAT MEANS WE WILL HAVE TO PERFORM ALL OF THE RESEARCH FOR OUR "PARTS" OURSELVES.

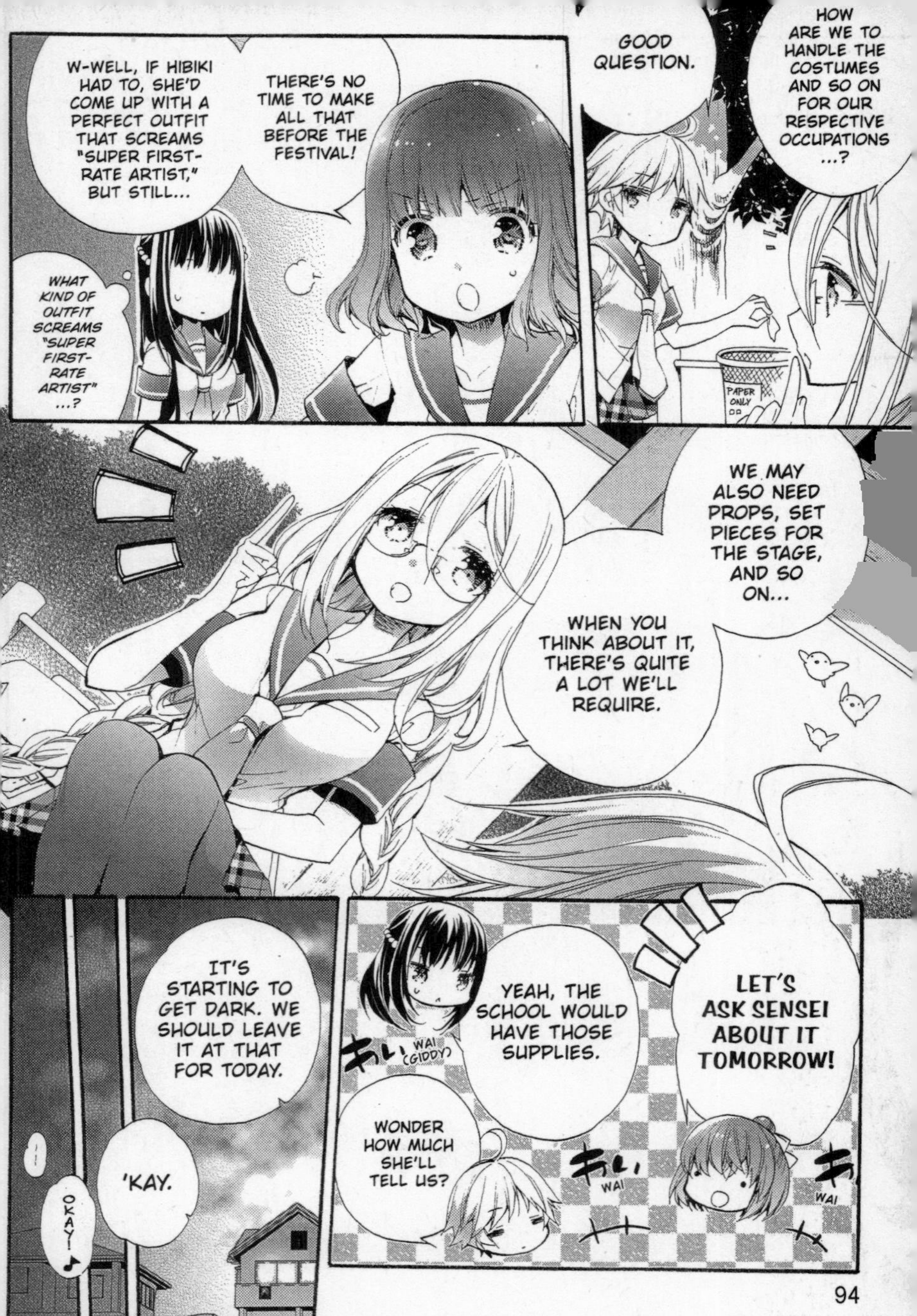
HOW ARE WE TO HANDLE THE COSTUMES AND SO ON FOR OUR RESPECTIVE OCCUPATIONS ...?
GOOD QUESTION.
PAPER ONLY
THERE'S NO TIME TO MAKE ALL THAT BEFORE THE FESTIVAL!
W-WELL, IF HIBIKI HAD TO, SHE'D COME UP WITH A PERFECT OUTFIT THAT SCREAMS "SUPER FIRST-RATE ARTIST," BUT STILL...
WHAT KIND OF OUTFIT SCREAMS "SUPER FIRST-RATE ARTIST" ...?
WE MAY ALSO NEED PROPS, SET PIECES FOR THE STAGE, AND SO ON...
WHEN YOU THINK ABOUT IT, THERE'S QUITE A LOT WE'LL REQUIRE.
LET'S ASK SENSEI ABOUT IT TOMORROW!
YEAH, THE SCHOOL WOULD HAVE THOSE SUPPLIES.
WAI (GIDDY)
WAI
WAI
WONDER HOW MUCH SHE'LL TELL US?
IT'S STARTING TO GET DARK. WE SHOULD LEAVE IT AT THAT FOR TODAY.
'KAY.
OKAY!♪

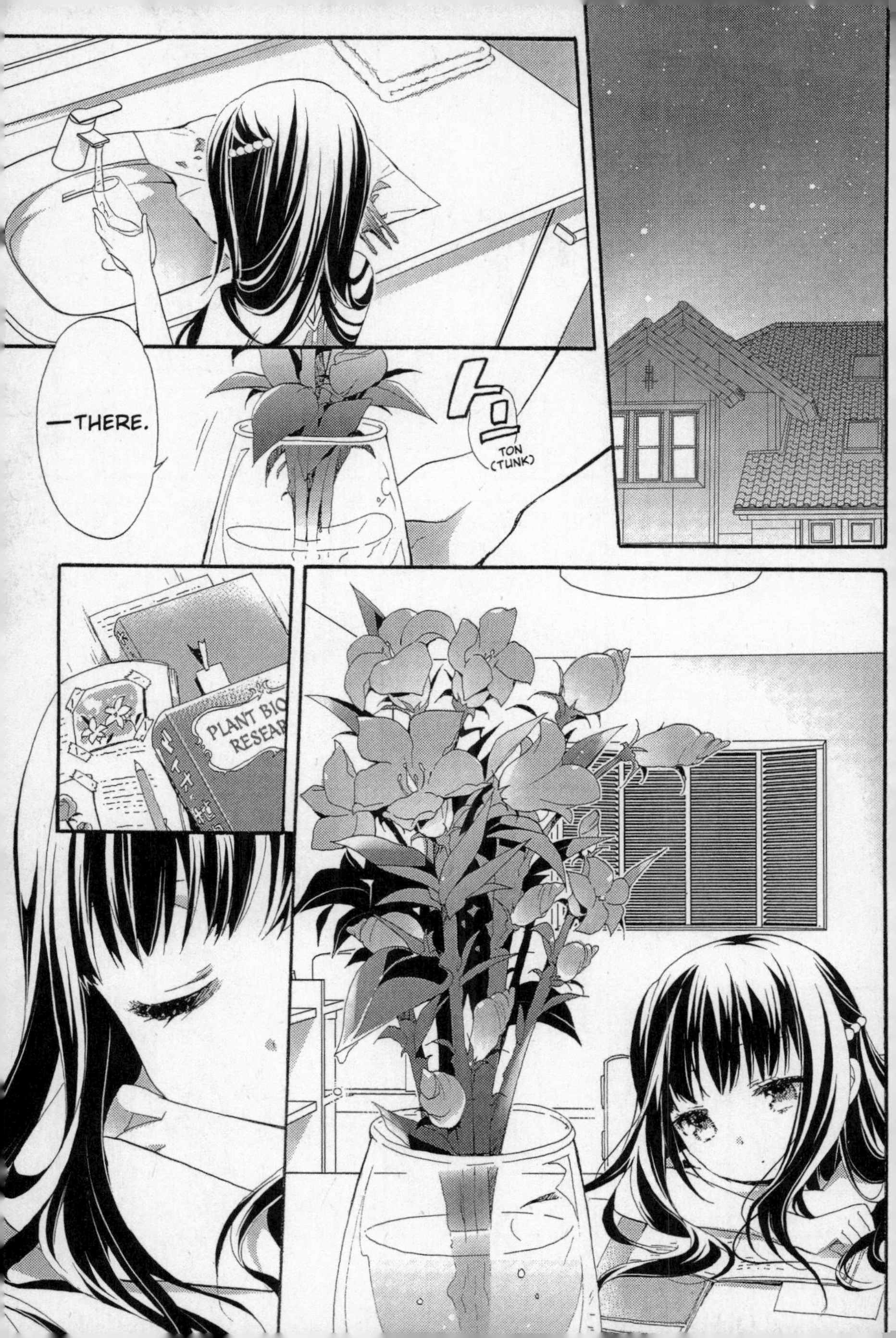

—THERE.
TON
(TUNK)
PLANT BIO
RESEAR

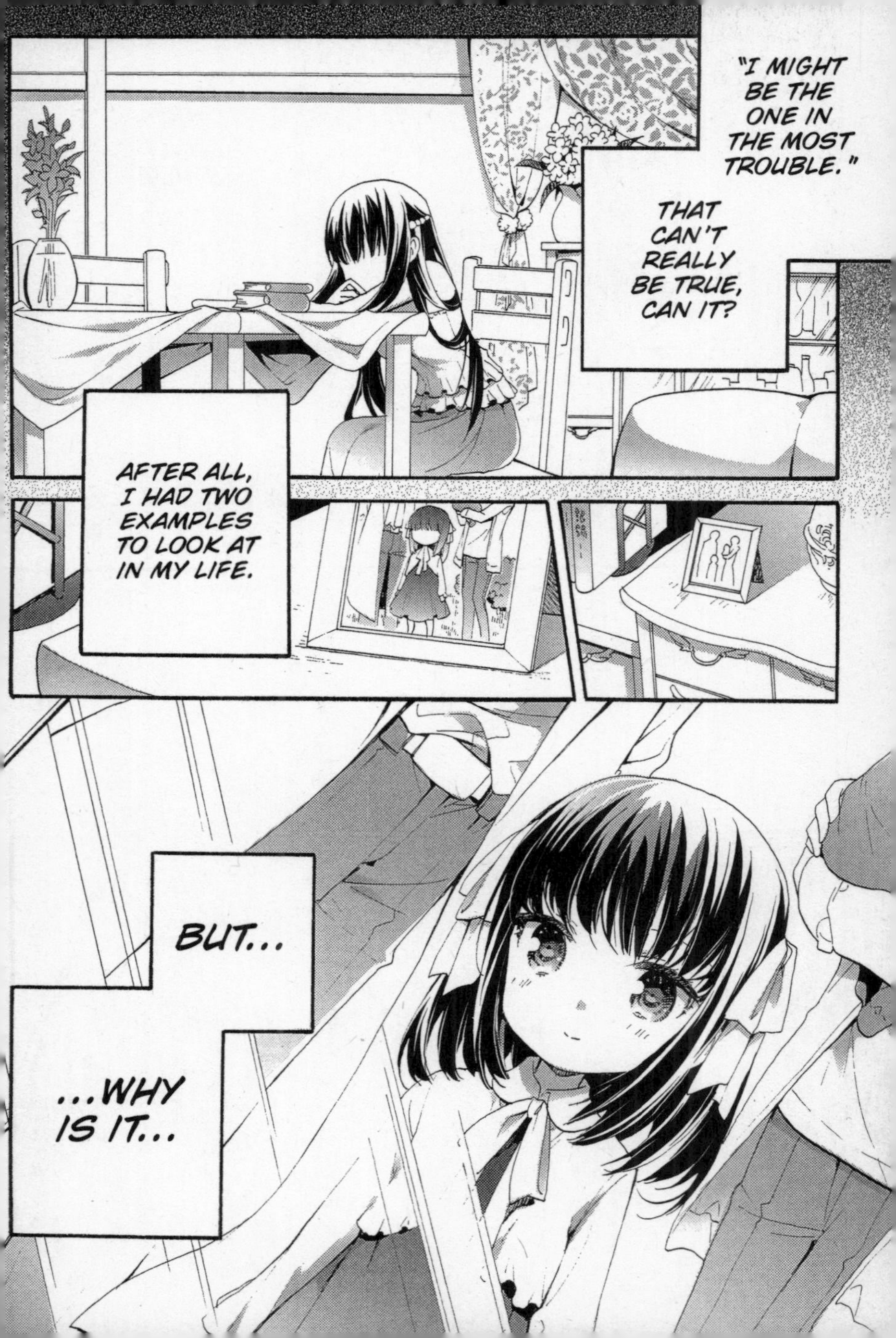
"I MIGHT BE THE ONE IN THE MOST TROUBLE."
THAT CAN'T REALLY BE TRUE, CAN IT?
AFTER ALL, I HAD TWO EXAMPLES TO LOOK AT IN MY LIFE.
BUT...
...WHY IS IT...

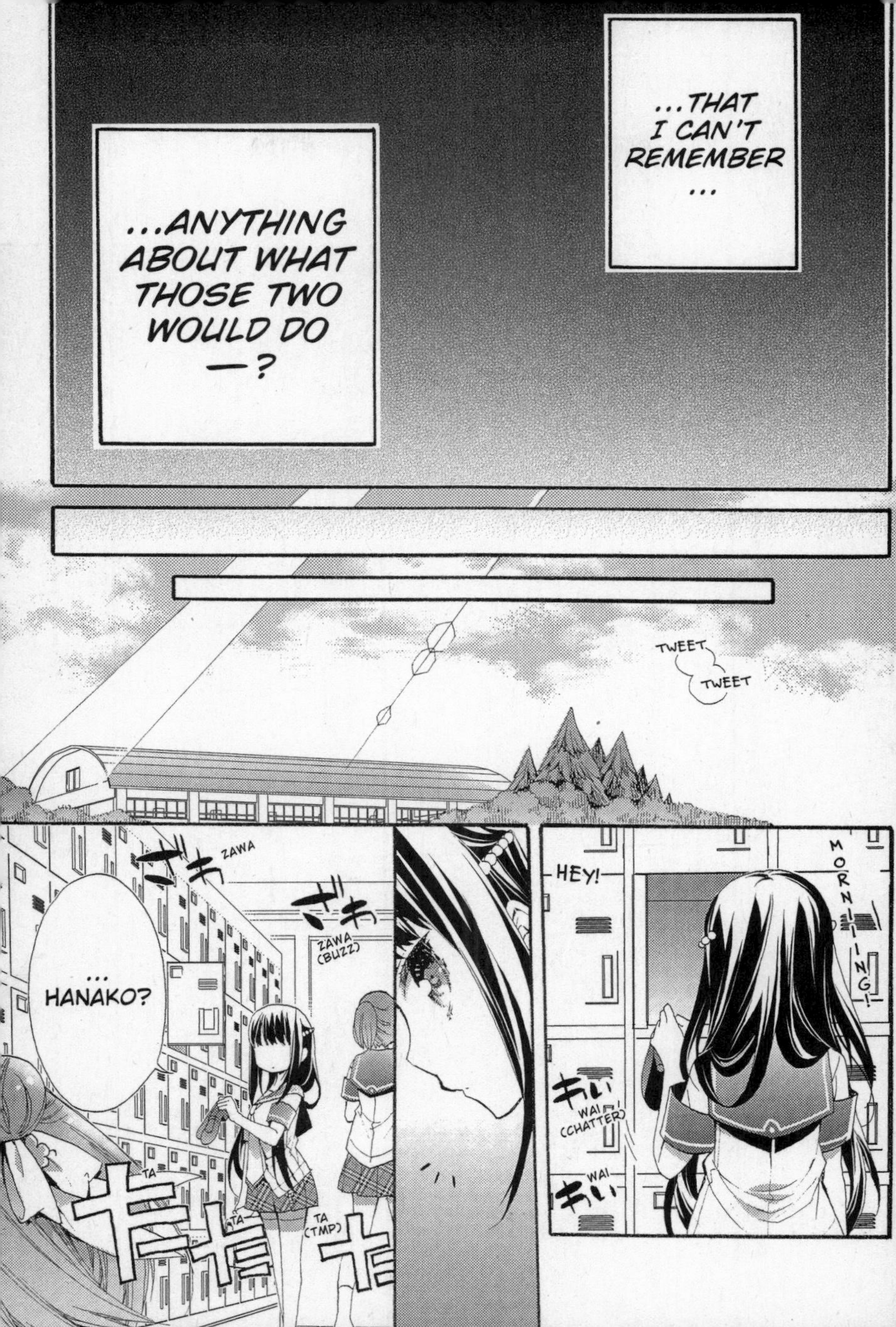
...THAT I CAN'T REMEMBER ...
...ANYTHING ABOUT WHAT THOSE TWO WOULD DO —?
TWEET
TWEET
MORNING!
HEY!
WAI (CHATTER)
WAI
ZAWA
ZAWA (BUZZ)
...HANAKO?
TA
TA
TA (TMP)

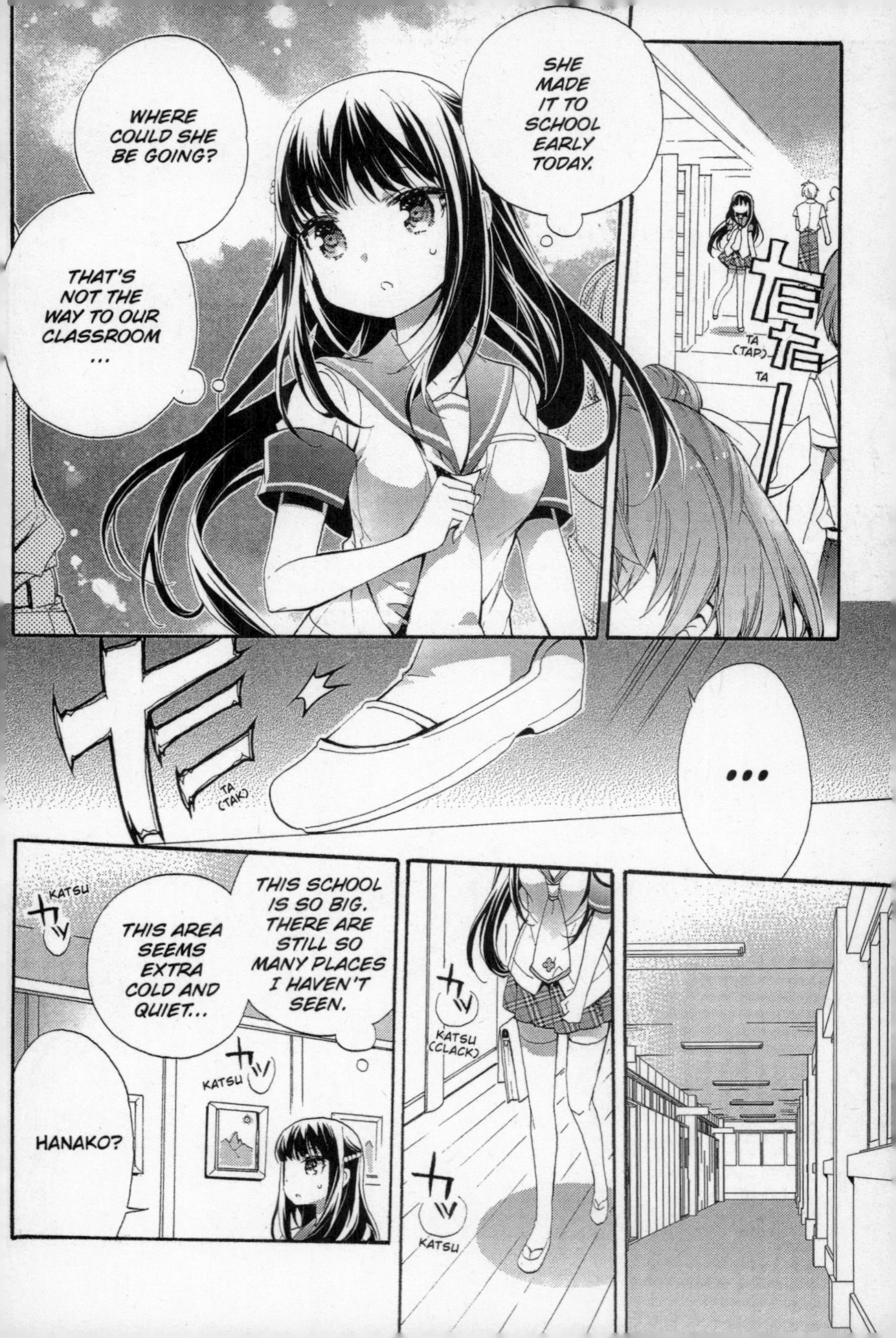
TA (TAP)
TA
SHE MADE IT TO SCHOOL EARLY TODAY.
WHERE COULD SHE BE GOING?
THAT'S NOT THE WAY TO OUR CLASSROOM ...
...
TA (TAK)
KATSU (CLACK)
KATSU
THIS SCHOOL IS SO BIG. THERE ARE STILL SO MANY PLACES I HAVEN'T SEEN.
THIS AREA SEEMS EXTRA COLD AND QUIET...
KATSU
KATSU
HANAKO?

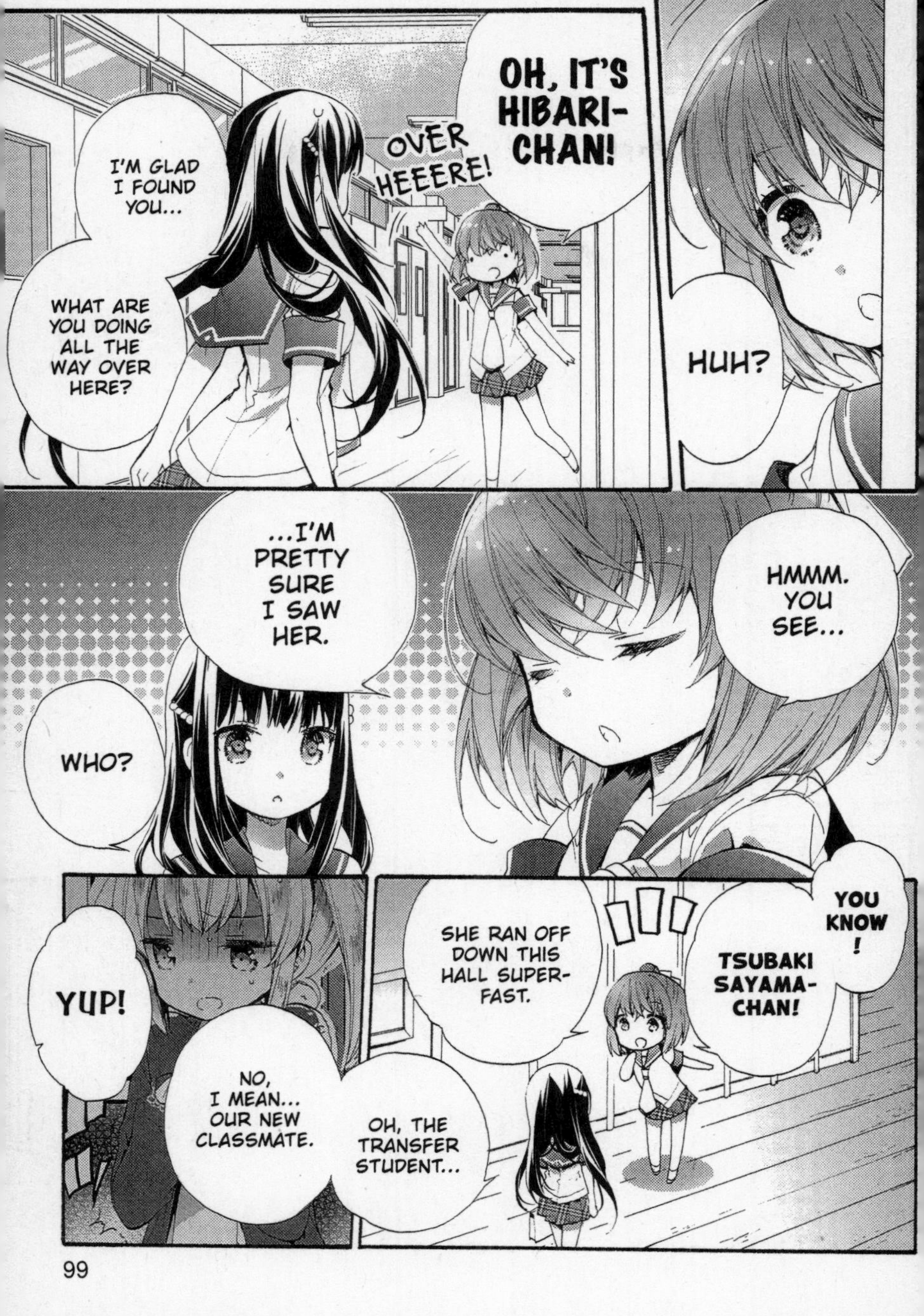
HUH?
OH, IT'S HIBARI-CHAN!
OVER HEEEERE!
I'M GLAD I FOUND YOU...
WHAT ARE YOU DOING ALL THE WAY OVER HERE?
HMMM. YOU SEE...
...I'M PRETTY SURE I SAW HER.
WHO?
YOU KNOW!
TSUBAKI SAYAMA-CHAN!
SHE RAN OFF DOWN THIS HALL SUPER-FAST.
OH, THE TRANSFER STUDENT...
NO, I MEAN... OUR NEW CLASSMATE.
YUP!

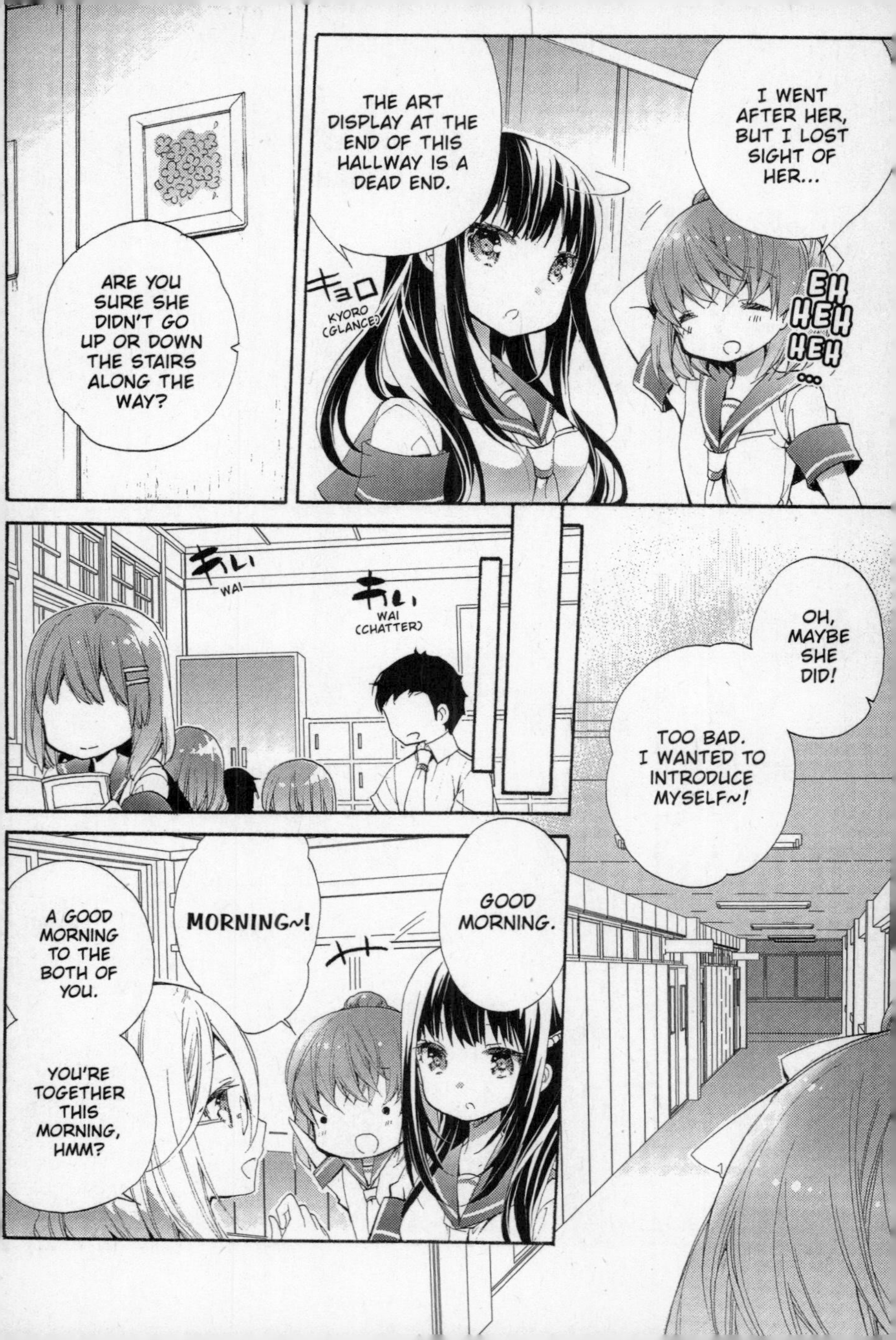
I WENT AFTER HER, BUT I LOST SIGHT OF HER...
EH HEH HEH...
THE ART DISPLAY AT THE END OF THIS HALLWAY IS A DEAD END.
キョロ
KYORO (GLANCE)
ARE YOU SURE SHE DIDN'T GO UP OR DOWN THE STAIRS ALONG THE WAY?
OH, MAYBE SHE DID!
TOO BAD. I WANTED TO INTRODUCE MYSELF~!
わい
WAI
わい
WAI (CHATTER)
GOOD MORNING.
MORNING~!
A GOOD MORNING TO THE BOTH OF YOU.
YOU'RE TOGETHER THIS MORNING, HMM?

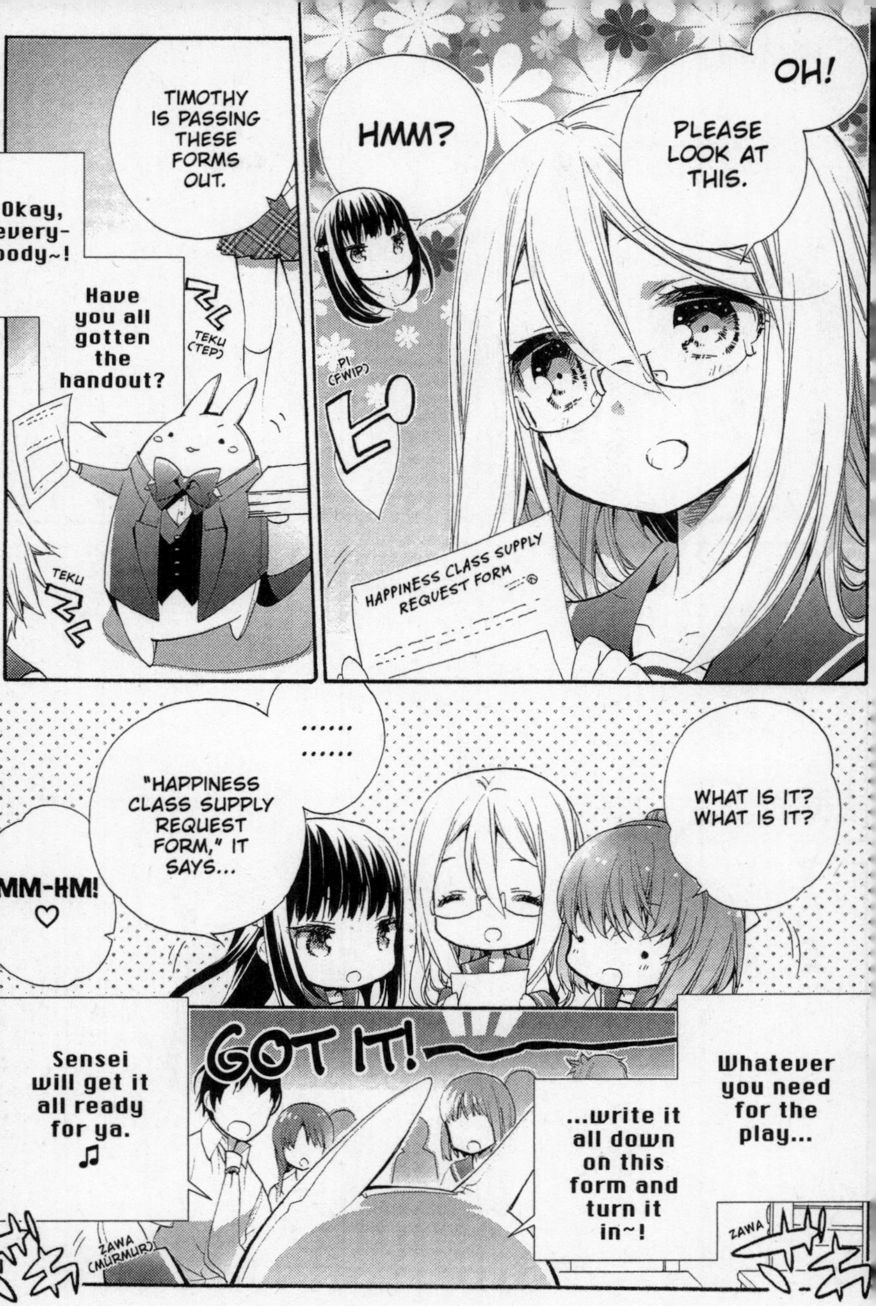
OH!
PLEASE LOOK AT THIS.
HMM?
PI (FWIP)
HAPPINESS CLASS SUPPLY REQUEST FORM
TIMOTHY IS PASSING THESE FORMS OUT.
Okay, every-body~!
Have you all gotten the handout?
TEKU (TEP)
TEKU
WHAT IS IT? WHAT IS IT?
......
......
"HAPPINESS CLASS SUPPLY REQUEST FORM," IT SAYS...
MM-HM! ♡
Whatever you need for the play...
...write it all down on this form and turn it in~!
ZAWA
GOT IT!
Sensei will get it all ready for ya. ♫
ZAWA (MURMUR)

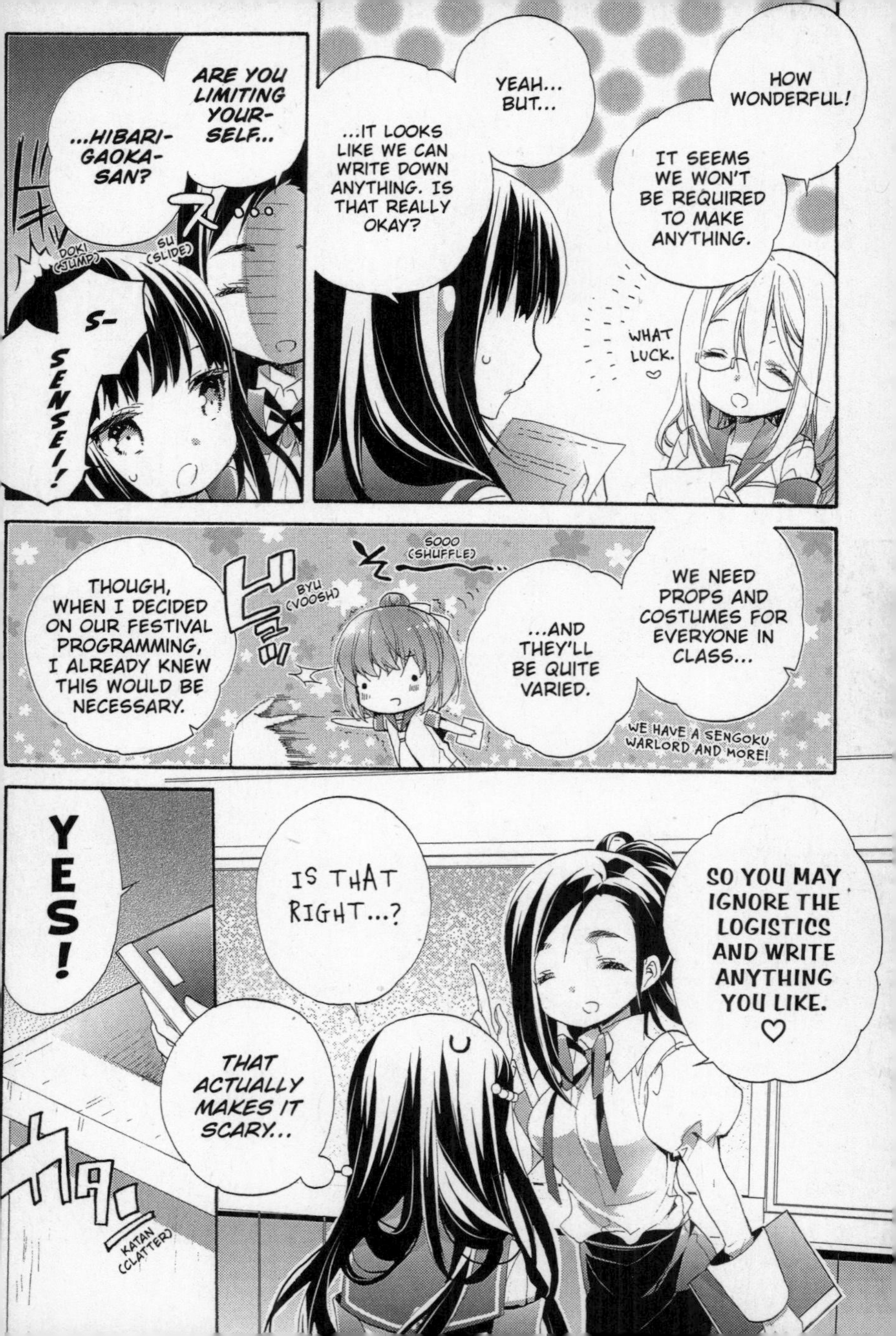
HOW WONDERFUL!
IT SEEMS WE WON'T BE REQUIRED TO MAKE ANYTHING.
WHAT LUCK. ♡
YEAH... BUT...
...IT LOOKS LIKE WE CAN WRITE DOWN ANYTHING. IS THAT REALLY OKAY?
ARE YOU LIMITING YOURSELF...
...HIBARIGAOKA-SAN?
SU (SLIDE)
DOKI (JUMP)
S-SENSEI!
WE NEED PROPS AND COSTUMES FOR EVERYONE IN CLASS...
...AND THEY'LL BE QUITE VARIED.
WE HAVE A SENGOKU WARLORD AND MORE!
SOOO (SHUFFLE)
BYU (VOOSH)
THOUGH, WHEN I DECIDED ON OUR FESTIVAL PROGRAMMING, I ALREADY KNEW THIS WOULD BE NECESSARY.
SO YOU MAY IGNORE THE LOGISTICS AND WRITE ANYTHING YOU LIKE. ♡
IS THAT RIGHT...?
THAT ACTUALLY MAKES IT SCARY...
YES!
KATAN (CLATTER)

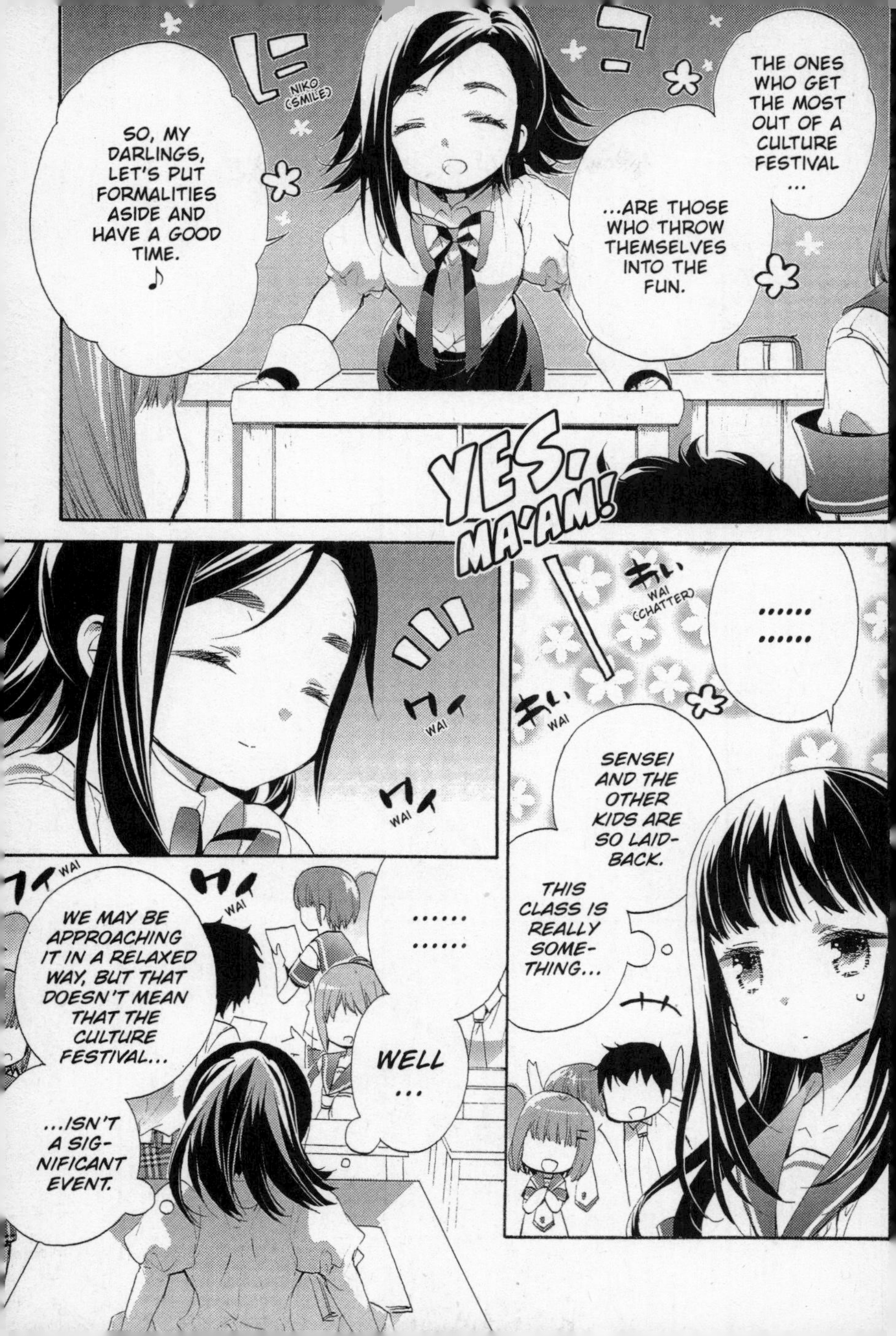

THE ONES WHO GET THE MOST OUT OF A CULTURE FESTIVAL ...
...ARE THOSE WHO THROW THEMSELVES INTO THE FUN.
NIKO (SMILE)
SO, MY DARLINGS, LET'S PUT FORMALITIES ASIDE AND HAVE A GOOD TIME. ♪
YES, MA'AM!
......
......
WAI (CHATTER)
WAI
SENSEI AND THE OTHER KIDS ARE SO LAID-BACK.
THIS CLASS IS REALLY SOME-THING...
WAI
WAI
......
......
WELL ...
WAI
WAI
WE MAY BE APPROACHING IT IN A RELAXED WAY, BUT THAT DOESN'T MEAN THAT THE CULTURE FESTIVAL...
...ISN'T A SIG-NIFICANT EVENT.

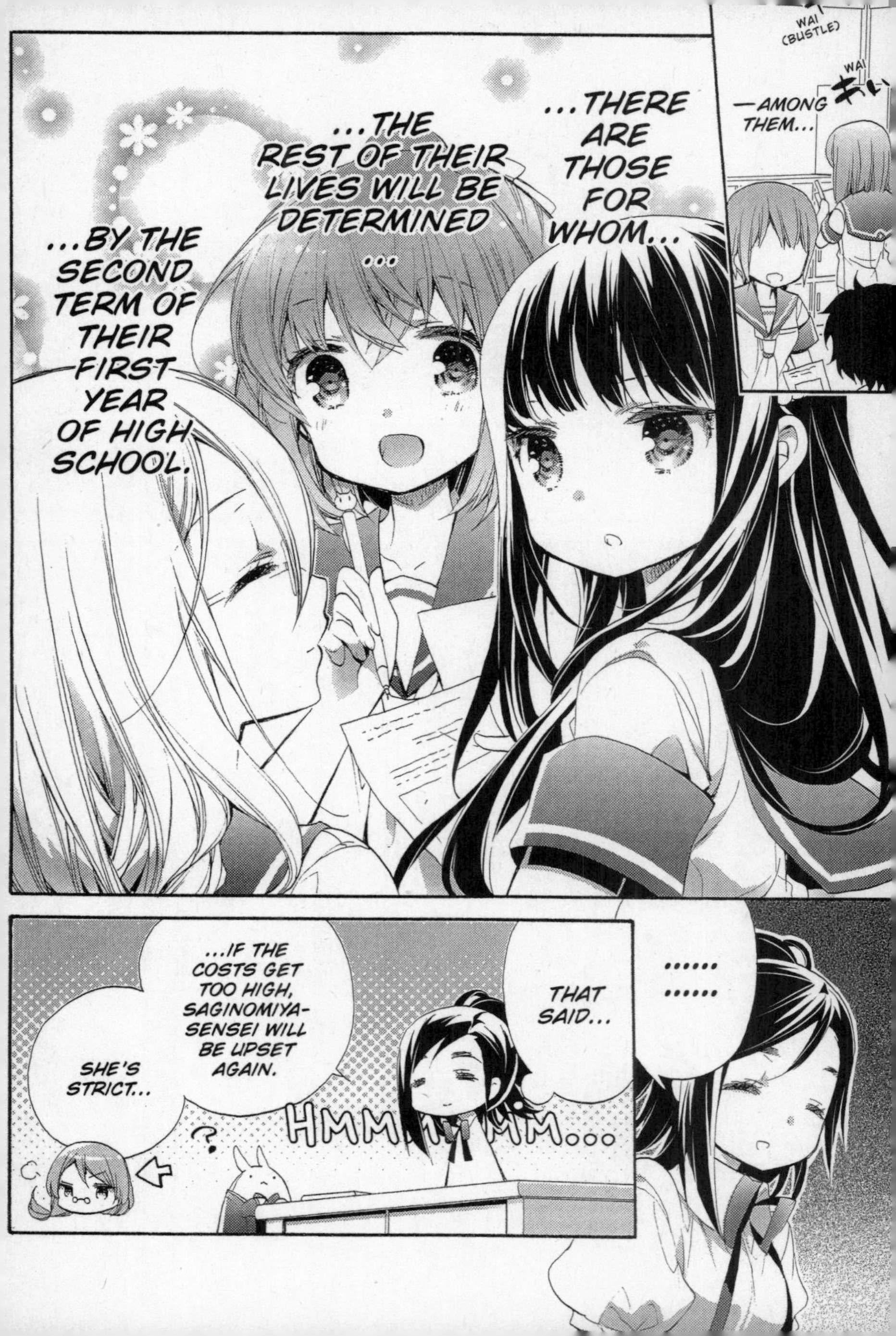
WAI (BUSTLE)
WAI
—AMONG THEM...
...THERE ARE THOSE FOR WHOM...
...THE REST OF THEIR LIVES WILL BE DETERMINED...
...BY THE SECOND TERM OF THEIR FIRST YEAR OF HIGH SCHOOL.
......
......
THAT SAID...
...IF THE COSTS GET TOO HIGH, SAGINOMIYA-SENSEI WILL BE UPSET AGAIN.
HMMMMMMM...
SHE'S STRICT...

AnneHappy♪

unhappy
go lucky!

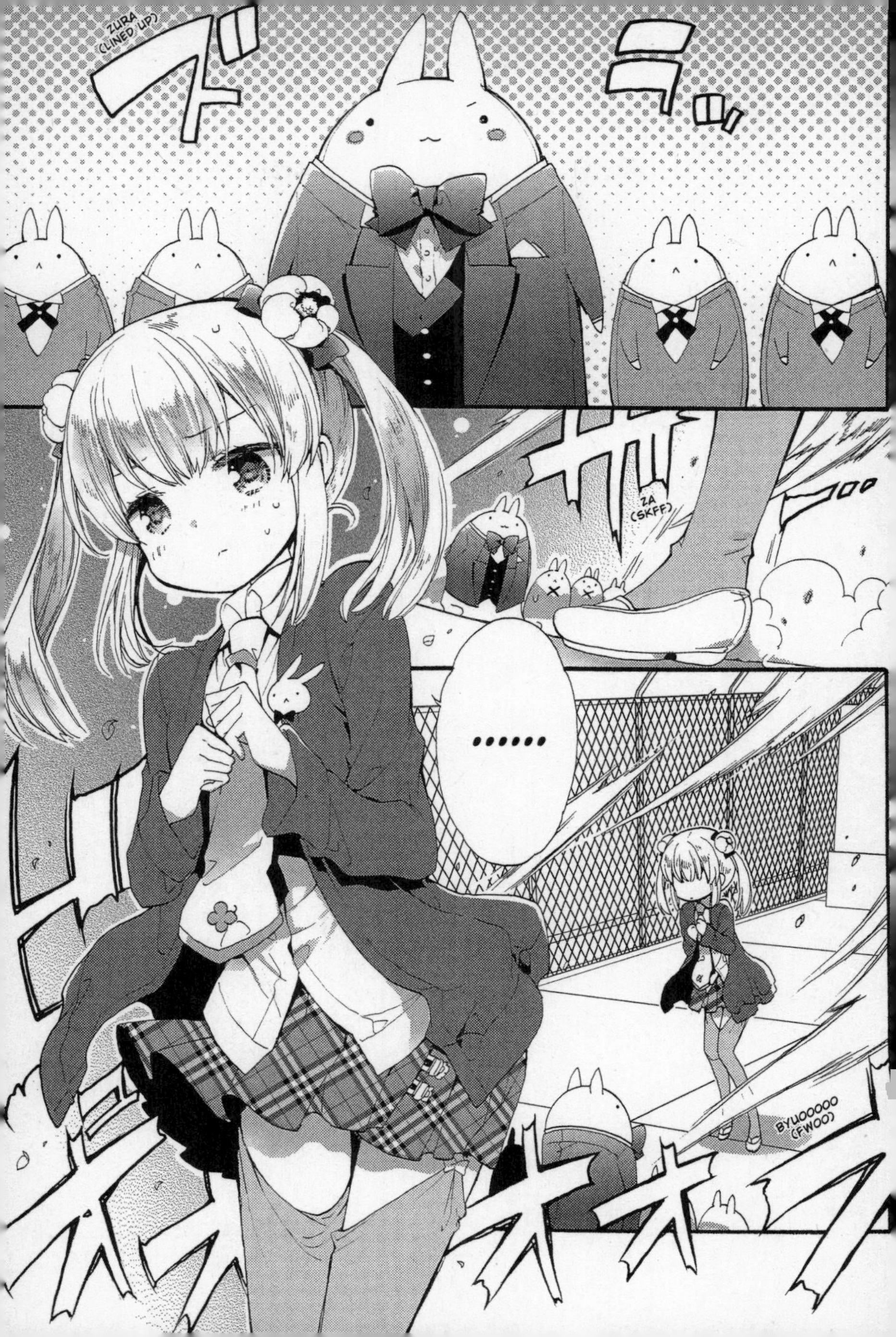
ZURA (LINED UP)
ZA (SKFF)
......
BYUOOOOO (FWOO)

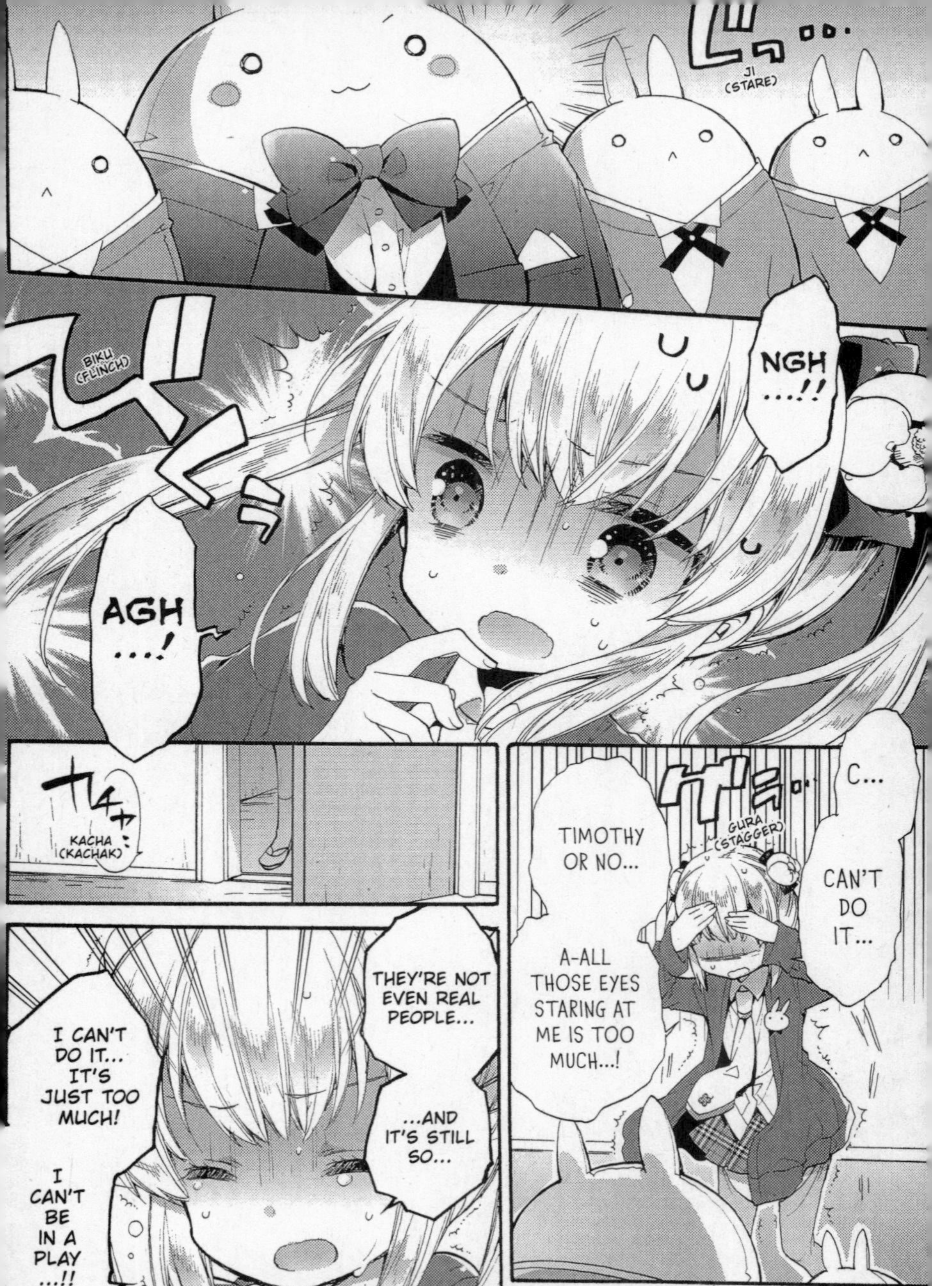
JI (STARE)
NGH ...!!
BIKU (FLINCH)
AGH ...!
C...
CAN'T DO IT...
GURA (STAGGER)
TIMOTHY OR NO...
A-ALL THOSE EYES STARING AT ME IS TOO MUCH...!
KACHA (KACHAK)
THEY'RE NOT EVEN REAL PEOPLE...
...AND IT'S STILL SO...
I CAN'T DO IT... IT'S JUST TOO MUCH!
I CAN'T BE IN A PLAY ...!!

Lucky. 34

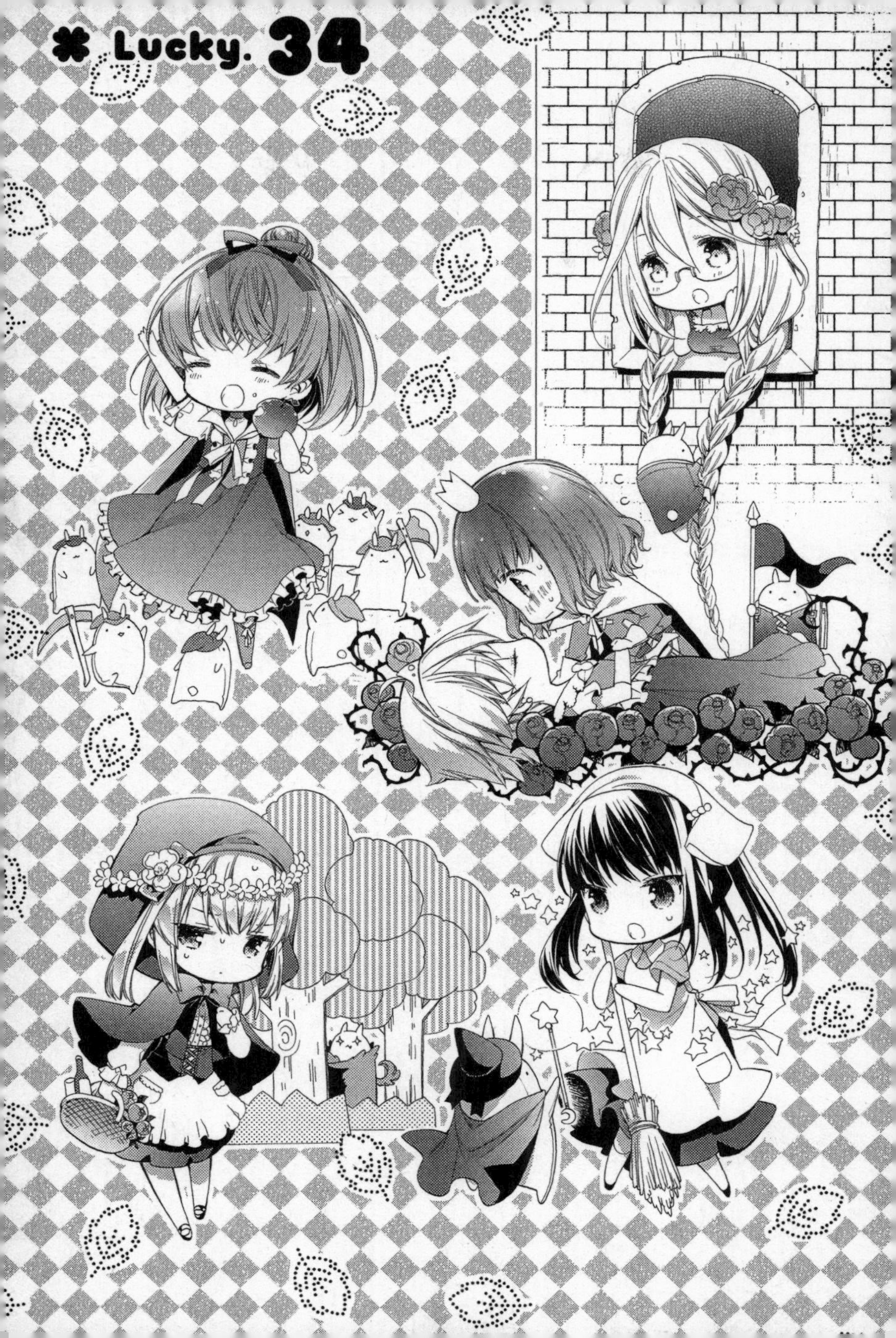

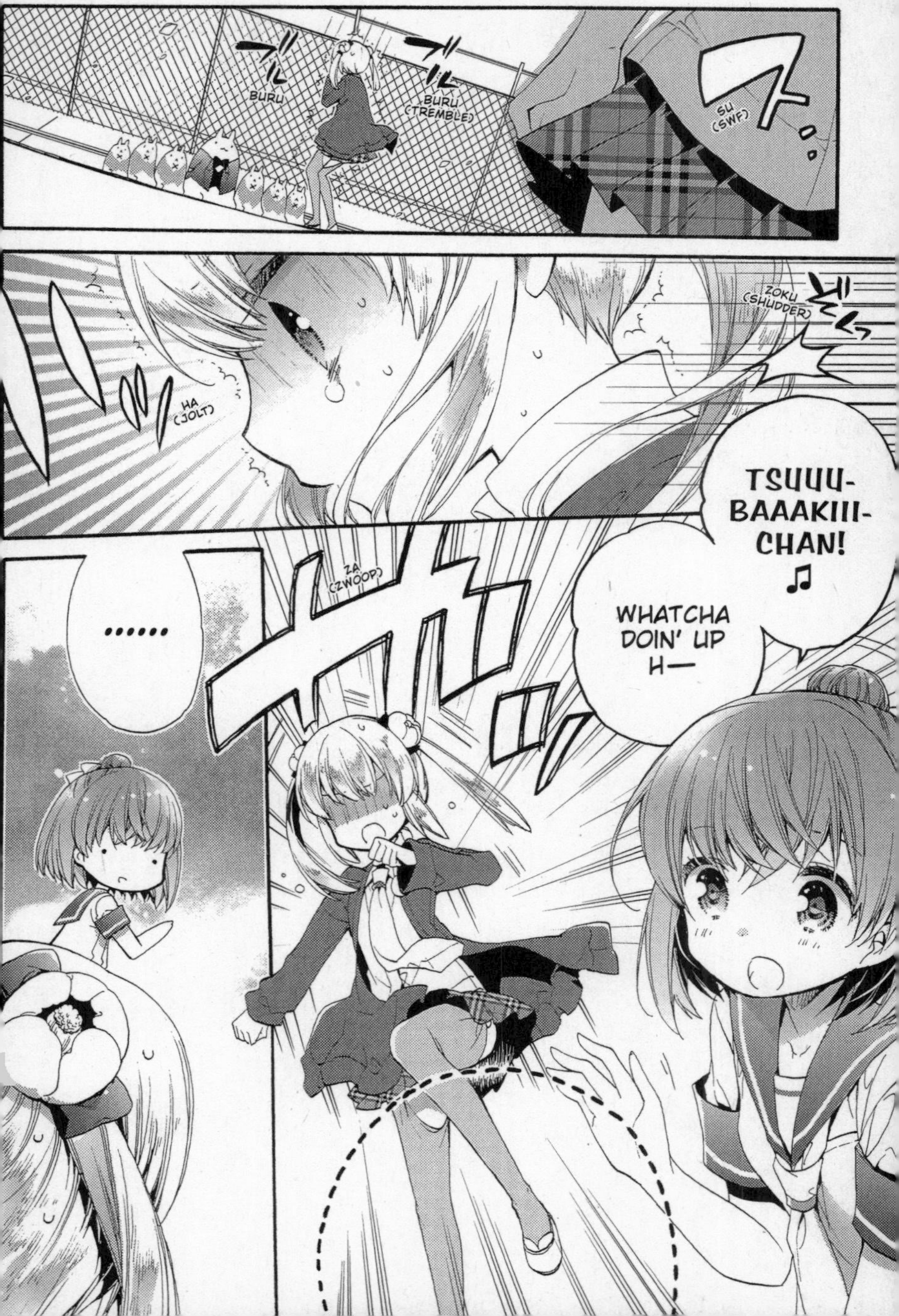
SU (SWF)
BURU (TREMBLE)
BURU
ZOKU (SHUDDER)
HA (JOLT)
TSUUU-BAAAKIII-CHAN! ♫
WHATCHA DOIN' UP H—
ZA (ZWOOP)
......

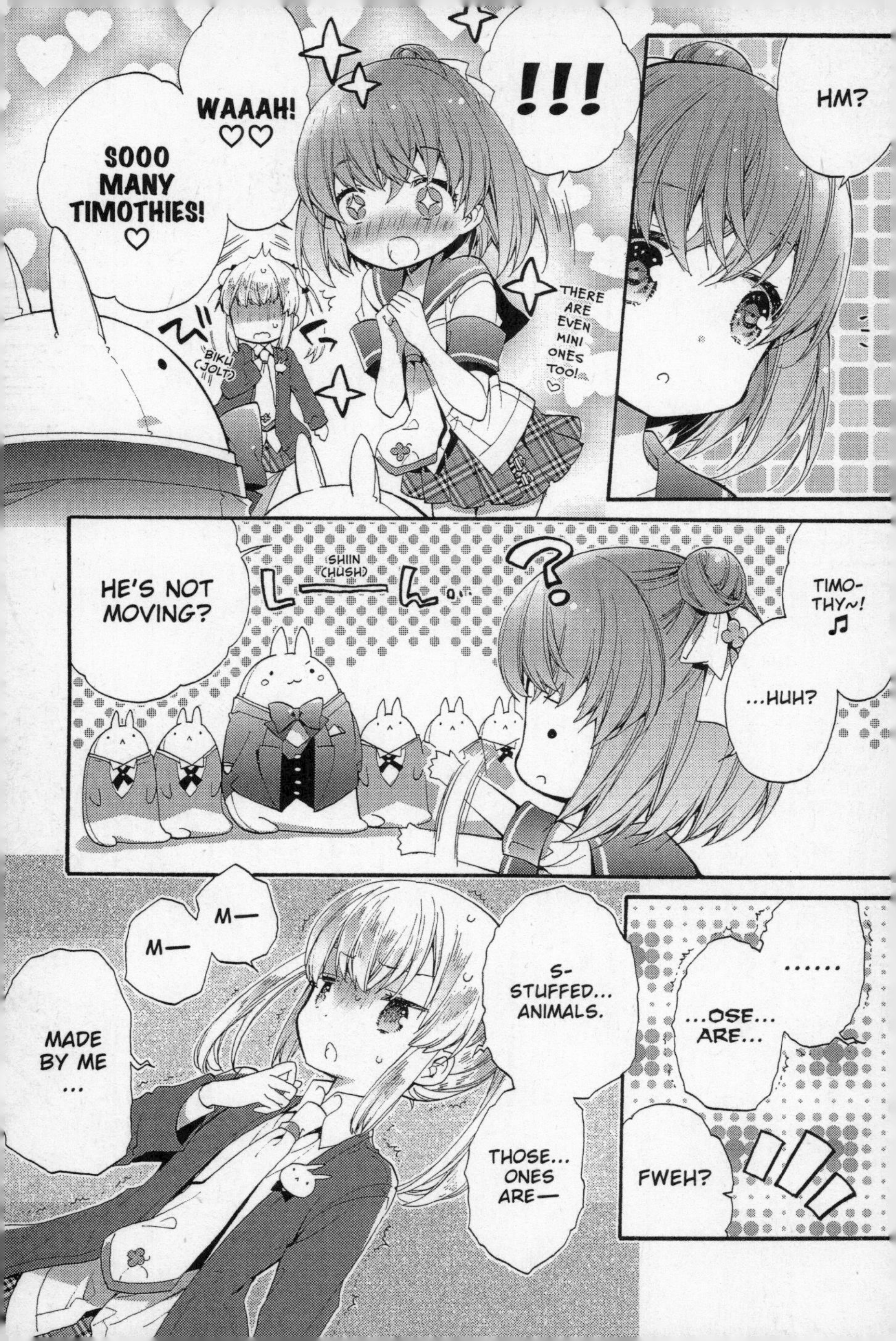
HM?
!!!
WAAAH! ♡♡
SOOO MANY TIMOTHIES! ♡
THERE ARE EVEN MINI ONES TOO! ♡
BIKU (JOLT)
TIMO-THY~! ♫
...HUH?
?
SHIIN (HUSH)
HE'S NOT MOVING?
......
...OSE... ARE...
FWEH?
S-STUFFED... ANIMALS.
M—
M—
THOSE... ONES ARE—
MADE BY ME ...

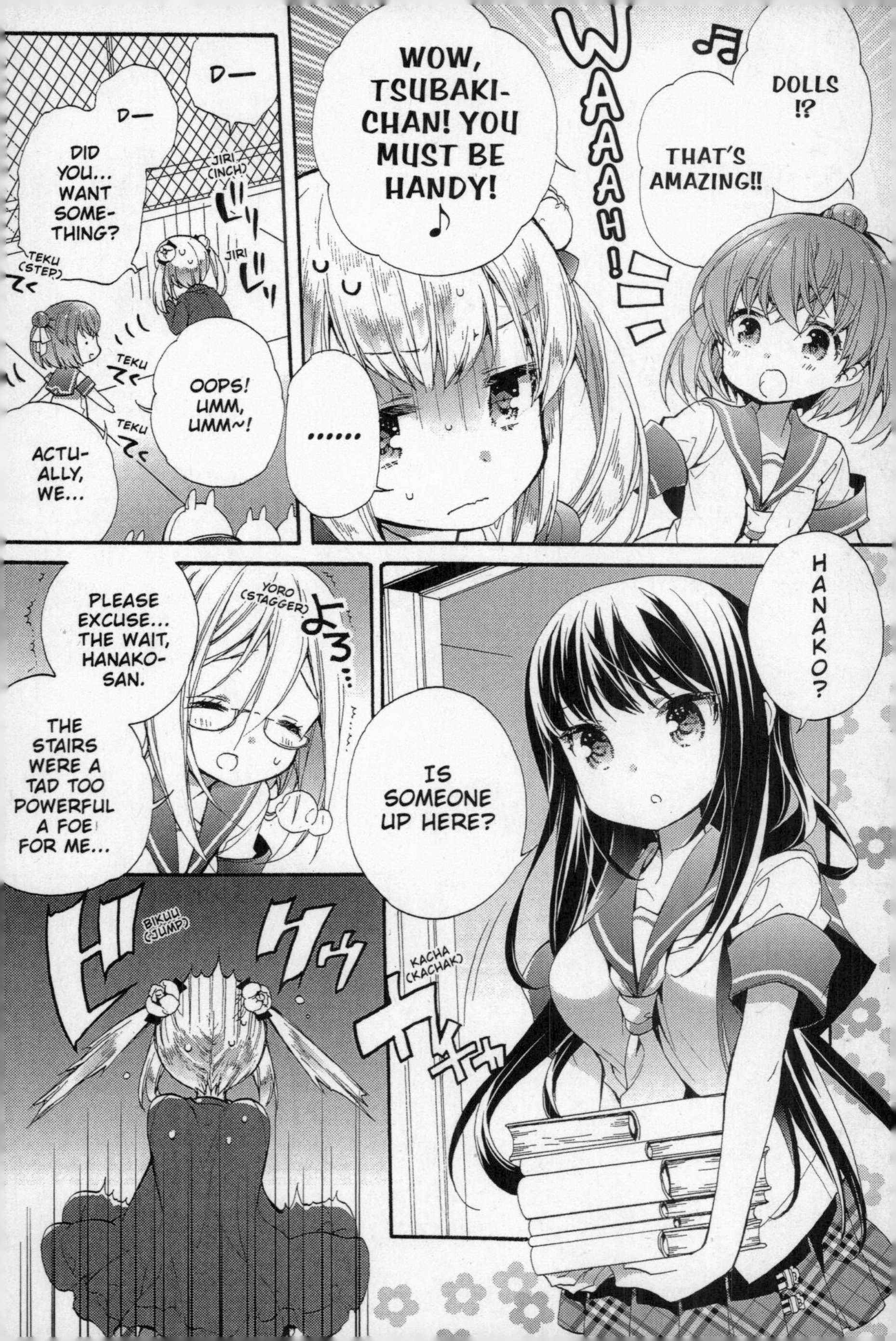
WAAAAH!
DOLLS!?
THAT'S AMAZING!!
WOW, TSUBAKI-CHAN! YOU MUST BE HANDY! ♪
......
D—
D—
DID YOU... WANT SOMETHING?
JIRI (INCH)
JIRI
TEKU (STEP)
TEKU
TEKU
OOPS! UMM, UMM~!
ACTUALLY, WE...
HANAKO?
IS SOMEONE UP HERE?
KACHA (KACHAK)
YORO (STAGGER)
PLEASE EXCUSE... THE WAIT, HANAKO-SAN.
THE STAIRS WERE A TAD TOO POWERFUL A FOE FOR ME...
BIKUU (JUMP)

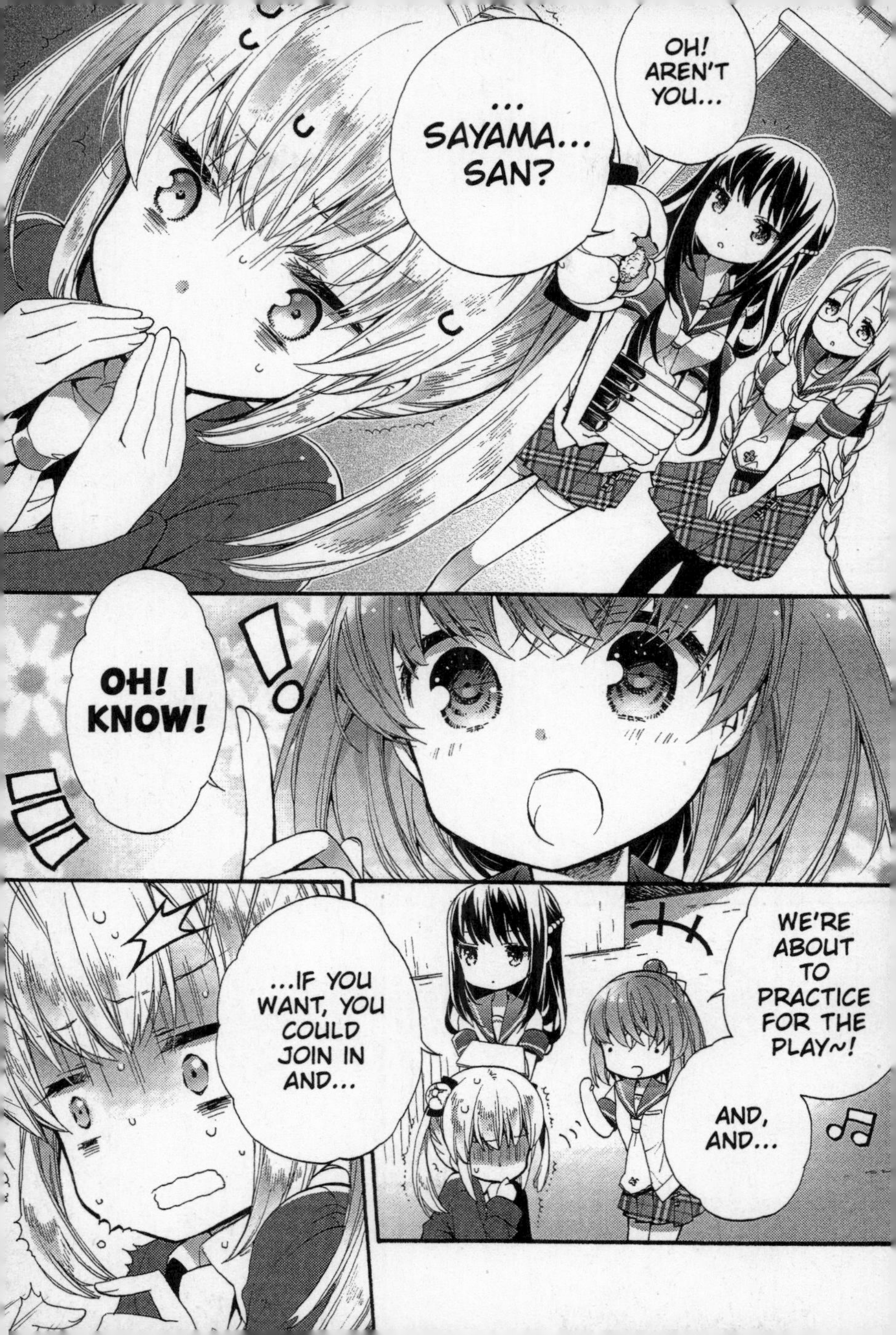
OH! AREN'T YOU...
... SAYAMA... SAN?
OH! I KNOW!
WE'RE ABOUT TO PRACTICE FOR THE PLAY~!
AND, AND...
...IF YOU WANT, YOU COULD JOIN IN AND...

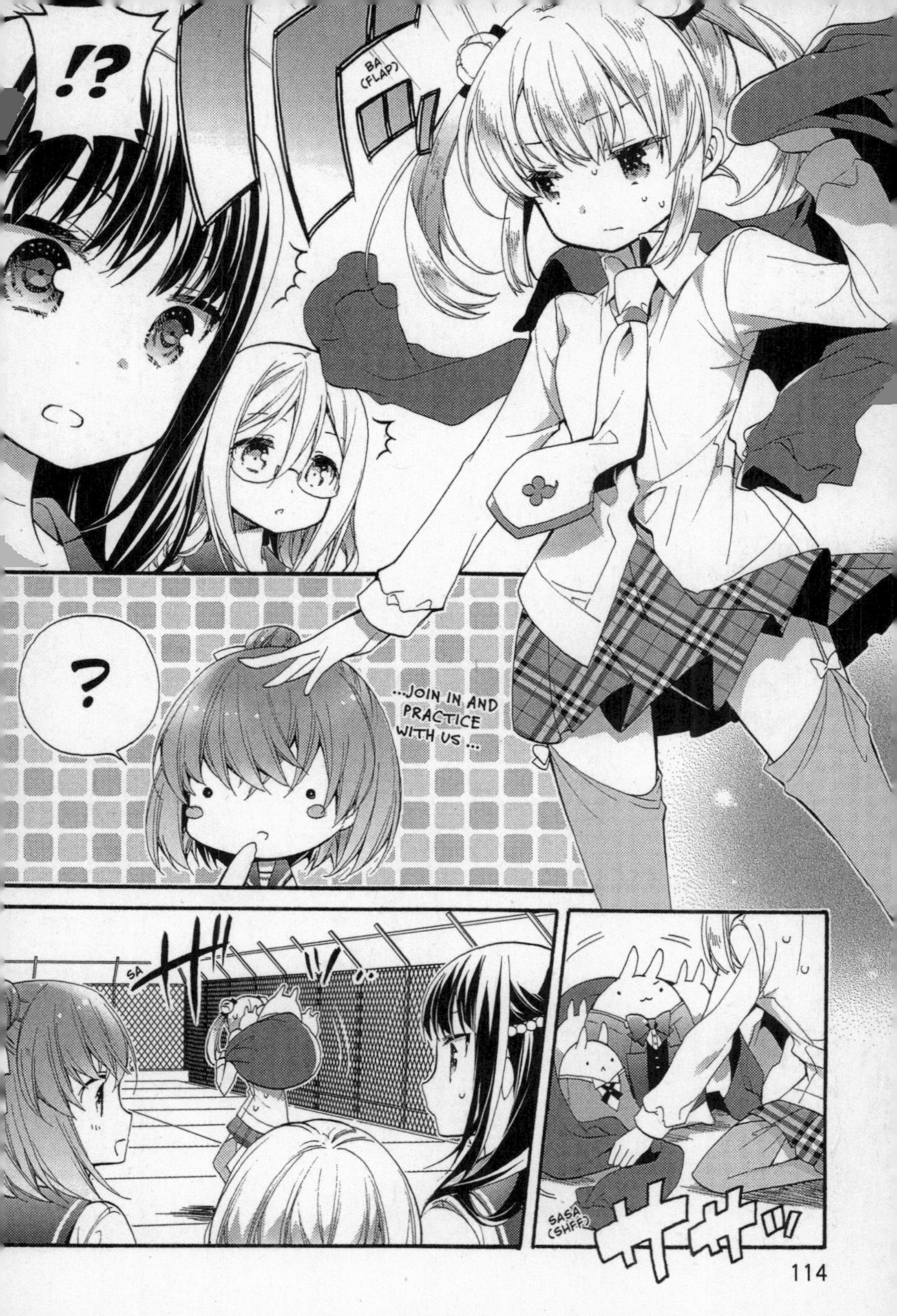
BA (FLAP)
!?
...JOIN IN AND PRACTICE WITH US...
?
SASA (SHFF)
SA

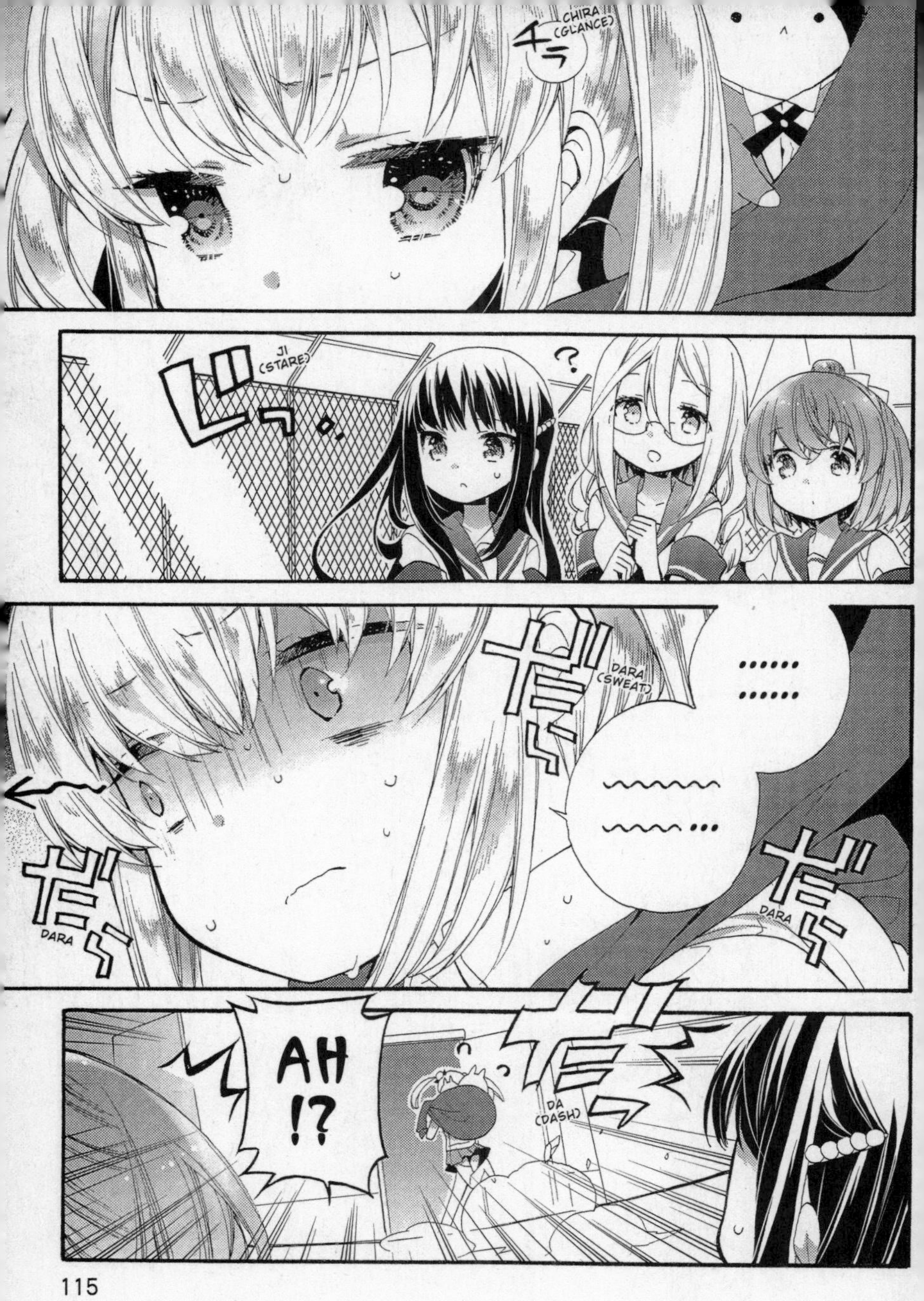

CHIRA (GLANCE)
JI (STARE)
?
DARA (SWEAT)
…… ……
DARA
DARA
DA (DASH)
AH !?

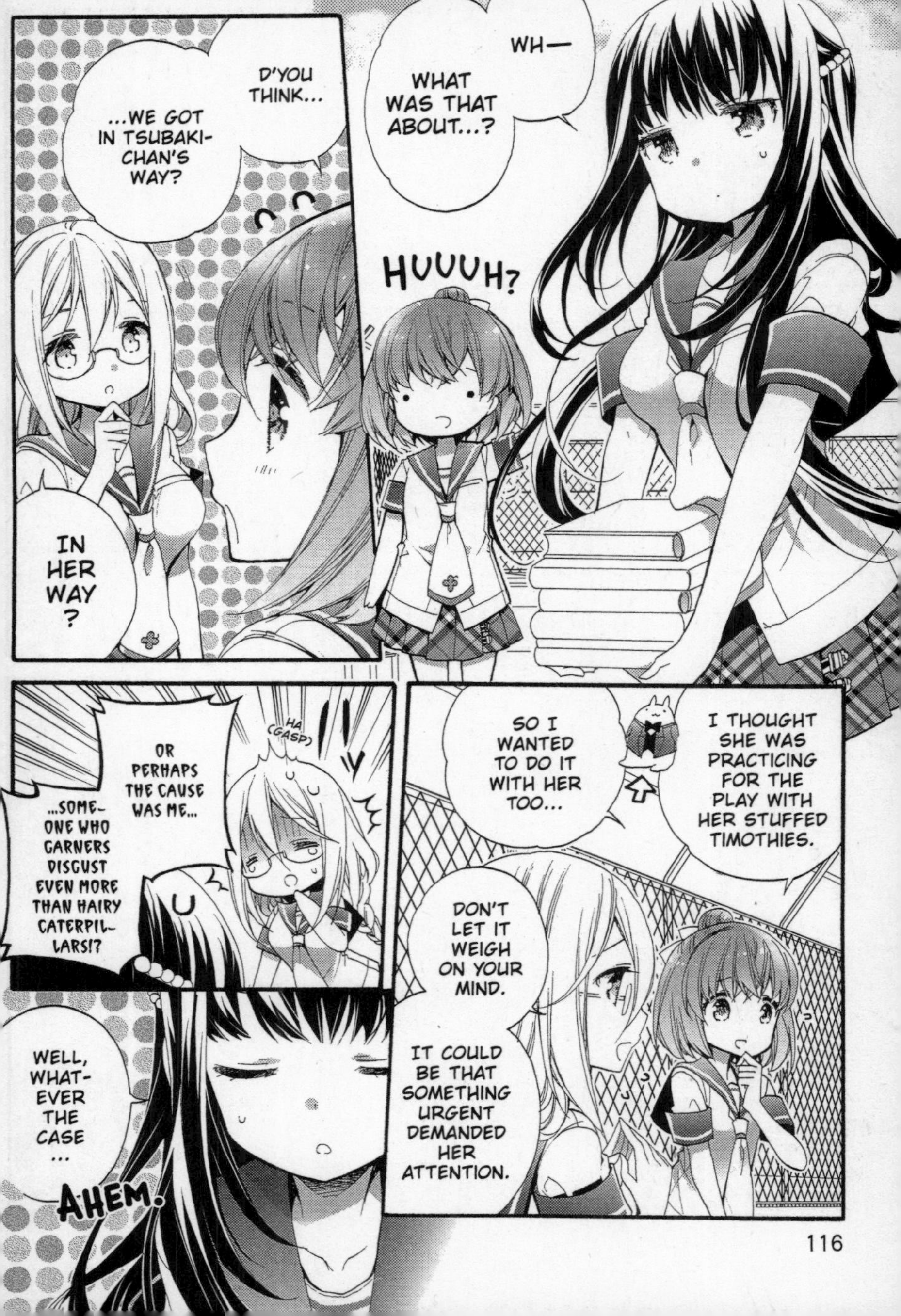
WH—
WHAT WAS THAT ABOUT...?
HUUUH?
D'YOU THINK...
...WE GOT IN TSUBAKI-CHAN'S WAY?
IN HER WAY?
I THOUGHT SHE WAS PRACTICING FOR THE PLAY WITH HER STUFFED TIMOTHIES.
SO I WANTED TO DO IT WITH HER TOO...
DON'T LET IT WEIGH ON YOUR MIND.
IT COULD BE THAT SOMETHING URGENT DEMANDED HER ATTENTION.
HA (GASP)
OR PERHAPS THE CAUSE WAS ME...
...SOMEONE WHO GARNERS DISGUST EVEN MORE THAN HAIRY CATERPILLARS!?
WELL, WHATEVER THE CASE...
AHEM.

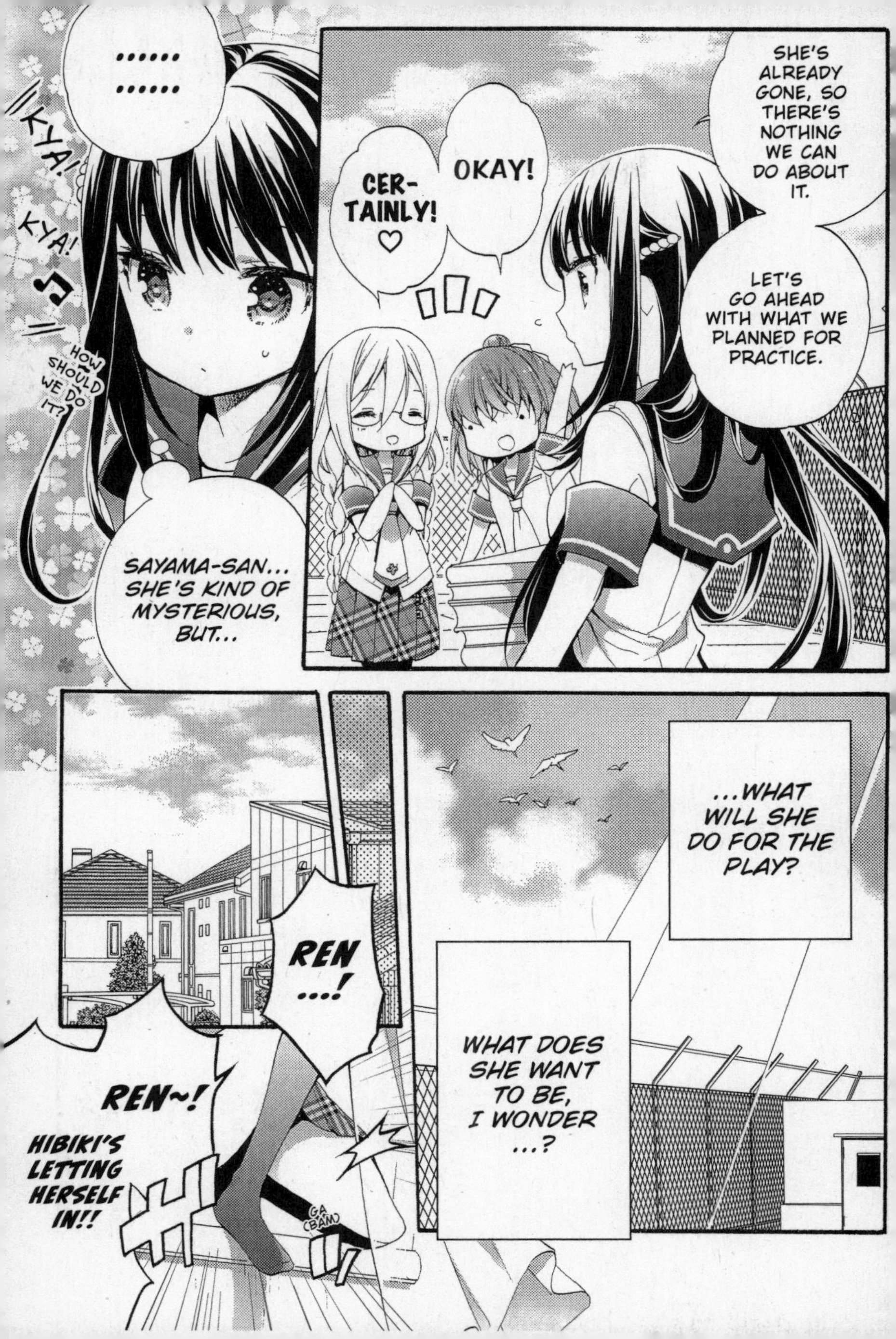
SHE'S ALREADY GONE, SO THERE'S NOTHING WE CAN DO ABOUT IT.
LET'S GO AHEAD WITH WHAT WE PLANNED FOR PRACTICE.
OKAY!
CER-TAINLY! ♡
......
......
KYA! KYA! ♪
HOW SHOULD WE DO IT?
SAYAMA-SAN... SHE'S KIND OF MYSTERIOUS, BUT...
...WHAT WILL SHE DO FOR THE PLAY?
WHAT DOES SHE WANT TO BE, I WONDER ...?
REN ...!
REN~!
HIBIKI'S LETTING HERSELF IN!!
GA (BAM)

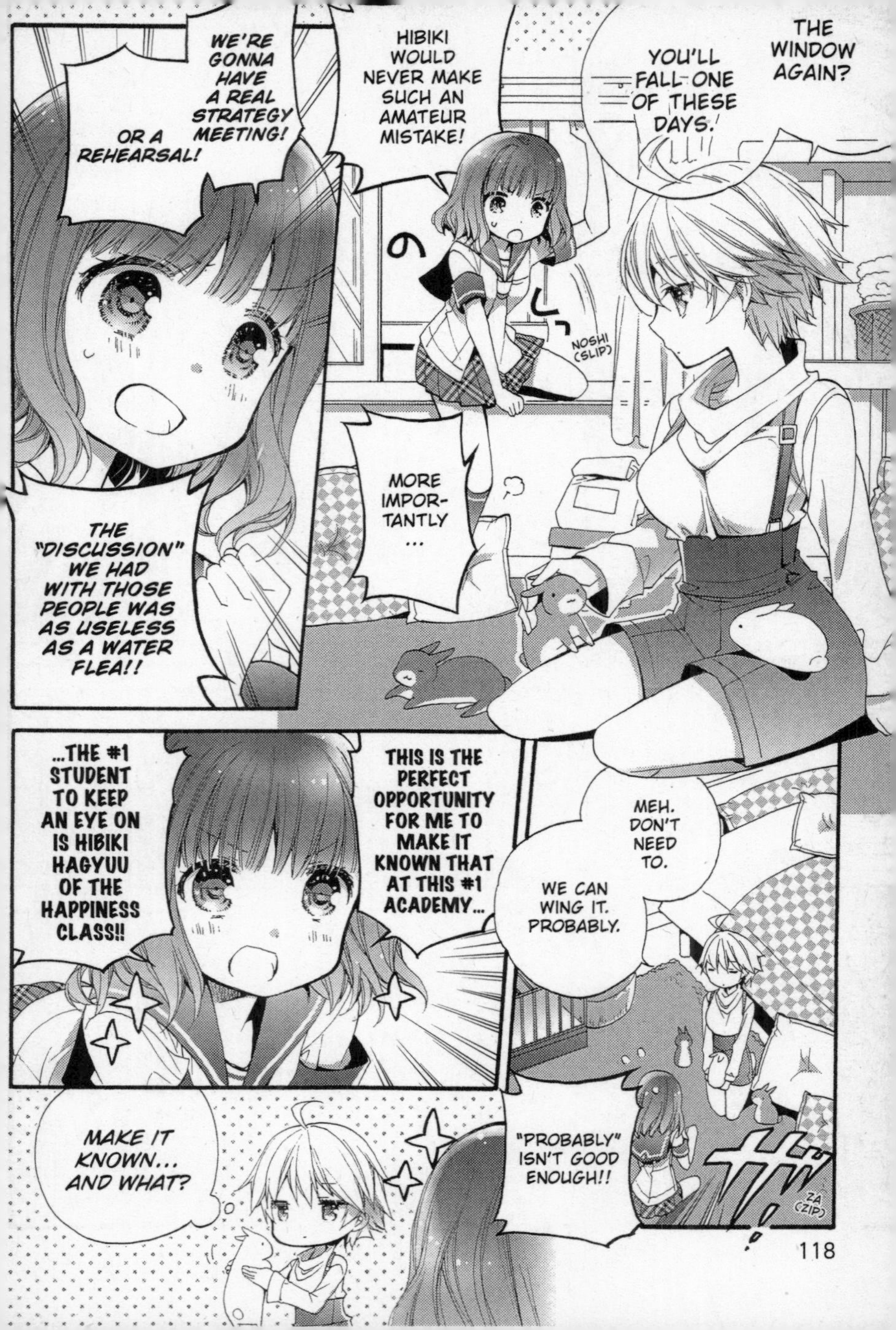

THE WINDOW AGAIN?
YOU'LL FALL ONE OF THESE DAYS.
HIBIKI WOULD NEVER MAKE SUCH AN AMATEUR MISTAKE!
NOSHI (SLIP)
MORE IMPORTANTLY...
THE "DISCUSSION" WE HAD WITH THOSE PEOPLE WAS AS USELESS AS A WATER FLEA!!
WE'RE GONNA HAVE A REAL STRATEGY MEETING!
OR A REHEARSAL!
MEH. DON'T NEED TO.
WE CAN WING IT. PROBABLY.
"PROBABLY" ISN'T GOOD ENOUGH!!
ZA (ZIP)
THIS IS THE PERFECT OPPORTUNITY FOR ME TO MAKE IT KNOWN THAT AT THIS #1 ACADEMY...
...THE #1 STUDENT TO KEEP AN EYE ON IS HIBIKI HAGYUU OF THE HAPPINESS CLASS!!
MAKE IT KNOWN... AND WHAT?

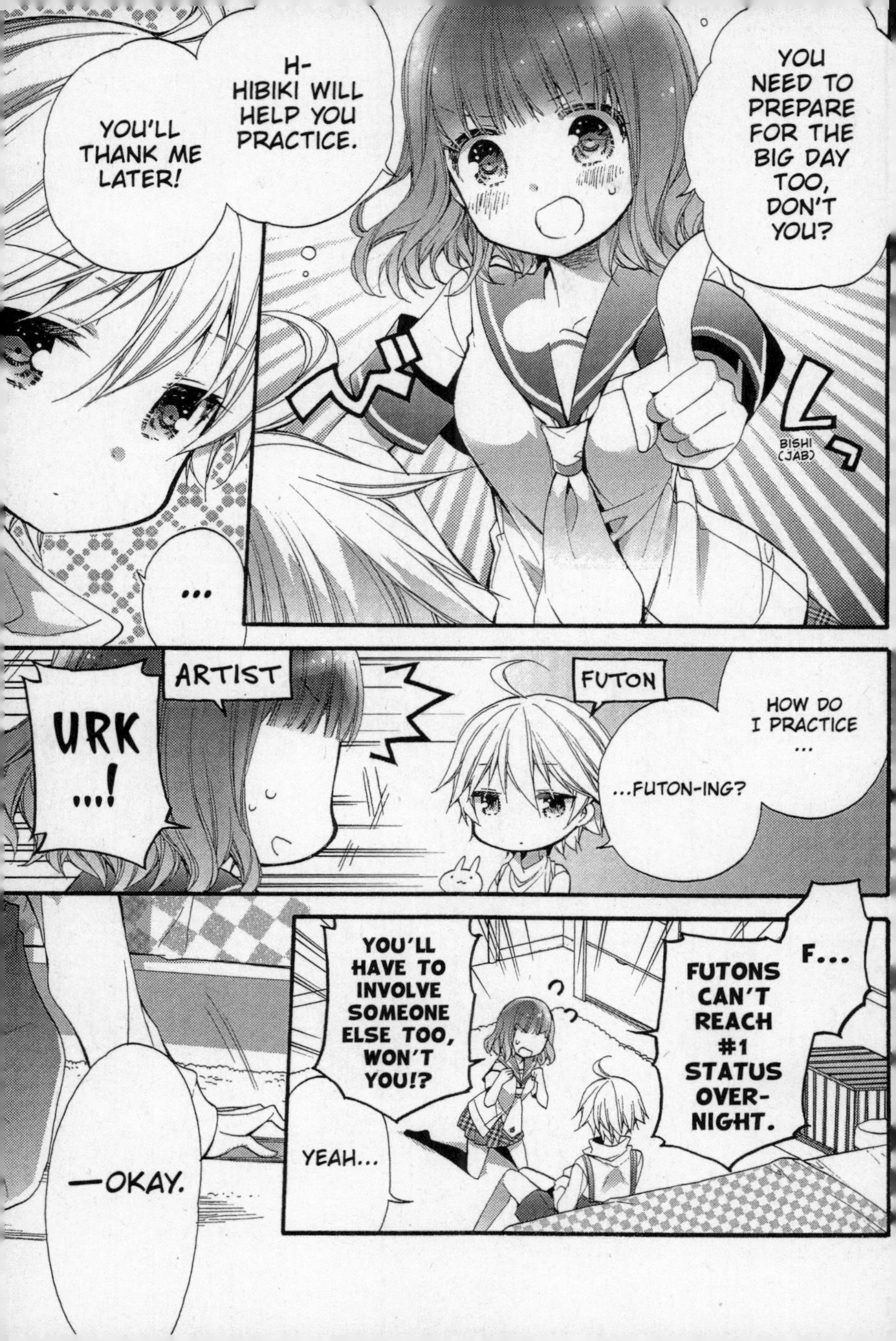
YOU NEED TO PREPARE FOR THE BIG DAY TOO, DON'T YOU?
H-HIBIKI WILL HELP YOU PRACTICE.
YOU'LL THANK ME LATER!
BISHI (JAB)
...
FUTON
HOW DO I PRACTICE ...
...FUTON-ING?
ARTIST
URK ...!
F...
FUTONS CAN'T REACH #1 STATUS OVER-NIGHT.
YOU'LL HAVE TO INVOLVE SOMEONE ELSE TOO, WON'T YOU!?
YEAH...
—OKAY.

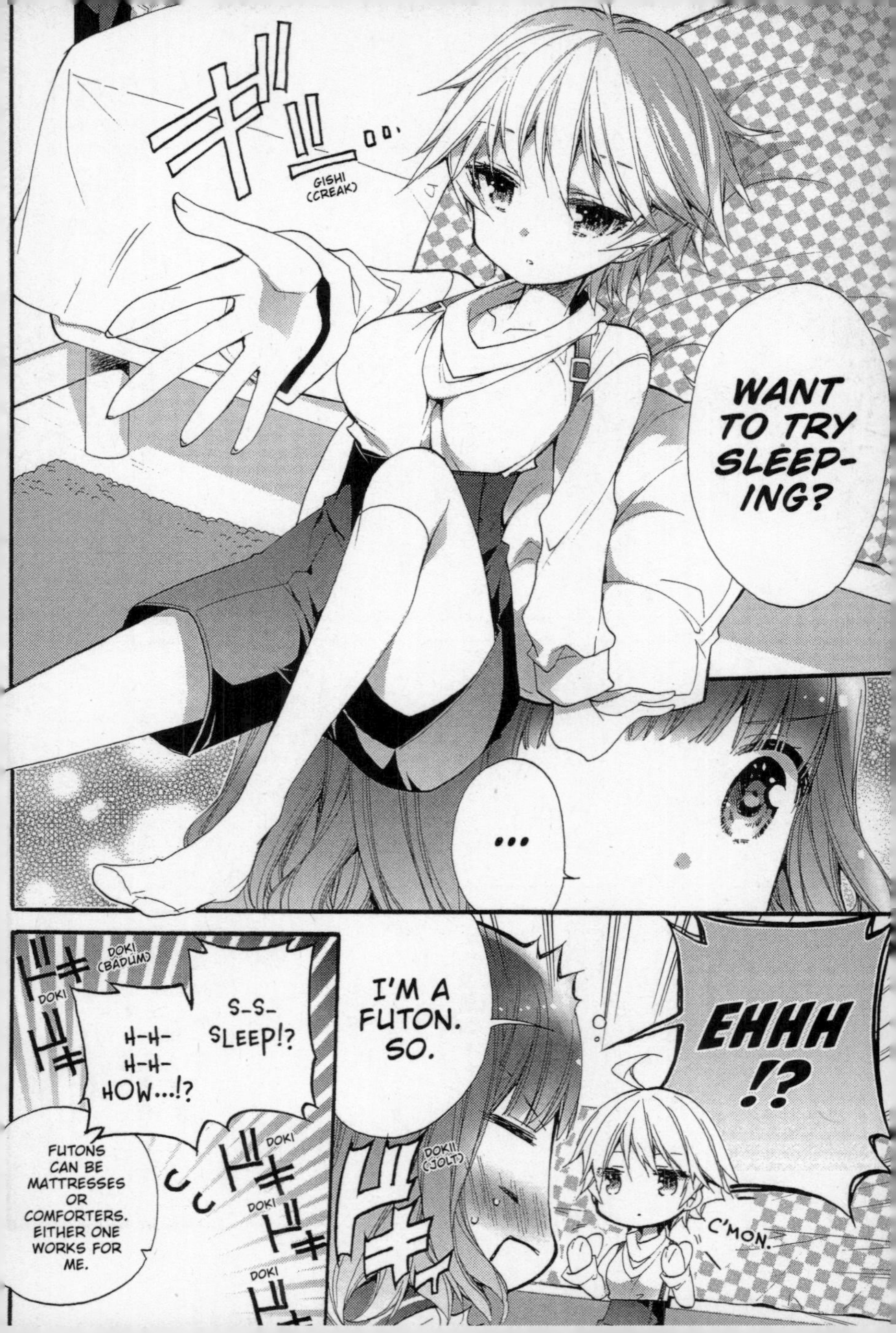
GISHI (CREAK)
WANT TO TRY SLEEPING?
...
EHHH!?
C'MON.
I'M A FUTON. SO.
DOKII (JOLT)
S-S-SLEEP!?
H-H-H-H-HOW...!?
DOKI (BADUM)
DOKI
DOKI
DOKI
DOKI
FUTONS CAN BE MATTRESSES OR COMFORTERS. EITHER ONE WORKS FOR ME.

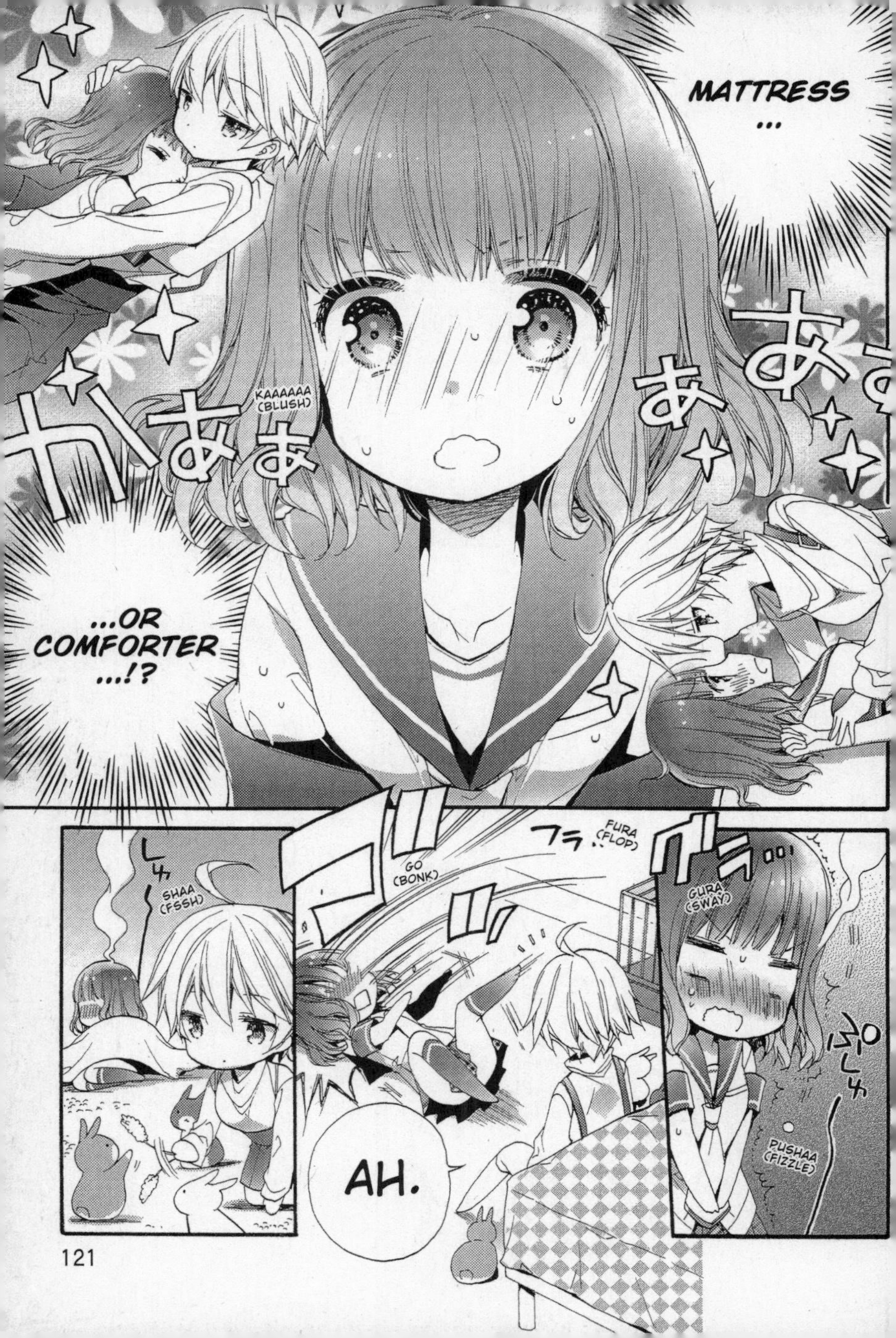

MATTRESS ...
かぁぁ
ぁぁ
KAAAAAA (BLUSH)
...OR COMFORTER ...!?
ぐら
GURA (SWAY)
ぷしゅー
PUSHAA (FIZZLE)
フラ
FURA (FLOP)
ゴッ
GO (BONK)
AH.
しゅ
SHAA (FSSH)

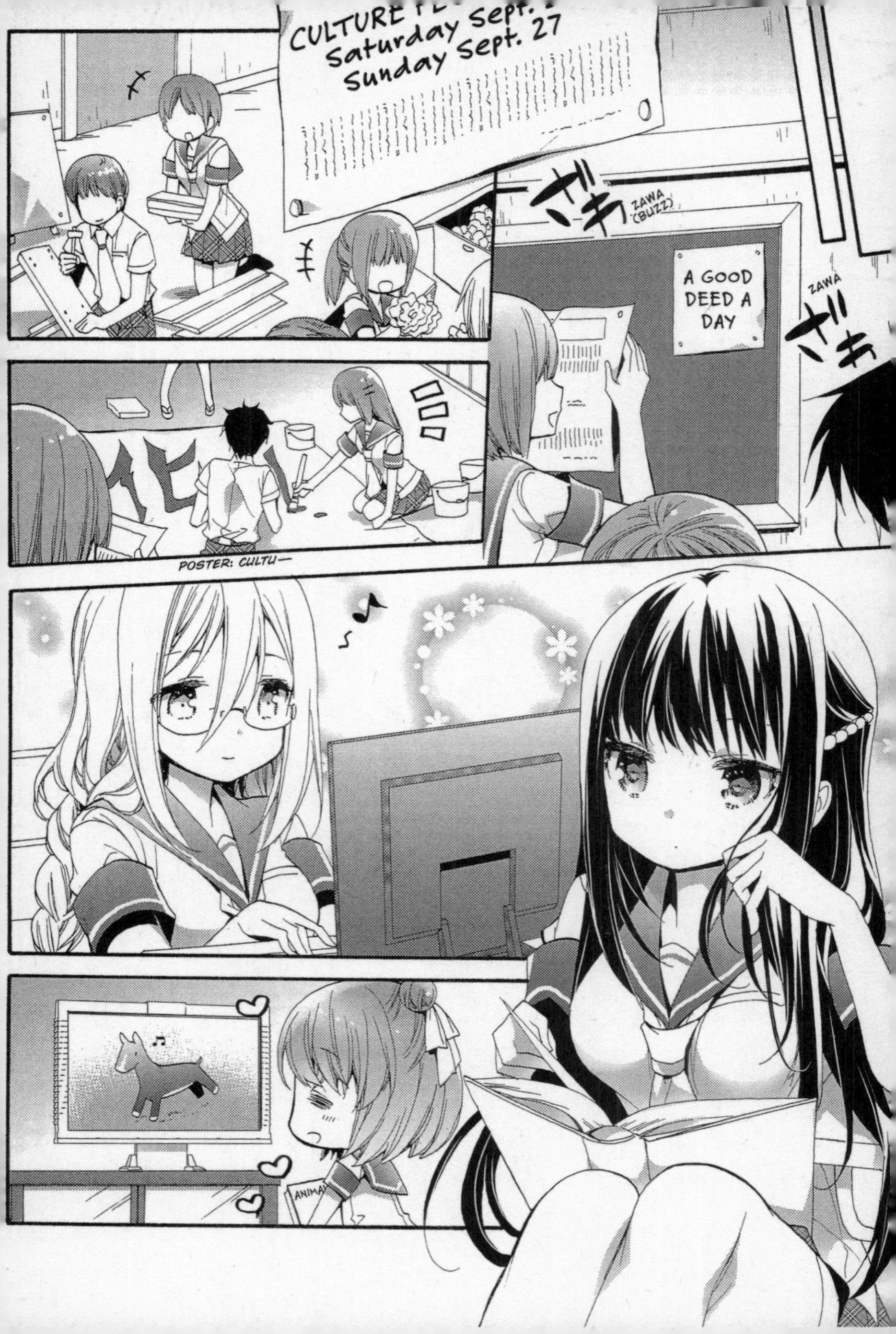
CULTURE
Saturday Sept.
Sunday Sept. 27
ざわ
ZAWA (BUZZ)
A GOOD DEED A DAY
ZAWA
ざわ
POSTER: CULTU—
ANIMA

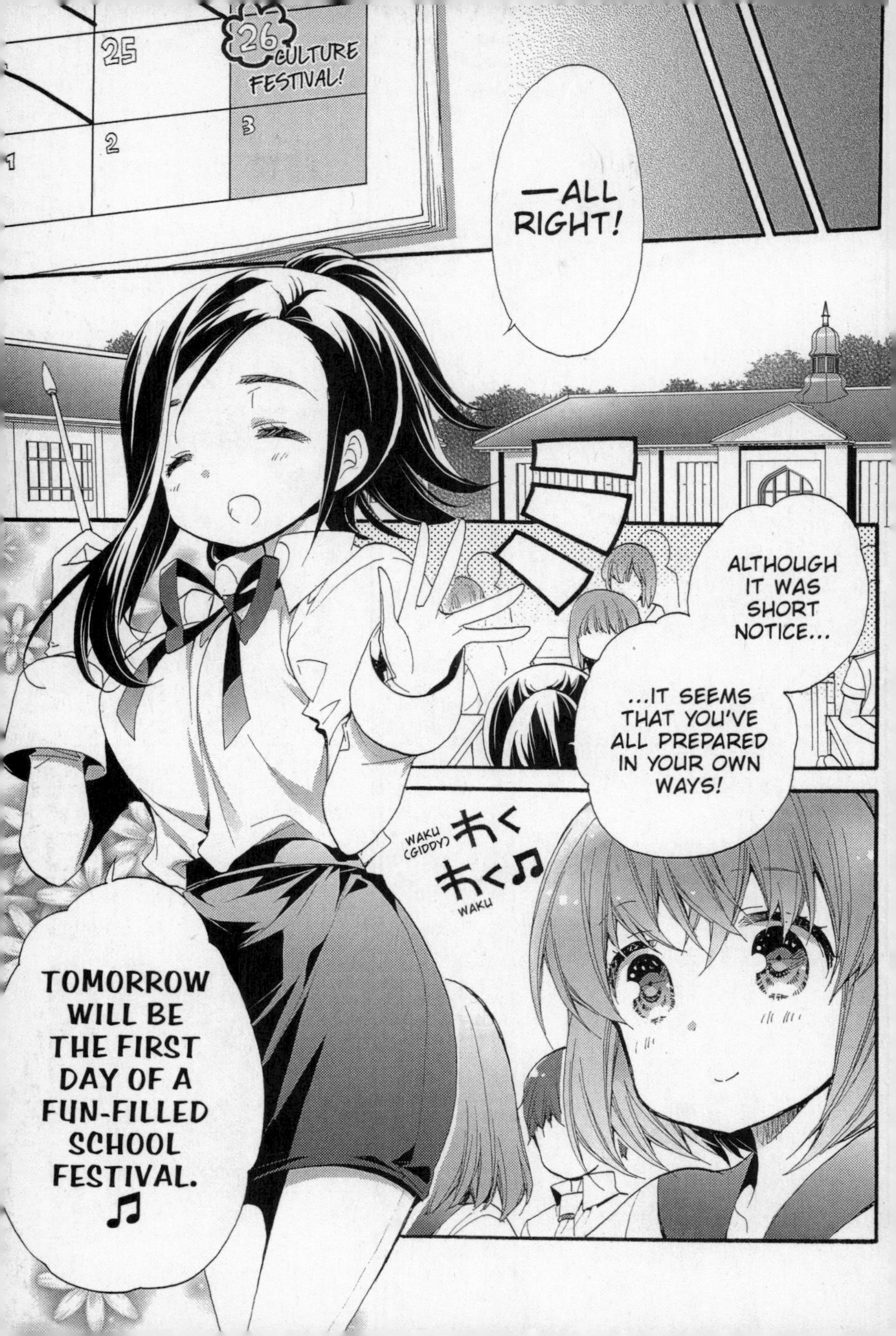

26 CULTURE FESTIVAL!
25
3
2
1
—ALL RIGHT!
ALTHOUGH IT WAS SHORT NOTICE...
...IT SEEMS THAT YOU'VE ALL PREPARED IN YOUR OWN WAYS!
わく わく♪
WAKU (GIDDY) WAKU
TOMORROW WILL BE THE FIRST DAY OF A FUN-FILLED SCHOOL FESTIVAL. ♫

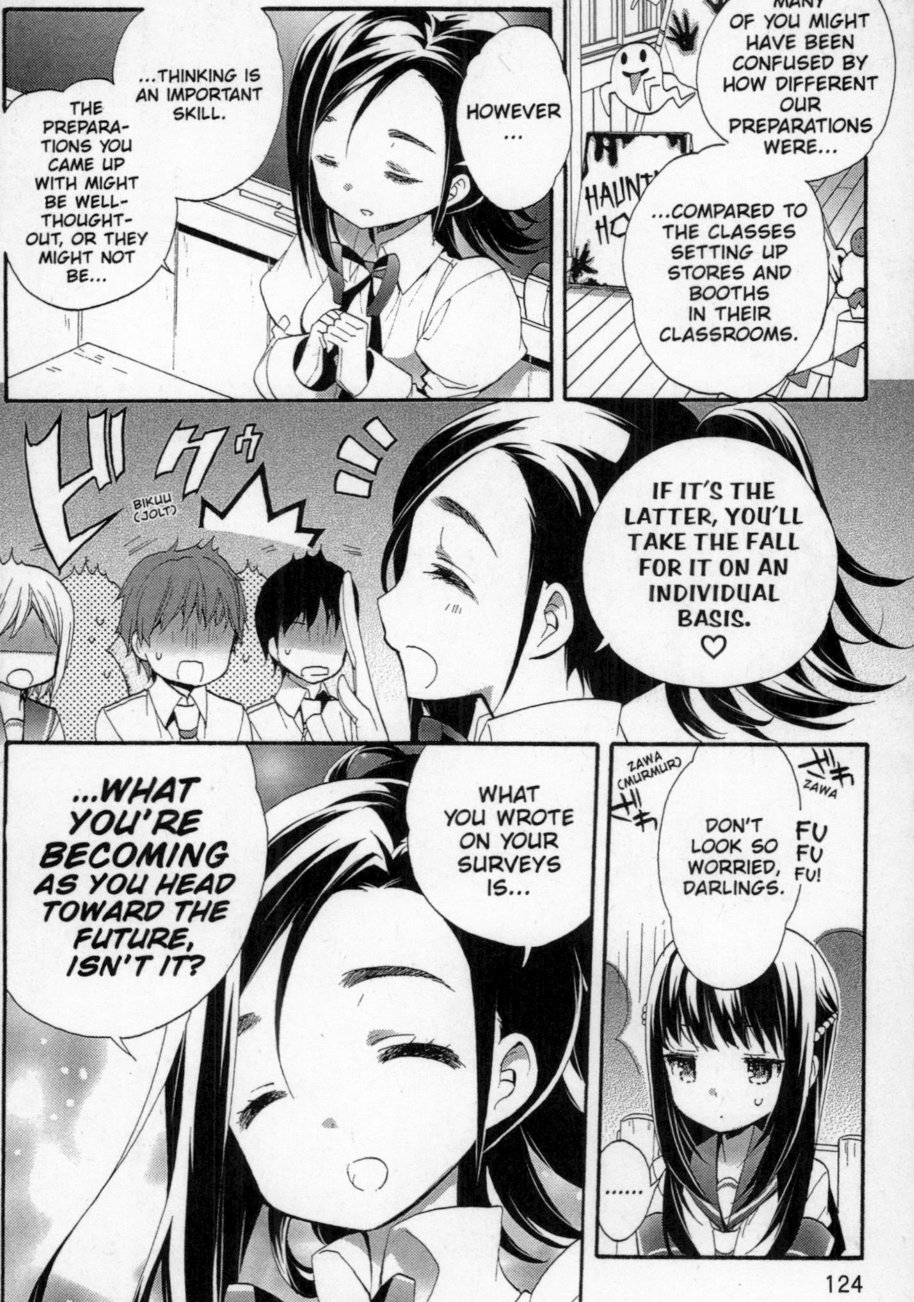
MANY OF YOU MIGHT HAVE BEEN CONFUSED BY HOW DIFFERENT OUR PREPARATIONS WERE...
...COMPARED TO THE CLASSES SETTING UP STORES AND BOOTHS IN THEIR CLASSROOMS.
HOWEVER ...
...THINKING IS AN IMPORTANT SKILL.
THE PREPARATIONS YOU CAME UP WITH MIGHT BE WELL-THOUGHT-OUT, OR THEY MIGHT NOT BE...
IF IT'S THE LATTER, YOU'LL TAKE THE FALL FOR IT ON AN INDIVIDUAL BASIS. ♡
BIKUU (JOLT)
ZAWA (MURMUR)
ZAWA
DON'T LOOK SO WORRIED, DARLINGS.
FU FU FU!
......
WHAT YOU WROTE ON YOUR SURVEYS IS...
...WHAT YOU'RE BECOMING AS YOU HEAD TOWARD THE FUTURE, ISN'T IT?

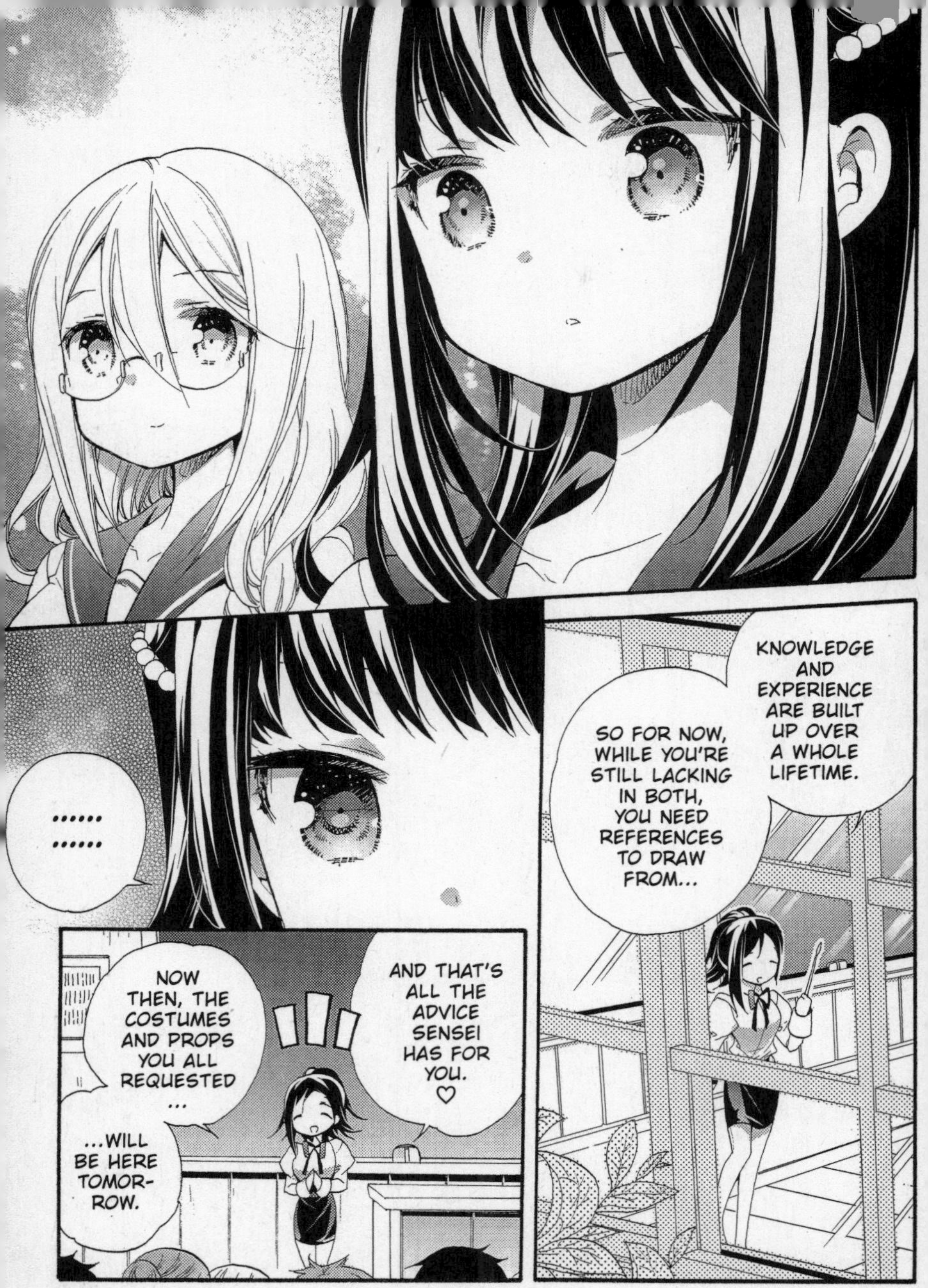
KNOWLEDGE AND EXPERIENCE ARE BUILT UP OVER A WHOLE LIFETIME.
SO FOR NOW, WHILE YOU'RE STILL LACKING IN BOTH, YOU NEED REFERENCES TO DRAW FROM...
......
......
AND THAT'S ALL THE ADVICE SENSEI HAS FOR YOU. ♡
NOW THEN, THE COSTUMES AND PROPS YOU ALL REQUESTED ...
...WILL BE HERE TOMORROW.

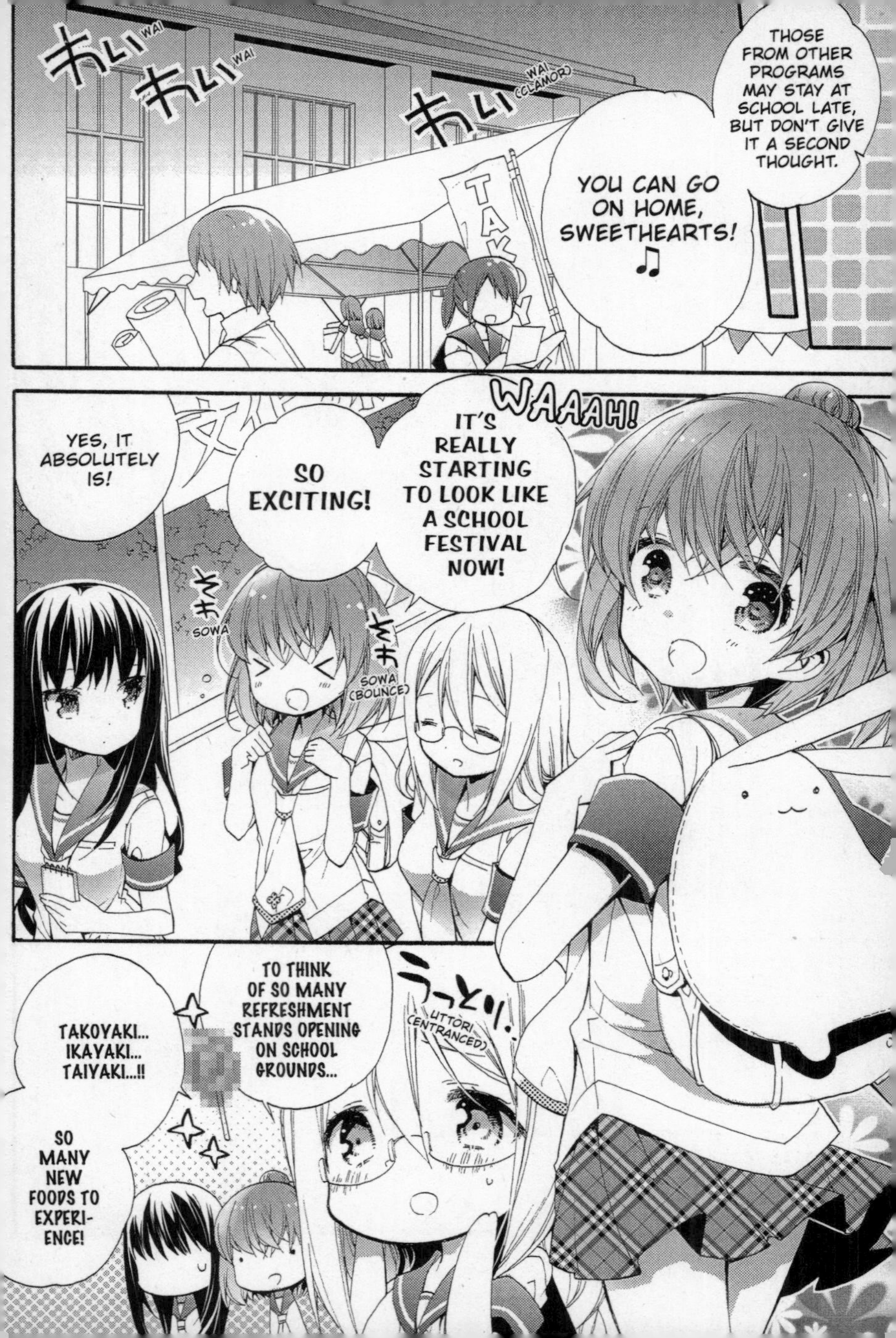
THOSE FROM OTHER PROGRAMS MAY STAY AT SCHOOL LATE, BUT DON'T GIVE IT A SECOND THOUGHT.
YOU CAN GO ON HOME, SWEETHEARTS! ♫
WAI
WAI
WAI (CLAMOR)
WAAAH!
IT'S REALLY STARTING TO LOOK LIKE A SCHOOL FESTIVAL NOW!
SO EXCITING!
YES, IT ABSOLUTELY IS!
SOWA (BOUNCE)
SOWA
UTTORI (ENTRANCED)
TO THINK OF SO MANY REFRESHMENT STANDS OPENING ON SCHOOL GROUNDS...
TAKOYAKI... IKAYAKI... TAIYAKI...!!
SO MANY NEW FOODS TO EXPERI-ENCE!

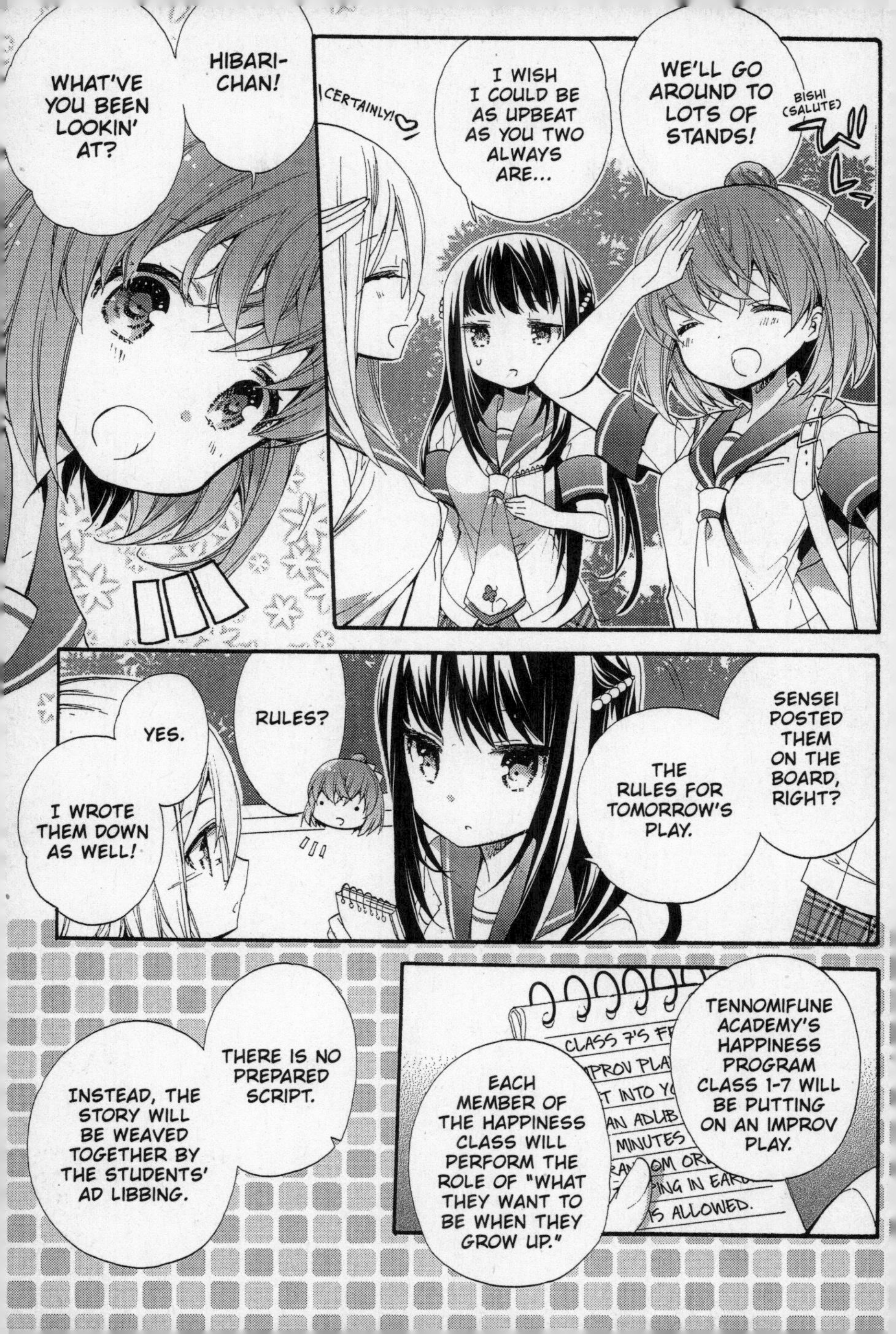
WE'LL GO AROUND TO LOTS OF STANDS!
BISHI (SALUTE)
I WISH I COULD BE AS UPBEAT AS YOU TWO ALWAYS ARE...
CERTAINLY!♡
HIBARI-CHAN!
WHAT'VE YOU BEEN LOOKIN' AT?
SENSEI POSTED THEM ON THE BOARD, RIGHT?
THE RULES FOR TOMORROW'S PLAY.
RULES?
YES.
I WROTE THEM DOWN AS WELL!
TENNOMIFUNE ACADEMY'S HAPPINESS PROGRAM CLASS 1-7 WILL BE PUTTING ON AN IMPROV PLAY.
EACH MEMBER OF THE HAPPINESS CLASS WILL PERFORM THE ROLE OF "WHAT THEY WANT TO BE WHEN THEY GROW UP."
THERE IS NO PREPARED SCRIPT.
INSTEAD, THE STORY WILL BE WEAVED TOGETHER BY THE STUDENTS' AD LIBBING.

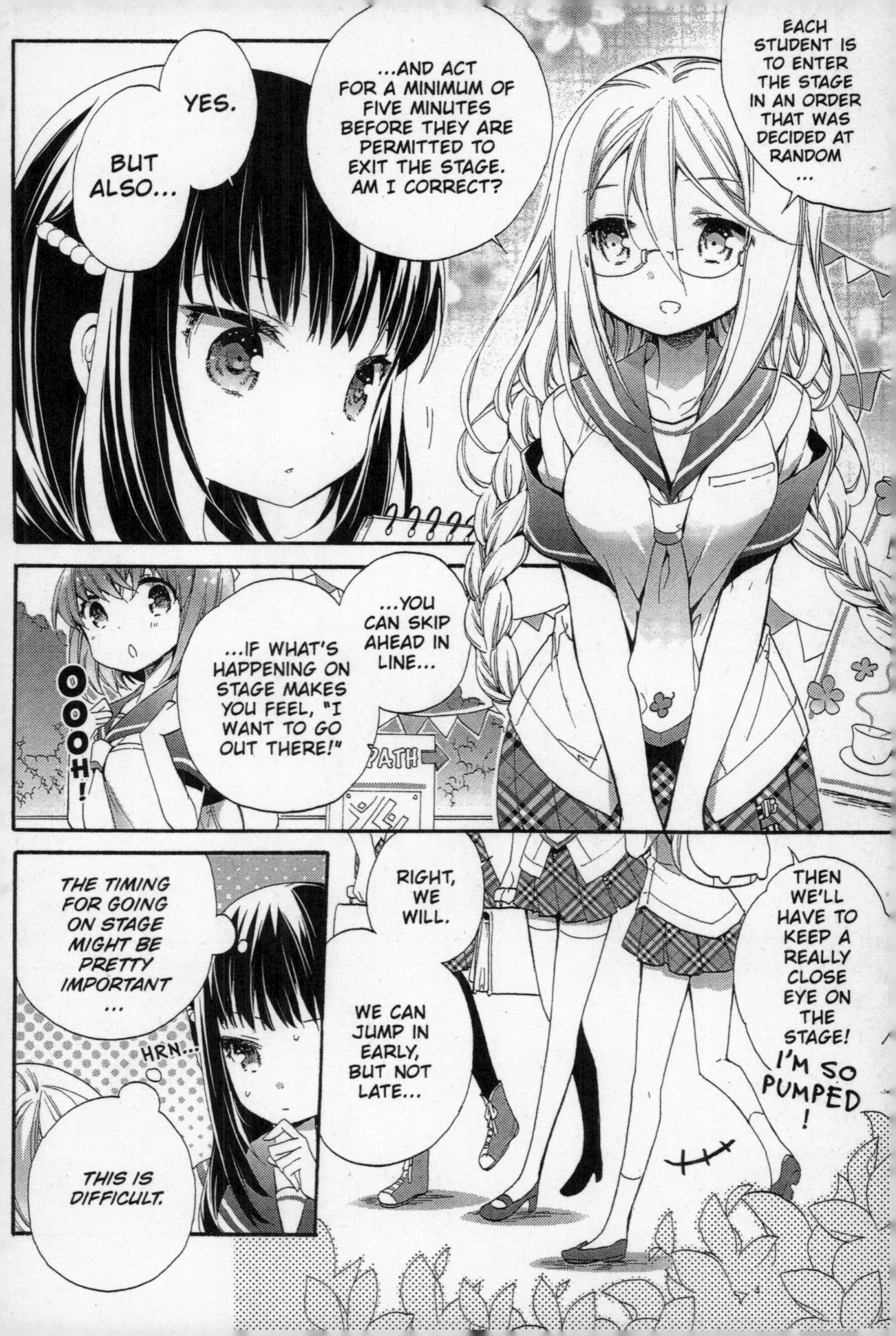
EACH STUDENT IS TO ENTER THE STAGE IN AN ORDER THAT WAS DECIDED AT RANDOM ...
...AND ACT FOR A MINIMUM OF FIVE MINUTES BEFORE THEY ARE PERMITTED TO EXIT THE STAGE. AM I CORRECT?
YES.
BUT ALSO...
...YOU CAN SKIP AHEAD IN LINE...
...IF WHAT'S HAPPENING ON STAGE MAKES YOU FEEL, "I WANT TO GO OUT THERE!"
PATH
OOOOH!
THEN WE'LL HAVE TO KEEP A REALLY CLOSE EYE ON THE STAGE!
I'M SO PUMPED!
RIGHT, WE WILL.
WE CAN JUMP IN EARLY, BUT NOT LATE...
THE TIMING FOR GOING ON STAGE MIGHT BE PRETTY IMPORTANT ...
HRN...
THIS IS DIFFICULT.

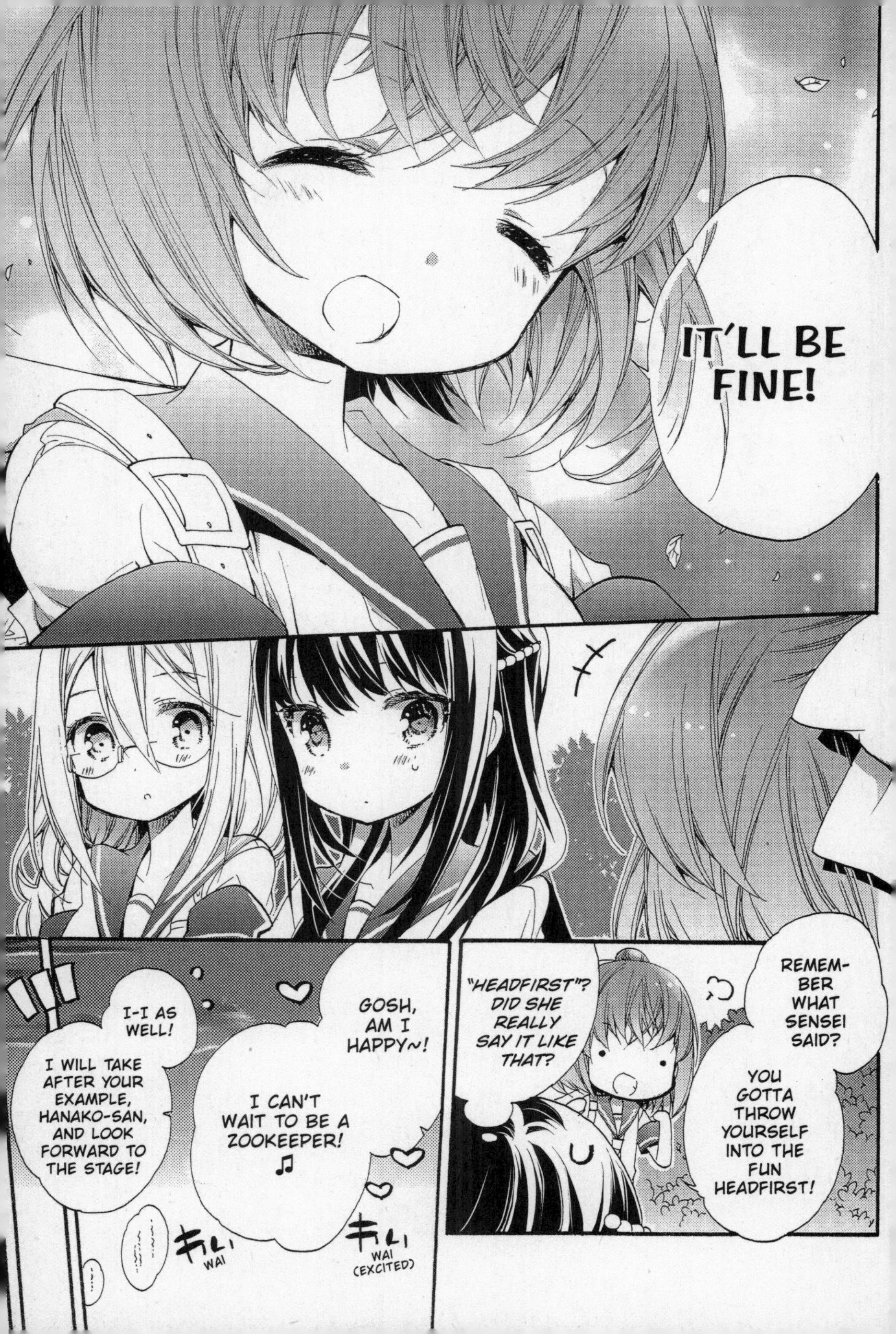
IT'LL BE FINE!
REMEM-BER WHAT SENSEI SAID?
YOU GOTTA THROW YOURSELF INTO THE FUN HEADFIRST!
"HEADFIRST"? DID SHE REALLY SAY IT LIKE THAT?
GOSH, AM I HAPPY~!
I CAN'T WAIT TO BE A ZOOKEEPER! ♫
WAI (EXCITED)
I-I AS WELL!
I WILL TAKE AFTER YOUR EXAMPLE, HANAKO-SAN, AND LOOK FORWARD TO THE STAGE!
WAI

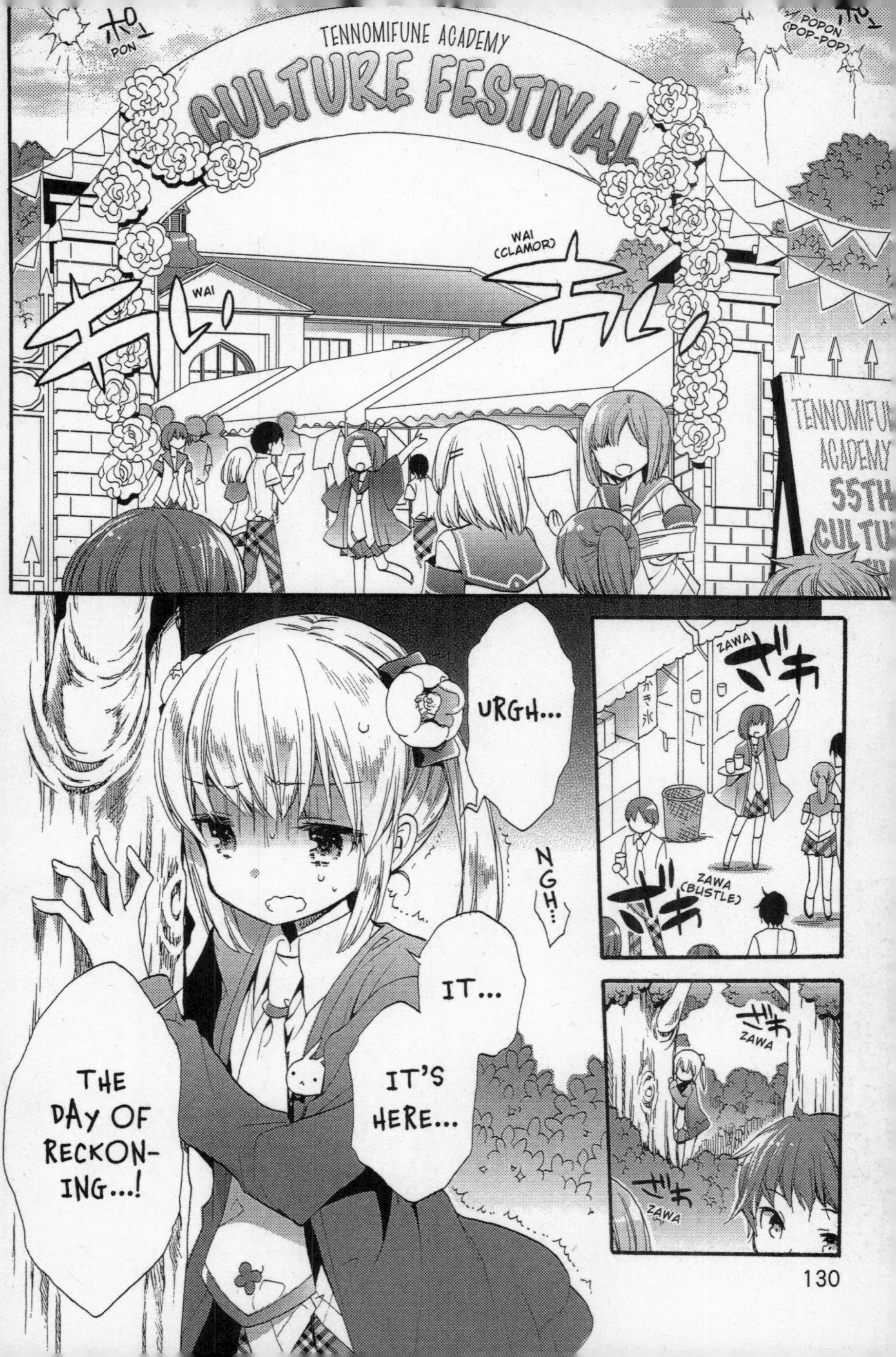

ポン
POPON (POP-POP)
TENNOMIFUNE ACADEMY
CULTURE FESTIVAL
WAI (CLAMOR)
TENNOMIFU
ACADEMY
55TH
CULTU
WAI
ポン
PON
ざわ
ZAWA
かき氷
ざわ
ZAWA (BUSTLE)
ざわ
ZAWA
ざわ
ZAWA
URGH...
NGH...
IT...
IT'S HERE...
THE DAY OF RECKON-ING...!

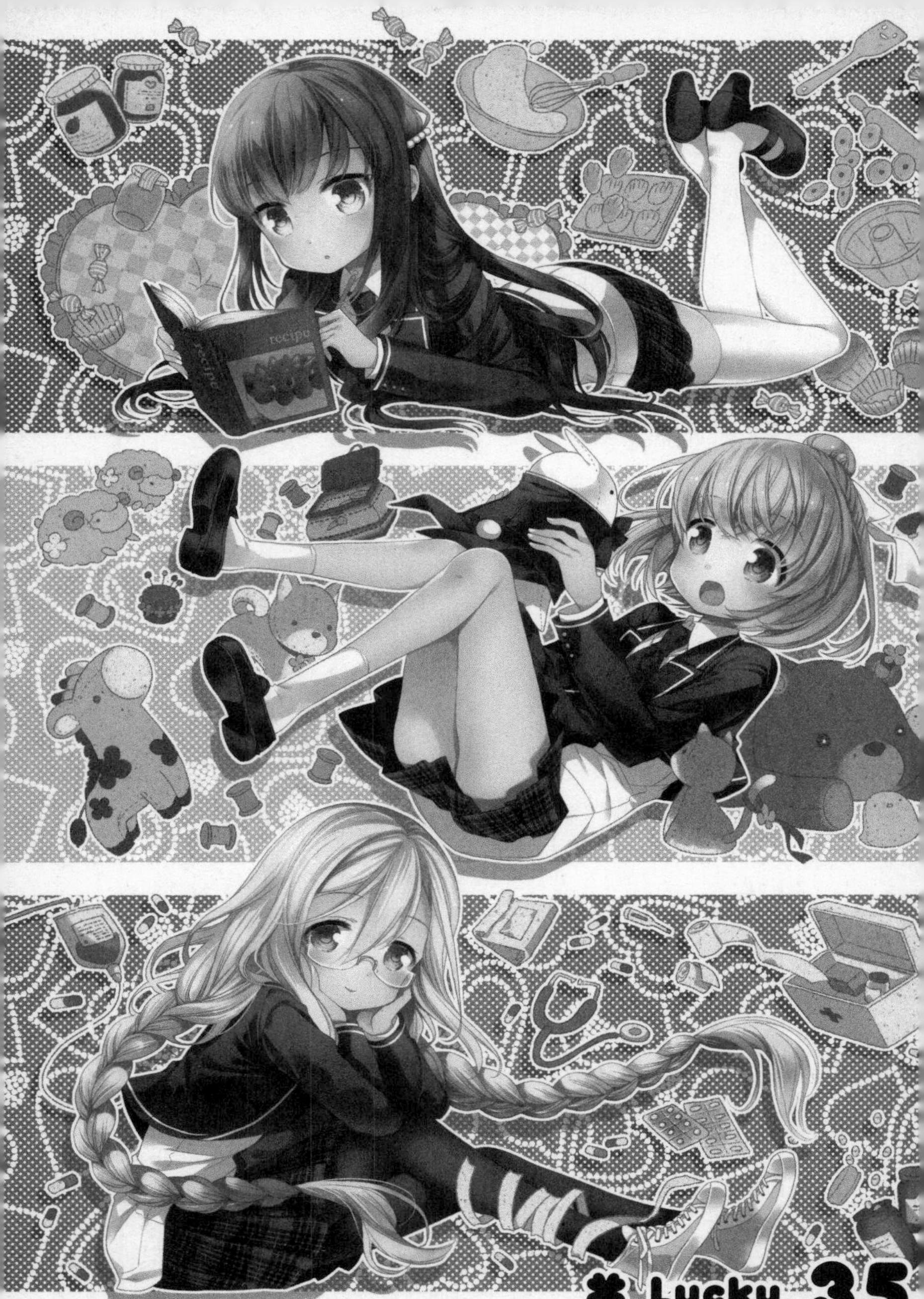
recipe
recipe

Lucky. 35

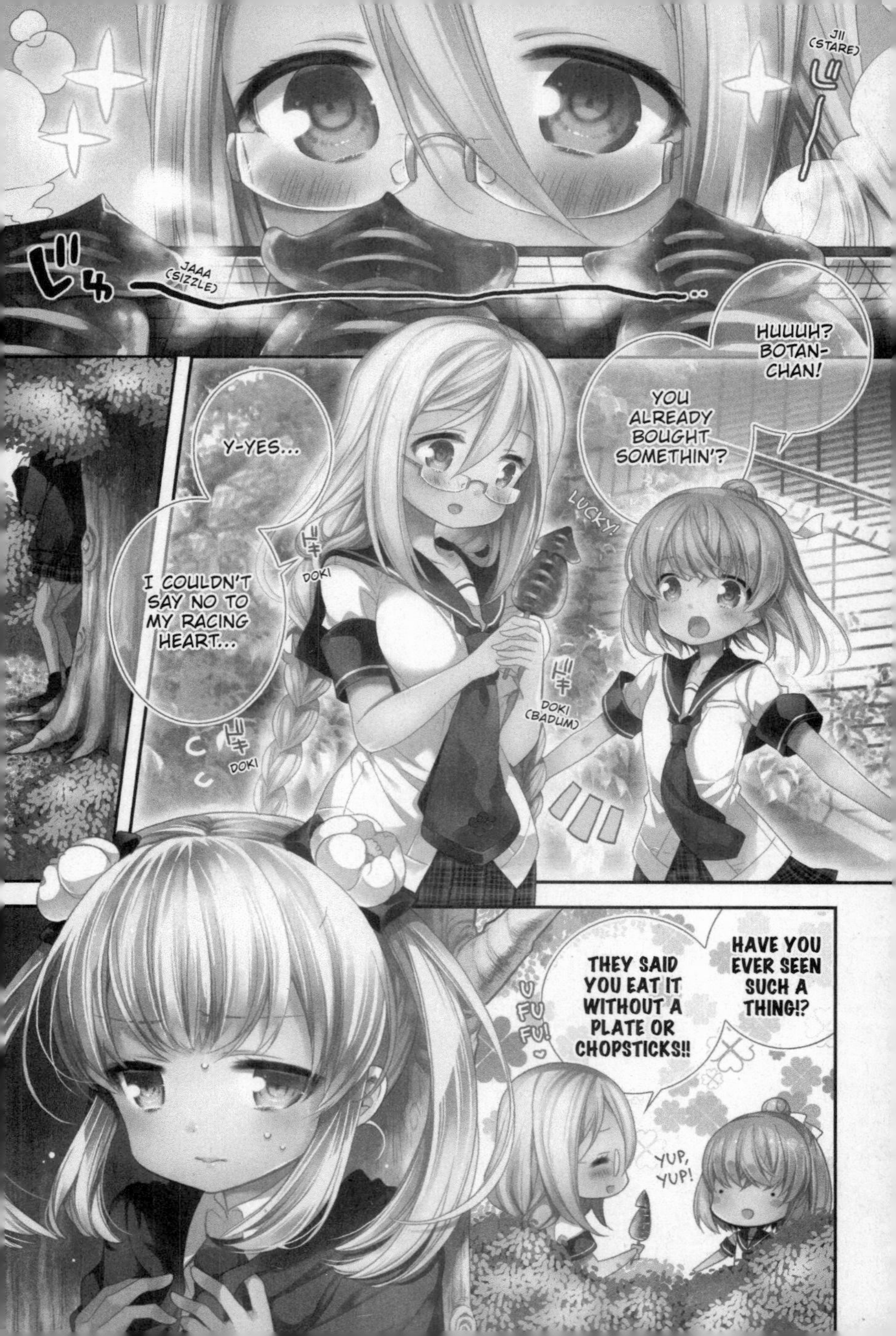
JII (STARE)
JAAA (SIZZLE)
HUUUH? BOTAN-CHAN!
YOU ALREADY BOUGHT SOMETHIN'?
LUCKY!
DOKI (BADUM)
Y-YES...
DOKI
I COULDN'T SAY NO TO MY RACING HEART...
DOKI
HAVE YOU EVER SEEN SUCH A THING!?
THEY SAID YOU EAT IT WITHOUT A PLATE OR CHOPSTICKS!!
UFUFU!
YUP, YUP!

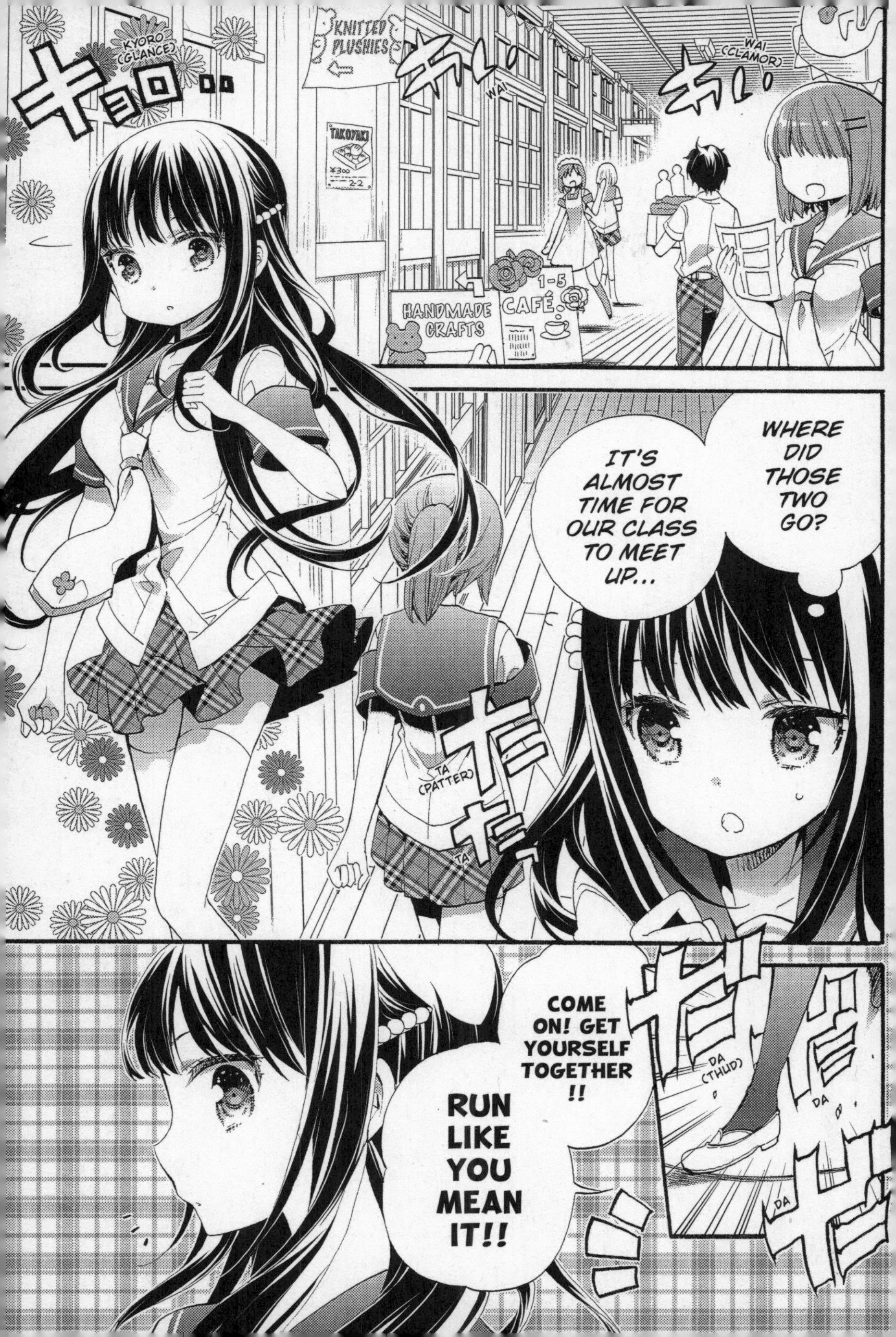
WAI (CLAMOR)
WAI
KNITTED PLUSHIES
TAKOYAKI ¥300 2-2
1-5 CAFÉ
HANDMADE CRAFTS
KYORO (GLANCE)
WHERE DID THOSE TWO GO?
IT'S ALMOST TIME FOR OUR CLASS TO MEET UP...
TA (PATTER)
TA
DA (THUD)
DA
DA
COME ON! GET YOURSELF TOGETHER!!
RUN LIKE YOU MEAN IT!!

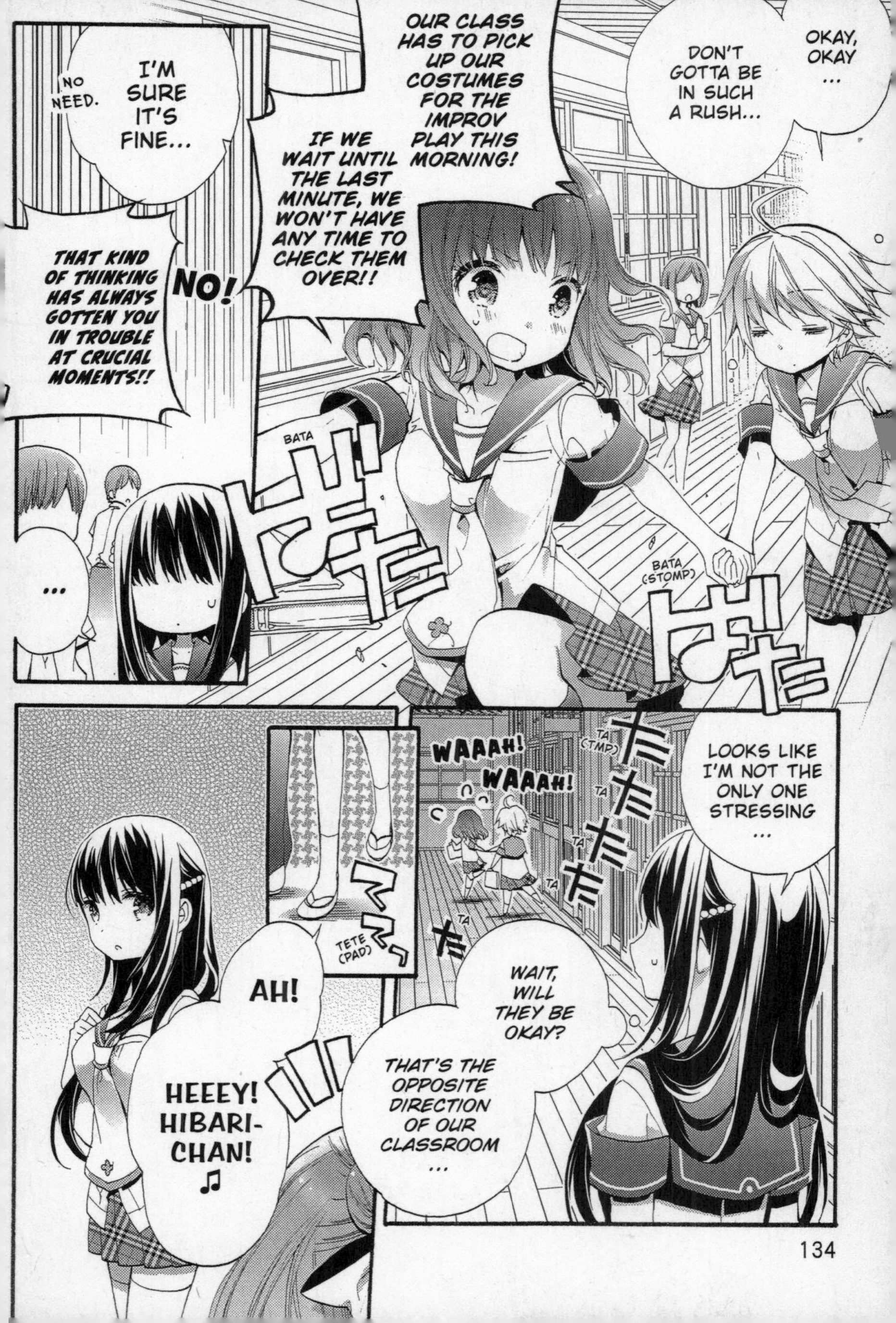
OKAY, OKAY ...
DON'T GOTTA BE IN SUCH A RUSH...
OUR CLASS HAS TO PICK UP OUR COSTUMES FOR THE IMPROV PLAY THIS MORNING!
IF WE WAIT UNTIL THE LAST MINUTE, WE WON'T HAVE ANY TIME TO CHECK THEM OVER!!
BATA
BATA (STOMP)
I'M SURE IT'S FINE...
NO NEED.
NO!
THAT KIND OF THINKING HAS ALWAYS GOTTEN YOU IN TROUBLE AT CRUCIAL MOMENTS!!
...
LOOKS LIKE I'M NOT THE ONLY ONE STRESSING ...
TA (TMP)
TA
TA
TA
TA
WAAAH!
WAAAH!
WAIT, WILL THEY BE OKAY?
THAT'S THE OPPOSITE DIRECTION OF OUR CLASSROOM ...
TETE (PAD)
AH!
HEEEY! HIBARI-CHAN! ♫

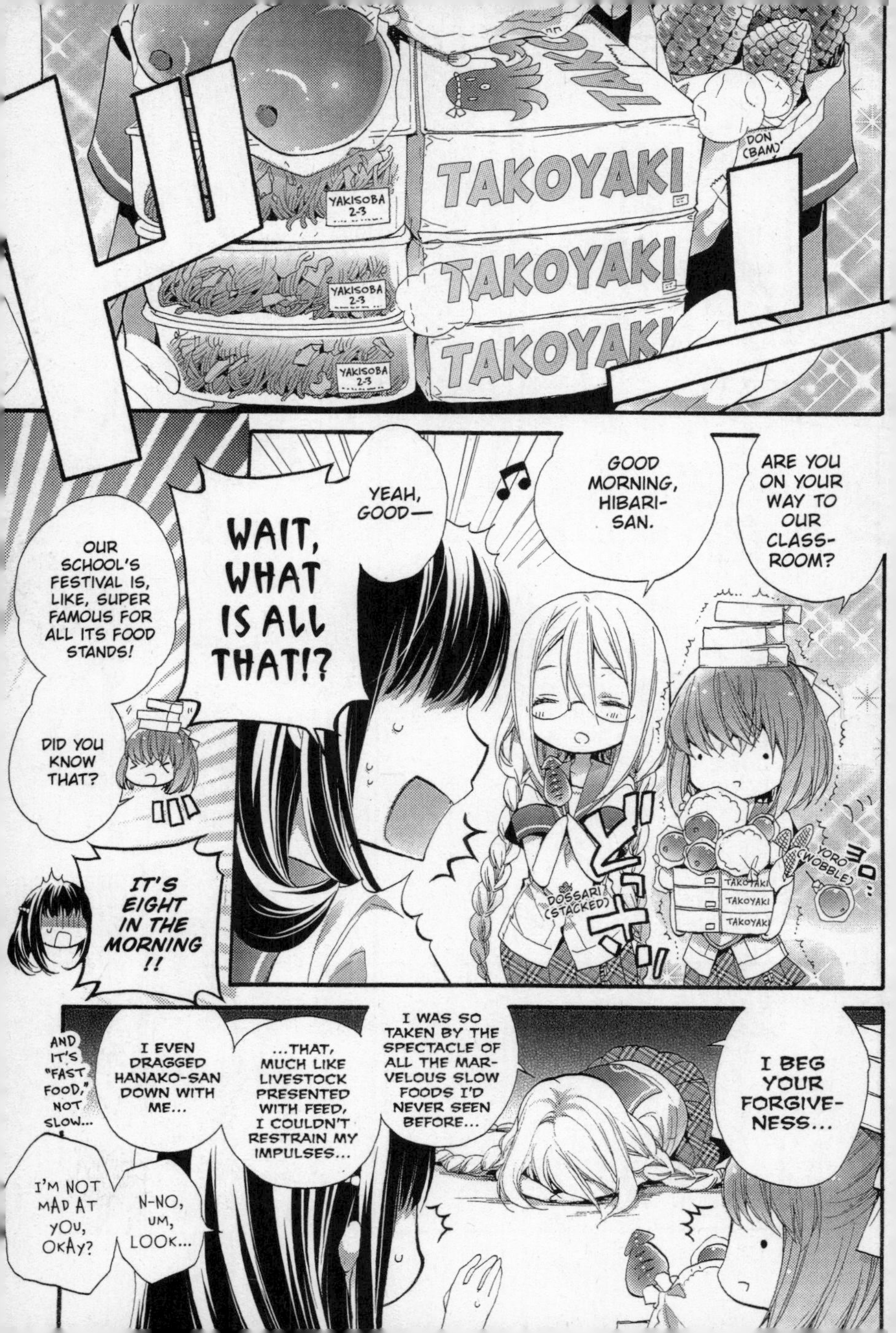
TAKOYAKI
TAKOYAKI
TAKOYAKI
YAKISOBA 2-3
YAKISOBA 2-3
YAKISOBA 2-3
DON (BAM)
ARE YOU ON YOUR WAY TO OUR CLASSROOM?
GOOD MORNING, HIBARI-SAN.
YEAH, GOOD—
WAIT, WHAT IS ALL THAT!?
YORO (WOBBLE)
TAKOYAKI
TAKOYAKI
TAKOYAKI
DOSSARI (STACKED)
OUR SCHOOL'S FESTIVAL IS, LIKE, SUPER FAMOUS FOR ALL ITS FOOD STANDS!
DID YOU KNOW THAT?
IT'S EIGHT IN THE MORNING!!
I BEG YOUR FORGIVENESS...
I WAS SO TAKEN BY THE SPECTACLE OF ALL THE MARVELOUS SLOW FOODS I'D NEVER SEEN BEFORE...
...THAT, MUCH LIKE LIVESTOCK PRESENTED WITH FEED, I COULDN'T RESTRAIN MY IMPULSES...
I EVEN DRAGGED HANAKO-SAN DOWN WITH ME...
AND IT'S "FAST FOOD," NOT SLOW...
N-NO, UM, LOOK...
I'M NOT MAD AT YOU, OKAY?

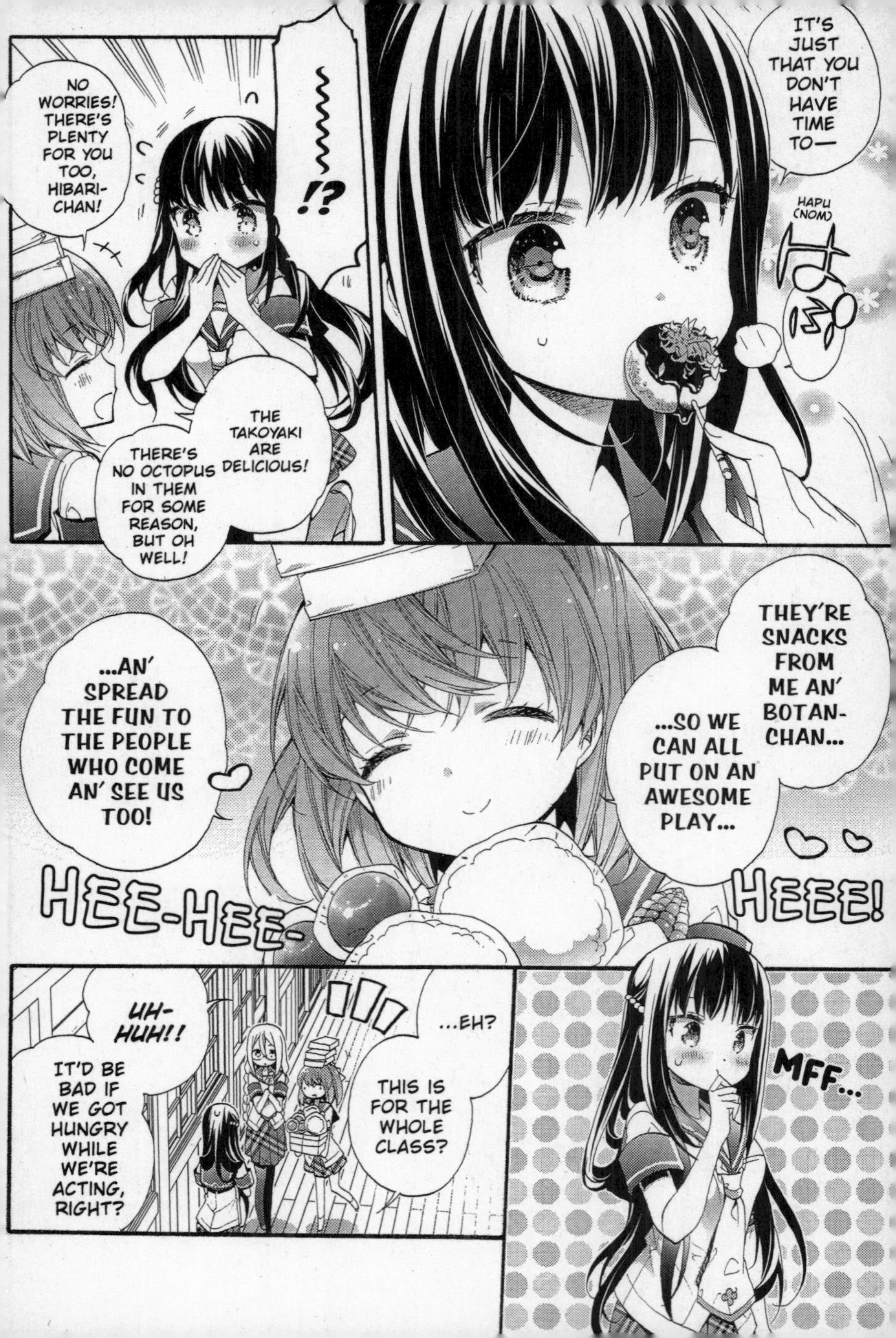
IT'S JUST THAT YOU DON'T HAVE TIME TO—
HAPU (NOM)
はふ
~~~~
!?
NO WORRIES! THERE'S PLENTY FOR YOU TOO, HIBARI-CHAN!
THE TAKOYAKI ARE DELICIOUS!
THERE'S NO OCTOPUS IN THEM FOR SOME REASON, BUT OH WELL!
THEY'RE SNACKS FROM ME AN' BOTAN-CHAN...
...SO WE CAN ALL PUT ON AN AWESOME PLAY...
...AN' SPREAD THE FUN TO THE PEOPLE WHO COME AN' SEE US TOO!
HEE-HEE-HEEE!
MFF...
...EH?
THIS IS FOR THE WHOLE CLASS?
UH-HUH!!
IT'D BE BAD IF WE GOT HUNGRY WHILE WE'RE ACTING, RIGHT?
~~~~

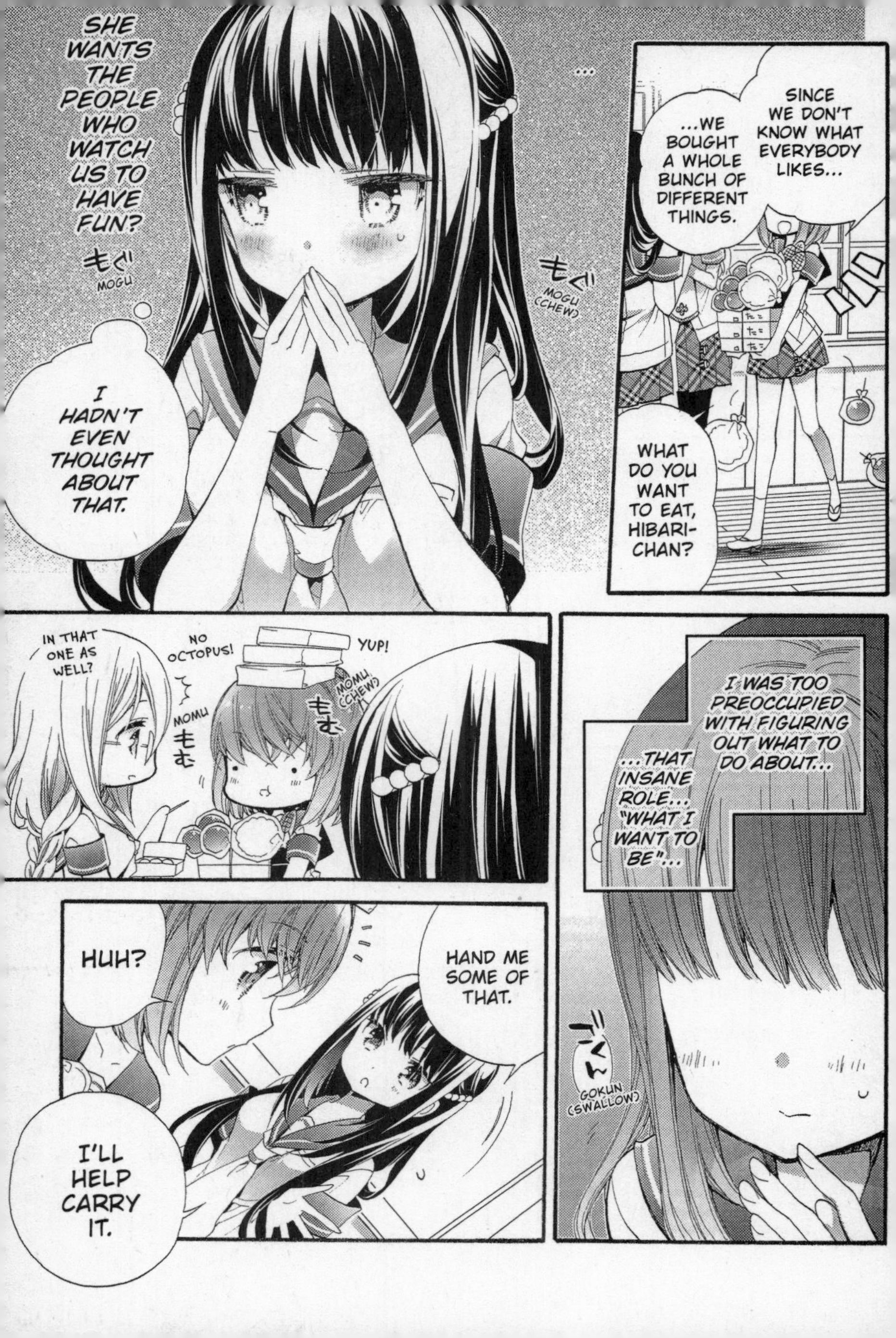
SINCE WE DON'T KNOW WHAT EVERYBODY LIKES...
...WE BOUGHT A WHOLE BUNCH OF DIFFERENT THINGS.
WHAT DO YOU WANT TO EAT, HIBARI-CHAN?
...
もぐ
MOGU (CHEW)
SHE WANTS THE PEOPLE WHO WATCH US TO HAVE FUN?
もぐ
MOGU
I HADN'T EVEN THOUGHT ABOUT THAT.
I WAS TOO PREOCCUPIED WITH FIGURING OUT WHAT TO DO ABOUT...
...THAT INSANE ROLE... "WHAT I WANT TO BE"...
ごくん
GOKUN (SWALLOW)
YUP!
もむ
MOMU (CHEW)
NO OCTOPUS!
MOMU
もむ
IN THAT ONE AS WELL?
HAND ME SOME OF THAT.
HUH?
I'LL HELP CARRY IT.

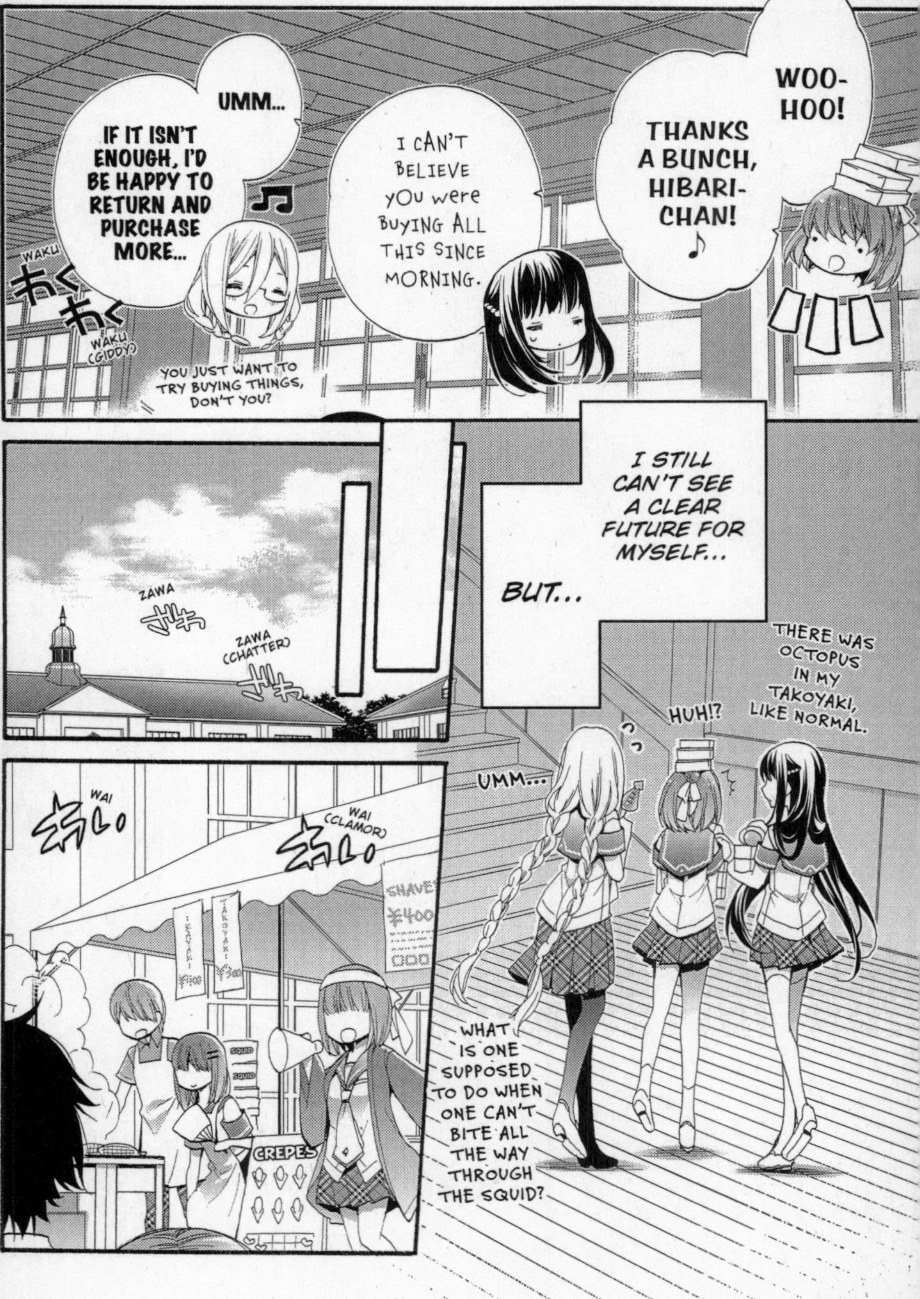
WOO-HOO!
THANKS A BUNCH, HIBARI-CHAN! ♪
I CAN'T BELIEVE yOu were BUYING ALL THIS SINCE MORNING.
UMM...
IF IT ISN'T ENOUGH, I'D BE HAPPY TO RETURN AND PURCHASE MORE... ♫
WAKU
WAKU (GIDDY)
YOU JUST WANT TO TRY BUYING THINGS, DON'T YOU?
I STILL CAN'T SEE A CLEAR FUTURE FOR MYSELF...
BUT...
THERE WAS OCTOPUS IN MY TAKOYAKI, LIKE NORMAL.
HUH!?
UMM...
WHAT IS ONE SUPPOSED TO DO WHEN ONE CAN'T BITE ALL THE WAY THROUGH THE SQUID?
ZAWA
ZAWA (CHATTER)
WAI
WAI (CLAMOR)
SQUID
SQUID
CREPES

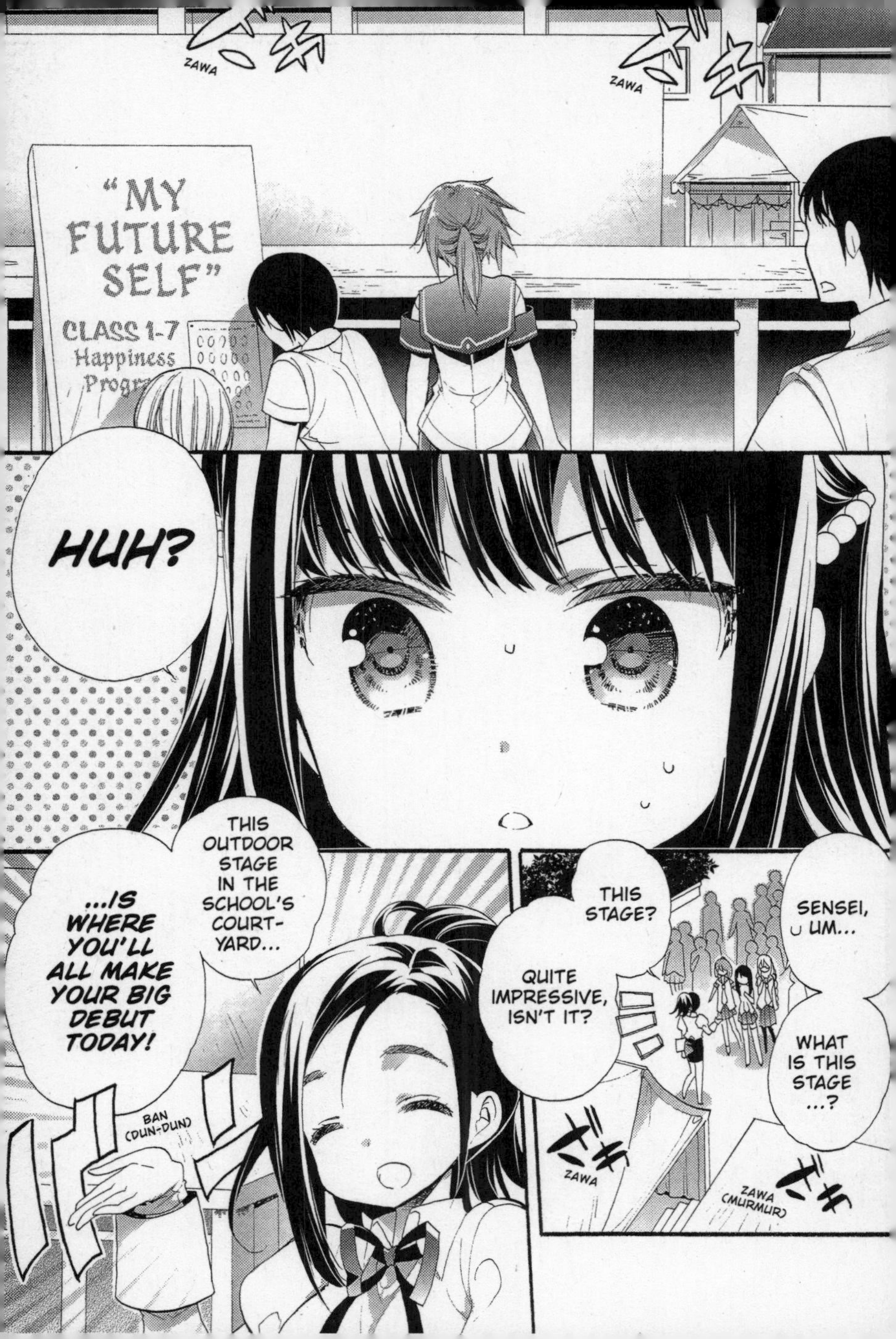
ZAWA
ZAWA
"MY FUTURE SELF"
CLASS 1-7
Happiness
Progra
HUH?
SENSEI, UM...
WHAT IS THIS STAGE ...?
THIS STAGE?
QUITE IMPRESSIVE, ISN'T IT?
ZAWA (MURMUR)
ZAWA
THIS OUTDOOR STAGE IN THE SCHOOL'S COURT-YARD...
...IS WHERE YOU'LL ALL MAKE YOUR BIG DEBUT TODAY!
BAN (DUN-DUN)

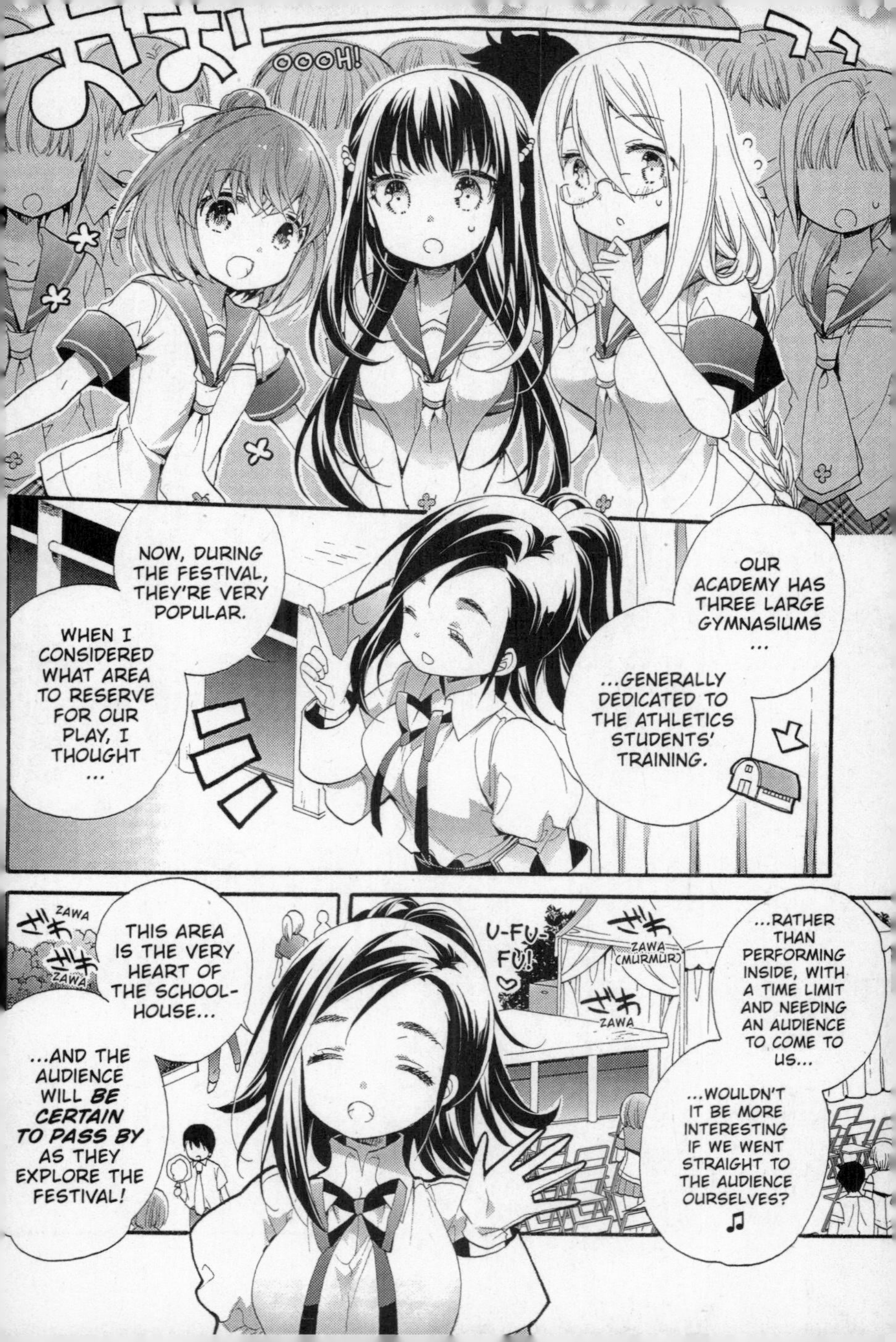
おおお——っっ
OOOH!
OUR ACADEMY HAS THREE LARGE GYMNASIUMS ...
...GENERALLY DEDICATED TO THE ATHLETICS STUDENTS' TRAINING.
NOW, DURING THE FESTIVAL, THEY'RE VERY POPULAR.
WHEN I CONSIDERED WHAT AREA TO RESERVE FOR OUR PLAY, I THOUGHT ...
...RATHER THAN PERFORMING INSIDE, WITH A TIME LIMIT AND NEEDING AN AUDIENCE TO COME TO US...
...WOULDN'T IT BE MORE INTERESTING IF WE WENT STRAIGHT TO THE AUDIENCE OURSELVES? ♫
ざわ
ZAWA (MURMUR)
U-FU-FU! ♡
ざわ
ZAWA
ざわ
ZAWA
ざわ
ZAWA
THIS AREA IS THE VERY HEART OF THE SCHOOL-HOUSE...
...AND THE AUDIENCE WILL *BE CERTAIN TO PASS BY* AS THEY EXPLORE THE FESTIVAL!

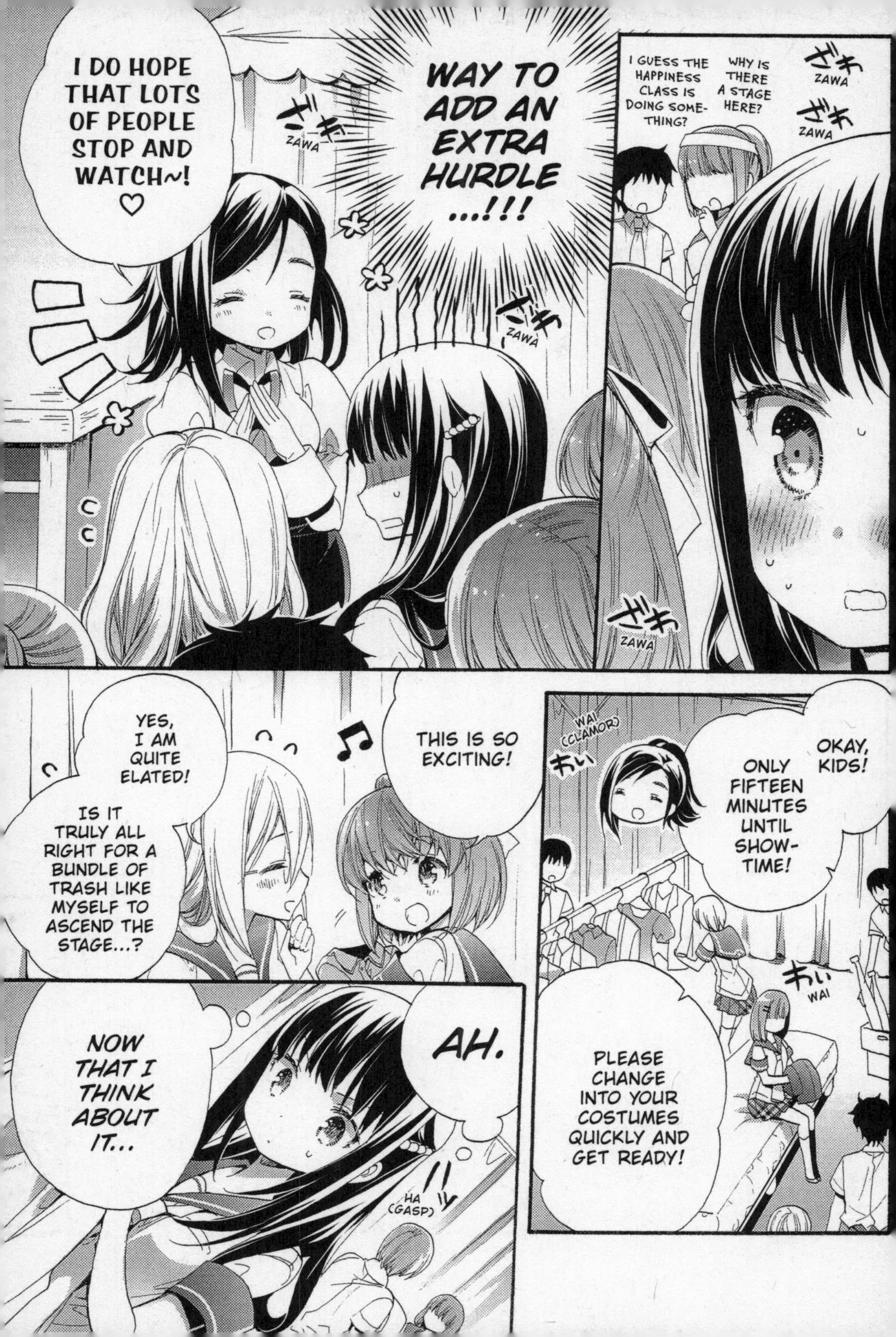
ZAWA
ZAWA
WHY IS THERE A STAGE HERE?
I GUESS THE HAPPINESS CLASS IS DOING SOME-THING?
ZAWA
WAY TO ADD AN EXTRA HURDLE ...!!!
ZAWA
ZAWA
I DO HOPE THAT LOTS OF PEOPLE STOP AND WATCH~! ♡
OKAY, KIDS! ONLY FIFTEEN MINUTES UNTIL SHOW-TIME!
WAI (CLAMOR)
WAI
PLEASE CHANGE INTO YOUR COSTUMES QUICKLY AND GET READY!
THIS IS SO EXCITING!
YES, I AM QUITE ELATED!
IS IT TRULY ALL RIGHT FOR A BUNDLE OF TRASH LIKE MYSELF TO ASCEND THE STAGE...?
AH.
HA (GASP)
NOW THAT I THINK ABOUT IT...

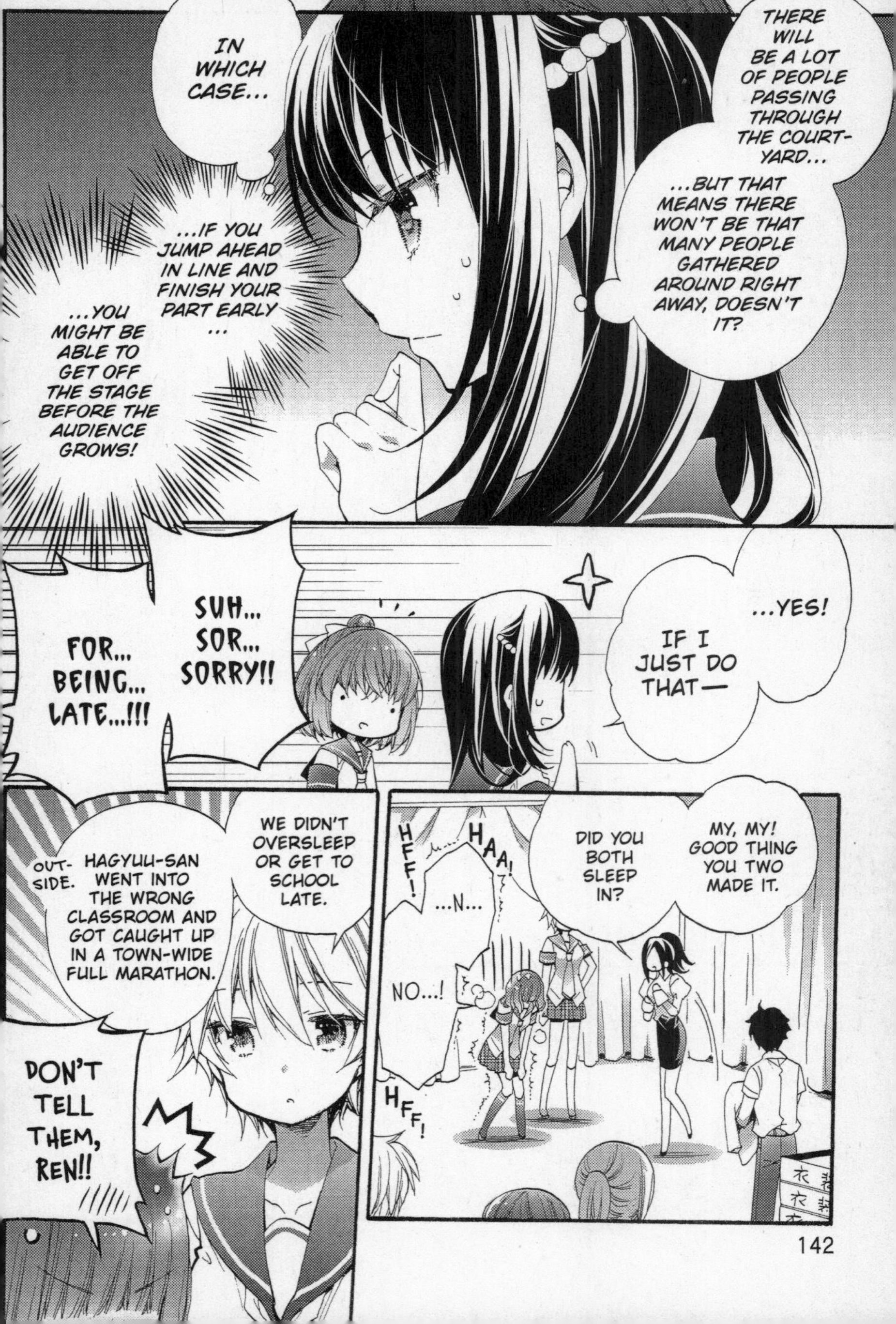
THERE WILL BE A LOT OF PEOPLE PASSING THROUGH THE COURT-YARD...
...BUT THAT MEANS THERE WON'T BE THAT MANY PEOPLE GATHERED AROUND RIGHT AWAY, DOESN'T IT?
IN WHICH CASE...
...IF YOU JUMP AHEAD IN LINE AND FINISH YOUR PART EARLY ...
...YOU MIGHT BE ABLE TO GET OFF THE STAGE BEFORE THE AUDIENCE GROWS!
...YES!
IF I JUST DO THAT—
SUH... SOR... SORRY!!
FOR... BEING... LATE...!!!
MY, MY! GOOD THING YOU TWO MADE IT.
DID YOU BOTH SLEEP IN?
HAA!
HFF!
...N...
NO...!
HFF!
WE DIDN'T OVERSLEEP OR GET TO SCHOOL LATE.
HAGYUU-SAN WENT INTO THE WRONG CLASSROOM AND GOT CAUGHT UP IN A TOWN-WIDE FULL MARATHON.
OUT-SIDE.
DON'T TELL THEM, REN!!

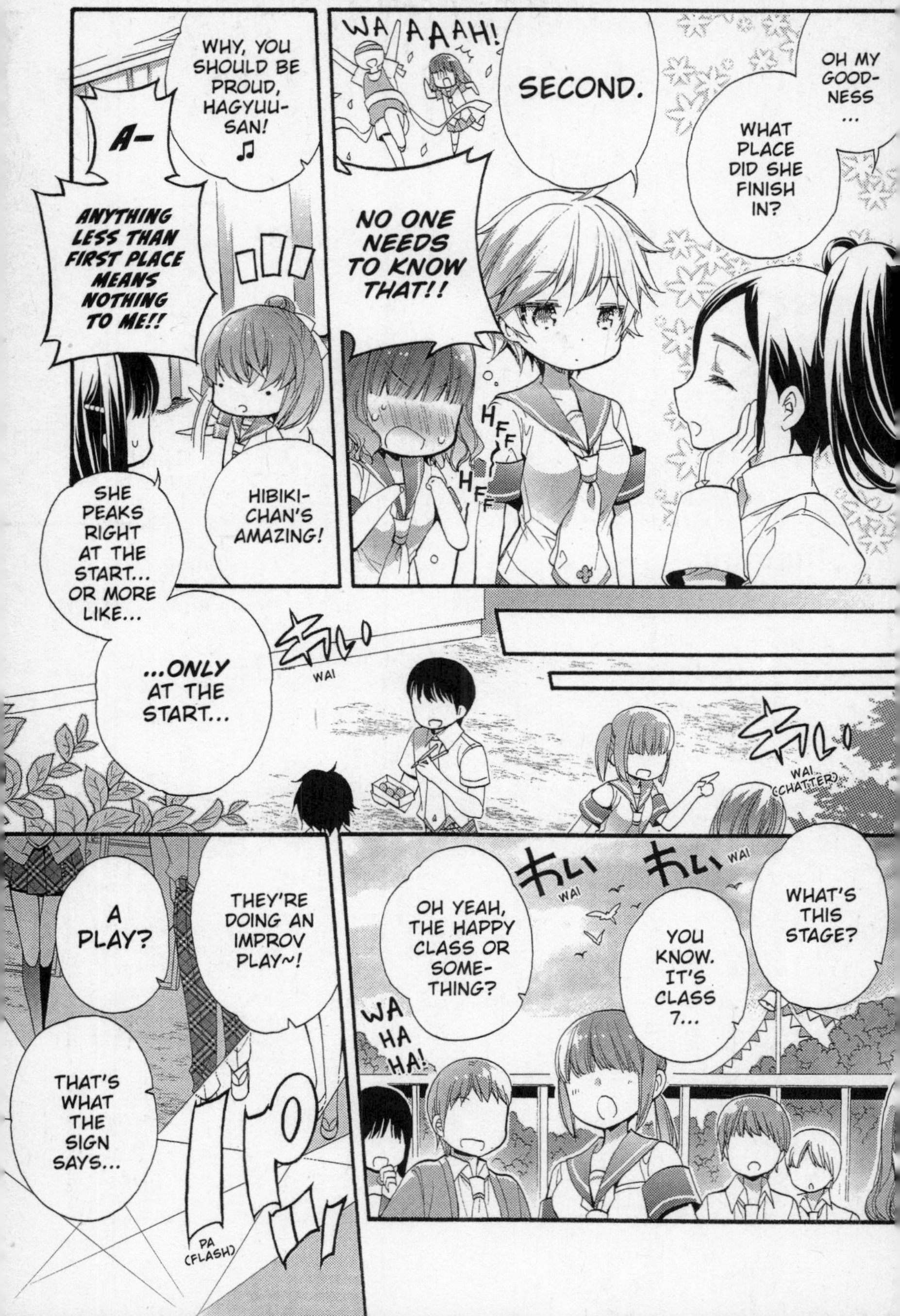
OH MY GOODNESS...
WHAT PLACE DID SHE FINISH IN?
SECOND.
WA AAAH!
NO ONE NEEDS TO KNOW THAT!!
HFF HFF
WHY, YOU SHOULD BE PROUD, HAGYUU-SAN! ♫
A-
ANYTHING LESS THAN FIRST PLACE MEANS NOTHING TO ME!!
HIBIKI-CHAN'S AMAZING!
SHE PEAKS RIGHT AT THE START... OR MORE LIKE...
...ONLY AT THE START...
WAI (CHATTER)
WAI
わい わい
WAI WAI
WHAT'S THIS STAGE?
YOU KNOW. IT'S CLASS 7...
OH YEAH, THE HAPPY CLASS OR SOMETHING?
WA HA HA!
THEY'RE DOING AN IMPROV PLAY~!
A PLAY?
THAT'S WHAT THE SIGN SAYS...
PA (FLASH)

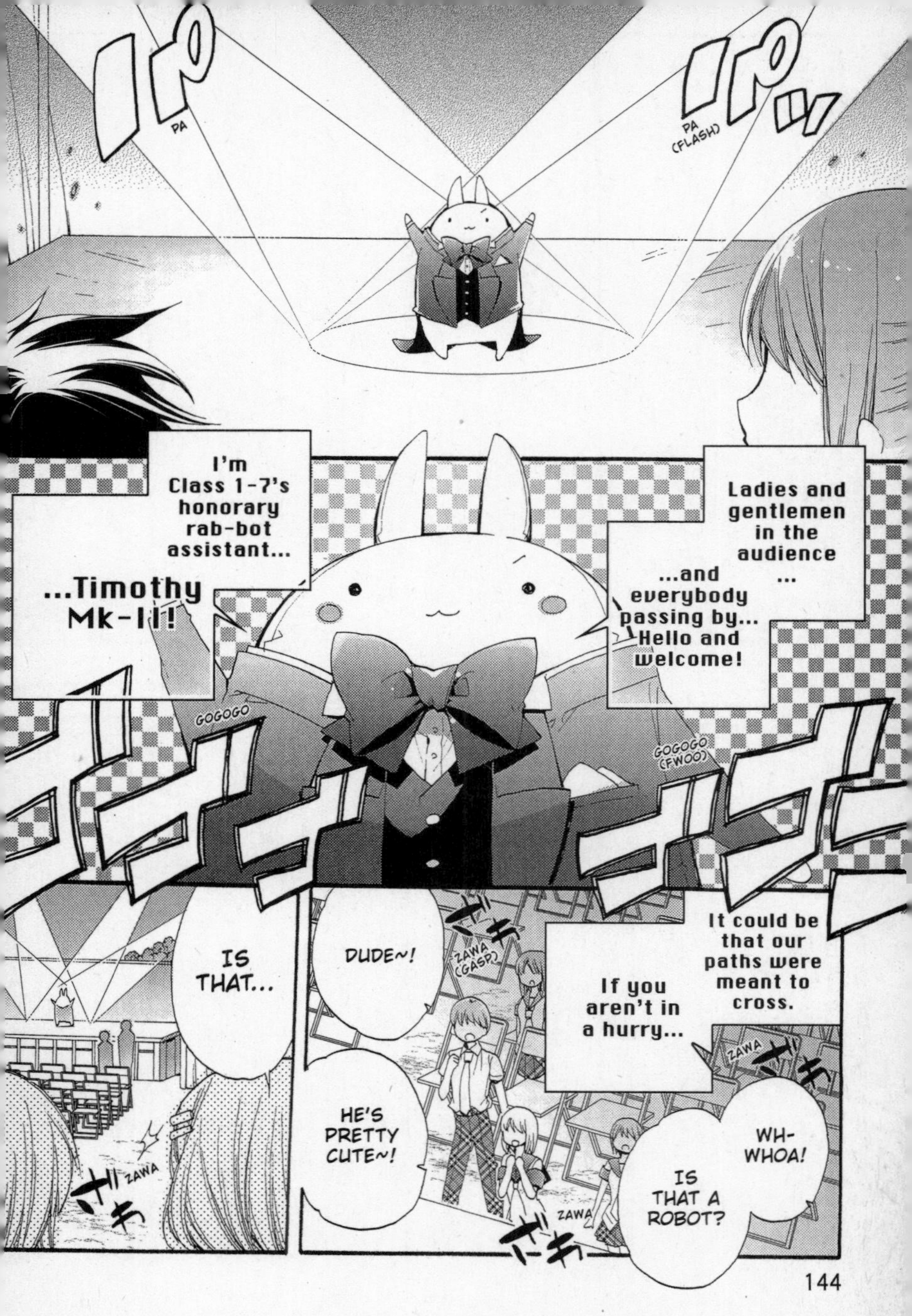
PA (FLASH)
PA
Ladies and gentlemen in the audience ...
...and everybody passing by... Hello and welcome!
I'm Class 1-7's honorary rab-bot assistant...
...Timothy Mk-II!
GOGOGO (FWOO)
GOGOGO
It could be that our paths were meant to cross.
If you aren't in a hurry...
ZAWA
WH-WHOA!
IS THAT A ROBOT?
ZAWA (GASP)
DUDE~!
HE'S PRETTY CUTE~!
ZAWA
IS THAT...
ZAWA

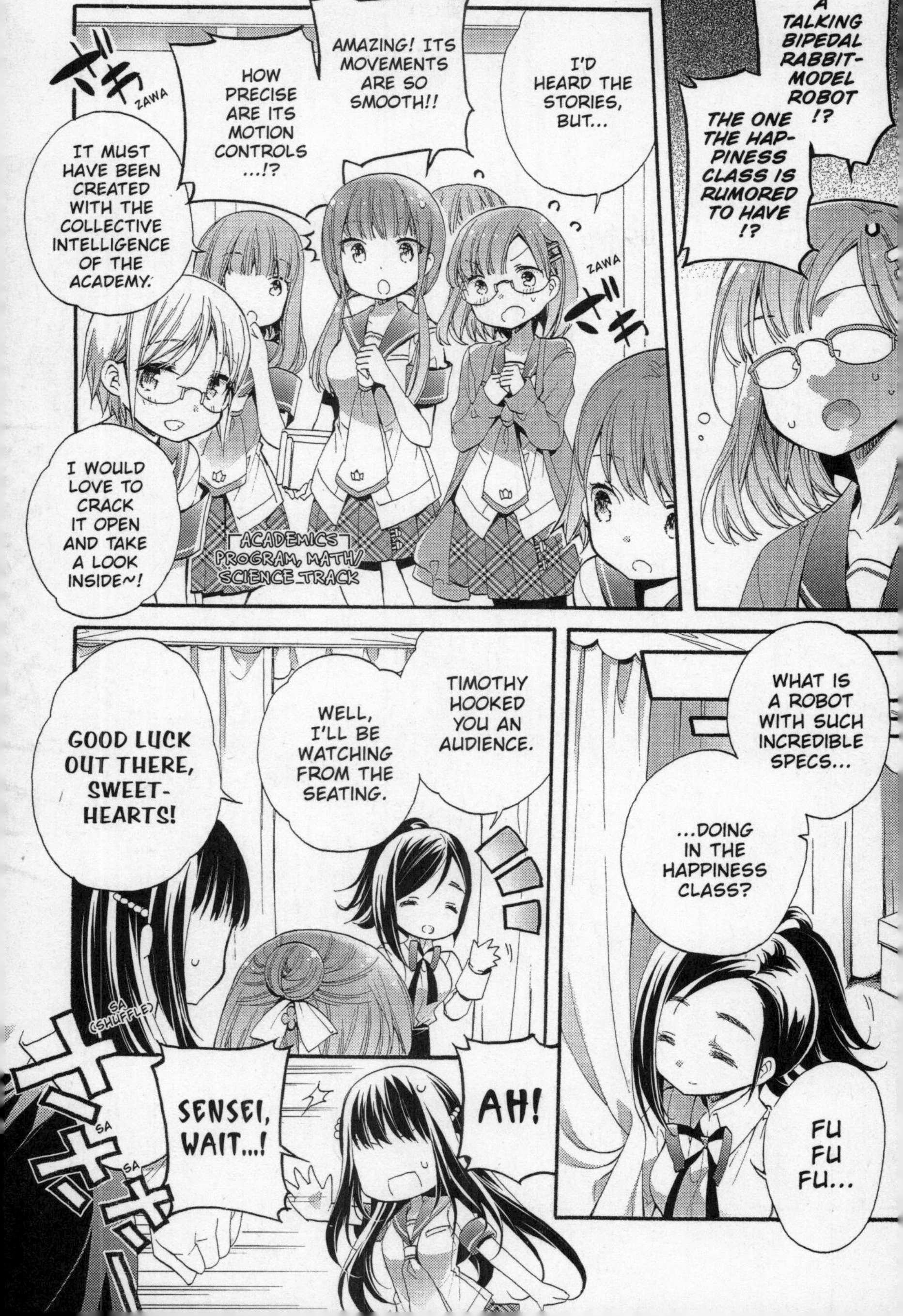
A TALKING BIPEDAL RABBIT-MODEL ROBOT!?
THE ONE THE HAPPINESS CLASS IS RUMORED TO HAVE!?
I'D HEARD THE STORIES, BUT...
AMAZING! ITS MOVEMENTS ARE SO SMOOTH!!
HOW PRECISE ARE ITS MOTION CONTROLS ...!?
ZAWA
ZAWA
IT MUST HAVE BEEN CREATED WITH THE COLLECTIVE INTELLIGENCE OF THE ACADEMY.
I WOULD LOVE TO CRACK IT OPEN AND TAKE A LOOK INSIDE~!
ACADEMICS PROGRAM, MATH/SCIENCE TRACK
WHAT IS A ROBOT WITH SUCH INCREDIBLE SPECS...
...DOING IN THE HAPPINESS CLASS?
FU FU FU...
TIMOTHY HOOKED YOU AN AUDIENCE.
WELL, I'LL BE WATCHING FROM THE SEATING.
GOOD LUCK OUT THERE, SWEETHEARTS!
AH!
SENSEI, WAIT...!
SA (SHUFFLE)
SA
SA

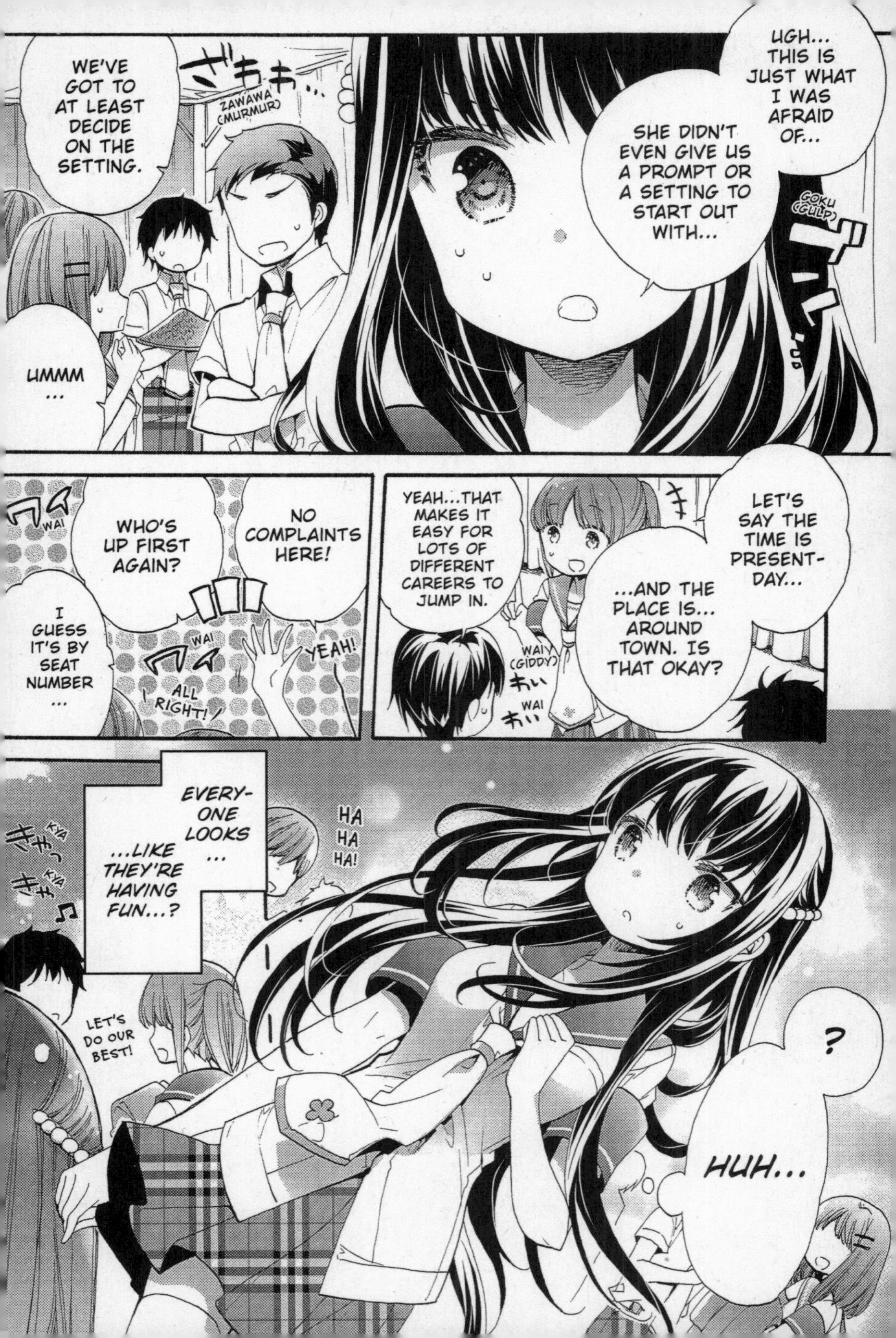
UGH... THIS IS JUST WHAT I WAS AFRAID OF...
SHE DIDN'T EVEN GIVE US A PROMPT OR A SETTING TO START OUT WITH...
GOKU (GULP)
ZAWAWA (MURMUR)
WE'VE GOT TO AT LEAST DECIDE ON THE SETTING.
UMMM...
LET'S SAY THE TIME IS PRESENT-DAY...
...AND THE PLACE IS... AROUND TOWN. IS THAT OKAY?
YEAH...THAT MAKES IT EASY FOR LOTS OF DIFFERENT CAREERS TO JUMP IN.
WAI (GIDDY)
WAI
NO COMPLAINTS HERE!
WHO'S UP FIRST AGAIN?
WAI
YEAH!
WAI
ALL RIGHT!
I GUESS IT'S BY SEAT NUMBER...
?
HUH...
HA HA HA!
EVERY-ONE LOOKS...
...LIKE THEY'RE HAVING FUN...?
KYA KYA
LET'S DO OUR BEST!

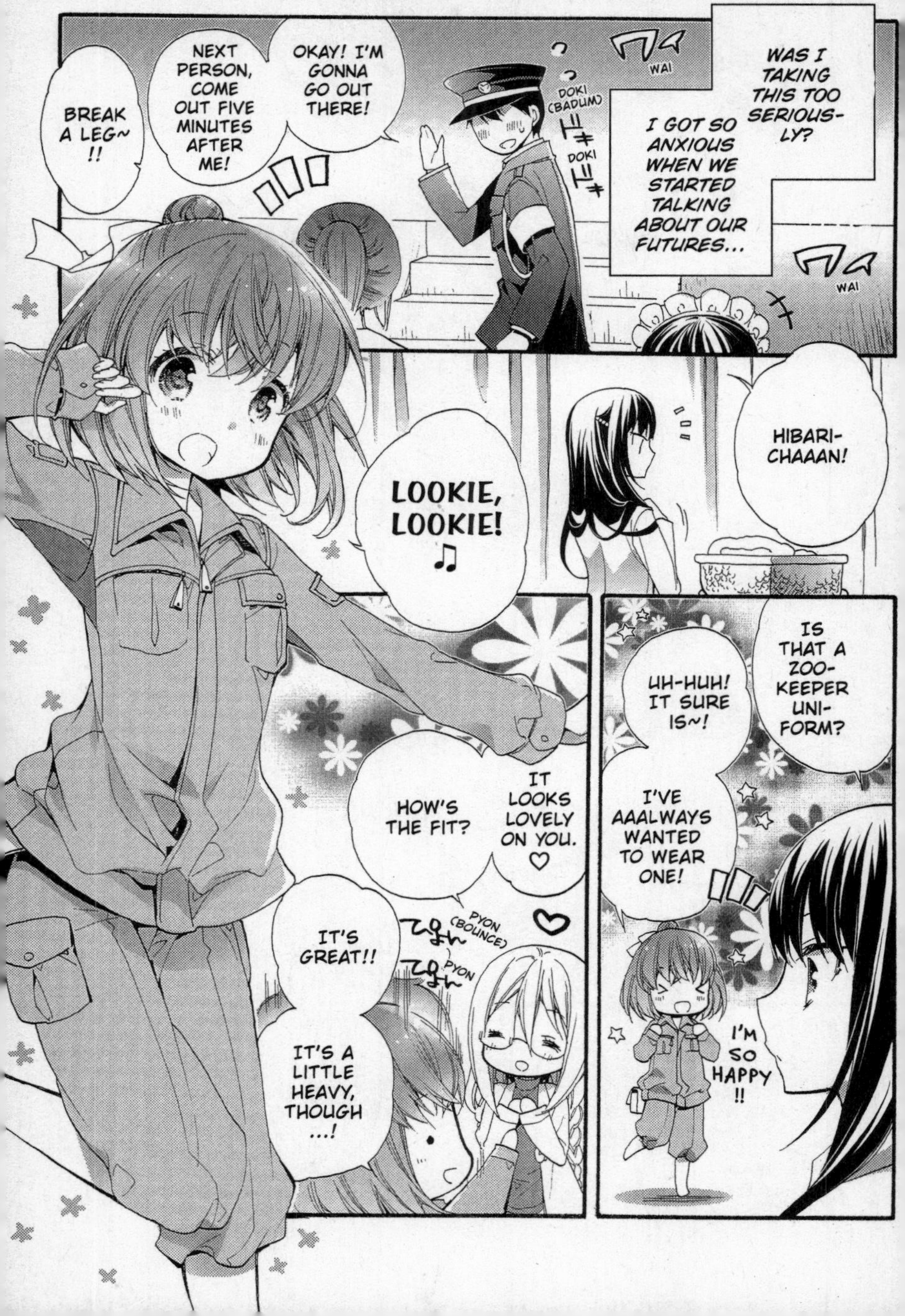
WAS I TAKING THIS TOO SERIOUSLY?
I GOT SO ANXIOUS WHEN WE STARTED TALKING ABOUT OUR FUTURES...
WAI
WAI
DOKI (BADUM)
DOKI
OKAY! I'M GONNA GO OUT THERE!
NEXT PERSON, COME OUT FIVE MINUTES AFTER ME!
BREAK A LEG~ !!
HIBARI-CHAAAN!
LOOKIE, LOOKIE! ♫
IS THAT A ZOO-KEEPER UNI-FORM?
UH-HUH! IT SURE IS~!
I'VE AAALWAYS WANTED TO WEAR ONE!
I'M SO HAPPY !!
IT LOOKS LOVELY ON YOU. ♡
HOW'S THE FIT?
PYON (BOUNCE)
PYON
IT'S GREAT!!
IT'S A LITTLE HEAVY, THOUGH ...!

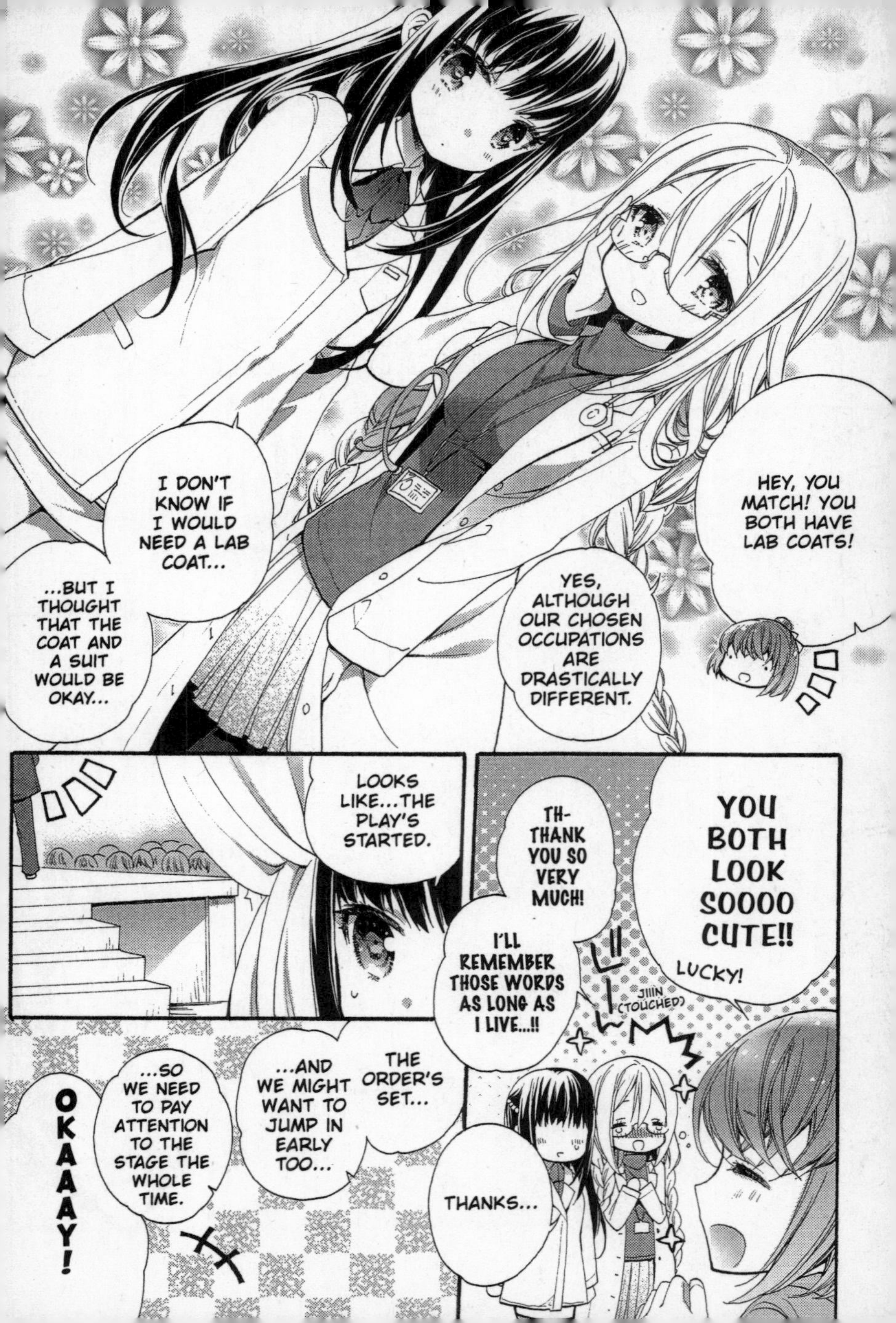
HEY, YOU MATCH! YOU BOTH HAVE LAB COATS!
YES, ALTHOUGH OUR CHOSEN OCCUPATIONS ARE DRASTICALLY DIFFERENT.
I DON'T KNOW IF I WOULD NEED A LAB COAT...
...BUT I THOUGHT THAT THE COAT AND A SUIT WOULD BE OKAY...
YOU BOTH LOOK SOOOO CUTE!!
LUCKY!
TH-THANK YOU SO VERY MUCH!
I'LL REMEMBER THOSE WORDS AS LONG AS I LIVE...!!
JIIIN (TOUCHED)
THANKS...
LOOKS LIKE...THE PLAY'S STARTED.
THE ORDER'S SET...
...AND WE MIGHT WANT TO JUMP IN EARLY TOO...
...SO WE NEED TO PAY ATTENTION TO THE STAGE THE WHOLE TIME.
OKAAAY!

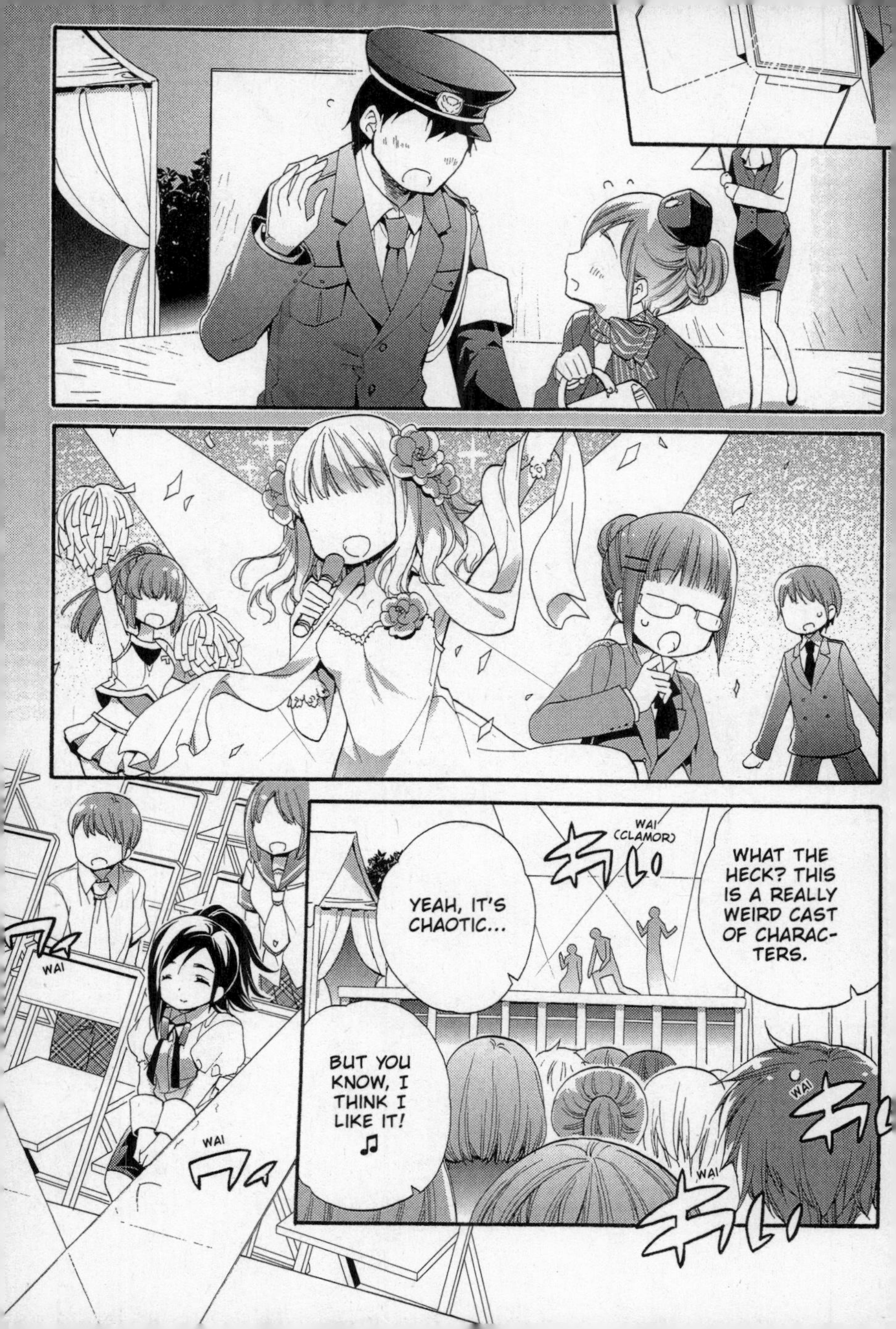
WHAT THE HECK? THIS IS A REALLY WEIRD CAST OF CHARAC-TERS.
WAI (CLAMOR)
YEAH, IT'S CHAOTIC...
WAI
BUT YOU KNOW, I THINK I LIKE IT! ♫
WAI
WAI
WAI

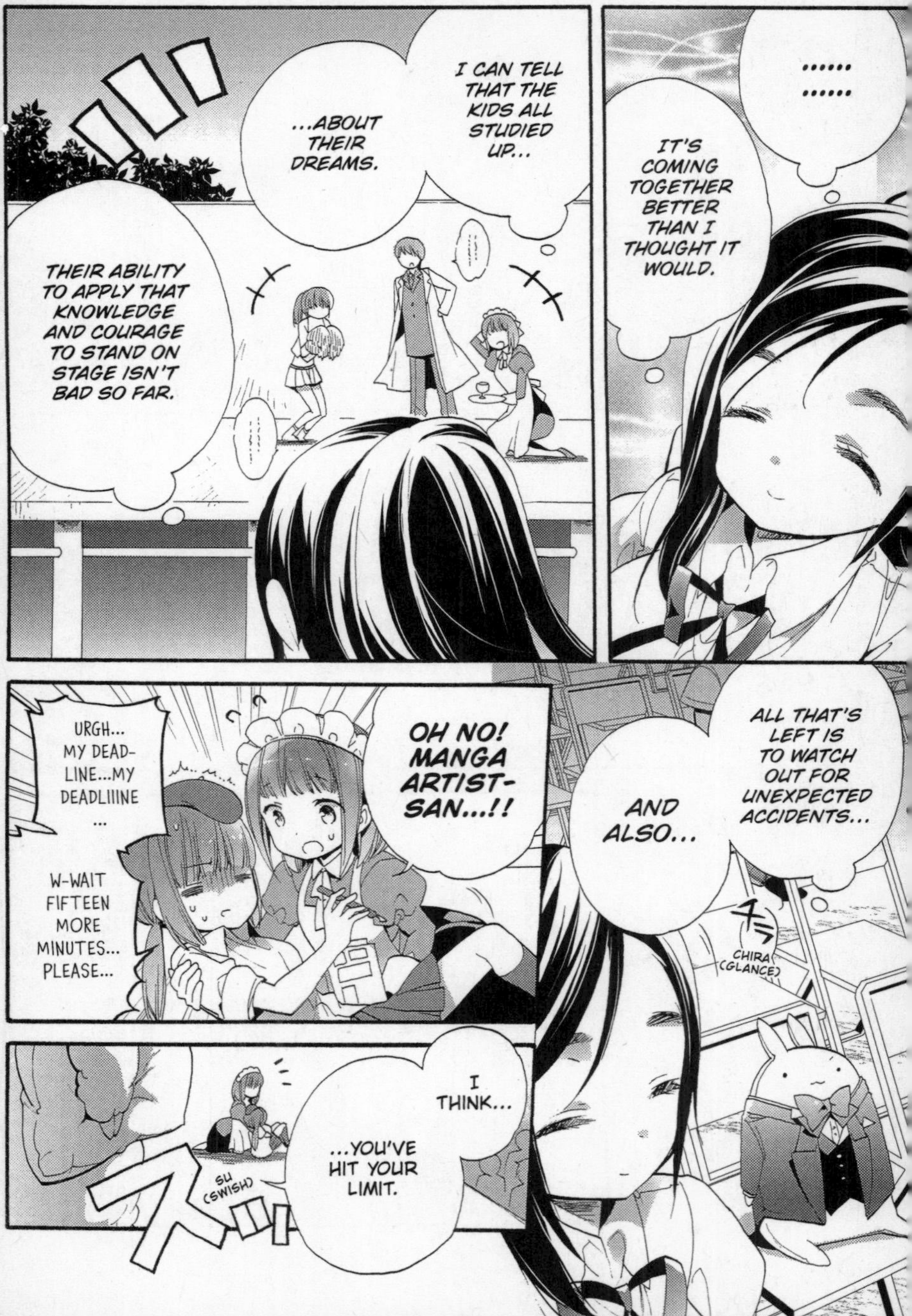
......
......
IT'S COMING TOGETHER BETTER THAN I THOUGHT IT WOULD.
I CAN TELL THAT THE KIDS ALL STUDIED UP...
...ABOUT THEIR DREAMS.
THEIR ABILITY TO APPLY THAT KNOWLEDGE AND COURAGE TO STAND ON STAGE ISN'T BAD SO FAR.
ALL THAT'S LEFT IS TO WATCH OUT FOR UNEXPECTED ACCIDENTS...
AND ALSO...
CHIRA (GLANCE)
OH NO! MANGA ARTIST-SAN...!!
URGH... MY DEAD-LINE...MY DEADLIIINE ...
W-WAIT FIFTEEN MORE MINUTES... PLEASE...
I THINK...
...YOU'VE HIT YOUR LIMIT.
SU (SWISH)

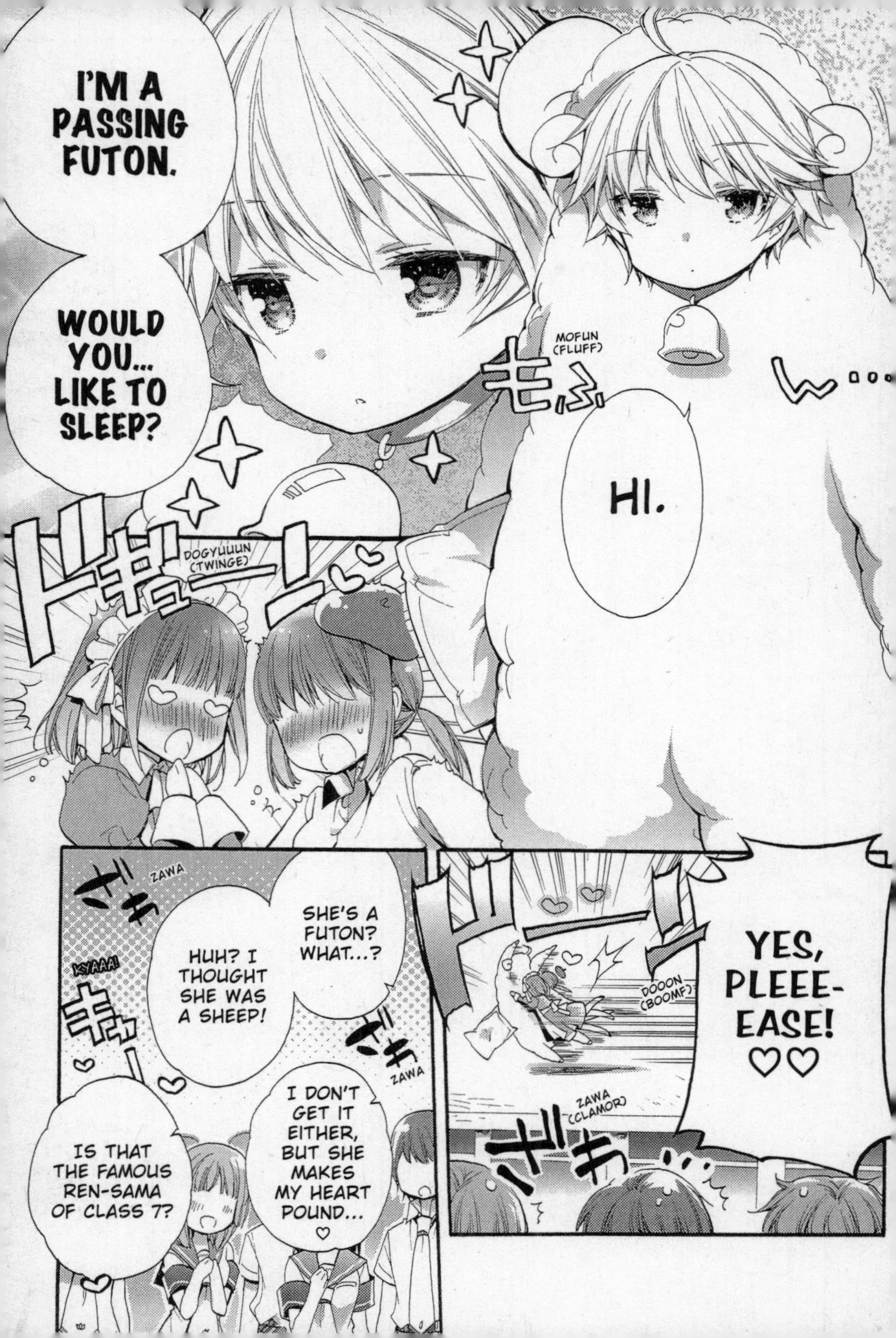
MOFUN (FLUFF)
HI.
I'M A PASSING FUTON.
WOULD YOU... LIKE TO SLEEP?
DOGYUUUN (TWINGE)
YES, PLEEE-EASE! ♡♡
DOOON (BOOMF)
ZAWA (CLAMOR)
ZAWA
SHE'S A FUTON? WHAT...?
HUH? I THOUGHT SHE WAS A SHEEP!
KYAAA!
ZAWA
I DON'T GET IT EITHER, BUT SHE MAKES MY HEART POUND... ♡
IS THAT THE FAMOUS REN-SAMA OF CLASS 7?

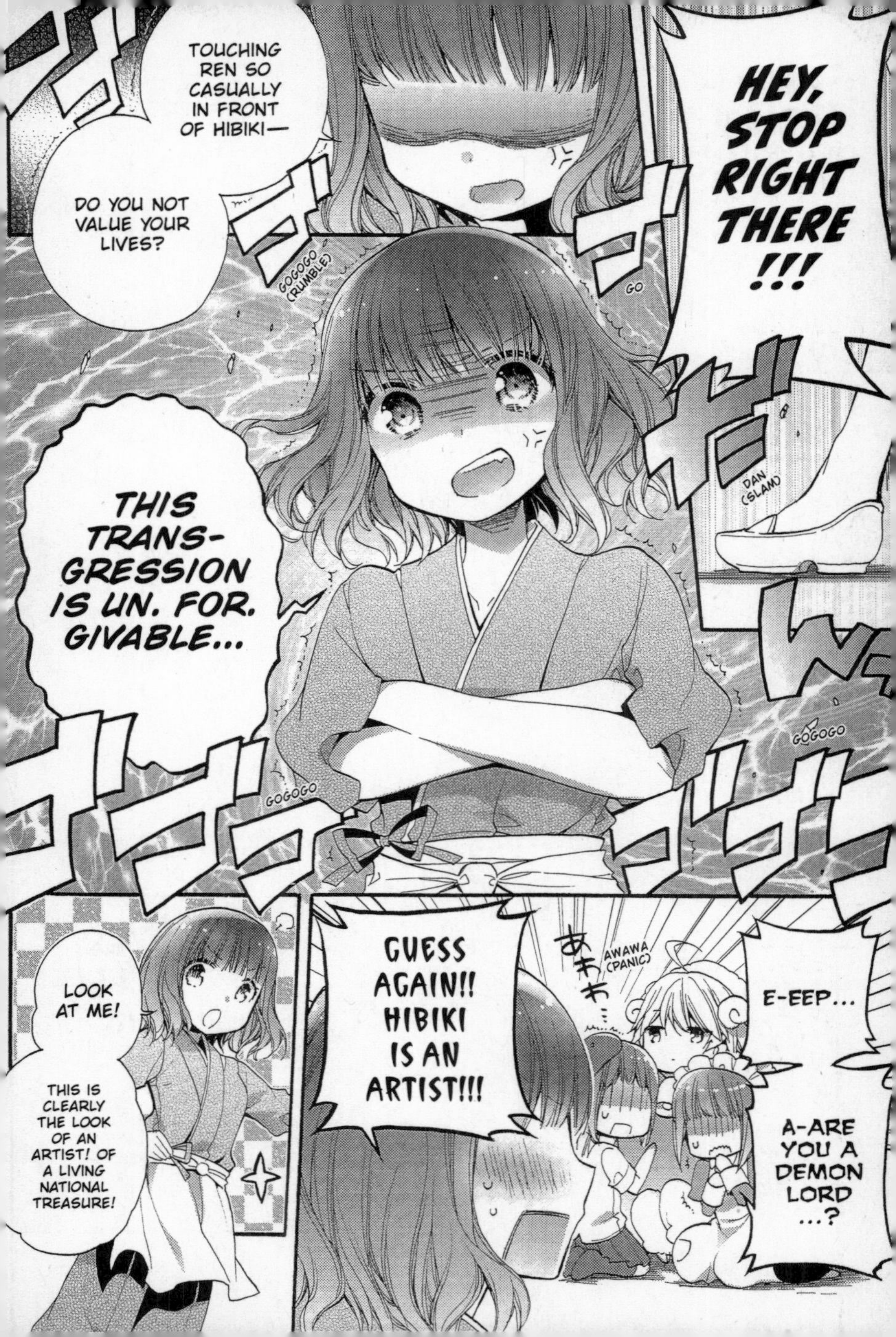
HEY, STOP RIGHT THERE!!!
TOUCHING REN SO CASUALLY IN FRONT OF HIBIKI—
DO YOU NOT VALUE YOUR LIVES?
GOGOGO (RUMBLE)
GO
DAN (SLAM)
THIS TRANS-GRESSION IS UN. FOR. GIVABLE...
GOGOGO
GOGOGO
E-EEP...
A-ARE YOU A DEMON LORD ...?
あわわ
AWAWA (PANIC)
GUESS AGAIN!! HIBIKI IS AN ARTIST!!!
LOOK AT ME!
THIS IS CLEARLY THE LOOK OF AN ARTIST! OF A LIVING NATIONAL TREASURE!

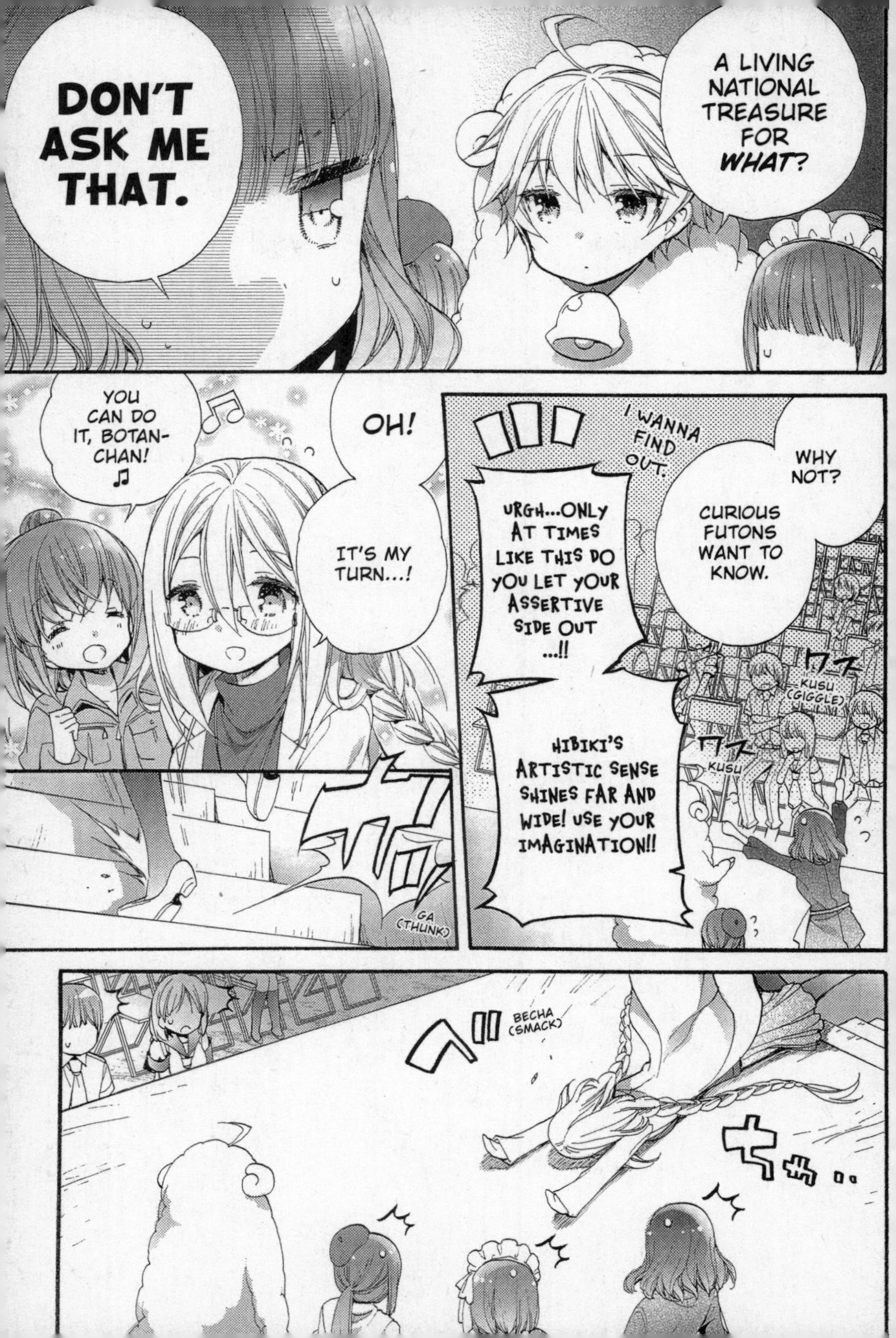
A LIVING NATIONAL TREASURE FOR *WHAT*?
DON'T ASK ME THAT.
WHY NOT?
CURIOUS FUTONS WANT TO KNOW.
I WANNA FIND OUT.
URGH...ONLY AT TIMES LIKE THIS DO YOU LET YOUR ASSERTIVE SIDE OUT ...!!
HIBIKI'S ARTISTIC SENSE SHINES FAR AND WIDE! USE YOUR IMAGINATION!!
KUSU (GIGGLE)
KUSU
OH!
IT'S MY TURN...!
YOU CAN DO IT, BOTAN-CHAN! ♫
GA (THUNK)
BECHA (SMACK)

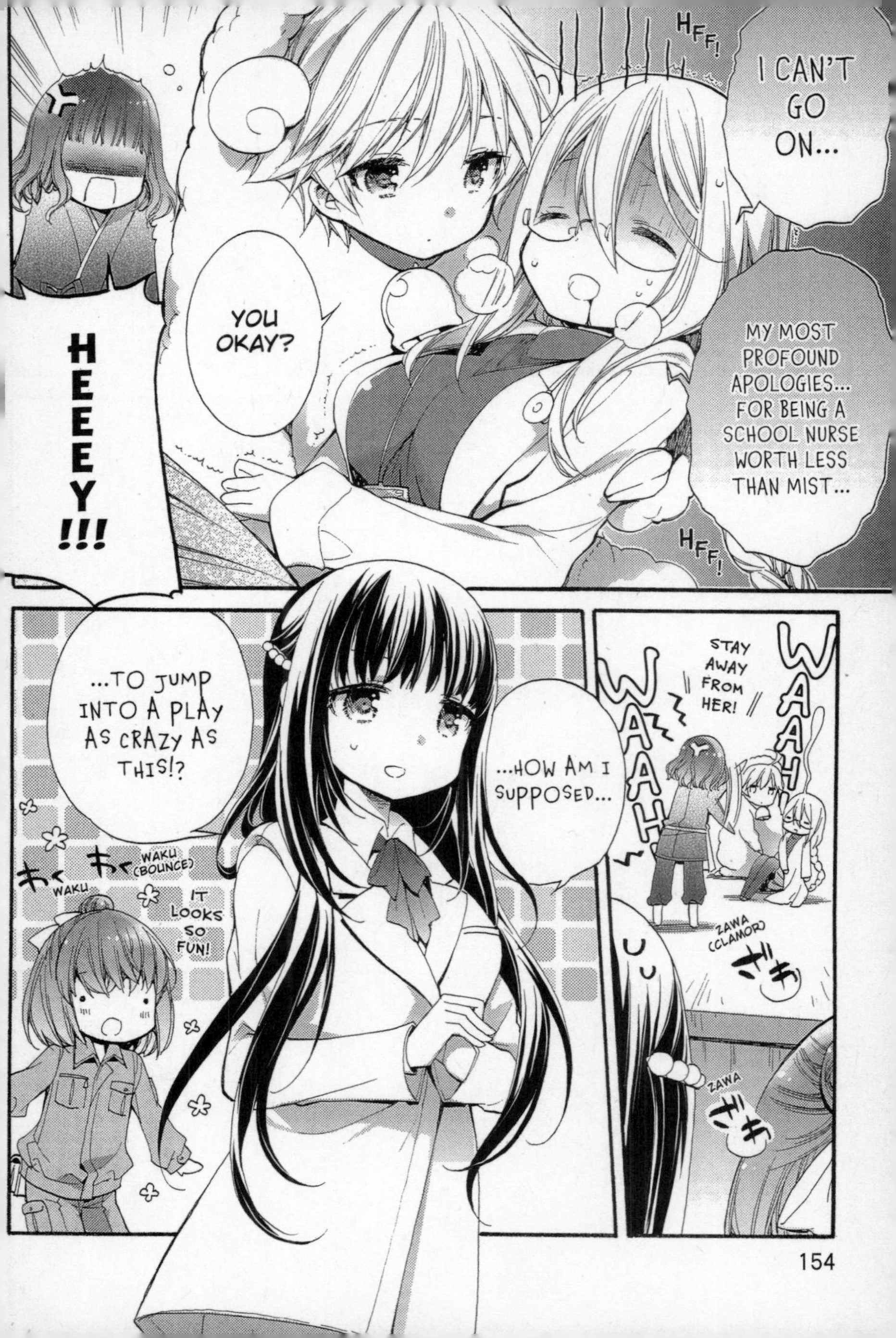
HFF!
I CAN'T GO ON...
MY MOST PROFOUND APOLOGIES... FOR BEING A SCHOOL NURSE WORTH LESS THAN MIST...
HFF!
YOU OKAY?
HEEEY!!!
WAAH!
STAY AWAY FROM HER!
WAAAH!
ZAWA (CLAMOR)
ZAWA
...HOW AM I SUPPOSED...
...TO JUMP INTO A PLAY AS CRAZY AS THIS!?
WAKU (BOUNCE)
WAKU
IT LOOKS SO FUN!

Anne Happy

unhappy go lucky!

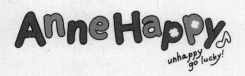

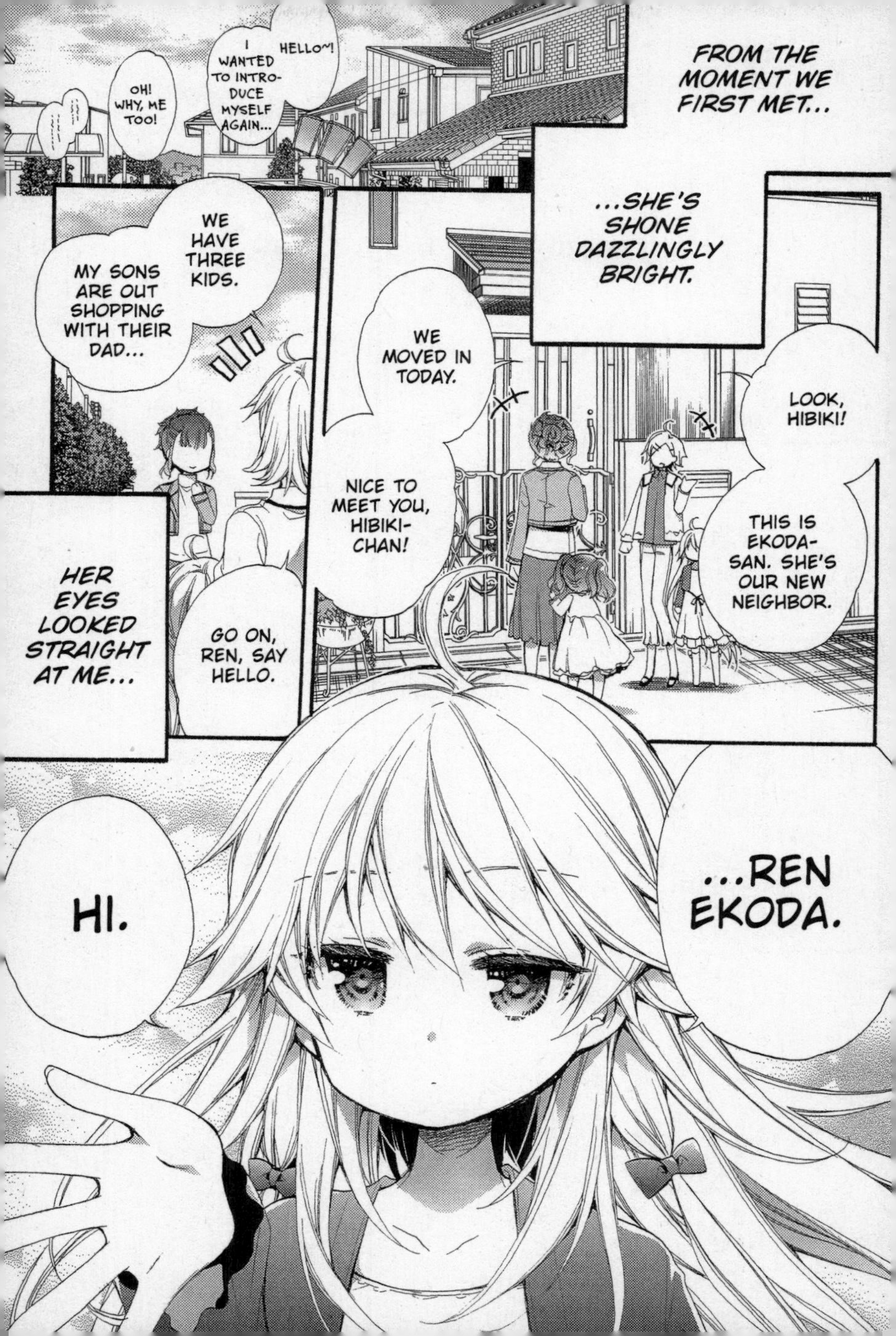
FROM THE MOMENT WE FIRST MET...
HELLO~!
I WANTED TO INTRO-DUCE MYSELF AGAIN...
OH! WHY, ME TOO!
...SHE'S SHONE DAZZLINGLY BRIGHT.
LOOK, HIBIKI!
THIS IS EKODA-SAN. SHE'S OUR NEW NEIGHBOR.
WE MOVED IN TODAY.
NICE TO MEET YOU, HIBIKI-CHAN!
WE HAVE THREE KIDS.
MY SONS ARE OUT SHOPPING WITH THEIR DAD...
GO ON, REN, SAY HELLO.
HER EYES LOOKED STRAIGHT AT ME...
...REN EKODA.
HI.

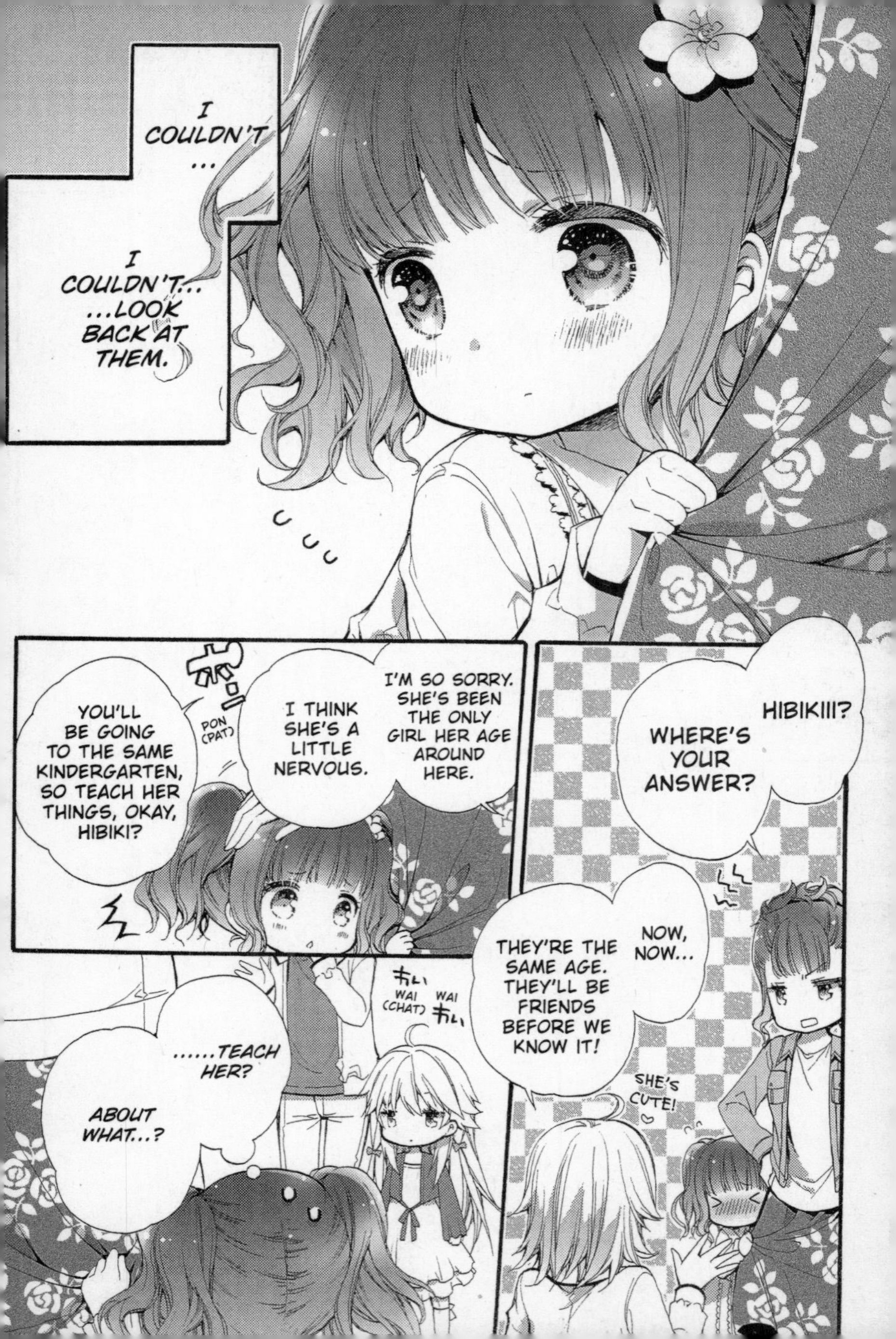
I COULDN'T ...
I COULDN'T... ...LOOK BACK AT THEM.
HIBIKIII?
WHERE'S YOUR ANSWER?
NOW, NOW...
THEY'RE THE SAME AGE. THEY'LL BE FRIENDS BEFORE WE KNOW IT!
SHE'S CUTE!
I'M SO SORRY. SHE'S BEEN THE ONLY GIRL HER AGE AROUND HERE.
I THINK SHE'S A LITTLE NERVOUS.
PON (PAT)
YOU'LL BE GOING TO THE SAME KINDERGARTEN, SO TEACH HER THINGS, OKAY, HIBIKI?
WAI WAI (CHAT)
......TEACH HER?
ABOUT WHAT...?

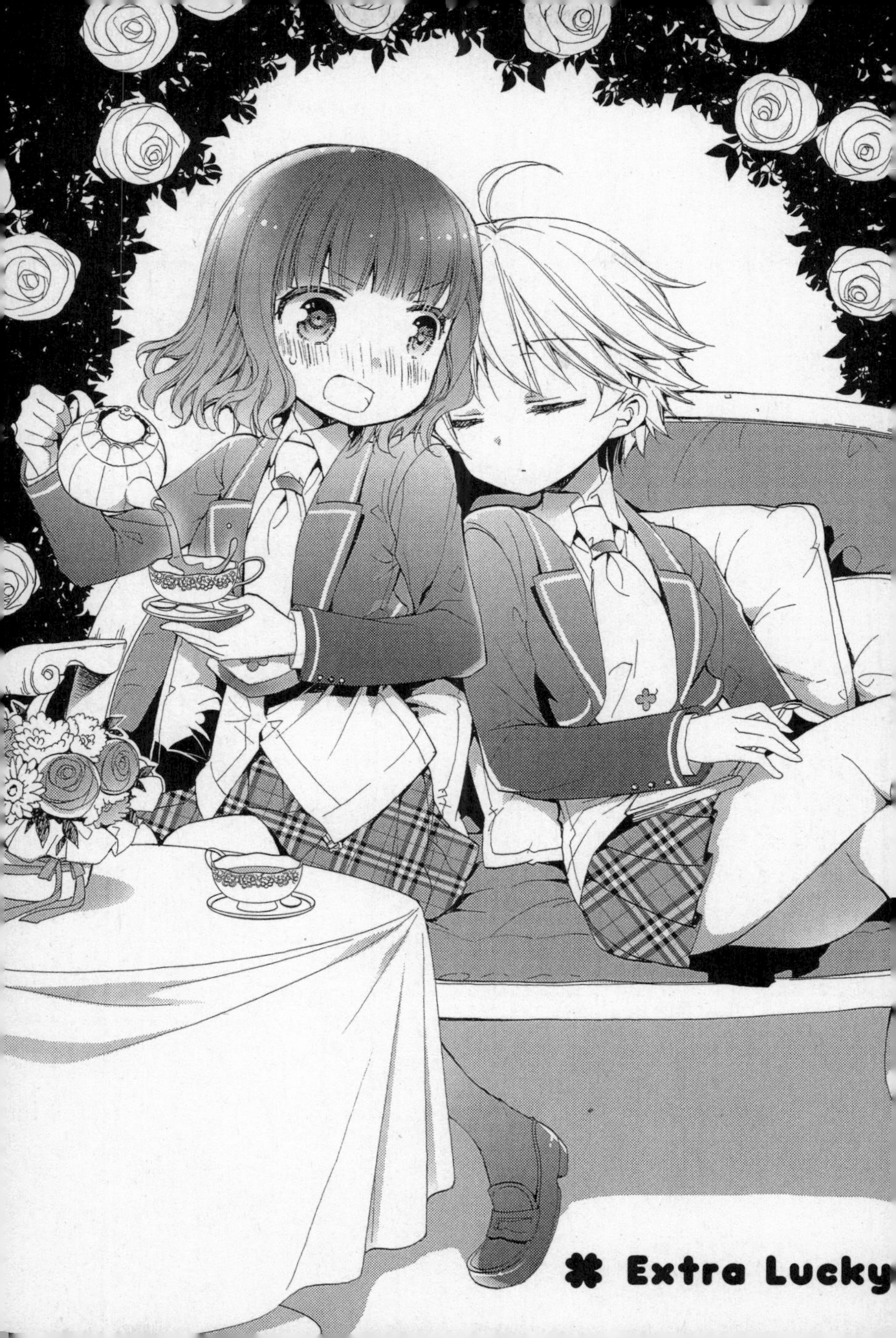
✤ Extra Lucky

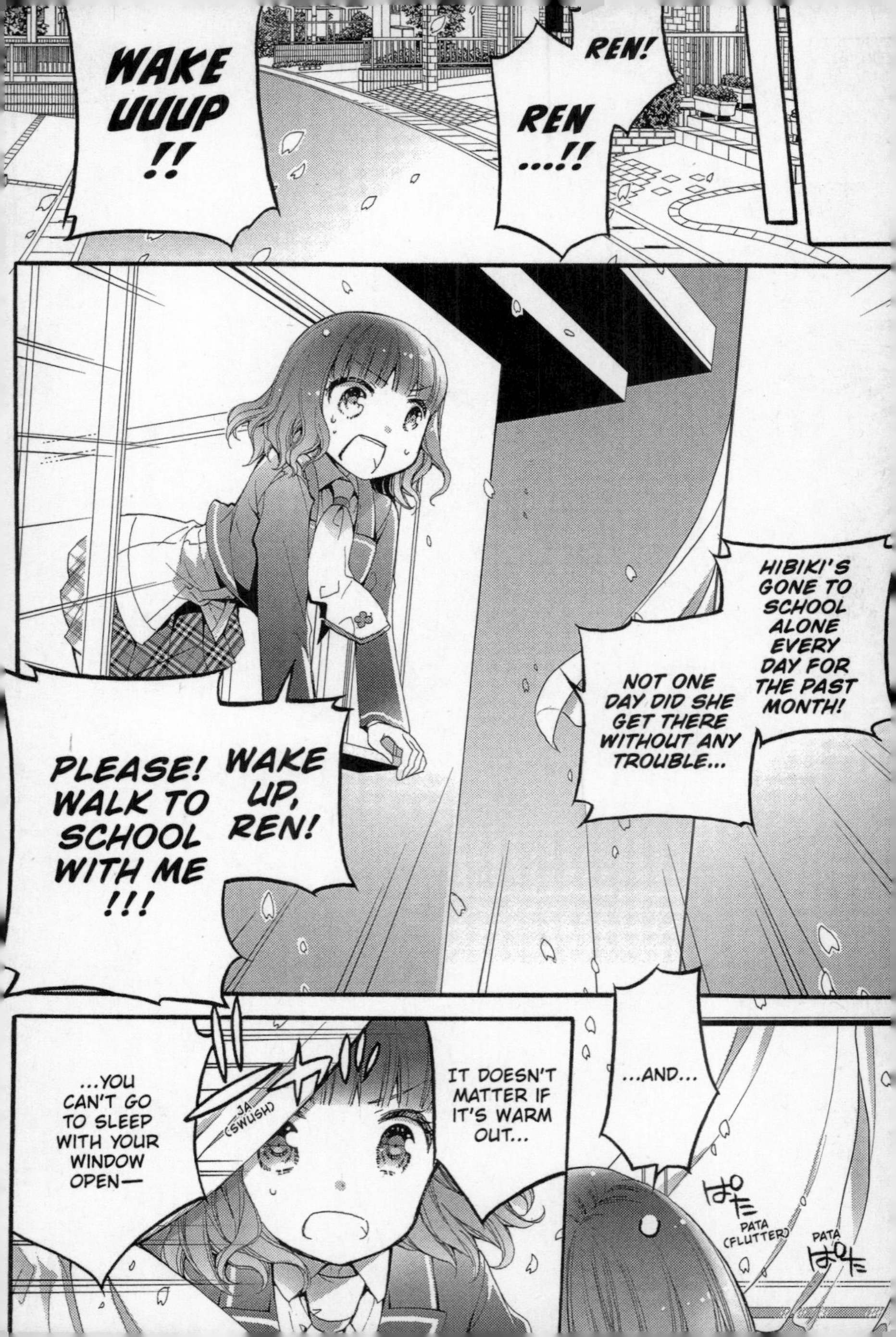
REN! REN...!!
WAKE UUUP!!
HIBIKI'S GONE TO SCHOOL ALONE EVERY DAY FOR THE PAST MONTH!
NOT ONE DAY DID SHE GET THERE WITHOUT ANY TROUBLE...
WAKE UP, REN!
PLEASE! WALK TO SCHOOL WITH ME!!!
...AND...
ぱた PATA (FLUTTER)
PATA ぱた
IT DOESN'T MATTER IF IT'S WARM OUT...
JA (SWUSH)
...YOU CAN'T GO TO SLEEP WITH YOUR WINDOW OPEN—

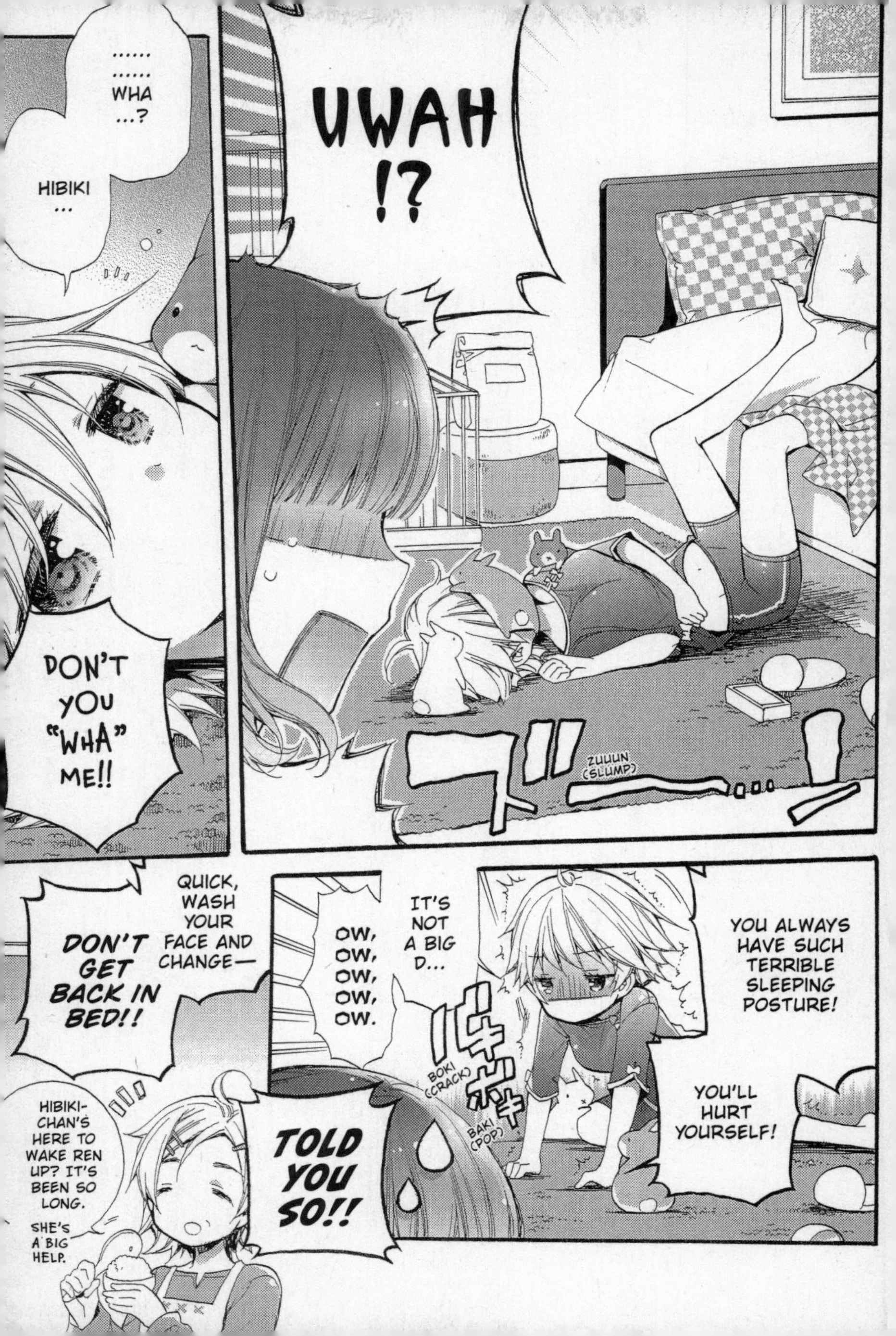
UWAH !?
ZUUUN (SLUMP)
.... WHA ...?
HIBIKI ...
DON'T YOU "WHA" ME!!
YOU ALWAYS HAVE SUCH TERRIBLE SLEEPING POSTURE!
YOU'LL HURT YOURSELF!
IT'S NOT A BIG D...
BOKI (CRACK)
BAKI (POP)
OW, OW, OW, OW, OW.
TOLD YOU SO!!
QUICK, WASH YOUR FACE AND CHANGE—
DON'T GET BACK IN BED!!
HIBIKI-CHAN'S HERE TO WAKE REN UP? IT'S BEEN SO LONG.
SHE'S A BIG HELP.

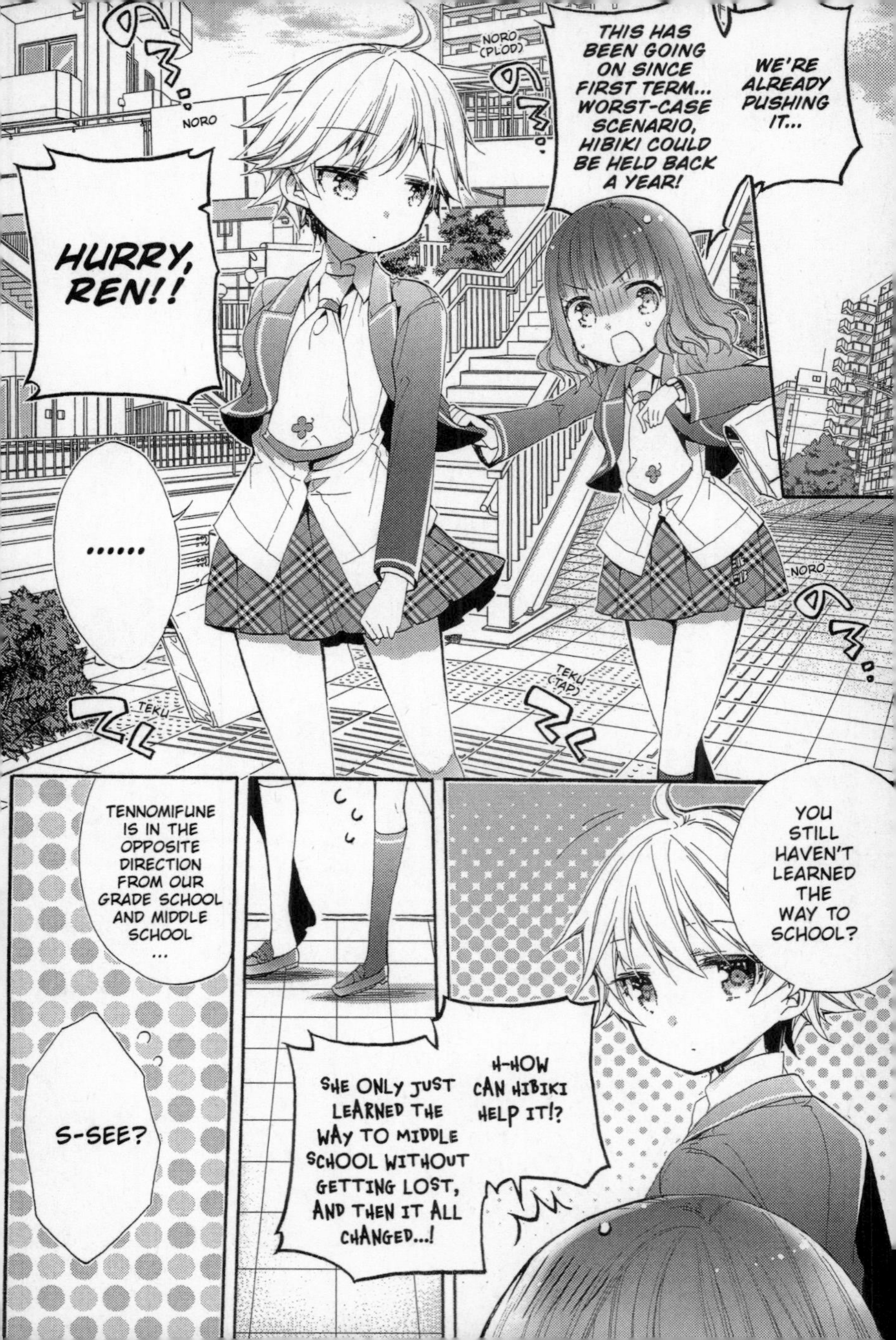
WE'RE ALREADY PUSHING IT...
THIS HAS BEEN GOING ON SINCE FIRST TERM... WORST-CASE SCENARIO, HIBIKI COULD BE HELD BACK A YEAR!
NORO (PLOD)
NORO
HURRY, REN!!
......
NORO
TEKU (TAP)
TEKU
YOU STILL HAVEN'T LEARNED THE WAY TO SCHOOL?
H-HOW CAN HIBIKI HELP IT!?
SHE ONLY JUST LEARNED THE WAY TO MIDDLE SCHOOL WITHOUT GETTING LOST, AND THEN IT ALL CHANGED...!
TENNOMIFUNE IS IN THE OPPOSITE DIRECTION FROM OUR GRADE SCHOOL AND MIDDLE SCHOOL...
S-SEE?

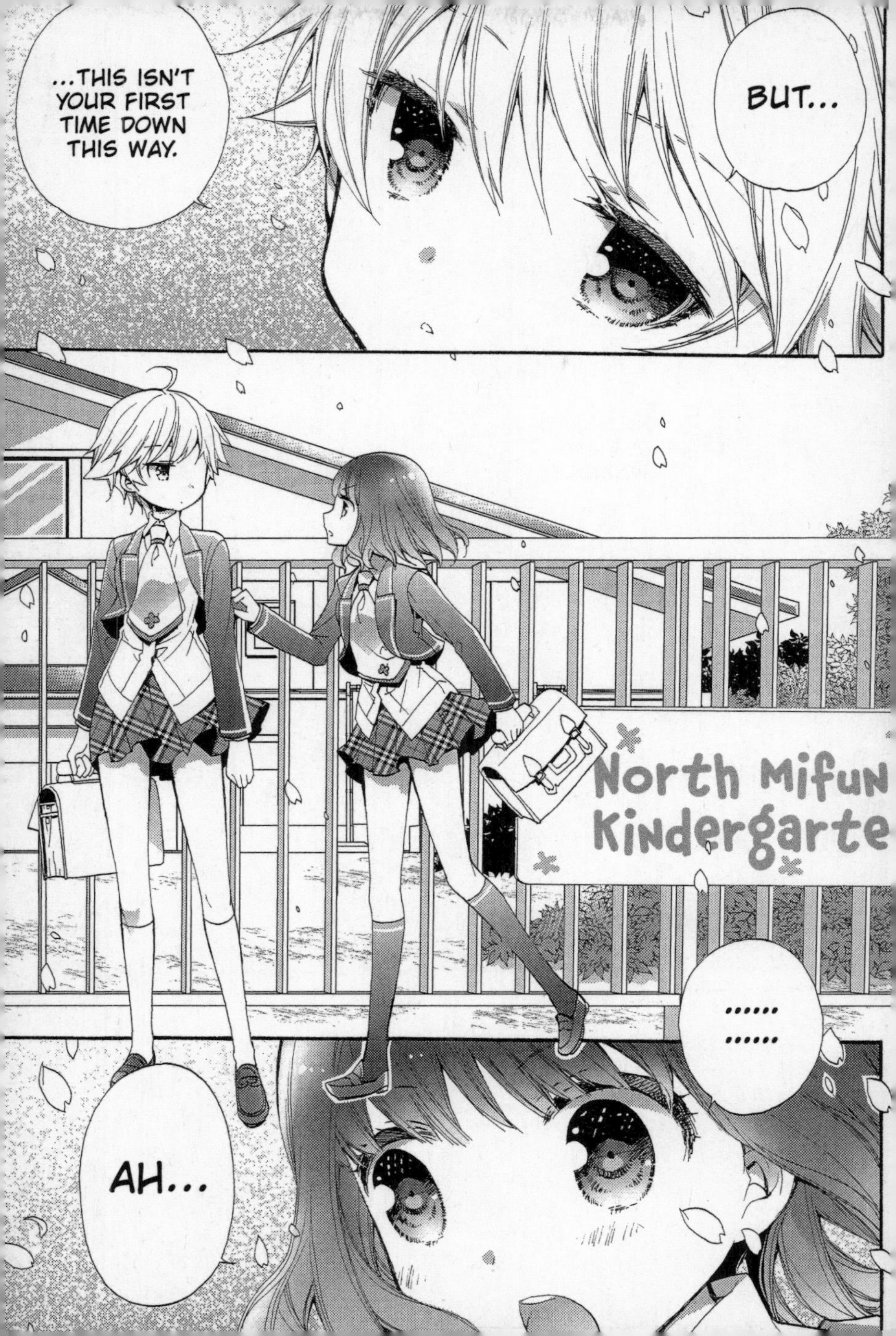
BUT...
...THIS ISN'T YOUR FIRST TIME DOWN THIS WAY.
North Mifun Kindergarte
......
......
AH...

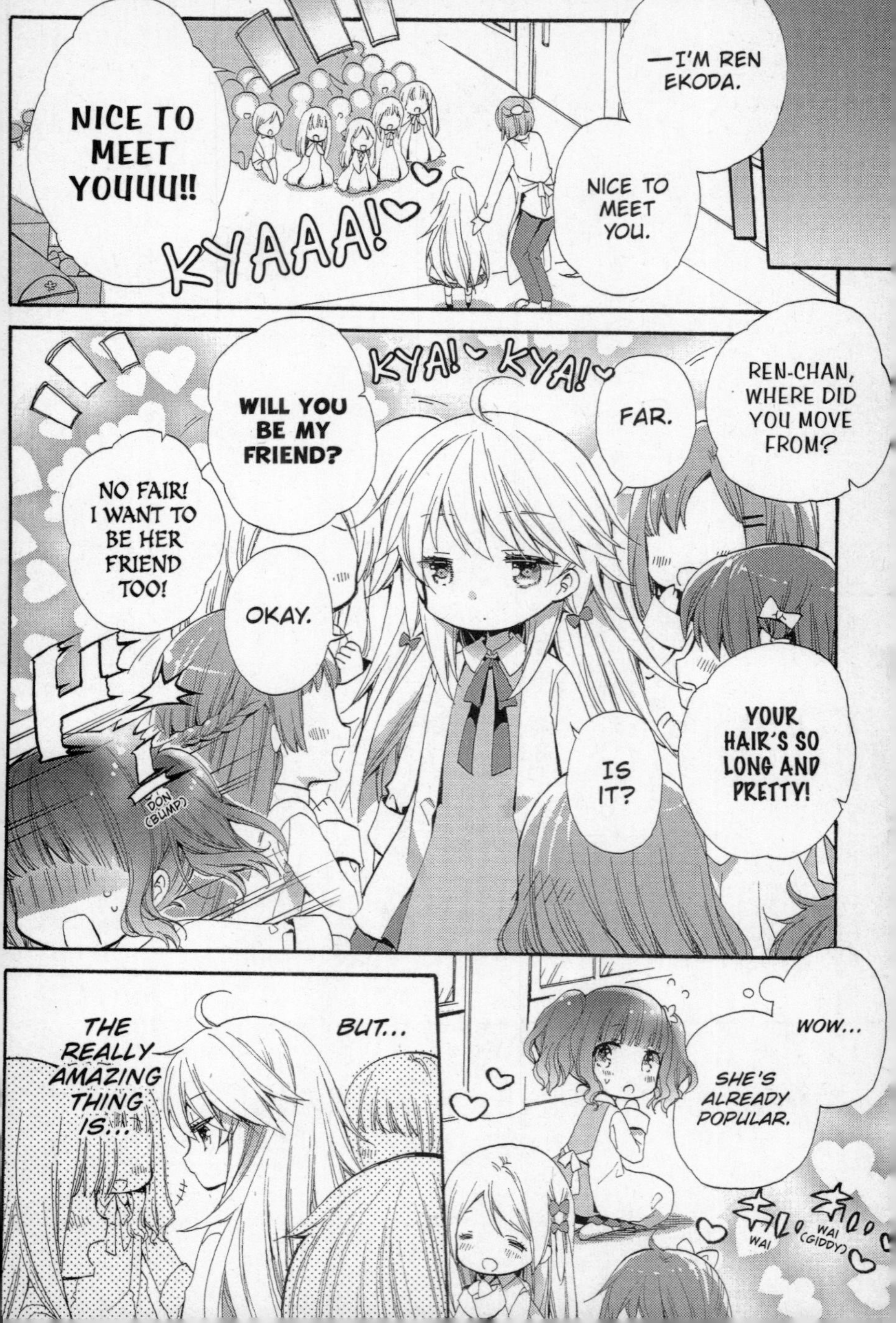
—I'M REN EKODA.
NICE TO MEET YOU.
NICE TO MEET YOUUU!!
KYAAA!
REN-CHAN, WHERE DID YOU MOVE FROM?
FAR.
KYA! KYA!
WILL YOU BE MY FRIEND?
NO FAIR! I WANT TO BE HER FRIEND TOO!
OKAY.
YOUR HAIR'S SO LONG AND PRETTY!
IS IT?
DON (BUMP)
WOW...
SHE'S ALREADY POPULAR.
WAI
WAI (GIDDY)
BUT...
THE REALLY AMAZING THING IS...

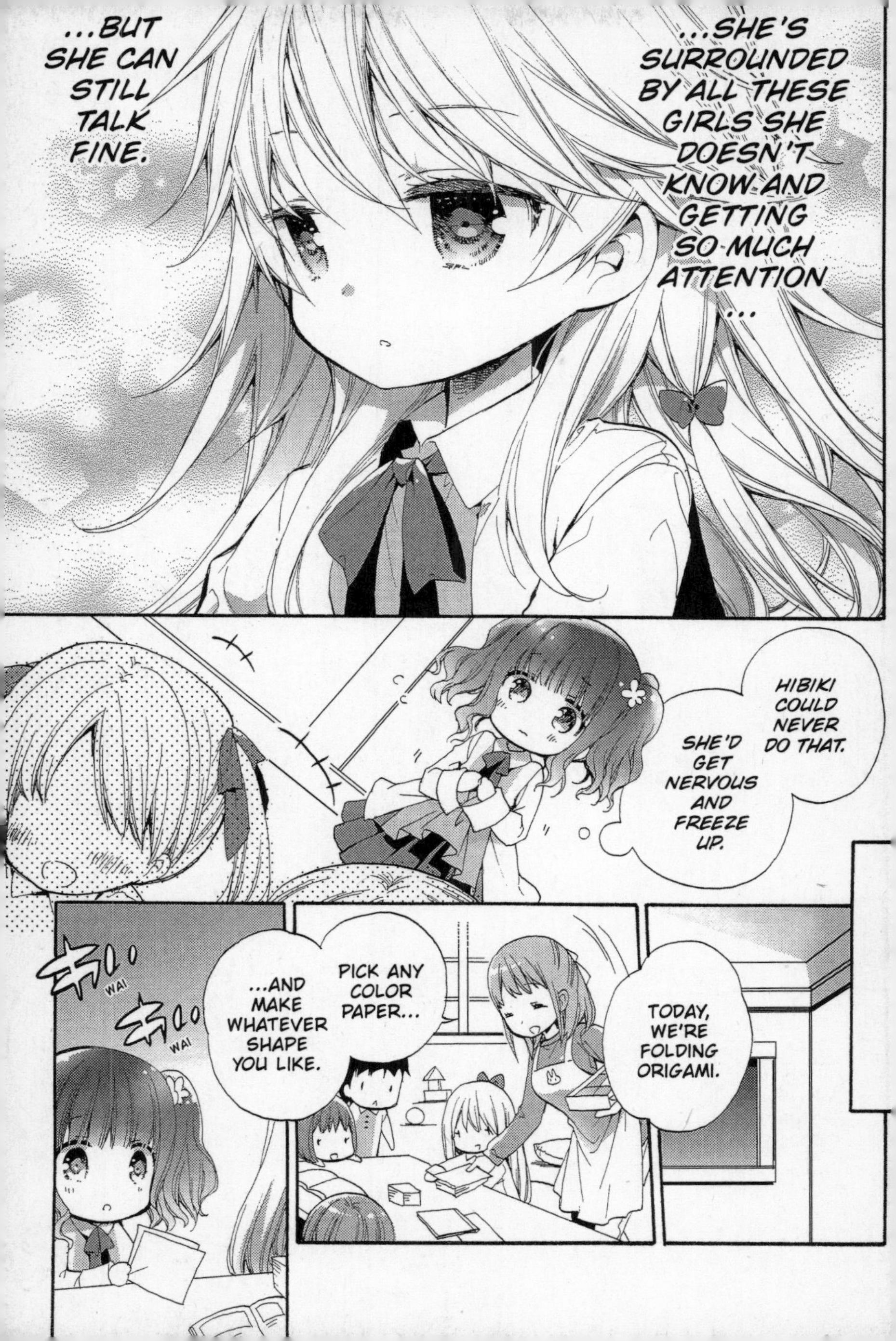
...SHE'S SURROUNDED BY ALL THESE GIRLS SHE DOESN'T KNOW AND GETTING SO MUCH ATTENTION...
...BUT SHE CAN STILL TALK FINE.
HIBIKI COULD NEVER DO THAT.
SHE'D GET NERVOUS AND FREEZE UP.
TODAY, WE'RE FOLDING ORIGAMI.
PICK ANY COLOR PAPER...
...AND MAKE WHATEVER SHAPE YOU LIKE.
WAI
WAI

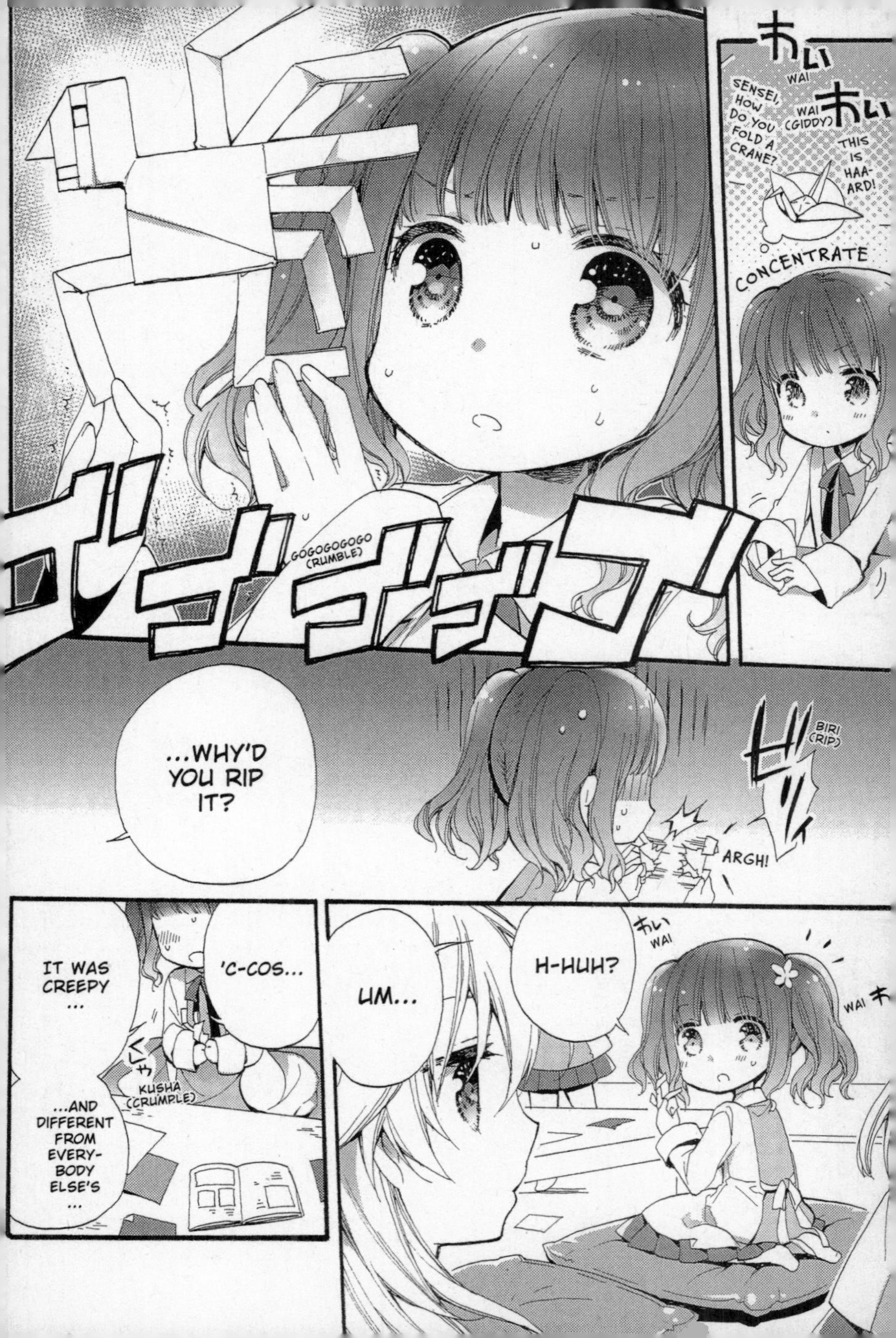

WAI
SENSEI, HOW DO YOU FOLD A CRANE?
WAI (GIDDY)
THIS IS HAA-ARD!
CONCENTRATE
GOGOGOGOGO (RUMBLE)
BIRI (RIP)
ARGH!
...WHY'D YOU RIP IT?
WAI
WAI
H-HUH?
UM...
'C-COS...
IT WAS CREEPY ...
KUSHA (CRUMPLE)
...AND DIFFERENT FROM EVERY-BODY ELSE'S ...

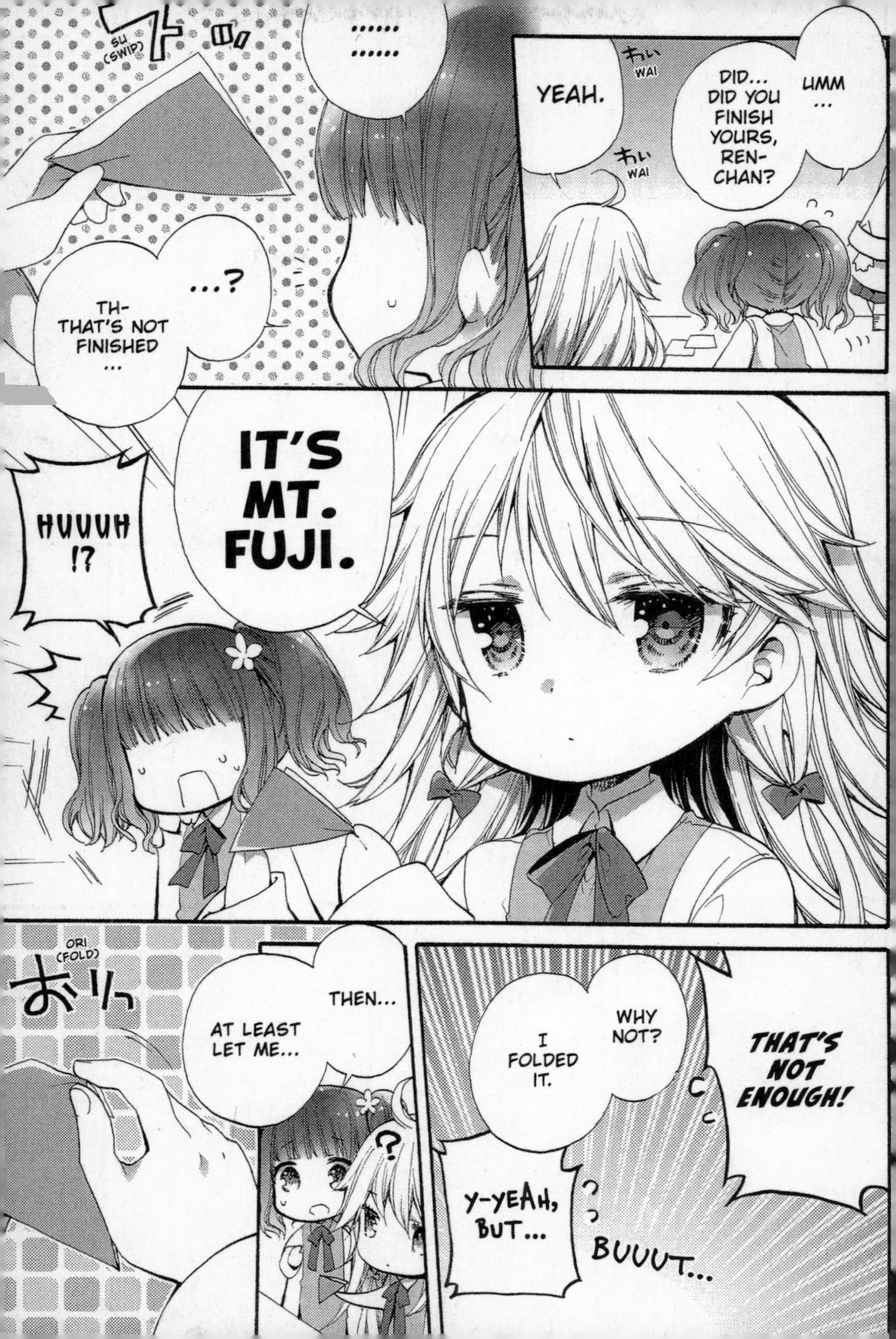
UMM ...
DID... DID YOU FINISH YOURS, REN-CHAN?
わい WAI
YEAH.
わい WAI
......
......
SU (SWIP)
...?
TH- THAT'S NOT FINISHED ...
IT'S MT. FUJI.
HUUUH !?
THAT'S NOT ENOUGH!
WHY NOT? I FOLDED IT.
Y-YEAH, BUT...
BUUUT...
THEN... AT LEAST LET ME...
ORI (FOLD)
おりっ

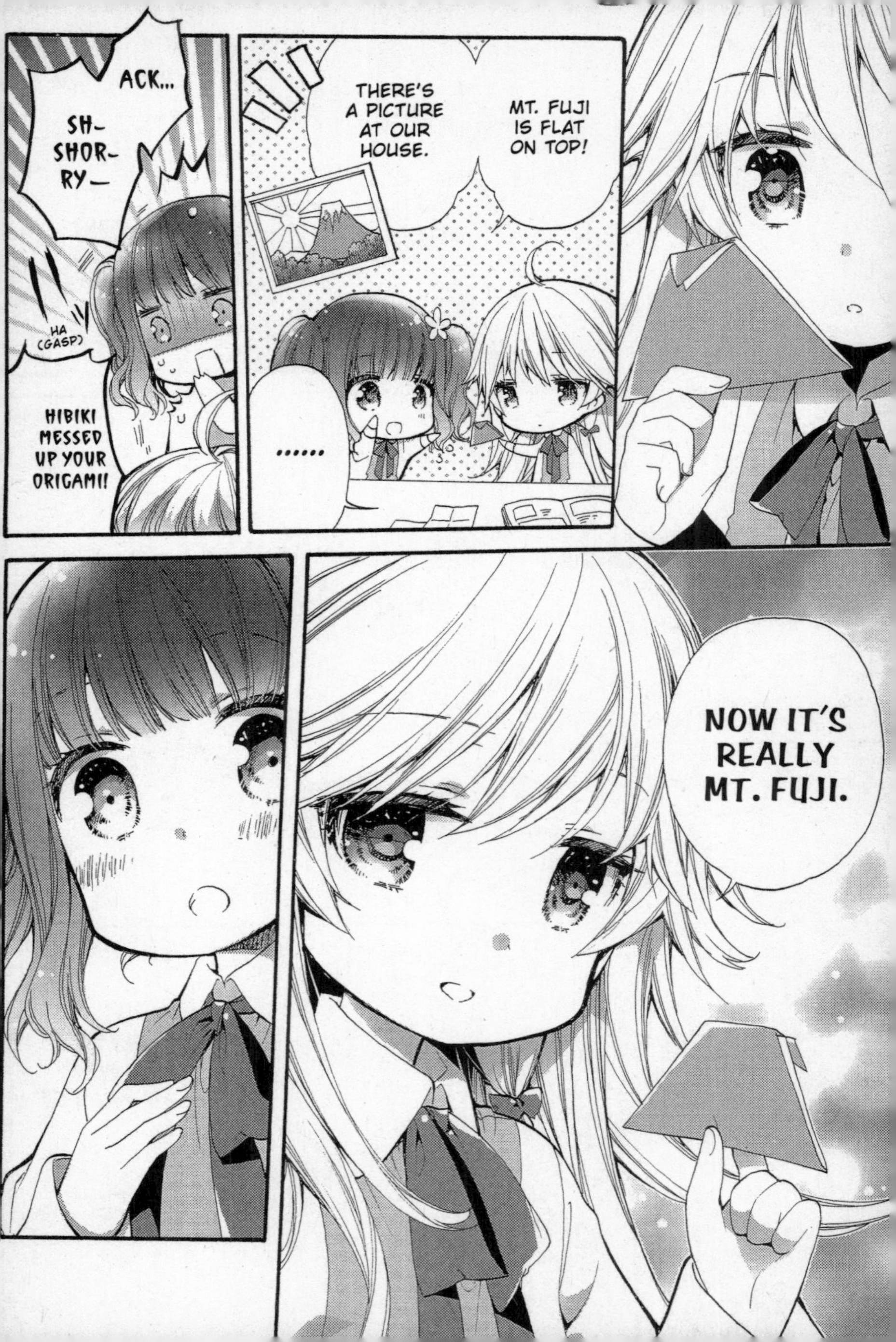
MT. FUJI IS FLAT ON TOP!
THERE'S A PICTURE AT OUR HOUSE.
......
ACK...
SH-SHORRY—
HA (GASP)
HIBIKI MESSED UP YOUR ORIGAMI!
NOW IT'S REALLY MT. FUJI.

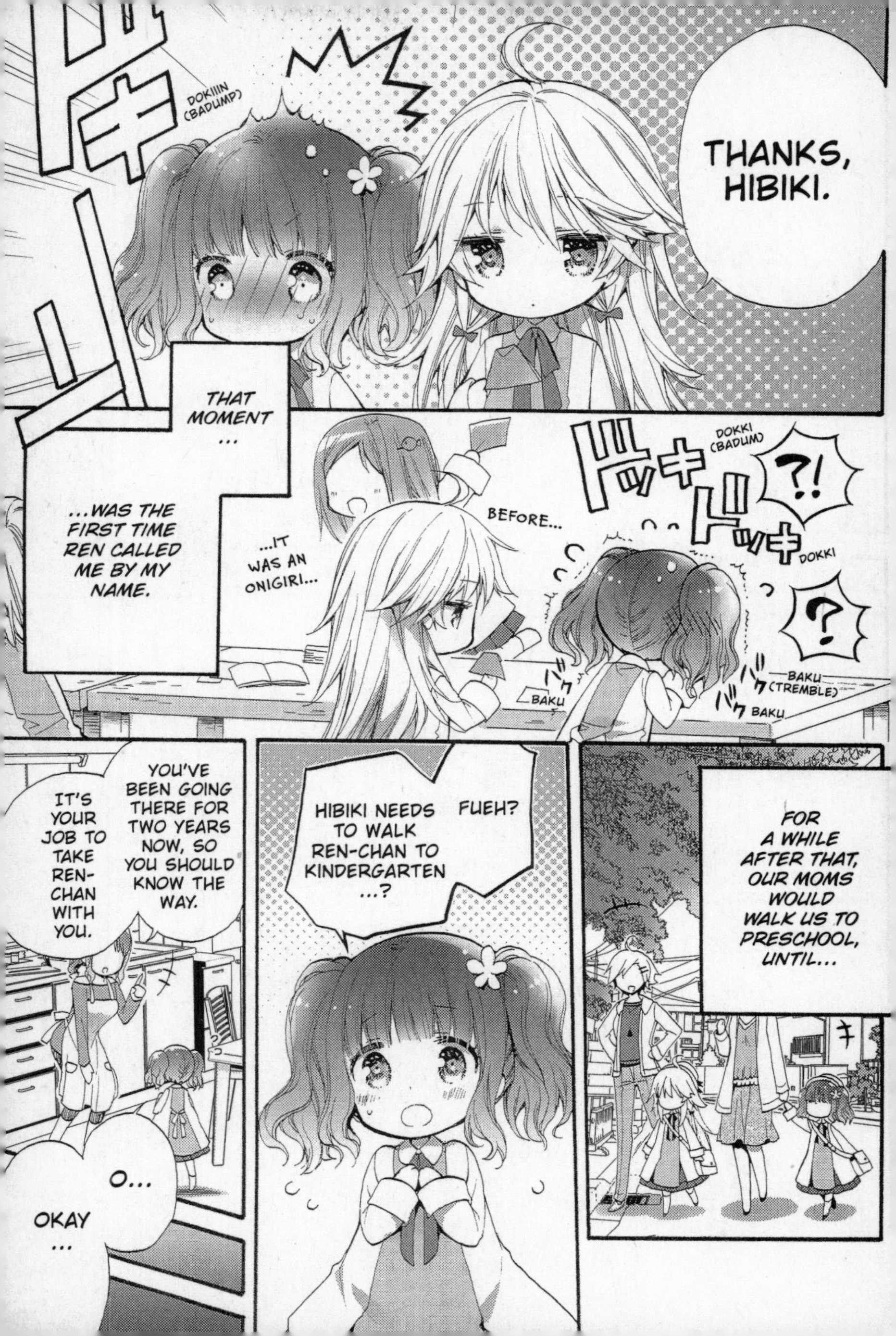
THANKS, HIBIKI.
DOKIIIN (BADUMP)
THAT MOMENT ...
...WAS THE FIRST TIME REN CALLED ME BY MY NAME.
DOKKI (BADUM)
?!
DOKKI
?
BEFORE...
...IT WAS AN ONIGIRI...
BAKU (TREMBLE)
BAKU
BAKU
FOR A WHILE AFTER THAT, OUR MOMS WOULD WALK US TO PRESCHOOL, UNTIL...
FUEH?
HIBIKI NEEDS TO WALK REN-CHAN TO KINDERGARTEN ...?
YOU'VE BEEN GOING THERE FOR TWO YEARS NOW, SO YOU SHOULD KNOW THE WAY.
IT'S YOUR JOB TO TAKE REN-CHAN WITH YOU.
O...
OKAY ...

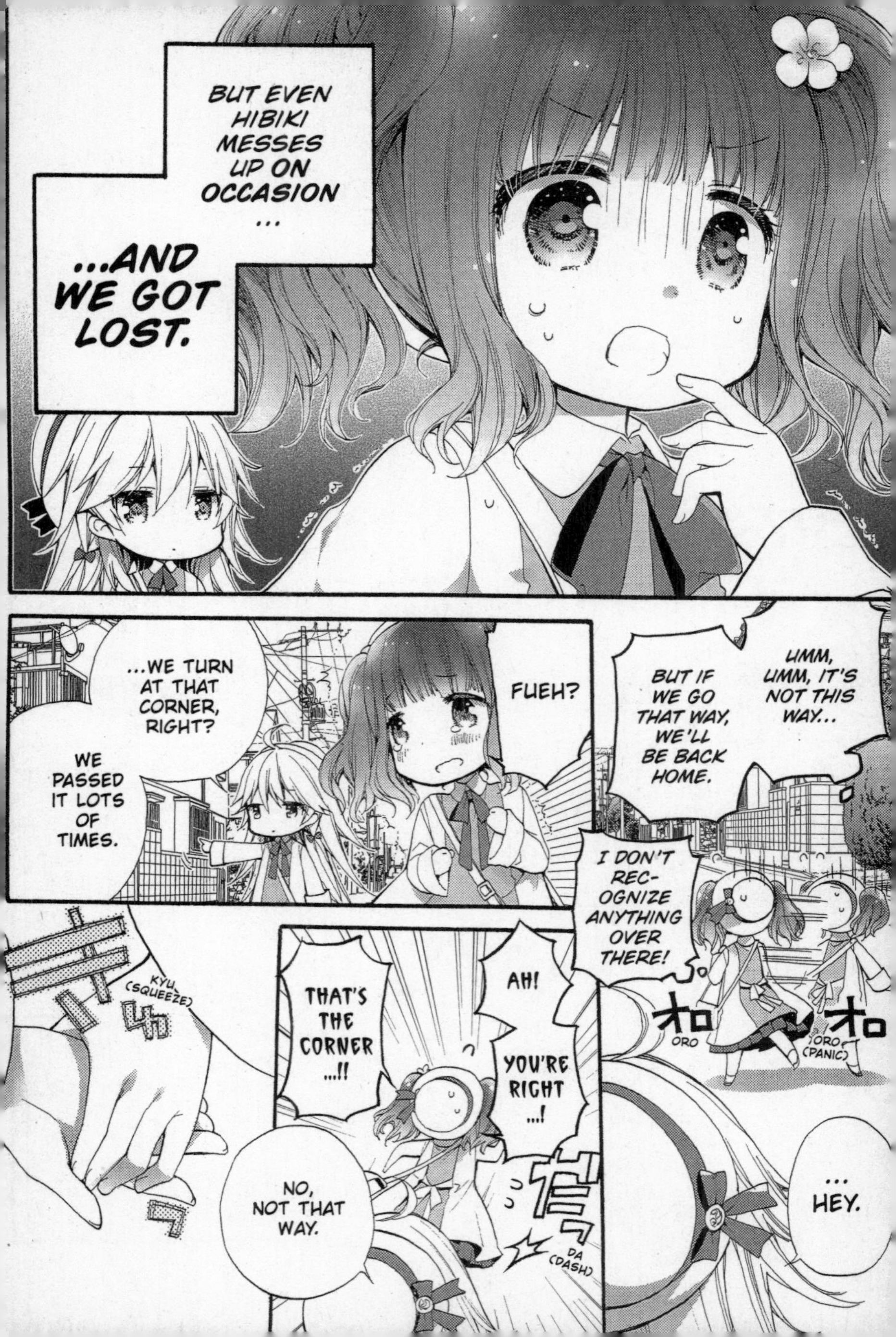
BUT EVEN HIBIKI MESSES UP ON OCCASION ...
...AND WE GOT LOST.
UMM, UMM, IT'S NOT THIS WAY...
BUT IF WE GO THAT WAY, WE'LL BE BACK HOME.
I DON'T RECOGNIZE ANYTHING OVER THERE!
オロ
ORO
オロ
ORO (PANIC)
FUEH?
...WE TURN AT THAT CORNER, RIGHT?
WE PASSED IT LOTS OF TIMES.
... HEY.
AH!
THAT'S THE CORNER ...!!
YOU'RE RIGHT ...!
DA (DASH)
NO, NOT THAT WAY.
KYU (SQUEEZE)

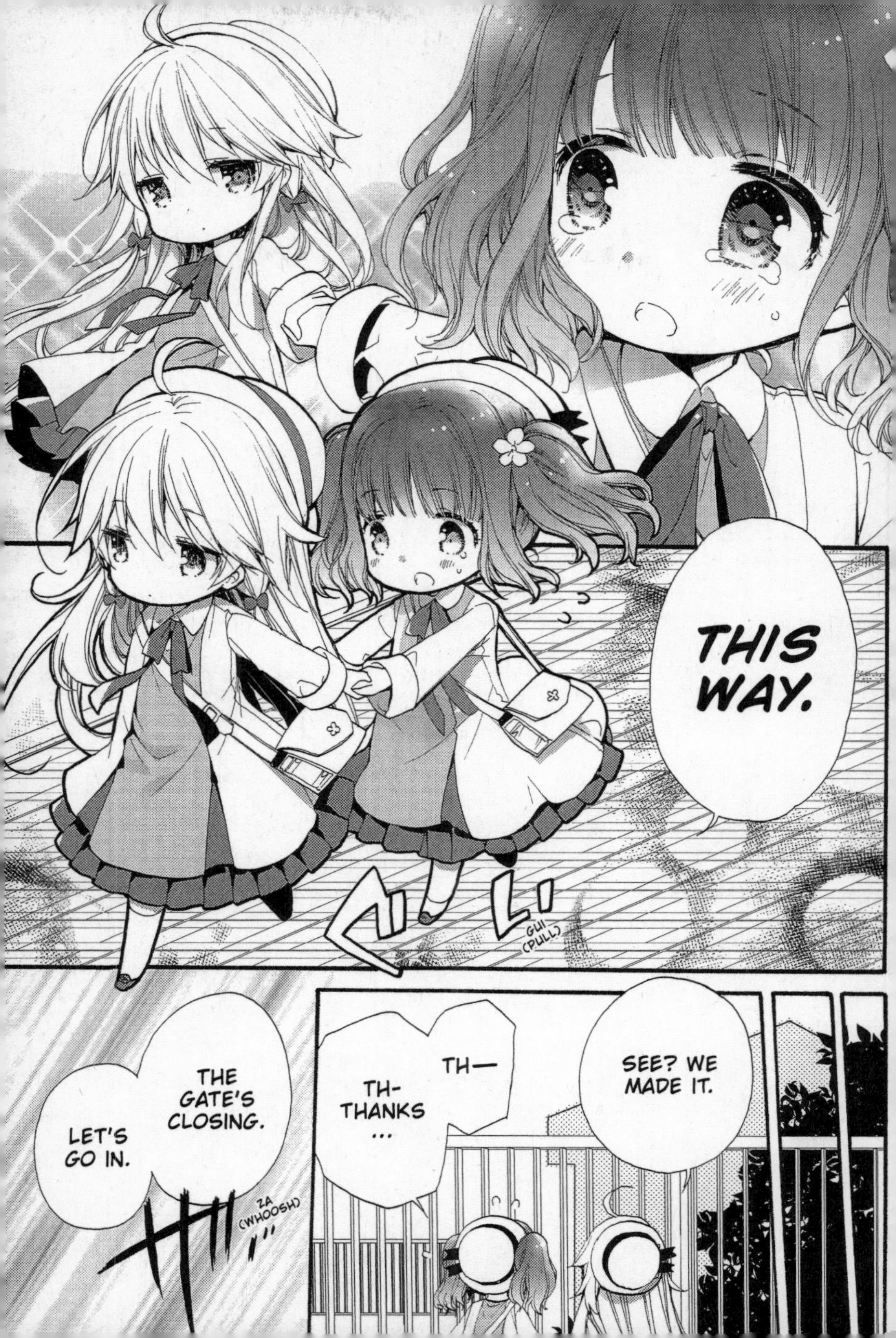
THIS WAY.
GUI (PULL)
SEE? WE MADE IT.
TH—
TH- THANKS ...
THE GATE'S CLOSING.
LET'S GO IN.
ZA (WHOOSH)

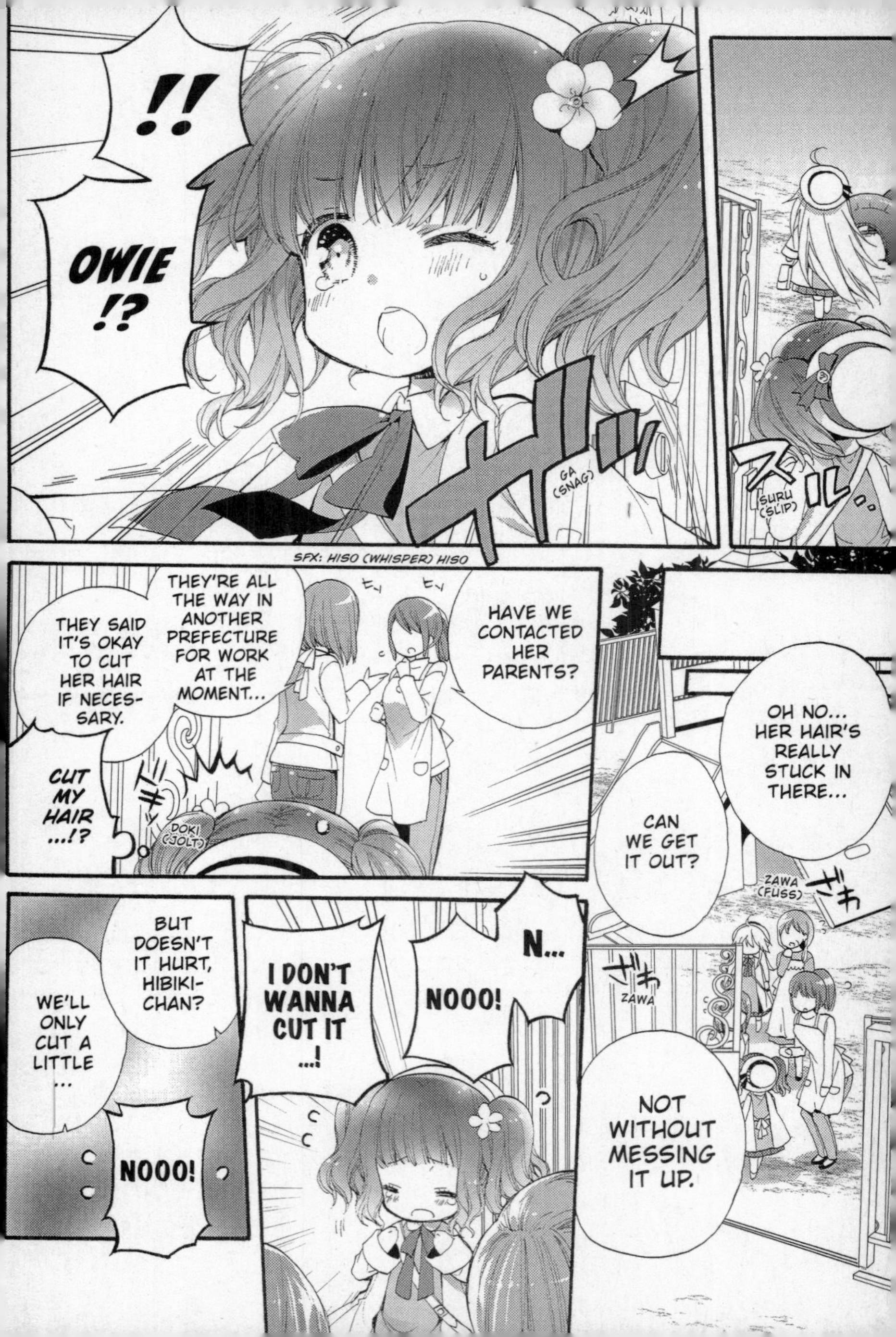
SURU (SLIP)
!!
OWIE !?
GA (SNAG)
SFX: HISO (WHISPER) HISO
OH NO... HER HAIR'S REALLY STUCK IN THERE...
CAN WE GET IT OUT?
ZAWA (FUSS)
ZAWA
NOT WITHOUT MESSING IT UP.
HAVE WE CONTACTED HER PARENTS?
THEY'RE ALL THE WAY IN ANOTHER PREFECTURE FOR WORK AT THE MOMENT...
THEY SAID IT'S OKAY TO CUT HER HAIR IF NECES-SARY.
CUT MY HAIR ...!?
DOKI (JOLT)
N...
NOOO!
I DON'T WANNA CUT IT ...!
BUT DOESN'T IT HURT, HIBIKI-CHAN?
WE'LL ONLY CUT A LITTLE ...
NOOO!

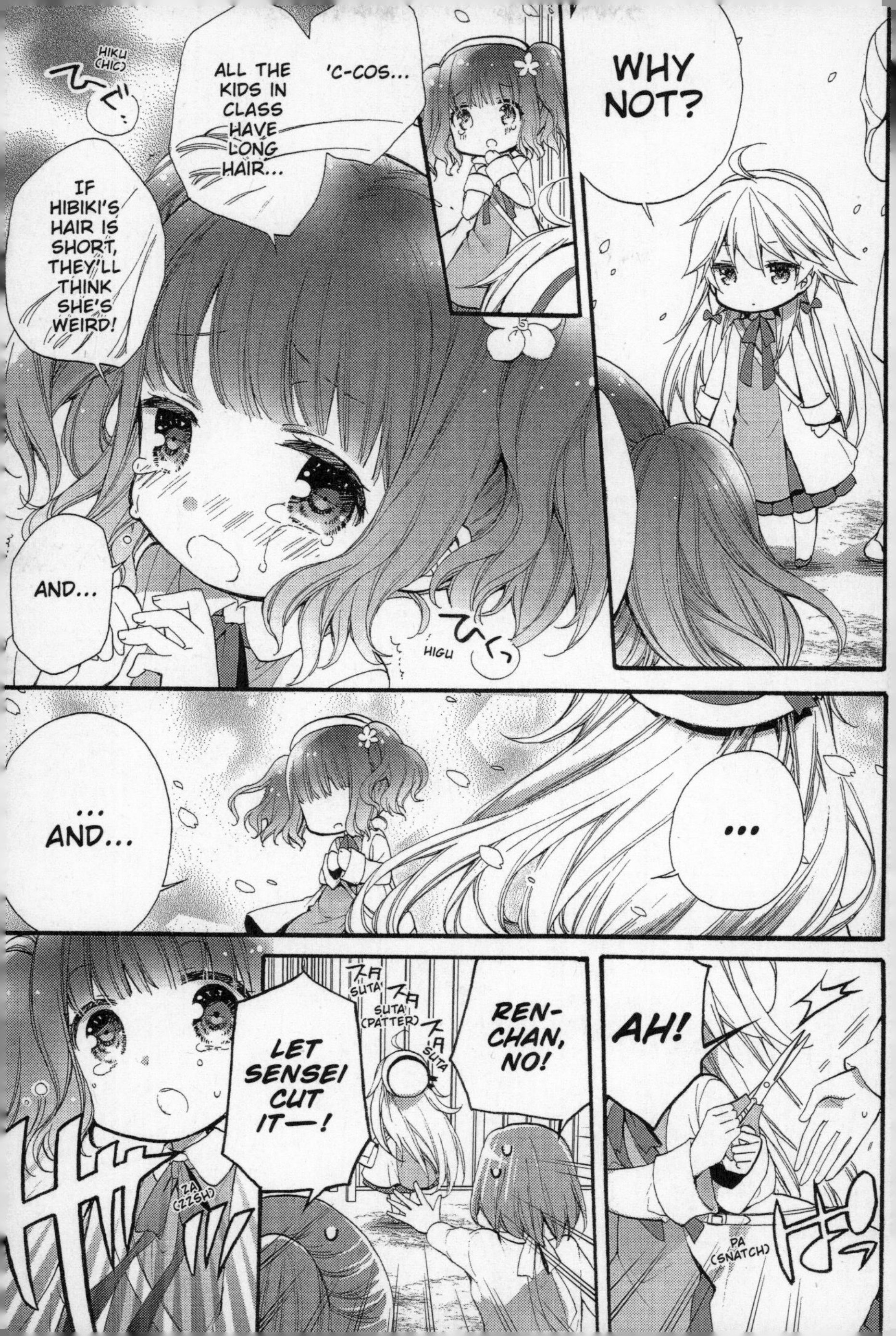
WHY NOT?
'C-COS...
ALL THE KIDS IN CLASS HAVE LONG HAIR...
HIKU (HIC)
IF HIBIKI'S HAIR IS SHORT, THEY'LL THINK SHE'S WEIRD!
HIGU
AND...
...
... AND...
AH!
PA (SNATCH)
REN-CHAN, NO!
SUTA SUTA (PATTER) SUTA
LET SENSEI CUT IT—!
ZA (ZZSH)

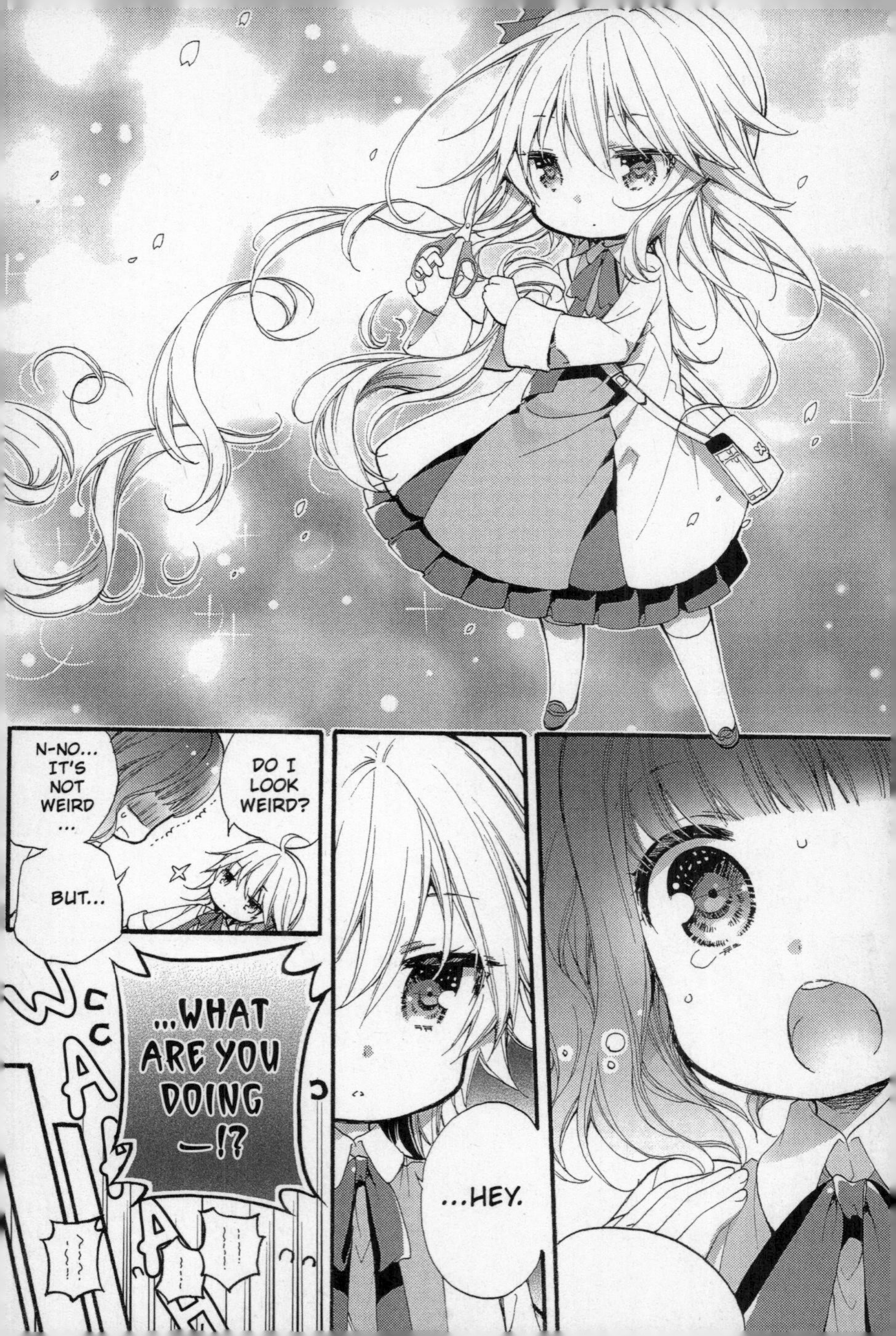
...HEY.
DO I LOOK WEIRD?
N-NO... IT'S NOT WEIRD ...
BUT...
...WHAT ARE YOU DOING—!?

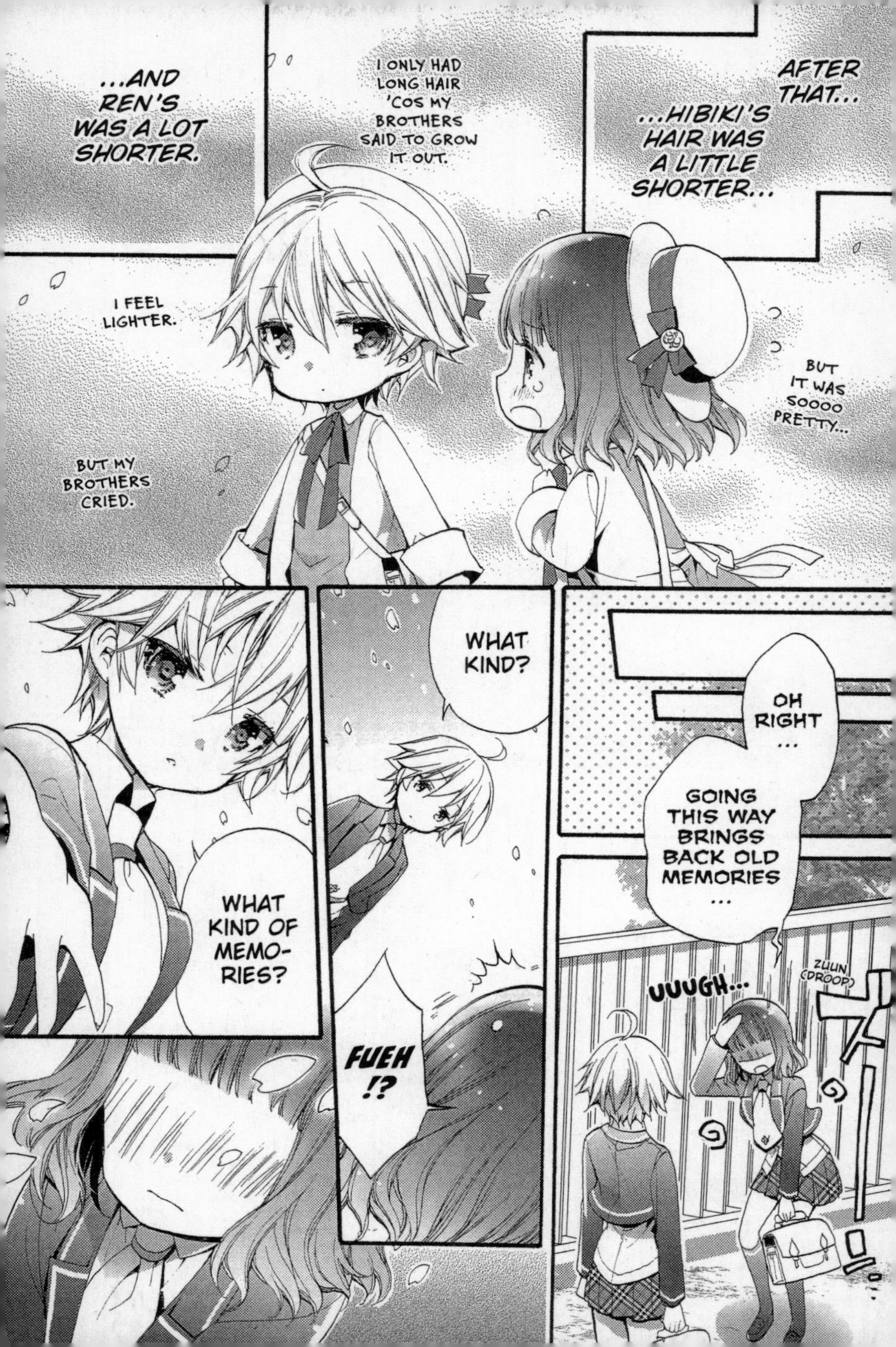
AFTER THAT...
...HIBIKI'S HAIR WAS A LITTLE SHORTER...
I ONLY HAD LONG HAIR 'COS MY BROTHERS SAID TO GROW IT OUT.
...AND REN'S WAS A LOT SHORTER.
I FEEL LIGHTER.
BUT IT WAS SOOOO PRETTY...
BUT MY BROTHERS CRIED.
OH RIGHT...
GOING THIS WAY BRINGS BACK OLD MEMORIES...
ZUUN (DROOP)
UUUGH...
WHAT KIND?
WHAT KIND OF MEMORIES?
FUEH !?

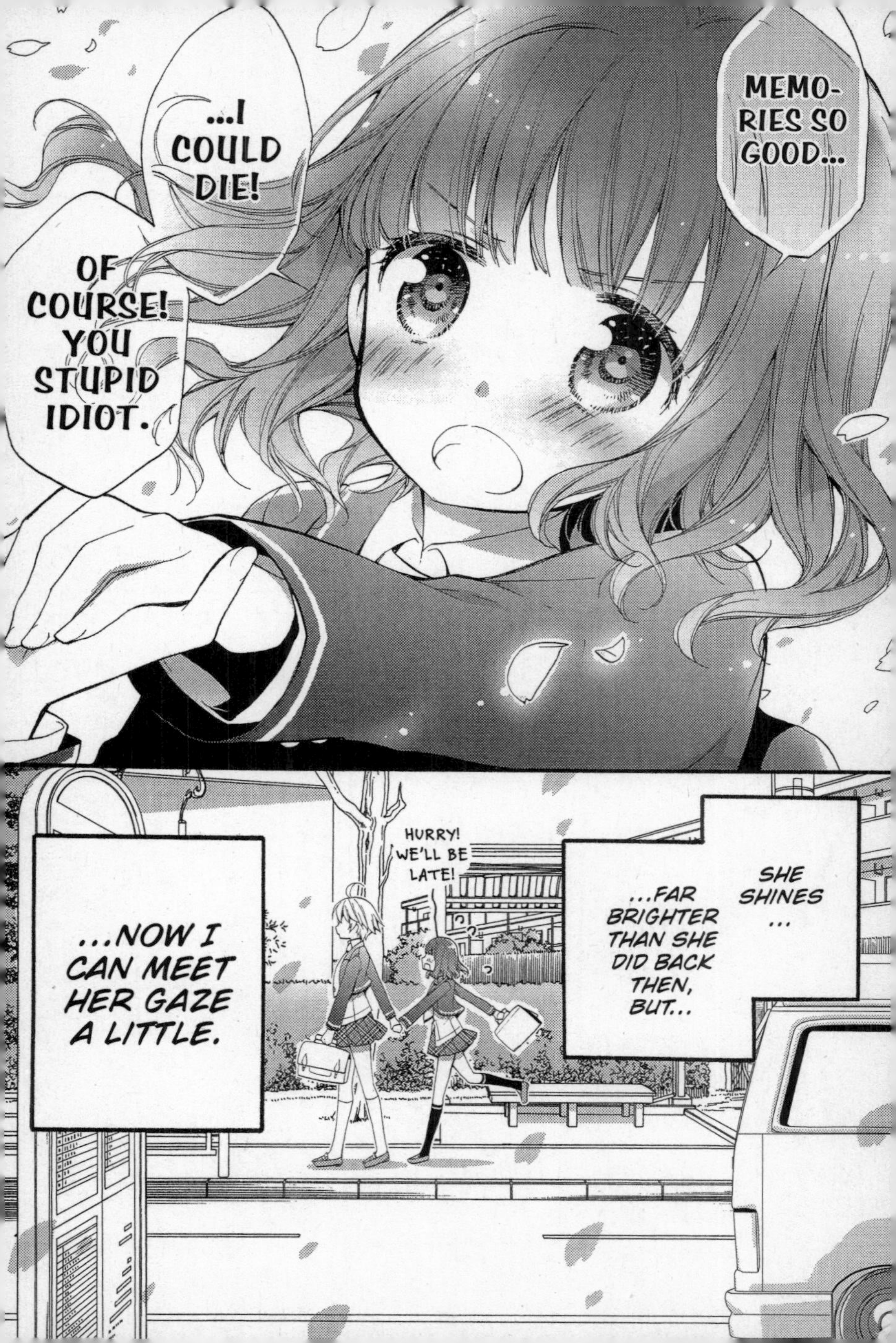
MEMORIES SO GOOD...
...I COULD DIE!
OF COURSE! YOU STUPID IDIOT.
SHE SHINES...
...FAR BRIGHTER THAN SHE DID BACK THEN, BUT...
HURRY! WE'LL BE LATE!
...NOW I CAN MEET HER GAZE A LITTLE.

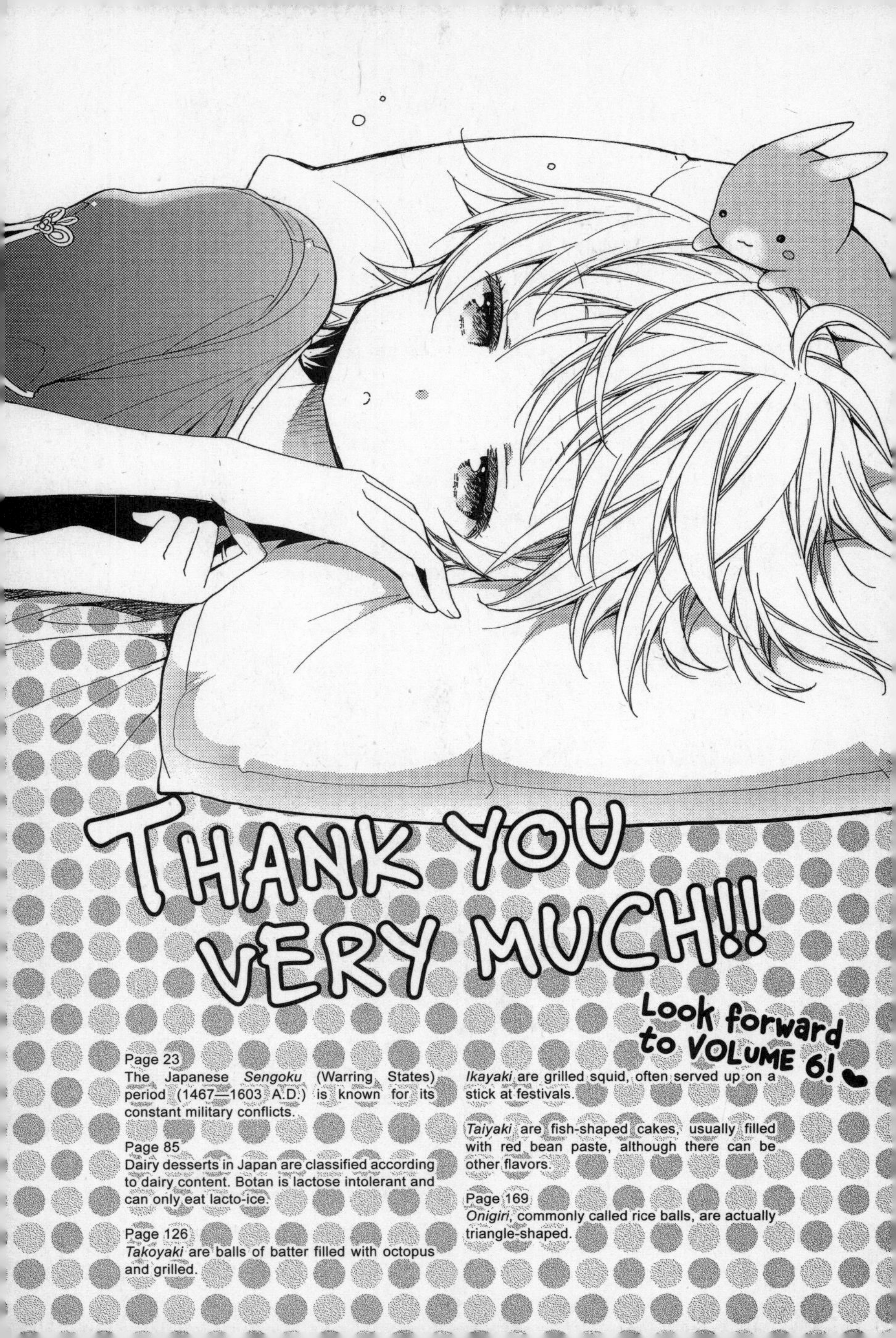
THANK YOU VERY MUCH!!
Look forward to VOLUME 6!

Page 23
The Japanese *Sengoku* (Warring States) period (1467—1603 A.D.) is known for its constant military conflicts.

Page 85
Dairy desserts in Japan are classified according to dairy content. Botan is lactose intolerant and can only eat lacto-ice.

Page 126
Takoyaki are balls of batter filled with octopus and grilled.

Ikayaki are grilled squid, often served up on a stick at festivals.

Taiyaki are fish-shaped cakes, usually filled with red bean paste, although there can be other flavors.

Page 169
Onigiri, commonly called rice balls, are actually triangle-shaped.

Anne Happy ♪
unhappy go lucky!

COTOJI

Translation: Amanda Haley
Lettering: Rochelle Gancio

This book is a work of fiction. Names, characters, places, and incidents are the product of the author's imagination or are used fictitiously. Any resemblance to actual events, locales, or persons, living or dead, is coincidental.

ANNE HAPPY ♪ VOL. 5
© 2016 Cotoji. All rights reserved. First published in Japan in 2016 by HOUBUNSHA CO., LTD., TOKYO. English translation rights in United States, Canada, and United Kingdom arranged with HOUBUNSHA CO., LTD. through Tuttle-Mori Agency, Inc., Tokyo.

English translation © 2017 by Yen Press, LLC

Yen Press
1290 Avenue of the Americas
New York, NY 10104

Visit us at yenpress.com
facebook.com/yenpress
twitter.com/yenpress
yenpress.tumblr.com
instagram.com/yenpress

First Yen Press Edition: May 2017

Yen Press is an imprint of Yen Press, LLC.
The Yen Press name and logo are trademarks of Yen Press, LLC.

The publisher is not responsible for websites (or their content) that are not owned by the publisher.

Library of Congress Control Number: 2016931012

ISBNs: 978-0-316-47163-3 (paperback)
       978-0-316-55970-6 (ebook)

10 9 8 7 6 5 4 3 2 1

BVG

Printed in the United States of America